McCormack's G
make life in Alameda
happier and understan
accurate information in a readable, entertaining style.

School Rankings, including the latest academic rankings (STAR test) for public schools, college placements by high school, SAT scores, a directory of private schools.

Community profiles. Home prices, rents. Descriptions of cities, towns and neighborhoods.

The perfect guide for parents or people shopping for homes or apartments or just interested in finding out more about Alameda, Merced, San Joaquin and Stanislaus counties and their weather, schools and communities.

Hospital services and medical care. Directory of hospitals.

Child Care. Directory of infant-care and day-care centers. Most popular names for babies.

Places to visit, things to do.

Local Colleges and Unemployment Figures.

Vital statistics. Population and income by town. Republicans and Democrats. Presidential votes. Crime, history, trivia and much more.

McCormack's Guides, edited by former newspaper reporters and editors, was established in 1984 and publishes the most popular general-interest guides to California counties. For a list of our other guides and an order form, see the last page. Or visit: www.mccormacks.com

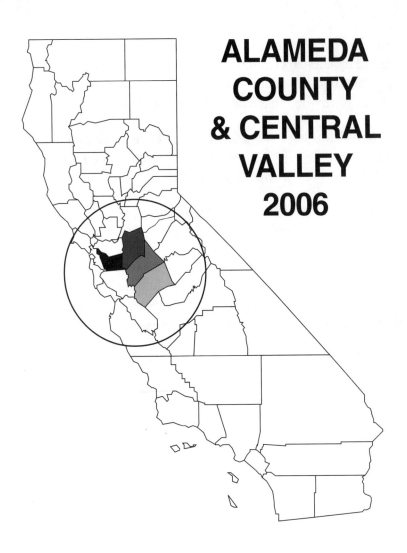

ALAMEDA COUNTY & CENTRAL VALLEY 2006

Edited by Don McCormack

 3211 Elmquist Court, Martinez, CA 94553
Phone: (800) 222-3602 & Fax: (925) 228-7223
bookinfo@mccormacks.com • www.mccormacks.com

Publisher and editor Don McCormack formed McCormack's Guides in 1984 to publish annual guides to California counties. A graduate of the University of California-Berkeley, McCormack joined the Contra Costa Times in 1969 and covered police, schools, politics, planning, courts and government. Later with the Richmond Independent and Berkeley Gazette, he worked as a reporter, then editor and columnist.

Maps illustrator Louis Liu attended the Academy of Art College in San Francisco, where he majored in illustration.

Many thanks to the people who write, edit, layout and help publish McCormack's Guides: Martina Bailey, Paul Fletcher, Mary Jennings, Meghan McCormack, John VanLandingham

DISCLAIMER

Indexed   ISBN 1-929365-68-3

Contents

On the Cover:
U.C. Berkeley, one of the leading universities in the U.S.

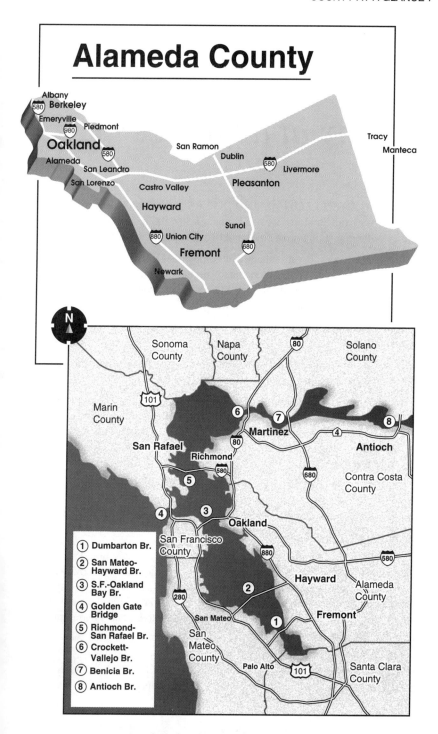

Alameda County

Chapter 1

County at a Glance

ENERGETIC, INTELLECTUAL AND DIVERSE, Alameda County is located across the bay from San Francisco and counts 1,507,500 residents, the great majority of them residing in 14 cities and two unincorporated towns.

In recent decades, because mainly of home prices, many people who work in Alameda County and the Bay Area have purchased homes in the nearby counties of San Joaquin, Stanislaus and Merced. These counties are also covered in this book, under Central Valley.

Alameda County also includes — a point of confusion — a city called "Alameda."

Just north of Alameda County is Contra Costa County. Together the two counties make up what is known locally as the East Bay.

In land, Alameda encompasses 733 square miles, about one-third the size of Delaware. North to south, the county runs from Albany to Fremont and east to west from Oakland to Livermore and the edge of the San Joaquin Valley. Discovery Peak, located south of Livermore-Pleasanton, is the highest mountain, 3,841 feet.

With the exception of Livermore, Pleasanton, Dublin and the hamlet of Sunol, all cities are located on or near the Bay. Tall hills divide the Bay cities from the inland towns and create different weather patterns.

Temperate with a Punch

The weather is balmy, one of the great attractions of the region. Rarely do temperatures roast or freeze. Rarely does humidity cause discomfort. Many shore cities, however, are too cool for outdoor pools. On some summer days, when the fog barrels through the Golden Gate, the Oakland hills can be plain cold. If you travel a few miles inland, over the ridge into Dublin-Pleasanton, you're in swimming pool country.

In the fall, dry winds called Diablos occasionally roar through the Berkeley-Oakland hills. In 1991, a Diablo-blown fire killed 25 and destroyed 2,500 homes and apartments, a loss of about $1.5 billion.

COUNTY AT A GLANCE 9

The East Bay

CONTRA COSTA & ALAMEDA COUNTIES

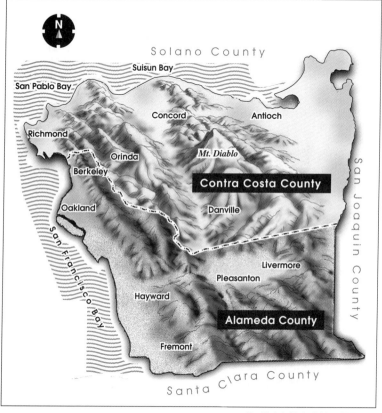

Map Illustrated By Louis Liu • 925.779.0394

Fingertip Facts

Three bridges connect Alameda County with the "Peninsula" (San Francisco and San Mateo counties). They are the Bay, the San Mateo and the Dumbarton. Of the three, the Bay, with its spectacular views of San Francisco, is by far the prettiest.

But if you commute to San Francisco, you may come to hate the Bay Bridge, a notorious bottleneck, that for the next few years will be an even

Alameda County Population

City or Area	1990	2000	2005*
Alameda	76,459	72,259	74,581
Albany	16,327	16,444	16,743
Berkeley	102,724	102,743	104,534
Castro Valley	48,619	57,292	NA
Dublin	23,229	29,973	39,931
Emeryville	5,740	6,882	8,261
Fremont	173,339	203,413	210,445
Hayward	111,498	140,030	146,027
Livermore	56,741	73,345	80,723
Newark	37,861	42,471	43,708
Oakland	372,242	399,484	412,318
Piedmont	10,602	10,952	11,055
Pleasanton	50,553	63,654	67,650
San Leandro	68,223	79,452	81,442
San Lorenzo	19,987	21,898	NA
Union City	53,762	66,869	70,685
Countywide	1,279,18	1,443,741	1,507,500

Source: 1990 census, 2000 census. *City population estimates by California Dept. of Finance, 2005. Castro Valley and San Lorenzo are unincorporated towns and do not get annually population estimates.

bigger pain. The east span is being replaced and the west span overhauled and rewired.

The largest and most populous city is Oakland. The richest is Piedmont, the smallest, Emeryville, the most exciting and stimulating, Berkeley, with Oakland a close second.

Berkeley is home to one of the most successful universities on the planet, the University of California at Berkeley, enrollment about 33,000 (grads and undergrads). The university is called "Cal." Its mascot is a Golden Bear. When fans urge Cal players to get hopping, they chant, "Go Bears." Cal's colors are blue and gold. Its alumni are Old Blues. Cal's arch rival is Stanford University, down and across the Bay. Colors: red. Nicknamed: The Cardinal. When Cal beats Stanford, especially in football or basketball, the hearts of young and old Blues go thumpety-thump.

Berkeley's politics are quite liberal and to some people "Berkeley" epitomizes the zaniness of California. The town makes no apologies for its politics or its policies. If you think that you are secure in your beliefs, Berkeley will offer someone who will differ, in a challenging way. The town, in lesser numbers, also has its conservatives and its moderates.

Alameda County is generally considered suburbia but 100-percent bedroom communities are few: Piedmont and maybe Castro Valley and San Lorenzo.

The other communities blend business, industry or government with residential, and this helps shorten the commute for many.

Oakland has an international airport that specializes in economy airlines (Southwest, United, JetBlue), one of the busiest shipping ports in the nation and a high-rise downtown.

On its south, Alameda County borders Santa Clara County, home of the original Silicon Valley. Short of space, Silicon Valley jumped its borders about 30 years ago and started building offices, plants and research facilities throughout Alameda County, particularly at Fremont, Hayward, Union City, Dublin and Pleasanton.

In the local economy, the university, which employs about 21,000 full and part timers, has been enormously beneficial. Berkeley graduates staff or manage thousands of firms, high tech to high finance, and government institutions. Biotech, one of the coming industries, has a firm hold in the East Bay, thanks in large measure to the university.

At Livermore, the university manages a large laboratory, 8,000 employees, that researches and develops weapons. The lab has its critics and its supporters.

In politics, Alameda County, foremost Berkeley and Oakland, is quite liberal and invariably goes head-over-heels for anyone the Democrats trot out as president. But many people approach politics in a pragmatic and sometimes contradictory way. The communities welcome jobs but often argue over residential development. Both put more cars on the road, a sore point, but housing is considered more intrusive.

Protecting the environment is a big thing in Alameda County. Over the past 40 years, pollution laws have been tightened, development controls installed and hundreds of millions spent to clean up the Bay. Quality-of-life issues are also big. Berkeley blocks many of its residential streets to force motorists onto arterial boulevards. Suburbanites argue for open space to keep the country feeling that they find so pleasing.

In its annual tally of housing, the state counted 558,840 residential units in Alameda County. This included 300,016 single homes, 39,146 single attached, 212,048 apartments or condos and 7,630 mobile homes.

A Diverse Lot

The residents are a diverse lot: all sorts of colors and creeds, rich and poor but mostly middle class, home-owners and renters, white collars and blue, homeless and Nobel winners. Thanks to the university and its labs, the county boasts a large collection of Big Brains.

The 2000 census tallied 215,598 African Americans, 9,146 American Indians, 309,013 Asians, 591,095 Caucasians, 273,910 Hispanics, and 9,142 Native Hawaiian or Pacific Islanders.

Average Household Income

City	1990	2000	2005*
Alameda	$70,600	$85,500	$87,200
Albany	60,900	75,900	79,300
Berkeley	63,500	76,100	79,300
Castro Valley	76,200	93,200	95,100
Dublin	83,400	101,700	102,900
Emeryville	61,300	76,600	80,200
Fremont	85,200	103,100	104,600
Hayward	61,200	72,300	74,000
Livermore	78,500	97,800	99,800
Newark	77,700	88,100	90,600
Oakland	54,800	65,500	67,400
Piedmont	180,800	218,800	230,800
Pleasanton	98,100	121,500	123,900
San Leandro	59,800	71,400	72,400
San Lorenzo	63,200	73,400	75,500
Union City	74,800	84,100	88,300
Remainder	115,700	150,400	180,500
Countywide	68,000	82,500	84,200

Source: Association of Bay Area Governments, "*Projections 2002*" Average income per household includes wages and salaries, dividends, interest, rent and transfer payments such as Social Security or public assistance. *Projections.

Schools, churches, businesses and government agencies do a good job of encouraging everyone to respect and celebrate differences. There are, and probably always will be, arguments over policies such as profiling and affirmative action. Alameda County is very much of the modern world but this said, the county and its residents strongly favor inclusive politics and practices to bring people together.

Charm, Beauty, Amusements

The Bay charms the eye. The hills command sweeping views. If you wish to swim, boat, fish, hit a baseball or a softball or a golf ball or a tennis ball, if you wish to shoot or weave a basket, if you wish to watch the best (or near best) in basketball or baseball or football, if you wish to study painting, or paint a nude or paint the town, Alameda County can accommodate. All the towns field sports for the kids and the adults. Soccer is particularly popular.

If you wish to pursue your ambitions, Alameda County offers the chance. Besides the University of California, the county boasts a state university, two large private universities, seven community colleges, an arts college and many vocational and specialty schools.

California Cuisine was invented in Alameda County by Alice Waters in her Berkeley restaurant Chez Panisse. Berkeley, Albany and Oakland are loaded with first-class restaurants and recently restaurants that pride themselves on fine cooking have moved out into the suburbs. Livermore and Pleasanton are noted for their wines.

Top 30 Baby Names

Alameda County

Boys

Name	Count
Daniel	143
Joshua	121
Alexander	105
Ryan	93
Jacob	88
Anthony	87
Matthew	87
Michael	86
Angel	81
Jose	81
Ethan	80
Diego	79
Kevin	77
Nathan	76
Andrew	74
David	74
Jonathan	74
Brandon	72
Christopher	72
Joseph	70
Tyler	69
William	68
Nicholas	67
Benjamin	65
Gabriel	64
Justin	63
James	62
Luis	60
Julian	58
Dylan	55

Girls

Name	Count
Emily	109
Sophia	79
Ashley	78
Isabella	77
Jessica	69
Samantha	67
Natalie	53
Alexandra	51
Emma	51
Michelle	50
Alyssa	49
Hannah	48
Jennifer	47
Elizabeth	46
Jasmine	46
Olivia	46
Sarah	46
Abigail	45
Grace	45
Kayla	44
Isabel	42
Madison	42
Maya	42
Andrea	41
Angelina	40
Alexis	39
Julia	39
Ariana	38
Anna	36
Lauren	36

California

Boys

Name	Count
Daniel	4157
Anthony	3797
Andrew	3464
Jose	3379
Jacob	3327
Joshua	3292
David	3246
Angel	3232
Matthew	2853
Michael	2844
Christopher	2754
Jonathan	2541
Ryan	2511
Alexander	2440
Joseph	2430
Ethan	2356
Nathan	2302
Brandon	2208
Kevin	2133
Juan	2106
Christian	2022
Jesus	2012
Nicholas	1999
Diego	1977
Luis	1957
Adrian	1824
Dylan	1757
Gabriel	1735
Isaac	1722
Carlos	1638

Girls

Name	Count
Emily	3388
Ashley	2922
Samantha	2474
Isabella	2435
Natalie	1942
Alyssa	1808
Emma	1740
Sophia	1715
Jessica	1700
Jasmine	1666
Elizabeth	1595
Madison	1572
Jennifer	1483
Kimberly	1460
Alexis	1434
Andrea	1374
Abigail	1314
Hannah	1310
Sarah	1304
Vanessa	1299
Mia	1270
Stephanie	1246
Brianna	1221
Michelle	1152
Olivia	1149
Kayla	1147
Leslie	1137
Grace	1127
Maria	1099
Victoria	1083

Source: California Department of Health Services, 2004 birth records. Some names would move higher on the list if the state grouped essentially same names with slightly different spellings, for example, Sarah and Sara. But state computer goes by exact spellings.

Oakland has a first-class museum and three professional teams — the Warriors (basketball), the Athletics (baseball) and the Raiders (football) — a zoo and a first-class night life built around Jack London Village, which is being improved. For college football and basketball, there's the university. The Sharks (professional hockey) play in San Jose, the Giants and the Forty Niners in San Francisco.

Plays, regular movies, offbeat movies, night clubs, jazz clubs, dance recitals, art galleries and art museums, chamber orchestras, symphonies, operas

VOTE Voter Registration

City	Demo.	Repub.	NP
Alameda	20,494	7,958	8,315
Albany	6,016	912	1,862
Berkeley	45,199	4,413	16,680
Dublin	6,187	5,113	3,248
Emeryville	2,487	387	1,051
Fremont	39,263	20,953	21,200
Hayward	28,521	8,270	9,231
Livermore	15,158	16,272	7,316
Newark	8,895	3,708	3,456
Oakland	128,251	14,948	38,728
Piedmont	3,958	2,235	1,274
Pleasanton	13,379	14,262	6,739
San Leandro	21,483	6,886	7,074
Union City	13,937	4,616	5,983
Unincorporated	33,913	15,917	11,159
Countywide	387,141	126,850	143,316

Source: Alameda County Registrar of Voters, California Secretary of State: Cities 2004. **Key**. Demo. (Democrat); Repub. (Republican). NP (Non-Partisan).

Presidential Voting in Alameda County

Year	Democrat	D-Votes	Republican	R-Votes
1948	Truman*	154,549	Dewey	150,588
1952	Stevenson	173,583	Eisenhower*	192,941
1956	Stevenson	174,033	Eisenhower*	192,911
1960	Kennedy*	217,172	Nixon	183,354
1964	Johnson*	283,833	Goldwater	142,988
1968	Humphrey	219,545	Nixon*	153,285
1972	McGovern	259,254	Nixon*	201,862
1976	Carter*	235,988	Ford	155,280
1980	Carter	201,720	Reagan*	158,531
1984	Mondale	282,041	Reagan*	192,408
1988	Dukakis	273,780	Bush*	139,618
1992	Clinton*	314,761	Bush	100,574
1996	Clinton*	303,702	Dole	106,534
2000	Gore	310,519	Bush*	106,137
2004	Kerry	326,675	Bush*	107,489

Source: County Registrar of Voters. * Election winner.

— they are all there. Many high culture events are presented in Berkeley or Oakland but art and culture groups are found throughout the other cities.

The East Bay is hip enough and populous enough to attract the top acts — Madonna, McCartney, Dylan — touring the country. What the East Bay doesn't have, San Francisco does.

Problems

Alameda County's elementary and secondary schools score among the top in the state and among the lowest. In 2003, Oakland school district, having lost track of its finances, was forced to declare bankruptcy. The state loaned it $100 million and put its own administrator in charge of the district.

In recent years, the state and local voters have greatly increased school funding and adopted programs that, all hope, will help students learn more. Many suburban schools score well above the 50th percentile.

In the early 1990s, Alameda County was recording over 200 homicides a year. Later in the decade, homicides dropped sharply but several years ago made a comeback. In 2001, the county counted 108 homicides; in 2002, the number was 144, in 2003, 139. In 2004, homicides tallied 117. Many of the homicides occur in Oakland which in 2004 passed a tax to add more cops..

In the 1990s, billions were spent to improve local freeways and mass transit. BART (suburban rail) runs trains to San Francisco and San Mateo County and down to Fremont. The line also runs up to Richmond and Pittsburg and out to Dublin-Pleasanton. The Altamont Commuter Express (a new rail service) carries passengers from the inland cities down to San Jose.

In 2003, BART began service to San Francisco International Airport, a plus for penny-pinching travelers and for people who work at or near the airport.

For several years, Oakland has been renovating its airport and the approach roads. The job continues but now it's much easier to get to and from the airport.

But no matter how much money is spent, traffic jams don't go away. The main reason: more people, more cars. In 2000, the state tallied within Alameda County 1,114,591 vehicles. If you take out everyone under age 16 and over age 85, you come up with just about one vehicle for every functioning adult.

With the economy souring, rents have softened but, perversely, thanks to low interest rates, home prices have risen. Alameda County offers lower home prices and rents than San Francisco, Santa Clara and San Mateo counties. But it's easy to spend $575,000 on a modest home and fork over $1,200 a month on a one-bedroom apartment. Newcomers to California are shocked by the home prices and rents.

Alameda County has its rich neighborhoods and its poor neighborhoods but the great majority of the housing was built for the middle class or upper middle. Because of the hills, many homes have views of the Bay.

Quakes a Fact of Life

The Hayward and Calaveras faults run right through the county. A major earthquake is not a matter of if. It's a matter of when. For some good information about preparing for a quake and what to do in one, read the beginning of your phone directory.

In the quake of 1989, many Oakland buildings were damaged, about 40 people were killed, a portion of a freeway collapsed, and the Bay Bridge, the main connection to San Francisco, was knocked out of service. A section of the top deck fell to the lower deck. The freeway has been redesigned; the part of the Bay Bridge that collapsed was repaired and is being replaced.

A Little History

The Spanish arrived in 1772, the expedition led by Lt. Pedro Fages and Father Juan Crespi. European diseases (cholera, measles and smallpox) and settler hostility and indifference just about obliterated the Indians and almost all their culture.

Then followed the Ranchero interlude, 1820 to about 1860. To secure California for Spain and later Mexico, large land grants were made to soldiers and civil servants.

Luis Peralta got Berkeley, Albany and Oakland; Jose Estudillo, San Leandro; Don Guillermo Castro, Hayward and Castro Valley; Jose Amador, Dublin; Juan and Augustin Bernal, Pleasanton.

Superb horsemen, the dons raised cattle, staged rodeos and lived in the grand style. Their parties lasted for days, their hospitality was renown.

But few in number and only recently endowed (the Castro and Estudillo grants were not made until the 1840s), they were unable to resist the Yankee invasion. What they didn't sell, they lost to swindlers, squatters and lawyers.

Gold Fever

Gold lured the Yankees to California, but the many who did not strike it rich turned to farming and commerce. Within a few decades of statehood (1850), Alameda County was well on its way to modern life. Horace Carpentier, sly lawyer, and friends incorporated Oakland as a city in 1852, much to surprise of rest of community. In 1853, the county of Alameda was formed, population 3,000. The first county seat was at Union City, the second at San Leandro. Finally, Oakland's votes carried the seat to that city in 1873.

Berkeley

"Westward the course of empire takes its way." Written by Bishop George Berkeley, the words charmed Frederick Billings. Billings was a trustee of the College of California, opened in 1860 in wild Oakland.

Favoring a more secluded and peaceful spot, trustees purchased land north of Oakland and, at Billings' suggestion, named the town "Berkeley." A few years later the college was offered to the state as the cornerstone of a public university system. The University of California at Berkeley went on to become one of the finest universities in the world.

Meanwhile, the trading posts and ranches in the hinterland were growing into small towns that would later burgeon into suburban cities.

The 20th Century

Ships and electric trains, planes and automobiles. The early 20th century saw many changes in Alameda County transportation. Borax Smith, of 20-mule-team fame, for a while beat Southern Pacific at the commuting race to San Francisco. His electrified trains, with the aid of ferries, crossed the Bay in 35 minutes.

In 1926, Oakland purchased 692 acres on Bay Farm Island for an airport.

Bridges

The first bridge was the railroad Dumbarton (Newark to Redwood City), 1910; the second, automotive Dumbarton, 1927. On Oct. 23, 1936, the last rivet was driven on the Bay Bridge. In 1967, Hayward and San Mateo were joined by the San Mateo Bridge. Finally, the Dumbarton, which used to infuriate motorists by raising the drawbridge during rush hour, was replaced with a higher bridge in 1982.

The bridges, World War II and the freeways changed the face of modern Alameda County. War brought people who liked what they saw. The bridges and freeways allowed them to spread over the countryside and travel long distances to work. In World War II, UC-Berkeley helped build the A-bomb dropped on Nagasaki.

Wild Years

Sixties and Seventies. Free speech. Student protests. Vietnam. War protests and marches. Black Panthers. Hell's Angels. People's Park. Marijuana and LSD. Super Bowl and World Series victories. BART (commuter rail) begins service. Port of Oakland, containerized, takes off. Symbionese Liberation Army. Oakland school superintendent assassinated. Patty Hearst kidnapped. Oakland elects first black mayor.

The Eighties. Raiders depart. Smoking down, cocaine up. Yuppies. Business follows people to suburbs (Pleasanton, Fremont). Japanese, GM join hands in NUMMI auto plant in Fremont. Gene splicing. Herpes and AIDS. Wild sex out, safe sex in. Babies in. Money in. Food in. U.S. veers right, Berkeley stays left but tilts toward center. Drug abuse remains a problem.

Oct. 17, 1989, the earthquake that won't be forgotten for a long time.

The county's demographics change. Revisions in the federal law greatly increased the number of immigrants from the Philippine Islands, China, India and Southeast Asia. The new Alameda County is much more international, cosmopolitan.

The Nineties

Oakland rebuilds from the earthquake.

BART in 1997 extended its line and opened stations in Castro Valley and Dublin, welcome alternatives to congested freeways.

The military pulls out of the Bay Area, the logical outcome to the end of the Cold War. Alameda Naval Air Station, home for decades to the giant carriers, closes and is now being used for civilian purposes. Also closed: the Oakland army base, a supply depot. Lawrence Livermore National Lab survives the shutdowns and finds ways to prove its benefits.

In 1995, cold-shouldered by L.A., the Raiders return to Oakland and after years of losing seem to have found their winning ways — until 2004 and 2005. El floppo! The A's made the playoffs in 2000, 2001 and 2002 and 2003.

2000 Plus

In the late 1990s and in 2000, the California economy boomed and millions were allocated to reduce class sizes and improve instruction.

In 2002, people were saying that many schools were in the best shape they have been in 25 years.

In 2003, with the state deficit hitting $38 billion and Sacramento warning of steep cuts coming to schools, colleges and universities, the cheering turned to fretting. As mentioned, the Oakland school district declared bankruptcy. Retrospectively, the failings seem obvious but in the heady days of 2000 and 2001, Oakland may have assumed that the good-time dollars would keep rolling in.

When the U.S. invaded Iraq, many in Berkeley protested but the days of sustained protests seem over. The hippies of old are now in their 50s and 60s; the younger generation perhaps less interested in politics.

Suburbs and Small Towns

In the suburbs and smaller towns, conservative or middle-of-the-road politics hold greater appeal but many a Democrat resides in towns like Fremont, Union City, Hayward and San Leandro. Growth and development tend to dominate suburban politics because billions of dollars and thousands of jobs ride on development and because the builders are the great moneybags of local politics.

With the passage of Prop. 13 in the 1970s, the funding base of local agencies, especially schools, shifted to Sacramento. Each year, heated arguments fill the Sacramento air as local groups try to squeeze money out of the governor and legislature.

Here are the groups making and carrying out local policy in the county:

The Board of Supervisors

Five members are elected countywide but by districts (Oakland votes for its supervisor, the Fremont area for its supervisor, and so on.) Supervisors are regional and municipal governors. They control spending for courts, social services and public health, including hospitals for the poor.

In their municipal hats, they build roads, decide zonings and, through the sheriff, provide police protection for unincorporated areas.

If you live in Castro Valley, San Lorenzo or outside any city limits, you will be governed from Oakland, seat of the county government, but often county officials follow the advice of local leaders.

City Councils

Generally, five members (Berkeley has nine) are elected, one council for each of the county's 14 cities. Some cities (Berkeley, Oakland) have directly elected mayors who share power with the councils. Councils are responsible for repairing roads, keeping neighborhoods safe, maintaining parks, providing recreation and doing other municipal chores.

Education Level of Population Age 25 & Over
(Percent of Population)

City or Town	ND	HS	SC	AA	BA	Grad
Alameda City	8%	7%	23%	7%	27%	15%
Albany	4	11	14	5	30	34
Berkeley	4	9	15	4	30	34
Castro Valley	8	24	26	8	20	11
Dublin	11	21	25	8	24	9
Emeryville	8	11	20	5	28	25
Fremont	7	17	20	8	27	17
Hayward	14	26	3	7	14	5
Livermore	7	20	29	9	20	12
Newark	11	23	25	7	17	7
Oakland	13	18	20	6	18	13
Piedmont	1	4	12	5	37	41
Pleasanton	4	15	24	9	32	16
San Leandro	11	26	25	8	17	7
San Lorenzo	12	33	26	7	11	4
Union City	10	21	22	8	21	8
Alameda County	10	19	22	7	21	14

Source: 2000 Census. Figures are percent of population age 25 and older, rounded to the nearest whole number. **Key:** ND (Less than 9th grade or some high school but no degree); HS (adults with high school diploma or GED only, no college); SC (adults with some college education); AA (adults with an associate degree); BA (adults with a bachelor's degree only); Grad (adults with a master's or higher degree).

Utility Districts

California grew so fast and chaotically that some regional needs, such as sewer and water, were met on an emergency basis by forming taxing districts with their own elected directors. The East Bay Municipal Utility District provides water to large portions of Alameda and Contra Costa counties and sewage treatment to six Alameda cities.

East Bay Regional Parks

If the park is big, chances are it's owned by the East Bay Regional Park District, one of the most successful park agencies nationally. The district, through its elected board, manages parks in Alameda and Contra Costa counties. Cities and special districts manage the small, municipal parks.

School Boards

Generally composed of five persons. There are 20 school districts in Alameda County, each with an elected school board.

Members hire or fire principals and superintendents, negotiate teacher salaries and decide policy matters and how much should be spent on computers and shop. The everyday running of schools is left to superintendents. Major funding decisions are made in Sacramento.

BART & Other Transit Districts

Elected Bay Area Rapid Transit District (BART) directors are responsible for making the trains run on time, providing parking at the stations and deciding where to extend BART.

Other transit agencies, such as AC Transit, run buses.

Regional Governments

As the Bay Area grew, it became apparent that many political boundaries either didn't make sense or else were too restrictive to solve regional problems, such as air and water pollution. Regional agencies were formed to deal with these problems.

Among the more important are, the Bay Conservation and Development Commission (shore protection), the Bay Area Air Quality Management District, the Regional Water Quality Control Board, the Association of Bay Area Governments and the Metropolitan Transportation Commission

Miscellenous:

• Responding to the cutback in state funds to the schools, several school districts in 2004 and 2005 passed funding measures to build and renovate schools or retain programs.

www.mccormacks.com

McCormack's Guides are published for:

ALAMEDA-CENTRAL VALLEY • CONTRA COSTA-SOLANO
• SANTA CLARA-SANTA CRUZ-SILICON VALLEY
• SAN FRANCISCO-SAN MATEO-MARIN-SONOMA
• SAN DIEGO • ORANGE COUNTY • GREATER SACRAMENTO

Available in e-book format at www.mccormacks.com:

LOS ANGELES • RIVERSIDE • SANTA BARBARA
• SAN BERNARDINO • VENTURA

Before you move ... buy

Also from McCormack's Guides:
How California Schools Work
1•800•222•3602

Chapter 2a

State School Rankings

HERE ARE COMPARISON RANKINGS from the 2005 STAR tests taken by almost every public-school student in California. This test is administered annually by the California Department of Education.

We have broken out the results in a way that makes comparisons between schools easy.

The rankings, based on the scores, range from 1 (the lowest) to 99 (the highest). A school that scores in the 20th percentile is landing in the bottom 20 percent of the state. A school that scores in the 95th percentile is placing among the top 5 percent of schools in the state.

These rankings should be considered rough measures of how the schools and their students are performing.

Many low- and middle-scoring schools have students who score high. Many high-scoring schools have students who land below the 25th percentile.

A few schools post average scores but turn out many high-scoring students. These schools often will have many students at the bottom and many at the top and few in the middle.

For more information, visit the school or go on the web and check out reports about individual schools. For more test results, go to www.star.cde.ca.gov. See also the school accountability reports.

To flesh out these scores, we are including in Chapter 2B a ranking system issued by the California Department of Education and in Chapter 7 the SAT scores, math and verbal, for the regular high schools. These scores and a chart that presents SAT scores by state will give you some idea of how local schools compare to schools nationwide.

Scores range from 1-99. A school scoring 75 has done better than 75 percent of other public schools in California.

Key: Eng (English), Ma (Math), Sci (Science).

Grade	Eng	Ma	Sci

Alameda City Unified School Dist.

Alameda City Unified Programs

Grade	Eng	Ma	Sci
4	7	2	
5	3	3	10
10	2		

Alameda High

Grade	Eng	Ma	Sci
9	89		
10	89		
11	90		

Alameda Science & Technology

Grade	Eng	Ma	Sci
9	93		

Arthur Anderson Comm. Learning

Grade	Eng	Ma	Sci
6	77	36	
7	94	87	
8	85		
9	96		
10	85		
11	98		

Bay Area School

Grade	Eng	Ma	Sci
9	51		
10	42		
11	84		

Bay Farm Elem.

Grade	Eng	Ma	Sci
2	99	99	
3	95	95	
4	98	94	
5	99	96	97
6	97	95	

Chipman Middle

Grade	Eng	Ma	Sci
6	23	32	
7	41	52	
8	32		

Earhart Elem.

Grade	Eng	Ma	Sci
2	87	89	
3	88	85	
4	92	91	
5	92	93	95
6	73	64	

Edison Elem.

Grade	Eng	Ma	Sci
2	94	92	
3	98	90	
4	90	81	
5	97	86	91

Encinal High

Grade	Eng	Ma	Sci
9	55		
10	68		
11	72		

Franklin Elem.

Grade	Eng	Ma	Sci
2	95	81	
3	94	84	
4	84	68	
5	80	56	72

Haight Elem.

Grade	Eng	Ma	Sci
2	39	48	
3	69	63	
4	55	37	
5	64	57	49

Island High (Cont.)

Grade	Eng	Ma	Sci
11	31		

Lincoln Middle

Grade	Eng	Ma	Sci
6	88	92	
7	91	93	
8	81		

Longfellow Elem.

Grade	Eng	Ma	Sci
2	67	77	
3	96	95	
4	56	74	
5	30	35	14

Lum Elem.

Grade	Eng	Ma	Sci
2	78	69	
3	74	78	
4	79	76	
5	79	66	68

Miller Elem.

Grade	Eng	Ma	Sci
2	82	75	
3	47	32	
4	65	71	
5	36	30	56

Otis Elem.

Grade	Eng	Ma	Sci
2	93	81	
3	72	54	
4	84	77	
5	75	68	62

Paden Elem.

Grade	Eng	Ma	Sci
2	85	72	
3	74	75	
4	81	83	
5	88	79	77
6	84	89	
7	94	98	
8	82		

Washington Elem.

Grade	Eng	Ma	Sci
2	36	43	
3	79	78	
4	59	57	
5	39	23	24

Wood Middle

Grade	Eng	Ma	Sci
6	59	65	
7	56	63	
8	49		

Woodstock Elem.

Grade	Eng	Ma	Sci
2	34	30	
3	50	54	
4	54	83	
5	44	66	32

Albany City Unified School Dist.

Albany High

Grade	Eng	Ma	Sci
9	92		
10	94		
11	96		

Albany Middle

Grade	Eng	Ma	Sci
6	94	95	
7	89	92	
8	91		

Scores range from 1-99. A school scoring 75 has done better than 75 percent of other public schools in California.
Key: Eng (English), Ma (Math), Sci (Science).

Grade	Eng	Ma	Sci
Cornell Elem.			
2	78	79	
3	96	92	
4	90	85	
5	96	92	97
MacGregor High (Cont.)			
11	24		
Marin Elem.			
2	94	90	
3	92	82	
4	93	87	
5	98	94	98
Ocean View Elem.			
2	90	91	
3	94	96	
4	94	85	
5	90	94	93

Berkeley Unified School Dist.
Alameda City Unified Programs

Grade	Eng	Ma	Sci
11	89		
Berkeley Alt..			
9	12		
10	1		
11	4		
Berkeley High			
9	84		
10	84		
11	88		
Cragmont Elem.			
2	66	63	
3	81	83	
4	63	69	
5	74	80	78
Emerson Elem.			
2	49	45	
3	85	89	
4	82	57	
5	74	67	76
Jefferson Elem.			
2	67	54	
3	87	80	
4	81	66	
5	82	77	86
King Middle			
6	70	76	
7	58	58	
8	73		
Leconte Elem.			
2	23	39	
3	38	27	
4	60	70	
5	48	30	64
Longfellow Arts & Tech			
6	31	34	
7	54	80	
8	52		

Grade	Eng	Ma	Sci
Malcolm X Elem.			
2	77	70	
3	72	70	
4	48	49	
5	67	87	60
Muir Elem.			
2	99	98	
3	82	86	
4	76	54	
5	80	78	88
Oxford Elem.			
2	82	83	
3	83	69	
4	77	84	
5	79	97	83
Parks Magnet			
2	34	48	
3	47	25	
4	59	43	
5	48	21	52
Thousand Oaks Elem.			
2	42	43	
3	80	79	
4	52	65	
5	42	39	39
Washington Elem.			
2	78	67	
3	44	33	
4	54	71	
5	62	37	50
Whittier/Arts (Elem.)			
2	43	42	
3	69	70	
4	81	70	
5	71	53	55
6	59	59	
Willard Middle			
6	55	28	
7	40	41	
8	43		

California School for the Deaf-Northern
Cali. Sch. for the Deaf - N.

Grade	Eng	Ma	Sci
2	1	2	
3	7	37	
4	4	11	
5	70	41	
6	67	41	
7	94	67	
8	70	9	
9	82		
10	72		
11	81		

Castro Valley Unified School Dist.
Canyon Middle

Grade	Eng	Ma	Sci
6	86	86	
7	86	86	
8	84		

Scores range from 1-99. A school scoring 75 has done better than 75 percent of other public schools in California.
Key: Eng (English), Ma (Math), Sci (Science).

Grade	Eng	Ma	Sci
Castro Valley Elem.			
2	75	64	
3	70	56	
4	56	67	
5	46	55	63
Castro Valley High			
9	87		
10	84		
11	86		
Chabot Elem.			
2	86	94	
3	87	87	
4	87	91	
5	80	84	77
Creekside Middle			
6	85	92	
7	88	95	
8	85		
Independent Elem.			
2	97	92	
3	96	97	
4	92	98	
5	94	94	93
Jensen Ranch (Elem.)			
2	97	99	
3	98	99	
4	96	99	
5	98	99	99
Marshall Elem.			
2	76	69	
3	73	78	
4	57	64	
5	58	69	77
Palomares Elem.			
2	73	65	
3	93	98	
4	92	98	
5	83	83	79
Proctor Elem.			
2	94	93	
3	88	85	
4	91	92	
5	96	96	92
Redwood Alt. High			
9	33		
10	25		
11	16		
Stanton Elem.			
2	66	74	
3	71	77	
4	70	66	
5	70	77	78
Vannoy Elem.			
2	90	86	
3	75	70	
4	87	90	
5	96	90	94

Grade	Eng	Ma	Sci
Dublin Unified School Dist.			
Dougherty Elem.			
2	98	97	
3	95	96	
4	97	98	
5	96	94	96
Dublin Elem.			
2	76	75	
3	83	82	
4	79	81	
5	93	94	94
Dublin High			
9	83		
10	85		
11	86		
Frederiksen Elem.			
2	55	65	
3	82	73	
4	71	63	
5	81	79	69
Murray Elem.			
2	59	50	
3	65	58	
4	86	86	
5	83	59	89
Nielsen Elem.			
2	83	87	
3	87	88	
4	82	86	
5	81	79	85
Valley High (Cont.)			
10	36		
11	43		
Wells Middle			
6	75	77	
7	76	78	
8	80		
Emery Unified School Dist.			
Anna Yates Elem.			
2	38	18	
3	66	80	
4	29	28	
5	30	26	28
6	33	22	
Emery Secondary			
7	26	38	
8	16		
9	41		
10	40		
11	39		
Fremont Unified School Dist.			
Alameda City Unified Programs			
7	2	7	
8	11	17	

Scores range from 1-99. A school scoring 75 has done better than 75 percent of other public schools in California.
Key: Eng (English), Ma (Math), Sci (Science).

Grade	Eng	Ma	Sci		Grade	Eng	Ma	Sci
American High					**Durham Elem.**			
9	89				2	63	78	
10	91				3	43	42	
11	84				4	67	54	
Ardenwood Elem.					5	52	47	59
2	87	89			6	57	77	
3	91	96			**Forest Park Elem.**			
4	87	92			2	98	98	
5	92	94	92		3	99	99	
6	90	96			4	97	97	
Azevada Elem.					5	99	98	98
2	61	61			6	96	96	
3	63	64			**Glenmoor Elem.**			
4	69	87			2	90	82	
5	67	67	73		3	77	80	
6	67	67			4	94	95	
Blacow Elem.					5	72	61	65
2	45	50			6	79	83	
3	39	47			**Gomes Elem.**			
4	28	50			2	99	98	
5	38	57	48		3	99	99	
6	46	66			4	99	99	
Brier Elem.					5	99	99	99
2	79	71			6	99	99	
3	73	84			**Green Elem.**			
4	74	78			2	79	65	
5	62	58	66		3	72	62	
6	57	82			4	59	66	
Brookvale Elem.					5	58	68	72
2	76	55			6	72	76	
3	82	95			**Grimmer Elem.**			
4	82	84			2	33	32	
5	58	42	62		3	37	42	
6	81	76			4	53	60	
Cabrillo Elem.					5	37	46	43
2	29	23			6	34	42	
3	39	40			**Hirsch Elem.**			
4	47	56			2	69	54	
5	32	37	43		3	72	76	
6	55	47			4	73	60	
Centerville Jr. High					5	70	90	52
7	69	70			6	73	50	
8	72				**Hopkins Jr. High**			
Chadbourne Elem.					7	99	99	
2	99	99			8	99		
3	99	99			**Horner Jr. High**			
4	99	99			7	88	94	
5	98	97	98		8	88		
6	98	99			**Irvington High**			
Circle of Independent Learning					9	91		
2	60	56			10	85		
5	67	54	76		11	81		
6	69	59			**Kennedy High**			
7	74	73			9	69		
8	84				10	73		
9	82				11	69		
10	33							
11	64							

Scores range from 1-99. A school scoring 75 has done better than 75 percent of other public schools in California.
Key: Eng (English), Ma (Math), Sci (Science).

Grade	Eng	Ma	Sci
Leitch Elem.			
2	96	95	
Maloney Elem.			
2	88	89	
3	60	69	
4	66	54	
5	81	83	86
6	73	80	
Mattos Elem.			
2	89	78	
3	69	60	
4	75	73	
5	69	75	89
6	81	85	
Millard Elem.			
2	83	86	
3	78	88	
4	74	78	
5	86	92	86
6	53	62	
Mission San Jose Elem.			
2	99	99	
3	97	99	
4	99	99	
5	99	99	99
6	99	99	
Mission San Jose High			
9	99		
10	99		
11	99		
Mission Valley Elem.			
2	98	98	
3	98	99	
4	99	99	
5	99	99	99
6	98	98	
Niles Elem.			
2	90	86	
3	81	87	
4	93	88	
5	90	82	93
6	89	88	
Oliveira Elem.			
2	74	77	
3	57	66	
4	56	57	
5	34	14	25
6	63	61	
Parkmont Elem.			
2	98	96	
3	92	97	
4	94	95	
5	94	95	95
6	83	89	
Patterson Elem.			
2	73	55	
3	66	72	
4	64	62	
5	66	44	59
6	82	72	

Grade	Eng	Ma	Sci
Robertson High (Cont.)			
10	16		
11	18		
Thornton Jr. High			
7	84	88	
8	79		
Vallejo Mill Elem.			
2	62	75	
3	61	62	
4	62	49	
5	72	54	69
6	79	62	
Walters Jr. High			
7	61	64	
8	60		
Warm Springs Elem.			
3	95	97	
4	92	96	
5	95	96	96
6	94	96	
Warwick Elem.			
2	81	78	
3	78	81	
4	78	75	
5	74	69	81
6	85	85	
Washington High			
9	86		
10	87		
11	85		
Weibel Elem.			
2	99	98	
3	99	99	
4	99	99	
5	99	99	99
6	99	99	
Hayward Unified School Dist.			
Bowman Elem.			
2	47	81	
3	15	34	
4	34	77	
5	40	76	16
6	28	43	
Brenkwitz High			
10	2		
11	4		
Bret Harte Middle			
7	51	22	
8	46		
Burbank Elem.			
2	18	50	
3	6	27	
4	27	35	
5	10	52	30
6	22	36	
Chavez Middle			
7	35	49	
8	36		

Scores range from 1-99. A school scoring 75 has done better than 75 percent of other public schools in California.
Key: Eng (English), Ma (Math), Sci (Science).

Grade	Eng	Ma	Sci
Cherryland Elem.			
2	16	44	
3	10	12	
4	22	30	
5	33	25	35
6	36	28	
East Ave. Elem.			
2	77	91	
3	77	86	
4	61	43	
5	74	81	73
6	64	59	
Eden Gardens Elem.			
2	37	22	
3	46	64	
4	68	47	
5	46	44	46
6	44	33	
Eldridge Elem.			
2	54	56	
3	63	68	
4	57	70	
5	55	65	62
6	66	66	
Fairview Elem.			
2	50	77	
3	60	52	
4	19	9	
5	21	28	15
6	24	24	
Glassbrook Elem.			
2	7	19	
3	12	19	
Harder Elem.			
2	41	73	
3	26	47	
4	27	37	
5	26	43	30
6	34	44	
Hayward High			
9	41		
10	48		
11	46		
Hayward Project			
3	2	35	
4	9	6	
5	25	21	10
6	10	5	
7	35	24	
8	51		
Highland Elem.			
2	86	82	
3	72	57	
4	68	57	
5	51	34	69
6	59	55	

Grade	Eng	Ma	Sci
King Middle			
7	52	52	
8	35		
Longwood Elem.			
2	16	42	
3	13	7	
4	40	56	
5	26	28	30
6	20	20	
Lorin A. Eden Elem.			
2	34	28	
3	39	20	
4	47	38	
5	41	44	36
6	61	51	
Markham Elem.			
2	67	61	
3	31	29	
4	41	37	
5	29	49	24
6	24	13	
Mt. Eden High			
9	48		
10	58		
11	52		
Muir Elem.			
2	23	19	
3	33	20	
4	26	46	
5	15	16	20
6	28	44	
Ochoa Middle			
7	28	39	
8	24		
Palma Ceia Elem.			
2	58	64	
3	19	13	
4	21	13	
5	41	49	42
6	27	16	
Park Elem.			
2	13	15	
3	35	42	
4	32	13	
5	30	21	40
6	28	17	
Ruus Elem.			
2	18	30	
3	24	27	
4	24	9	
5	21	23	36
6	15	9	
Schafer Park Elem.			
2	14	27	
3	21	29	
4	21	32	
5	25	40	41
6	31	32	

Scores range from 1-99. A school scoring 75 has done better than 75 percent of other public schools in California.

Key: Eng (English), Ma (Math), Sci (Science).

Shepherd Elem.

Grade	Eng	Ma	Sci
2	5	18	
3	8	10	

Southgate Elem.

Grade	Eng	Ma	Sci
2	69	80	
3	60	54	
4	51	62	
5	62	36	67
6	56	69	

Strobridge Elem.

Grade	Eng	Ma	Sci
2	20	24	
3	52	53	
4	69	59	
5	46	28	36
6	50	49	

Tennyson High

Grade	Eng	Ma	Sci
9	34		
10	49		
11	43		

Treeview Elem.

Grade	Eng	Ma	Sci
2	47	35	
3	53	46	
4	52	47	
5	15	27	22
6	34	24	

Tyrrell Elem.

Grade	Eng	Ma	Sci
4	41	60	
5	24	26	20
6	31	40	

Winton Middle

Grade	Eng	Ma	Sci
7	35	40	
8	33		

Livermore Valley Joint Unif. School Dist.

Alt.amont Creek Elem.

Grade	Eng	Ma	Sci
2	74	68	
3	69	61	
4	81	69	
5	70	52	75

Arroyo Seco Elem.

Grade	Eng	Ma	Sci
2	86	78	
3	73	74	
4	91	92	
5	88	70	88

Christensen Middle

Grade	Eng	Ma	Sci
6	79	72	
7	80	74	
8	78		

Croce Elem.

Grade	Eng	Ma	Sci
2	83	96	
3	77	71	
4	80	64	
5	71	71	83

Del Valle Cont. High

Grade	Eng	Ma	Sci
11	34		

East Ave. Middle

Grade	Eng	Ma	Sci
6	81	74	
7	78	75	
8	84		

Granada High

Grade	Eng	Ma	Sci
9	89		
10	92		
11	92		

Jackson Ave. Elem.

Grade	Eng	Ma	Sci
2	71	73	
3	68	73	
4	77	76	
5	78	52	78

Junction Ave. Middle

Grade	Eng	Ma	Sci
6	48	57	
7	43	51	
8	44		

Livermore High

Grade	Eng	Ma	Sci
9	82		
10	81		
11	77		

Marylin Ave. Elem.

Grade	Eng	Ma	Sci
2	7	17	
3	22	20	
4	21	8	
5	41	23	54

Michell Elem.

Grade	Eng	Ma	Sci
2	51	35	
3	56	51	
4	66	46	
5	80	82	65

Phoenix High (Cont.)

Grade	Eng	Ma	Sci
10	28		
11	33		

Portola Elem.

Grade	Eng	Ma	Sci
2	38	44	
3	49	64	
4	43	49	
5	26	33	44

Rancho Las Positas Elem.

Grade	Eng	Ma	Sci
2	88	84	
3	70	56	
4	60	50	
5	80	75	84

Smith Elem.

Grade	Eng	Ma	Sci
2	90	88	
3	93	93	
4	84	75	
5	92	92	93

Sunset Elem.

Grade	Eng	Ma	Sci
2	93	91	
3	90	80	
4	93	86	
5	90	83	89

Vineyard Alt..

Grade	Eng	Ma	Sci
7	88	69	
8	61		
9	39		
10	32		
11	63		

Scores range from 1-99. A school scoring 75 has done better than 75 percent of other public schools in California.
Key: Eng (English), Ma (Math), Sci (Science).

Grade	Eng	Ma	Sci
William Mendenhall Middle			
6	84	83	
7	84	82	
8	87		

New Haven Unified School Dist. (Union City)

Alameda City Unified Programs

Grade	Eng	Ma	Sci
2	1	1	
3	2	2	
Alvarado Elem.			
2	47	59	
3	55	66	
4	52	57	
5	43	22	49
Alvarado Middle			
6	52	51	
7	70	66	
8	67		
Barnard-White Middle			
6	31	31	
7	49	40	
8	54		
Cabello Elem.			
2	44	60	
3	43	75	
4	37	61	
5	48	54	48
Chavez Middle			
6	64	64	
7	77	63	
8	75		
Eastin Elem.			
2	84	93	
3	83	93	
4	83	84	
5	86	93	81
Emanuele Elem.			
2	46	65	
3	44	67	
4	44	63	
5	50	69	75
Hillview Crest Elem. (Hayward)			
2	24	63	
3	52	61	
4	26	27	
5	42	29	44
James Logan High			
9	69		
10	65		
11	59		
Kitayama Elem.			
2	57	54	
3	61	72	
4	64	69	
5	73	63	76

Grade	Eng	Ma	Sci
Pioneer Elem.			
2	78	76	
3	72	85	
4	80	84	
5	81	86	86
Searles Elem.			
2	39	46	
3	47	49	
4	53	42	
5	60	63	59

Newark Unified School Dist.

Bridgepoint High (Cont.)

Grade	Eng	Ma	Sci
11	19		
Bunker Elem.			
2	62	64	
3	78	79	
4	70	74	
5	70	76	76
6	77	85	
Crossroads High (Alt..)			
10	21		
11	30		
Graham Elem.			
2	24	19	
3	41	54	
4	35	45	
5	44	37	49
6	43	49	
Kennedy Elem.			
2	52	53	
3	85	75	
4	61	51	
5	76	73	82
6	78	78	
Lincoln Elem.			
2	61	59	
3	61	67	
4	56	68	
5	48	41	59
6	73	68	
Milani Elem.			
2	28	36	
3	43	44	
4	40	19	
5	48	33	61
6	51	48	
Musick Elem.			
2	33	68	
3	44	62	
4	26	17	
5	32	19	61
6	62	45	
Newark Jr. High			
7	46	54	
8	47		
Newark Memorial High			
9	59		
10	62		
11	65		

Scores range from 1-99. A school scoring 75 has done better than 75 percent of other public schools in California.
Key: Eng (English), Ma (Math), Sci (Science).

Grade	Eng	Ma	Sci
Schilling (August) Elem.			
2	34	51	
3	24	23	
4	25	34	
5	49	42	48
6	34	37	
Snow Elem.			
2	55	69	
3	64	72	
4	58	72	
5	48	44	48
6	61	76	

Oakland Unified School Dist.

Grade	Eng	Ma	Sci
ACORN Woodland Elem.			
2	14	12	
3	20	56	
4	5	20	
5	15	31	4
Alameda City Unified Programs			
6	3	2	
9	1		
Allendale Elem.			
2	42	64	
3	39	40	
4	12	7	
5	23	16	26
American Indian Pub. Char.			
6	92	96	
7	95	95	
8	84		
ASCEND			
3	58	75	
5	27	24	17
6	19	26	
7	37	30	
8	33		
Bay Area Technology School			
6	29	16	
Bella Vista Elem.			
2	60	66	
3	47	69	
4	32	42	
5	38	37	11
Brewer Middle			
6	31	44	
7	29	59	
8	37		
Brookfield Elem.			
2	9	6	
3	23	26	
4	9	7	
5	16	12	8
Burchhalter Elem.			
2	37	12	
3	53	43	
4	39	11	
5	49	42	65

Grade	Eng	Ma	Sci
Business & Info. Technology			
9	25		
10	26		
11	28		
Carter Middle			
6	3	3	
7	20	12	
8	22		
Chabot Elem.			
2	96	90	
3	95	91	
4	94	89	
5	91	81	80
Claremont Middle			
6	19	8	
7	13	12	
8	40		
Cleveland Elem.			
2	93	95	
3	90	93	
4	66	79	
5	81	93	45
Cole Middle			
6	3	2	
7	16	11	
8	14		
College Prep. and Architecture			
9	21		
10	38		
11	40		
Cox Elem.			
2	2	2	
3	4	5	
4	5	5	
5	16	20	11
Crocker Highlands Elem.			
2	98	98	
3	74	71	
4	88	76	
5	92	95	87
Dewey Academy Sr. High			
9	7		
10	3		
11	11		
Dolores Huerta Learning Acad.			
2	4	27	
3	4	26	
4	10	10	
5	17	31	7
6	32	25	
7	14	15	
8	20		
E. Bay Consv. Corps Char.			
2	17	9	
3	67	33	
4	28	4	
5	42	15	33

Scores range from 1-99. A school scoring 75 has done better than 75 percent of other public schools in California.
Key: Eng (English), Ma (Math), Sci (Science).

Grade	Eng	Ma	Sci
East Oakland Comm. High			
9	27		
East Oakland Leadership Acad.			
6	19	7	
7	39	38	
East Oakland School of the Art			
9	15		
10	23		
11	18		
Elmhurst Middle			
6	4	6	
7	7	7	
8	11		
Emerson Elem.			
2	28	3	
3	35	30	
4	12	2	
5	22	9	4
EnCompass Acad.			
2	3	7	
Explorer Middle			
6	16	21	
Far West (Cont.)			
6	60	50	
7	22	6	
8	10		
9	29		
10	45		
11	26		
Franklin Elem.			
2	41	48	
3	63	84	
4	28	62	
5	44	65	49
Frick Middle			
6	7	7	
7	14	10	
8	21		
Fruitvale Elem.			
2	68	56	
3	38	34	
4	56	60	
5	55	71	44
Garfield Elem.			
2	21	38	
3	16	34	
4	30	42	
5	11	27	9
Glenview Elem.			
2	72	58	
3	60	54	
4	55	57	
5	69	74	63
Golden Gate Elem.			
2	11	3	
3	16	12	
4	21	4	
5	17	3	3

Grade	Eng	Ma	Sci
Grass Valley Elem.			
2	70	62	
3	54	44	
4	59	71	
5	71	89	47
Growing Children Char.			
2	1	5	
3	1	2	
4	2	2	
5	3	1	8
Harte Middle			
6	26	29	
7	26	26	
8	35		
Havenscourt Middle			
6	3	3	
7	8	7	
8	11		
Hawthorne Elem.			
2	6	7	
3	4	6	
4	8	20	
5	15	27	9
Highland Elem.			
2	2	4	
3	4	7	
4	3	5	
5	14	9	7
Hillcrest Elem.			
2	98	97	
3	97	89	
4	98	99	
5	94	99	85
6	99	94	
7	98	94	
8	98		
Hoover Elem.			
2	18	10	
3	19	5	
4	28	37	
5	12	53	22
Howard Elem.			
2	49	11	
3	51	18	
4	52	49	
5	8	12	30
International Comm.			
2	9	21	
3	20	42	
4	8	12	
5	30	36	22
Jefferson Elem.			
2	5	31	
3	7	8	
4	11	18	
5	6	10	3

Scores range from 1-99. A school scoring 75 has done better than 75 percent of other public schools in California.

Key: Eng (English), Ma (Math), Sci (Science).

Grade	Eng	Ma	Sci
Kaiser Elem.			
2	74	71	
3	95	84	
4	71	77	
5	81	94	72
King Estates Middle			
7	8	7	
8	14		
King Elem.			
2	12	8	
3	12	3	
4	7	2	
KIPP Prep.			
5	60	72	67
6	62	63	
7	76	94	
La Escuelita Elem.			
2	23	48	
3	13	23	
4	34	76	
5	65	88	54
Lafayette Elem.			
2	15	9	
3	8	24	
4	4	4	
5	12	3	3
Lakeview Elem.			
2	36	28	
3	59	53	
4	12	9	
5	26	9	36
Laney Middle (Opp.)			
7	5	3	
8	10		
9	31		
10	57		
11	48		
Laurel Elem.			
2	55	40	
3	37	43	
4	32	49	
5	52	64	39
Lazear Elem.			
2	7	23	
3	6	10	
4	16	25	
5	22	41	14
Leadership Preparatory High			
9	16		
10	28		
11	32		
LIFE Academy			
9	33		
10	51		
11	41		
Lighthouse Comm. Char.			
2	35	10	
6	12	10	
7	18	51	
8	17		

Grade	Eng	Ma	Sci
Lincoln Elem.			
2	92	99	
3	78	97	
4	66	94	
5	68	90	80
Lionel Wilson College Prep.			
6	7	34	
7	11	16	
8	32		
9	33		
10	38		
11	36		
Lockwood Elem.			
2	5	2	
3	4	6	
4	3	5	
5	4	5	2
Lowell Middle			
7	12	9	
8	11		
Madison Middle			
6	3	3	
7	4	5	
8	10		
Mandela High			
9	21		
10	25		
11	24		
Mann Elem.			
2	32	20	
3	8	5	
4	8	10	
5	9	11	3
Manzanita Elem.			
2	20	8	
3	15	6	
4	8	11	
5	11	15	8
Markham Elem.			
2	11	7	
3	7	4	
4	22	14	
5	21	36	12
Marshall Elem.			
2	83	84	
3	43	65	
4	39	33	
5	34	39	34
Maxwell Park Elem.			
2	11	3	
3	8	3	
4	11	4	
5	24	12	13
McClymonds Sr. High			
9	23		
10	27		
11	29		

Scores range from 1-99. A school scoring 75 has done better than 75 percent of other public schools in California.
Key: Eng (English), Ma (Math), Sci (Science).

Grade	Eng	Ma	Sci
Media College Preparatory			
9	14		
10	18		
11	37		
Melrose Elem.			
2	8	20	
3	11	61	
4	7	17	
5	26	58	14
Melrose Leadership Academy			
6	7	26	
7	27	47	
8	10		
Merritt Middle College High			
9	13		
10	18		
11	14		
MetWest High			
9	68		
10	67		
11	58		
Miller Elem.			
2	97	97	
3	94	85	
4	87	78	
5	94	94	90
Monarch Academy			
2	14	23	
3	19	22	
4	14	27	
5	9	36	17
6	7	17	
7	36	65	
8	42		
Montclair Elem.			
2	90	87	
3	90	83	
4	91	86	
5	93	92	91
Montera Middle			
6	73	71	
7	80	77	
8	78		
Munck Elem.			
2	61	54	
3	43	39	
4	45	64	
5	45	52	40
North Oakland Char.			
4	97	79	
Oakland Alt. School			
9	21		
10	6		
Oakland Char. Academy			
6	44	41	
7	57	64	
8	50		

Grade	Eng	Ma	Sci
Oakland Comm.. Day Middle			
8	7		
Oakland Military			
6	12	23	
7	30	35	
8	34		
9	64		
10	64		
Oakland School For The Arts			
9	93		
10	94		
11	82		
Oakland Sr. High			
9	30		
10	39		
11	42		
Oakland Technical Sr. High			
9	36		
10	41		
11	38		
Oakland Unity High			
9	41		
10	30		
11	60		
Parker Elem.			
2	32	14	
3	8	17	
4	10	4	
5	20	17	21
Paul Robeson College Prep.			
9	20		
10	31		
11	34		
Peralta Elem.			
2	87	96	
3	71	77	
4	86	91	
5	74	65	33
Piedmont Ave. Elem.			
2	56	38	
3	55	53	
4	37	39	
5	61	66	30
Prescott Elem.			
2	33	17	
3	31	22	
4	29	9	
5	6	7	7
Ralph Bunche Academy			
7	2	1	
8	2		
9	9		
10	1		
Redwood Heights Elem.			
2	89	92	
3	90	88	
4	89	87	
5	95	94	90

Scores range from 1-99. A school scoring 75 has done better than 75 percent of other public schools in California.

Key: Eng (English), Ma (Math), Sci (Science).

Grade	Eng	Ma	Sci
Reems Academy			
2	27	24	
3	75	68	
4	35	18	
5	35	35	44
6	31	73	
7	28	20	
8	12		
Roosevelt Middle			
6	21	32	
7	30	37	
8	27		
Rudsdale Academy			
8	4		
Santa Fe Elem.			
2	33	14	
3	12	4	
4	8	8	
5	10	7	10
Sequoia Elem.			
2	87	74	
3	28	27	
4	49	50	
5	52	56	31
Sherman Elem.			
2	48	9	
3	18	4	
4	32	17	
5	32	26	7
Simmons Middle			
6	3	3	
7	8	10	
8	8		
Skyline High			
9	67		
10	66		
11	67		
Sobrante Park Elem.			
2	9	6	
3	26	28	
4	72	77	
5	10	19	17
Stonehurst Elem.			
2	13	14	
3	24	24	
4	5	7	
5	12	35	17
Street Academy (Alt.)			
9	27		
10	41		
11	40		
Think College Now			
2	8	14	
3	6	23	
Thornhill Elem.			
2	98	95	
3	94	95	
4	95	92	
5	99	98	99

Grade	Eng	Ma	Sci
University Preparatory			
9	38		
10	67		
11	75		
Urban Promise			
6	14	24	
7	23	19	
8	13		
Washington Elem.			
2	37	18	
3	5	10	
4	16	5	
5	4	9	3
Webster Academy (K-6)			
2	2	2	
3	3	4	
4	2	3	
5	4	7	4
West Oakland Comm.			
8	49		
Westlake Middle			
6	31	59	
7	30	45	
8	30		
Whittier Elem.			
2	4	5	
3	6	8	
4	9	22	
5	8	29	5
YES			
9	19		
10	15		

Piedmont City Unified School Dist.

Grade	Eng	Ma	Sci
Beach Elem.			
2	97	95	
3	99	96	
4	98	98	
5	96	90	97
Havens Elem.			
2	99	98	
3	98	89	
4	97	95	
5	96	93	97
Millennium High (Cont.)			
10	56		
11	76		
Piedmont High			
9	99		
10	99		
11	99		
Piedmont Middle			
6	99	97	
7	97	95	
8	98		

Scores range from 1-99. A school scoring 75 has done better than 75 percent of other public schools in California.
Key: Eng (English), Ma (Math), Sci (Science).

Grade	Eng	Ma	Sci
Wildwood Elem.			
2	91	99	
3	96	87	
4	96	84	
5	95	95	92
Pleasanton Unified School Dist.			
Alisal Elem.			
2	90	90	
3	92	95	
4	87	88	
5	84	88	89
Amador Valley High			
9	95		
10	96		
11	96		
Donlon Elem.			
2	95	94	
3	93	90	
4	95	85	
5	89	72	89
Fairlands Elem.			
2	95	97	
3	95	96	
4	95	98	
5	94	94	96
Foothill High			
9	97		
10	97		
11	97		
Hart Middle			
6	92	90	
7	97	96	
8	96		
Harvest Park Int.			
6	95	95	
7	98	95	
8	97		
Hearst Elem.			
2	90	95	
3	95	95	
4	93	96	
5	94	97	92
Lydiksen Elem.			
2	85	88	
3	93	94	
4	94	96	
5	90	93	94
Mohr Elem.			
2	99	99	
3	98	98	
4	96	88	
5	98	99	98
Pleasanton Middle			
6	95	97	
7	98	98	
8	95		

Grade	Eng	Ma	Sci
Valley View Elem.			
2	87	88	
3	95	91	
4	89	96	
5	87	94	82
Village High			
10	33		
11	49		
Vintage Hills Elem.			
2	96	99	
3	97	97	
4	93	94	
5	96	95	98
Walnut Grove Elem.			
2	91	91	
3	95	92	
4	98	97	
5	98	97	98
San Leandro Unified School Dist.			
Bancroft Middle			
6	50	29	
7	52	35	
8	43		
Garfield Elem.			
2	55	53	
3	34	19	
4	35	6	
5	30	7	37
Jefferson Elem.			
2	32	39	
3	40	46	
4	40	24	
5	26	16	30
Lincoln High (Cont.)			
11	7		
Madison Elem.			
2	57	83	
3	55	54	
4	45	28	
5	64	64	67
McKinley Elem.			
2	43	33	
3	23	14	
4	35	20	
5	60	76	56
Monroe Elem.			
2	32	37	
3	33	32	
4	45	41	
5	64	49	51
Muir Middle			
6	41	40	
7	50	46	
8	56		
Roosevelt Elem.			
2	77	74	
3	61	46	
4	76	55	
5	72	74	74

Scores range from 1-99. A school scoring 75 has done better than 75 percent of other public schools in California.
Key: Eng (English), Ma (Math), Sci (Science).

Grade	Eng	Ma	Sci
San Leandro High			
9	56		
10	63		
11	69		
Washington Elem.			
2	22	46	
3	32	22	
4	43	27	
5	30	21	10
Wilson Elem.			
2	38	35	
3	35	41	
4	27	10	
5	23	19	24

San Lorenzo Unified School Dist.

Grade	Eng	Ma	Sci
Arroyo High			
9	70		
10	77		
11	72		
Bay Elem.			
2	51	58	
3	53	65	
4	67	46	
5	58	34	62
Bohannon Middle			
6	26	24	
7	40	39	
8	29		
Colonial Acres Elem.			
2	18	33	
3	24	13	
4	14	3	
5	20	9	26
Corvallis Elem.			
2	53	60	
3	63	71	
4	50	54	
5	61	66	66
Dayton Elem.			
2	51	58	
3	56	55	
4	63	44	
5	40	26	33
Del Rey Elem.			
2	39	51	
3	47	31	
4	27	14	
5	33	22	19
Edendale Middle			
6	10	7	
7	25	23	
8	22		
Grant Elem.			
2	30	26	
3	33	25	
4	51	38	
5	42	69	44

Grade	Eng	Ma	Sci
Hesperian Elem.			
2	32	41	
3	16	6	
4	36	16	
5	16	7	16
Hillside Elem.			
2	16	17	
3	34	48	
4	7	4	
5	9	4	3
Lorenzo Manor Elem.			
2	22	25	
3	29	18	
4	28	30	
5	41	53	36
Royal Sunset (Cont.)			
9	10		
10	4		
11	12		
San Lorenzo High			
9	37		
10	39		
11	33		
Washington Manor Middle			
6	47	43	
7	53	61	
8	54		

SBE KIPP Summit Academy

Grade	Eng	Ma	Sci
SBE KIPP Summit Academy			
5	56	76	76
6	74	92	

Sunol Glen Unified School Dist.

Grade	Eng	Ma	Sci
B.A.S.I.S. (Union City)			
2	48	61	
3	79	50	
4	64	39	
5	63	44	57
6	62	38	
7	56	47	
8	59		
9	65		
10	52		
11	47		
Sunol Glen Elem. (Sunol)			
2	70	79	
3	84	61	
4	80	70	
5	85	58	86
6	96	78	
7	98	95	
8	95		

Chapter 2b

State 1 to 10 Rankings

FOR EASE OF COMPREHENSION, the California Department of Education has worked out a system to rank schools by their test scores.

This system takes several forms, the simplest of which is a ranking of 1 to 10.

One is the lowest score, ten is the highest.

This chapter lists the rankings for just about every school in the county.

Keep in mind that this is a crude representation of how the schools are scoring. If you combine this data with the rankings in Chapter 2a and the SAT scores and other data in Chapter 7, you will have a more rounded picture of the scores at each school.

Nonetheless, the scores can still mislead. Almost every school, even those at the bottom, will graduate students who score at the top.

Almost every school with scores at the top will graduate kids who score at the bottom and the middle.

For a general discussion of scores and what they mean, read the chapter on How Public Schools Work.

School	District	City/Town	Rank
Bay Farm Elem.	Alameda City Unified	Alameda	10
Earhart Elem.	Alameda City Unified	Alameda	10
Edison Elem.	Alameda City Unified	Alameda	10
Franklin Elem.	Alameda City Unified	Alameda	9
Haight Elem.	Alameda City Unified	Alameda	6
Longfellow Elem.	Alameda City Unified	Alameda	5
Lum Elem.	Alameda City Unified	Alameda	8
Miller Elem.	Alameda City Unified	Alameda	7
Otis Elem.	Alameda City Unified	Alameda	8
Paden Elem.	Alameda City Unified	Alameda	9
Washington Elem.	Alameda City Unified	Alameda	5
Woodstock Elem.	Alameda City Unified	Alameda	5
Chipman Middle	Alameda City Unified	Alameda	5
Lincoln Middle	Alameda City Unified	Alameda	10
Wood Middle	Alameda City Unified	Alameda	7
Alameda Comm. Lrng. Ctr.	Alameda City Unified	Alameda	10
Alameda High	Alameda City Unified	Alameda	8
Encinal High	Alameda City Unified	Alameda	5
Cornell Elem.	Albany City Unfied	Albany	10
Marin Elem.	Albany City Unfied	Albany	10
Ocean View Elem.	Albany City Unfied	Albany	10
Albany Middle	Albany City Unfied	Albany	10
Albany High	Albany City Unfied	Albany	10
Cragmont Elem.	Berkeley Unified	Berkeley	8
Emerson Elem.	Berkeley Unified	Berkeley	8
Jefferson Elem.	Berkeley Unified	Berkeley	9
Leconte Elem.	Berkeley Unified	Berkeley	4
Malcolm X Elem.	Berkeley Unified	Berkeley	6
Muir Elem.	Berkeley Unified	Berkeley	8
Oxford Elem.	Berkeley Unified	Berkeley	7
Parks Environ. Science	Berkeley Unified	Berkeley	3
Thousand Oaks Elem.	Berkeley Unified	Berkeley	7
Washington Elem.	Berkeley Unified	Berkeley	5
Whittier/Arts Elem.	Berkeley Unified	Berkeley	7
King Middle	Berkeley Unified	Berkeley	7
Longfellow Arts & Tech. Mid.	Berkeley Unified	Berkeley	5
Willard Middle	Berkeley Unified	Berkeley	5
Berkeley High	Berkeley Unified	Berkeley	7

School	District	City/Town	Rank
Castro Valley Elem.	Castro Valley Unified	Castro Valley	7
Chabot Elem.	Castro Valley Unified	Castro Valley	9
Independent Elem.	Castro Valley Unified	Castro Valley	10
Jensen Ranch Elem.	Castro Valley Unified	Castro Valley	10
Marshall Elem.	Castro Valley Unified	Castro Valley	8
Proctor Elem.	Castro Valley Unified	Castro Valley	10
Stanton Elem.	Castro Valley Unified	Castro Valley	8
Vannoy Elem.	Castro Valley Unified	Castro Valley	9
Canyon Middle	Castro Valley Unified	Castro Valley	9
Creekside Middle	Castro Valley Unified	Castro Valley	10
Castro Valley High	Castro Valley Unified	Castro Valley	9
Dougherty Elem.	Dublin Unified	Dublin	10
Dublin Elem.	Dublin Unified	Dublin	9
Frederiksen Elem.	Dublin Unified	Dublin	8
Murray Elem.	Dublin Unified	Dublin	8
Nielsen Elem.	Dublin Unified	Dublin	9
Wells Middle	Dublin Unified	Dublin	9
Dublin High	Dublin Unified	Dublin	10
Anna Yates Elem.	Emery Unified	Emeryville	4
Emery Secondary Sch.	Emery Unified	Emeryville	2
Ardenwood Elem.	Fremont Unified	Fremont	10
Azeveda Elem.	Fremont Unified	Fremont	7
Blacow Elem.	Fremont Unified	Fremont	5
Brier Elem.	Fremont Unified	Fremont	7
Brookvale Elem.	Fremont Unified	Fremont	8
Cabrillo Elem.	Fremont Unified	Fremont	5
Chadbourne Elem.	Fremont Unified	Fremont	10
Durham Elem.	Fremont Unified	Fremont	7
Forest Park Elem.	Fremont Unified	Fremont	10
Glenmoor Elem.	Fremont Unified	Fremont	9
Gomes Elem.	Fremont Unified	Fremont	10
Green Elem.	Fremont Unified	Fremont	7
Grimmer Elem.	Fremont Unified	Fremont	4
Hirsch Elem.	Fremont Unified	Fremont	8
Leitch Elem.	Fremont Unified	Fremont	10
Maloney Elem.	Fremont Unified	Fremont	8
Mattos Elem.	Fremont Unified	Fremont	8
Millard Elem.	Fremont Unified	Fremont	8

School	District	City/Town	Rank
Mission San Jose Elem.	Fremont Unified	Fremont	10
Mission Valley Elem.	Fremont Unified	Fremont	10
Niles Elem.	Fremont Unified	Fremont	9
Oliveira Elem.	Fremont Unified	Fremont	6
Parkmont Elem.	Fremont Unified	Fremont	10
Patterson Elem.	Fremont Unified	Fremont	8
The Circle of Ind. Lrng.	Fremont Unified	Fremont	6
Vallejo Mill Elem.	Fremont Unified	Fremont	7
Warm Springs Elem.	Fremont Unified	Fremont	10
Warwick Elem.	Fremont Unified	Fremont	9
Weibel Elem.	Fremont Unified	Fremont	10
Centerville Jr. High	Fremont Unified	Fremont	8
Hopkins Jr. High	Fremont Unified	Fremont	10
Horner Jr. High	Fremont Unified	Fremont	9
Thornton Jr. High	Fremont Unified	Fremont	8
Walters Jr. High	Fremont Unified	Fremont	7
American High	Fremont Unified	Fremont	9
Irvington High	Fremont Unified	Fremont	9
Kennedy High	Fremont Unified	Fremont	6
Mission San Jose High	Fremont Unified	Fremont	10
Washington High	Fremont Unified	Fremont	9
Bowman Elem.	Hayward Unified	Hayward	2
Burbank Elem.	Hayward Unified	Hayward	2
Cherryland Elem.	Hayward Unified	Hayward	2
East Ave. Elem.	Hayward Unified	Hayward	8
Eden Gardens Elem.	Hayward Unified	Hayward	5
Eldridge Elem.	Hayward Unified	Hayward	6
Fairview Elem.	Hayward Unified	Hayward	3
Glassbrook Elem.	Hayward Unified	Hayward	1
Harder Elem.	Hayward Unified	Hayward	4
Hayward Project Elem.	Hayward Unified	Hayward	2
Highland Elem.	Hayward Unified	Hayward	7
Longwood Elem.	Hayward Unified	Hayward	2
Lorin A. Eden Elem.	Hayward Unified	Hayward	5
Markham Elem.	Hayward Unified	Hayward	2
Muir Elem.	Hayward Unified	Hayward	2
Palma Ceia Elem.	Hayward Unified	Hayward	4
Park Elem.	Hayward Unified	Hayward	2

School	District	City/Town	Rank
Ruus Elem.	Hayward Unified	Hayward	2
Schafer Park Elem.	Hayward Unified	Hayward	3
Shepherd Elem.	Hayward Unified	Hayward	2
Southgate Elem.	Hayward Unified	Hayward	5
Strobridge Elem.	Hayward Unified	Hayward	3
Treeview Elem.	Hayward Unified	Hayward	5
Tyrrell Elem.	Hayward Unified	Hayward	2
Bret Harte Middle	Hayward Unified	Hayward	4
Chavez Middle	Hayward Unified	Hayward	3
King Middle	Hayward Unified	Hayward	3
Ochoa Middle	Hayward Unified	Hayward	3
Winton Middle	Hayward Unified	Hayward	4
Hayward High	Hayward Unified	Hayward	4
Mt. Eden High	Hayward Unified	Hayward	4
Tennyson High	Hayward Unified	Hayward	2
Almond Ave. Elem.	Livermore Valley Jt. Unif.	Livermore	9
Altamont Creek Elem.	Livermore Valley Jt. Unif.	Livermore	8
Arroyo Mocho Elem.	Livermore Valley Jt. Unif.	Livermore	8
Arroyo Seco Elem.	Livermore Valley Jt. Unif.	Livermore	9
Croce Elem.	Livermore Valley Jt. Unif.	Livermore	9
Jackson Ave. Elem.	Livermore Valley Jt. Unif.	Livermore	7
Marylin Ave. Elem.	Livermore Valley Jt. Unif.	Livermore	3
Michell Elem.	Livermore Valley Jt. Unif.	Livermore	7
Portola Elem.	Livermore Valley Jt. Unif.	Livermore	4
Rancho Las Positas Elem.	Livermore Valley Jt. Unif.	Livermore	9
Smith Elem.	Livermore Valley Jt. Unif.	Livermore	9
Sunset Elem.	Livermore Valley Jt. Unif.	Livermore	10
Christensen Middle	Livermore Valley Jt. Unif.	Livermore	8
East Ave. Middle	Livermore Valley Jt. Unif.	Livermore	9
Junction Ave. Middle	Livermore Valley Jt. Unif.	Livermore	6
Mendenhall Middle	Livermore Valley Jt. Unif.	Livermore	10
Granada High	Livermore Valley Jt. Unif.	Livermore	7
Livermore High	Livermore Valley Jt. Unif.	Livermore	6
Alvarado Elem.	New Haven Unified	Union City	6
Cabello Elem.	New Haven Unified	Union City	6
Delaine Eastin Elem.	New Haven Unified	Union City	9
Emanuele Elem.	New Haven Unified	Union City	5
Hillview Crest Elem.	New Haven Unified	Hayward	5

School	District	City/Town	Rank
Kitayama Elem.	New Haven Unified	Union City	7
Pioneer Elem.	New Haven Unified	Union City	9
Searles Elem.	New Haven Unified	Union City	5
Alvarado Middle	New Haven Unified	Union City	8
Barnard-White Middle	New Haven Unified	Union City	6
Chavez Middle	New Haven Unified	Union City	7
James Logan High	New Haven Unified	Union City	6
Bunker Elem.	Newark Unified	Newark	7
Graham Elem.	Newark Unified	Newark	4
Kennedy Elem.	Newark Unified	Newark	7
Lincoln Elem.	Newark Unified	Newark	7
Milani Elem.	Newark Unified	Newark	5
Musick Elem.	Newark Unified	Newark	5
Schilling Elem.	Newark Unified	Newark	4
Snow Elem.	Newark Unified	Newark	7
Newark Jr. High	Newark Unified	Newark	7
Newark Memorial High	Newark Unified	Newark	5
ACORN Woodland Elem.	Oakland Unified	Oakland	1
Allendale Elem.	Oakland Unified	Oakland	3
ASCEND	Oakland Unified	Oakland	5
Bella Vista Elem.	Oakland Unified	Oakland	4
Brookfield Village Elem.	Oakland Unified	Oakland	2
Burbank Elem.	Oakland Unified	Oakland	1
Chabot Elem.	Oakland Unified	Oakland	10
Cleveland Elem.	Oakland Unified	Oakland	9
Cox Elem.	Oakland Unified	Oakland	1
Crocker Highlands Elem.	Oakland Unified	Oakland	9
E. Bay Consv. Corps Char.	Oakland Unified	Oakland	5
Emerson Elem.	Oakland Unified	Oakland	2
Foster Elem.	Oakland Unified	Oakland	1
Franklin Elem.	Oakland Unified	Oakland	5
Fruitvale Elem.	Oakland Unified	Oakland	5
Garfield Elem.	Oakland Unified	Oakland	2
Glenview Elem.	Oakland Unified	Oakland	5
Golden Gate Elem.	Oakland Unified	Oakland	1
Grass Valley Elem.	Oakland Unified	Oakland	8
Hawthorne Elem.	Oakland Unified	Oakland	1
Highland Elem.	Oakland Unified	Oakland	1

School	District	City/Town	Rank
Hillcrest Elem.	Oakland Unified	Oakland	10
Hoover Elem.	Oakland Unified	Oakland	3
Howard Elem.	Oakland Unified	Oakland	5
Huerta Lrng. Acad.	Oakland Unified	Oakland	1
International Comm.	Oakland Unified	Oakland	4
Jefferson Elem.	Oakland Unified	Oakland	1
Kaiser Elem.	Oakland Unified	Oakland	9
King Elem.	Oakland Unified	Oakland	1
KIPP: Oak College Prep.	Oakland Unified	Oakland	5
La Escuelita Elem.	Oakland Unified	Oakland	4
Lafayette Elem.	Oakland Unified	Oakland	2
Lakeview Elem.	Oakland Unified	Oakland	2
Laurel Elem.	Oakland Unified	Oakland	5
Lazear Elem.	Oakland Unified	Oakland	2
Lincoln Elem.	Oakland Unified	Oakland	9
Lockwood Elem.	Oakland Unified	Oakland	1
Mann Elem.	Oakland Unified	Oakland	1
Manzanita Elem.	Oakland Unified	Oakland	1
Markham Elem.	Oakland Unified	Oakland	3
Marshall Elem.	Oakland Unified	Oakland	1
Maxwell Park Elem.	Oakland Unified	Oakland	1
Melrose Elem.	Oakland Unified	Oakland	1
Miller Elem.	Oakland Unified	Oakland	9
Monarch Acad.	Oakland Unified	Oakland	2
Montclair Elem.	Oakland Unified	Oakland	10
Munck Elem.	Oakland Unified	Oakland	5
Parker Elem.	Oakland Unified	Oakland	1
Peralta Elem.	Oakland Unified	Oakland	7
Piedmont Ave. Elem.	Oakland Unified	Oakland	4
Prescott Elem.	Oakland Unified	Oakland	1
Redwood Heights Elem.	Oakland Unified	Oakland	10
Reems Acad.	Oakland Unified	Oakland	2
Santa Fe Elem.	Oakland Unified	Oakland	2
Sequoia Elem.	Oakland Unified	Oakland	4
Sherman Elem.	Oakland Unified	Oakland	1
Sobrante Park Elem.	Oakland Unified	Oakland	1
Stonehurst Elem.	Oakland Unified	Oakland	1
Swett Elem.	Oakland Unified	Oakland	2

School	District	City/Town	Rank
Thornhill Elem.	Oakland Unified	Oakland	10
Washington Elem.	Oakland Unified	Oakland	1
Webster Acad.	Oakland Unified	Oakland	1
Whittier Elem.	Oakland Unified	Oakland	1
American Indian Pub. Char.	Oakland Unified	Oakland	9
Brewer Middle	Oakland Unified	Oakland	4
Carter Middle	Oakland Unified	Oakland	1
Claremont Middle	Oakland Unified	Oakland	3
Cole Elem.	Oakland Unified	Oakland	1
Elmhurst Middle	Oakland Unified	Oakland	1
Frick Middle	Oakland Unified	Oakland	1
Harte Middle	Oakland Unified	Oakland	4
Havenscourt Middle	Oakland Unified	Oakland	1
King Estates Middle	Oakland Unified	Oakland	1
Lowell Middle	Oakland Unified	Oakland	1
Madison Middle	Oakland Unified	Oakland	1
Montera Middle	Oakland Unified	Oakland	8
Oakland Char. Acad.	Oakland Unified	Oakland	4
Roosevelt Middle	Oakland Unified	Oakland	2
Rudsdale Acad.	Oakland Unified	Oakland	1
Simmons Middle	Oakland Unified	Oakland	1
Urban Promise Acad.	Oakland Unified	Oakland	1
Westlake Middle	Oakland Unified	Oakland	3
Far West Cont. High	Oakland Unified	Oakland	1
Fremont Sr. High	Oakland Unified	Oakland	1
LIFE Acad.	Oakland Unified	Oakland	1
Lionel Wilson College Prep.	Oakland Unified	Oakland	1
McClymonds Sr. High	Oakland Unified	Oakland	1
Oakland Sch. For Arts	Oakland Unified	Oakland	9
Oakland Sr. High	Oakland Unified	Oakland	1
Skyline High	Oakland Unified	Oakland	3
Beach Elem.	Piedmont City Unified	Piedmont	10
Havens Elem.	Piedmont City Unified	Piedmont	10
Wildwood Elem.	Piedmont City Unified	Piedmont	10
Piedmont Middle	Piedmont City Unified	Piedmont	10
Piedmont High	Piedmont City Unified	Piedmont	10
Alisal Elem.	Pleasanton Unified	Pleasanton	9
Donlon Elem.	Pleasanton Unified	Pleasanton	10

School	District	City/Town	Rank
Fairlands Elem.	Pleasanton Unified	Pleasanton	10
Hearst Elem.	Pleasanton Unified	Pleasanton	10
Lydiksen Elem.	Pleasanton Unified	Pleasanton	10
Mohr Elem.	Pleasanton Unified	Pleasanton	10
Valley View Elem.	Pleasanton Unified	Pleasanton	10
Vintage Hills Elem.	Pleasanton Unified	Pleasanton	10
Walnut Grove Elem.	Pleasanton Unified	Pleasanton	10
Hart Middle	Pleasanton Unified	Pleasanton	10
Harvest Park Int.	Pleasanton Unified	Pleasanton	10
Pleasanton Middle	Pleasanton Unified	Pleasanton	10
Amador Valley High	Pleasanton Unified	Pleasanton	10
Foothill High	Pleasanton Unified	Pleasanton	10
Garfield Elem.	San Leandro Unified	San Leandro	3
Jefferson Elem.	San Leandro Unified	San Leandro	4
Madison Elem.	San Leandro Unified	San Leandro	6
McKinley Elem.	San Leandro Unified	San Leandro	4
Monroe Elem.	San Leandro Unified	San Leandro	6
Roosevelt Elem.	San Leandro Unified	San Leandro	7
Washington Elem.	San Leandro Unified	San Leandro	2
Wilson Elem.	San Leandro Unified	San Leandro	3
Bancroft Middle	San Leandro Unified	San Leandro	5
Muir Middle	San Leandro Unified	San Leandro	6
San Leandro High	San Leandro Unified	San Leandro	4
Bay Elem.	San Lorenzo Unified	San Lorenzo	8
Colonial Acres Elem.	San Lorenzo Unified	San Lorenzo	2
Corvallis Elem.	San Lorenzo Unified	San Lorenzo	6
Dayton Elem.	San Lorenzo Unified	San Lorenzo	6
Del Rey Elem.	San Lorenzo Unified	San Lorenzo	4
Grant Elem.	San Lorenzo Unified	San Lorenzo	6
Hesperian Elem.	San Lorenzo Unified	San Lorenzo	3
Hillside Elem.	San Lorenzo Unified	San Lorenzo	1
Lorenzo Manor Elem.	San Lorenzo Unified	San Lorenzo	4
Bohannon Middle	San Lorenzo Unified	San Lorenzo	5
Edendale Middle	San Lorenzo Unified	San Lorenzo	3
Washington Manor Middle	San Lorenzo Unified	San Lorenzo	7
Arroyo High	San Lorenzo Unified	San Lorenzo	6
San Lorenzo High	San Lorenzo Unified	San Lorenzo	1
Bay Area Sch. For Ind. Study	Sunol Glen Unified	Union City	3
Sunol Glen Elem.	Sunol Glen Unified	Sunol	8

BUY 10 OR MORE & SAVE!

If you order 10 or more books of any mix, price drops by about 50 percent.
1-800-222-3602. Or fill out form and send with check to:
McCormack's Guides, P.O. Box 190, Martinez, CA 94553. Or fax
order to (925) 228-7223. To order online go to www.mccormacks.com

1-800-222-3602

Next to title, write in number of copies ordered:

No.	McCormack's Guide	Single	Bulk
___	Alameda & Central Valley 2006	$13.95	$6.25
___	Contra Costa & Solano 2006	$13.95	$6.25
___	Orange County 2006	$13.95	$6.25
___	Greater Sacramento 2006	$13.95	$6.25
___	San Diego County 2006.	$13.95	$6.25
___	San Francisco, San Mateo,		
	Marin, Sonoma 2006	$13.95	$6.25
___	Santa Clara & Santa Cruz 2006	$13.95	$6.25
___	How California Schools Work	$15.95	$6.25

Subtotal $ _____

CA sales tax (8.25%) _____

Shipping* _____

Total Amount of Order $ _____

*For orders of 10 or more, shipping is 60 cents per book. For orders of fewer than 10, shipping is $4.50 for first book, $1.50 per book thereafter.

VISA **MasterCard** **◉** *Circle one: Check/Visa/MC/Am.Exp. or Bill Us*

Card No. _____ *Exp. Date* _____

Name _____

Company _____

Address _____

City _____ *State* _____ *Zip* _____

Phone: (_____) _____ *Fax (_____)* _____

The following guides are available online at www.mccormacks.com:
Los Angeles County 2006, Riverside County 2006, Ventura County 2006,
San Bernardino County 2006 and Santa Barbara County 2006.

☐ **Check here to receive advertising information**

Chapter 3

City & Town Profiles

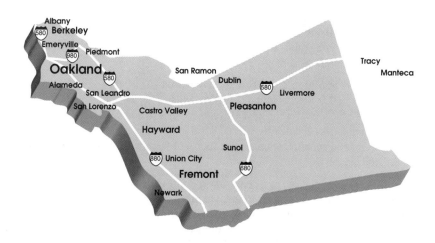

WHERE DO YOU want to live? What can you afford? What are the choices? What is the commute like? The following profiles may help. For more information on local cities, call chambers of commerce.

INDEX TO PROFILES

ALAMEDA

ISLAND-PENINSULA CITY. Located at one of the choicest spots in the Bay Area, population of 74,581. Site of many Victorians and stately homes. Charming. Also many small and modest homes and many apartments. Compared to other towns, a great commute.

School scores middle to high. In 2005, residents voted to extend and raise a tax to retain electives and keep class sizes small.

Crime low suburban average and may decline in the coming years. Alameda is attracting more college educated and more professionals. This should raise schools scores and lower crime.

A town in transition. In 1997, the Navy closed an airfield and naval base and turned over 2,000 acres to the city. Alameda has been debating what to build on the base and over the next 10 years expects to add 5,000 to 10,000 residents to the base and nearby streets. For the immediate, the city hopes to build on the base about 500 homes, one fourth of them with "affordable" subsidized prices.

Alameda is composed of a peninsula and three islands — one tiny, one a Coast Guard base, and the main island two miles wide and seven miles long where most of the housing is located. The main island, called Alameda, is separated from Oakland by an estuary. Immediately to the south of the main island is a peninsula called Bay Farm Island. Here is where you'll find some of the newest housing in the city, two 18-hole golf courses, a 9-hole course, a driving range, the training camp for the Oakland Raiders, and a modern, high-tech office park.

The town that tore down all its billboards boasts about 20 parks, seven marinas (over 2,000 berths), a skate park, five yacht clubs, three libraries, model airplane field, trails, many activities (soccer, football, etc.) for kids and adults, and over 100 clubs and service groups. Amenities include a shopping center, first-class restaurants, theater. Annual art and wine festival. Hometown stores that have won the affections of residents: Tucker's Ice Cream Parlor, Ole's Waffle House, the Boogie Woogie Bagel Boy and Pagano's hardware. Big party and parade on the Fourth of July. Annual sand castle contest. Two dog parks, one for big dogs, one for small. In planning, a movie complex.

Jazz and nightclubs nearby, in Jack London Village, Oakland. Movies. The delights of San Francisco are just across the Bay Bridge, a BART ride (from Oakland) of less than a half-hour. Or a drive of about 20 minutes.

Before you move … buy

$13⁹⁵
SINGLE COPY
VOLUME DISCOUNTS

McCormack's Guides are published for:

- ALAMEDA-CENTRAL VALLEY • CONTRA COSTA-SOLANO
- SANTA CLARA-SANTA CRUZ-SILICON VALLEY
- SAN FRANCISCO-SAN MATEO-MARIN-SONOMA
- SAN DIEGO • ORANGE COUNTY • GREATER SACRAMENTO

Available in e-book format at www.mccormacks.com:

LOS ANGELES • RIVERSIDE • SANTA BARBARA • SAN BERNARDINO • VENTURA

Also from McCormack's Guides:
How California Schools Work

www.mccormacks.com
1•800•222•3602

A few miles away, at the Oakland Coliseum, big-time professional sports (Warriors basketball, Athletics and Raiders). Alameda has what most East Bay cities lack — an open, approachable shore, about six miles of sandy beach, operated as a regional park. Historically, cities have surrendered the shore to industry and the railroad. Water is popular with sailors and windsurfers.

Alameda started out in 1900 connected to Oakland. At that time, it was considered a prestige address, attractive to the affluent who built stately homes. Then the-powers-that-be decided to cut a ship-channel and presto, an island came into existence. It is now connected to Oakland by three bridges and two tunnels. As the century progressed, the island gradually was built out with bungalows, apartments, and here and there, more mansions.

Alameda has about 3,500 Victorian and Queen Anne homes, more than San Francisco. Alameda codes protect Victorians and preserve other older buildings and historic shopping districts. Owners love their "Vics" and spend time and money to restore and maintain them. Tours available to visit a few. Streets clean. Graffiti absent. Many small shops. Good town for strolling. Many arguments over quality-of-life issues.

Alameda also has many older homes that are plain and small and some-times run down. It's expensive to upgrade an old home and many owners have just let things slide or done minimal repairs. Some homes have one-car garages. Some garages are converted horse barns.

Thousands of apartments have been built along the shore. After a rush of apartment construction in the 1980s, residents voted to forbid anything bigger than a duplex.

For the fairly new, drive to Harbor Bay, waterfront development on Bay Farm Island. Planned community built around five "villages." Most of the residential growth in the last 25 years has been at Harbor Bay, which also includes the business park, 300 acres. Some neighborhoods — notably Ballena Bay on the main island — feature homes with their own docks.

Housing units in 2005 totaled 32,112, of which 13,057 were single homes, 3,964 single attached, 14,791 multiples, and 300 mobile homes. Outside of the former base, few housing units are being built.

Traffic is sometimes sluggish on city arterials but the overall commute, compared to other East Bay cities, is good. Buses to Oakland and San Francisco and to BART (commute rail) station in downtown Oakland. Oakland Airport on southern border of Alameda. Commute ferry to Oakland and downtown San Francisco (ferries leave from Bay Farm Island and from main island, near Alameda Point.) Local jobs by the tens of thousands, in Berkeley, downtown Oakland, the Oakland Airport. For many residents, the commute is only a few miles.

Over the next five years or so, the east span of the Bay Bridge is to be replaced. In the best of times, the Bay Bridge is a mess during commute hours. Construction delays will make it worse but Alamedans have choices: the ferries and BART.

One homicide in 2004, zero in 2003, two in 2002 and 2001, one in 2000, zero in 1999, one in 1998, two in 1997. Counts for previous years are three, zero, one, one, two, six, three, zero, two, and two. Alameda, close to Oakland and San Francisco, gives you the conveniences of the city and the safety of the suburb (but take usual precautions: lock doors, etc.).

Jets take off from Oakland airport. Noise suppression measures have been taken. If purchasing a home or renting a place, spend a few hours listening, or talk to neighbors. Ask about night flights. Oakland airport is expanding its terminals but not its runways. With the expansion, night flights of cargo planes are supposed to be restricted.

School rankings middling to 90th percentile, compared to other California schools. Voters in 1989 approved a $48 million bond to repair schools, add classrooms. In 2002, another tax was approved, this one to fund salaries, enrich programs and decrease class size, and in 2005 a similar tax was passed. In 2004, another renovation bond was passed, $57 million. In 2005 work began on a replacement campus for Woodstock Elementary.

Some of these taxes require a two-thirds, which is hard to muster in California. Many districts try and fail. When a two-thirds tax passes, it indicates, we believe, strong educational values in the town.

Community college adds much to educational life.

Catholic high school. Three Catholic elementary schools.

Alameda started the 1990s with 76,459 residents and finished with 72,259 — the drop coming from the base closure. Many people lost their jobs. Stores closed or lost business. Since then, the West End, as the base area is known, has made a comeback. The old residents were blue-collar workers or sailors. The new residents tend to be young professionals. The Coast Guard retained housing for military personnel around the Bay Area.

The military base was one of the most famous in American history. From it, the carrier Hornet sailed in 1942 to venture close to Japan and launch the first bombing raid on that country. The raid shamed the Japanese Navy and influenced its disastrous decision to attack Midway Island, perhaps the decisive naval battle of World War II. In 1998, the city saved from the scrapper's torch the "new" Hornet, commissioned in 1943. The ship, as long as three football fields, was tidied up and turned into a museum.

Put the whole package together — the views, the jobs, the peace, the easy commute, the closeness to San Francisco, Oakland and Berkeley, the charm of the old — Alameda comes across as one of the best addresses in the East Bay. Chamber of commerce (510) 522-0414.

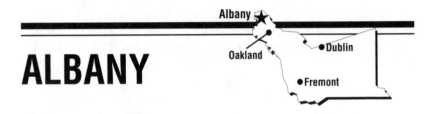

ALBANY

SMALL CITY, STABLE population of 16,743, on the shore, next to and influenced by Berkeley. The university and all it offers — art, music, theater, sports — are within 10 minutes. Quiet. Home to many professionals and married UC students. School rankings high. UC kids make up about 20 percent of school district enrollment. Crime low. One homicide in 2004, zero from 1997 through 2003. For previous years are, one, one, zero, one, zero, zero, one, zero, one.

Housing rises from Bay to hills with great views. Built out. Many homes are old and small, one and two bedrooms, yet command high prices. High-rise condos near freeway. UC has renovated its housing for students with children. In 2005, the state counted in Albany 7,315 residential units: 3,779 single homes, 197 single attached, 3,333 apartments, 6 mobile homes.

About 50 restaurants, 40 antique stores, many of them on Solano Avenue, loads of charm. From cheap to expensive, eateries offer international cuisines, gourmet hamburgers and more. Evenings full of amblers. The avenue has bookstores and two movie theaters, one leaning toward art-house. Annual "Solano Stroll" street fair draws 100,000. Golden Gate Fields offers trotters, thoroughbreds, satellite betting. City is thinking about turning part of race track parking into housing, park, plaza, other uses. Seniors center. Community center. Library. Teen center. Town pool. Soccer, Little League, many activities. Barnes and Noble Books, Trader Joe's closeby.

Academic rankings among top 15 percent in state, at high school, top 5 percent. Strong school support, what's expected from a university town. Five public schools enroll about 3,000 kids, many in walking distance. In 1993 and 2004, voters approved bond to renovate and rebuild schools, upgrade science labs and library. Parcel tax passed in 1999 to retain math, science and art classes, hire librarians and counselors and improve technology. Another parcel tax was passed in 2005 to retain electives, librarians and teachers. In 1999, district opened rebuilt elementary and middle schools. New state-of-the-art high school. Despite this, parents want more than school district can afford. Constant fund raising. Every year about three dozen schools in California crack the 600 mark in the math SAT. In 2003, Albany High hit 602. Many private schools in Berkeley-El Cerrito.

Ten minutes to Oakland, 20 minutes to San Fran. Freeway and Bay Bridge congested but an endurable commute. BART stations in Berkeley and El Cerrito. Buses to City and throughout East Bay. Chamber (510) 525-1771.

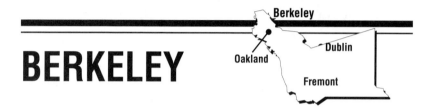

BERKELEY

ONE OF THE MOST famous cities in the world. Intellectually intense, charming and scenic. Hill homes look over the Bay and Golden Gate. Always encouraging the new and innovative but not dynamic in a corporate way. Population 104,534.

Too little land and Berkeley is suspicious of big business and Big Biz reciprocates. This said, the city near its waterfront has many small firms and some bio-tech firms, including a large Bayer facility.

About half of Berkeley's housing stock predates World War II, about 40 percent was built between 1940 and 1970. In the 1990s, Berkeley added just 1,200 housing units, according to 2000 census. Many students and people working at the university live in nearby towns.

A city of contrasts. On the south side of the university, People's Park and Telegraph Avenue, magnets for teenagers and the down and out (but new shops and restaurants are pushing this section a little up the scale). On the north, Holy Hill, a congregation of religious schools, and a quieter neighborhood.

Anchored by Spengers restaurant and fish market, Berkeley's newest flourishing commercial area spreads a few blocks south down Fourth Street. Boutiques offer shoppers European antiques, cafe-quality cappuccino machines, high-fashion shoes and clothing, imported curios and doggie beds fit for a well-to-do human. Cody's bookstore and a Peet's coffee shop keep the street connected to its Berkeley roots.

Also flourishing: an arts district in the downtown, along Shattuck Avenue. Opened in 2001 in this neighborhood, a home for the Berkeley Repertory, 600 seats, the Aurora Theater, 160 seats, and Jazz school, 600 students. Moving north, Shattuck becomes more upscale, but the concentration of exotic, varied and inexpensive restaurants has earned the area the moniker: "Gourmet Ghetto." Alice Waters invented "California cuisine" at Chez Panisse, located on the north. Berkeley also sustains butchers and bakeries, an upscale supermarket, Andronico's, and large markets that specialize in organic food, including the Berkeley Bowl and Whole Foods. There's also a farmers' market, very popular. Not all have succumbed to gourmet dining. Berkeley High kids, offered a tasty and nourishing menu, preferred french fries and fat but the fight continues.

A town that enjoys conversation and ideas. Berkeley is staunchly Democratic and liberal and if you followed the town solely through newspaper headlines, it would come across as extremely liberal.

Berkeley school district was one of the first in the nation to integrate its schools through mandated busing. Voters down through the years have passed funding measures to rebuild or overhaul every school in the district and to avoid cuts in academics and extra curricular activities. In 2004, they passed yet another funding measure to lower class sizes and improve teacher training and the music instruction and more.

Yet many parents send their children to private schools; one study put the number about 23 percent. Arguments abound over education and how the school district deals with problems, particularly at the high school. Berkeley mixes kids of diverse backgrounds. Scores vary by group. Many kids are struggling or doing so-so, many succeeding.

School district has revised attendance policies and boundaries to reduce busing and leave more children in their neighborhood schools but this is a situation where not everyone can be satisfied.

In state comparisons, even the low-scoring Berkeley schools do fairly well, rankings in the 40th to 60th percentile. Oakland would love to have these scores in many of its schools. For many Berkeley parents, however, these scores are not acceptable. They have high academic ambitions for their children — UC Berkeley, Harvard, Yale, Stanford, etc. On the high end, the school district generally delivers. Berkeley High School usually places second in Alameda County in moving students up to California public colleges, including the University of California. But parents remain critical and wary, and this, combined with the complexity of programs, has taken a toll on teachers and administrators. Berkeley district has a reputation of being tough to govern.

Although residents support education, many have little direct contact with the schools. Berkeley district enrolls about 8,900 students, 9 percent of the town's population. By contrast, Antioch, a bedroom town in neighboring Contra Costa County, has about 22 percent of its population enrolled in its local schools.

These numbers reflect another side of Berkeley: it is to a large extent a singles town, a renters' town. The state tally in 2005 showed 47,368 residential units: 20,148 single homes, 1,756 single attached, 25,405 apartments, 59 mobile homes.

Civic leaders and council members are always talking about laying out the welcome mat for businesses. But when the projects are big, the arguments are fierce. Berkeley council meetings are notorious for droning on and on. Everyone wants to "share." This style has its fans. Berkeley believes in bringing its citizens along through talk and cooperation.

But in other neighborhoods, notably Shattuck and Fourth Street, the city has been innovative and has made improvements. The town has a good employment base, foremost the university, about 12,000 local jobs.

Cultural-culinary mecca. Berkeley has loads of bookstores, restaurants, coffee shops, clubs, dance halls, art galleries and specialty stores. The university is brimming with activities, many of them open to the public — recitals, symphonies, dance, exhibits, plays, a great variety of classes (extension program), sporting events, notably basketball and football. Berkeley has a night life, for young people and for mature adults.

Many activities for kids. Lawrence Hall of Science. Fishing pier. Boating. Marina. Merry-Go-Round, trails, golf course, botanical garden, playing fields at Tilden Park, which borders Berkeley. City hall sponsors many activities.

Residents fix up their homes and fight for neighborhood quality. To stop speeders and curtail traffic through residential neighborhoods, the city blocked many streets with concrete pylons. Berkeley has its rundown streets near the water but even these will often have homes or apartments that show good care. The Berkeley hills command one of the prettiest vistas on the West Coast — the Golden Gate. Spectacular sunsets.

Berkeley nourishes its neighborhoods, which many will find charming and in character, almost European. In the flatlands, you are never far from a coffee shop or bakery. In 2000, voters approved spending $5 million to renovate the town's libraries. In its treatment of the disabled, Berkeley is miles ahead of many municipalities.

Good commute town. Interstate 80 runs along the shore. Highways 13 and 24 run through the hills and along the east side. BART (commute rail) has three stations in town; trains to Oakland and San Francisco. AC Transit runs buses throughout Alameda County and West Contra Costa. Berkeley is only five miles from the Bay Bridge. On the down side, internal traffic is a bear and Berkeley is short of parking.

Near campus, many students and young people live in old homes divided into small apartments. The university community years ago spread into Kensington, Oakland, Richmond, El Cerrito, Albany. UC Berkeley has rebuilt its married-student housing, located in Albany. Cal students looking for housing should call university housing and dining services. Phone (510) 642-2456.

Being opposite the Golden Gate, Berkeley gets the ocean breezes and sometimes the summer fog. It has its hot days and its cold but the general temperature is pleasantly cool. If you want to swim outdoors you can (at Lake Temescal or Lake Anza in Tilden Park) but many people head for the indoor pools around the city. In autumn, hot and dry Diablos blow into Bay Area. In 1991, a big chunk of the Berkeley-Oakland hills burned; 2,500 homes and apartments lost, 25 dead. If you buy in hills, clear away brush.

In recent years, homicides have dropped but always take care. Difficult to generalize about crime: many neighborhoods, flats and hills, have low crime. Senseless shooting in 2005: young woman home from Darmouth on vacation was unintentionally killed. Four homicides in 2004, six in 2003, seven in 2002, one in 2001, four in 2000, three in 1999, two in 1998. The counts for the previous years are 11, 8, 10, 8, 8, 12, 14, 11, 11, 14, 11. The university has its own police force. Miscellaneous:

• New foot-bike bridge crossing Interstate 80 to the water.

• Piece by piece, park lovers and government agencies are putting together a trail-park system that one day, they hope, will run from the Bay Bridge to the Delta.

• Good place for gossip and meeting people: the YMCA gym-exercise club.

• Campus is always adding or remodeling buildings. The City of Berkeley and the university at times relate to each other as the cat relates to the dog but on many projects they stumble into detente. Berkeley would like the university to pay more city taxes. If it could, the university would roll its eyes but mostly it replies by listing all the good it does the town — jobs, payroll, etc.

• Smoke out. No smoking at bus stops or within 20 feet of stops or at building entrances.

• Just a few years ago, everyone, it seemed, wanted to live in Berkeley. Rents shot up, available apartments seem to disappear. And now ... it's amazing what the collapse of dotcoms will do to a community. It also helped that the private sector and the university built more units. The result: not a glut but rents have dropped and choice has returned.

• Free parking on campus — but only if you have won a Nobel. The city in 2005 was debating whether to award free parking to hybrid cars.

• Chamber of commerce (510) 549-7003.

CASTRO VALLEY

BEDROOM TOWN WITH COUNTRY ATMOSPHERE in hills east of San Leandro and Hayward. Many lovely homes, not opulent, but often large and well cared for. Some homes have great views of Bay and sunset and this has pushed town up market. In the canyons and on the outskirts, horse ranches. Castro Valley also has many ordinary tract homes.

School scores high, top 20 percent in state. Many professionals move into Castro Valley for its schools. A large state university just about borders Castro Valley and boosts education values. Also nearby, a community college. School and community boundaries differ. Call school district for boundaries, (510) 537-3000. Since 1990, residents have passed five renovation-construction bonds, indicating strong support for schools. In 2003, science labs added at all elementary schools. High school has added classrooms, expanded gym, library and cafeteria and constructed science and math buildings. Recent addition: a performing arts center that the high school will share with the town. The latest bond, 2005, will provide money to expand libraries, add classrooms, upgrade sixth grade science labs and improve sports fields so they can be used by town's people.

Unincorporated, which means Castro Valley is governed from Oakland by the county board of supervisors. In reality, much local control has devolved to community groups. A master plan for future development is being prepared. Many new homes are going up east of Castro Valley and at times it looks like suburbia will extend uninterrupted all the way over the hills to Pleasanton. In recent years, the town has done a good job of sprucing up its downtown. Major medical center, Eden, in downtown.

Castro Valley is part of the Hayward Area Recreation District. Many activities: soccer, baseball, tennis, little theater, dance, community center, art and exercise classes, more. Castro Valley is within a few minutes' drive of large regional parks, including Lake Chabot. Public golf course. Fall arts festival. Annual rodeo. Archery range. Many university classes open to public.

The FBI doesn't track unincorporated towns but communities with Castro Valley's demographics are usually low in crime.

Fast shot to Oakland, Berkeley, Pleasanton by Interstate 580. Buses. BART, which has stations in Hayward and San Leandro, extended its line to Dublin and built a station in Castro Valley. This helps commute. Complaints about traffic along Crow Canyon Road, a short cut to Contra Costa suburbs. Chamber of commerce (510) 537-5300.

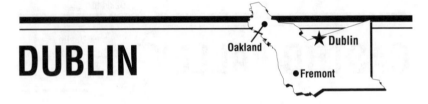

DUBLIN

BEDROOM TOWN that started millennium with high hopes of roaring into high tech, then got a blast of new market reality. Nonetheless, if premature, the hopes will probably be fulfilled. Location, location, location. Good town if you are in the market for a new home or apartment.

Population 39,931. School scores high, crime low, commute easy if you have a local job, amusements and shopping plentiful and getting better. A modern and in many ways a progressive town.

In 2004, shot down one measure to boost school operating funding and at the end the year approved a measure for school construction funds.

Also in 2004, the town cleared the way for a giant Ikea store to be built near the freeway and an existing mall, Hacienda Crossings. (As of 2005, however, Ikea seemed in no rush to start construction). Inspired by all the retail bucks that will change hands in this neighborhood, more stores are moving in. The result: a cornucopia of tax revenue that will allow Dublin to do more in the way of parks, rec and civic amenities.

Dublin is located at the junction of Interstates 680 and 580 in a bowl called the Amador Valley. Pleasanton, which borders Dublin to the south, and Livermore, to the east, are also located in the Amador Valley. Immediately north of Dublin another valley, the San Ramon, begins. It takes in the Contra Costa County towns of San Ramon, Danville, Alamo and Blackhawk. The region is often referred to as the I-680 corridor.

Danville, Alamo and Blackhawk are upscale to rich. San Ramon, Dublin, Pleasanton and Livermore are middle-class affluent, high-tech, bedroom towns. San Ramon has Bishop Ranch, 350 firms employing 30,000; major tenants include SBC, Chevron and Toyota. Pleasanton has Hacienda Business Park; major tenants, Oracle, AT&T, Safeway headquarters, Kaiser Permanente. Livermore has the Lawrence Livermore Lab, a large weapons and nuclear research facility run by the University of California, Berkeley.

In all of these towns, school scores are generally high, crime low. Many residents are college educated, some are brilliant. The setting is pretty. Hills and valleys, Mt. Diablo to the northeast. Green in spring and winter, gold in summer and fall. The less enlightened might call the gold "dried-out grass" but no matter, the region cast its charms. Wineries dot the east side of the Amador Valley, cachet by the vat.

Over the past 25 years or so the region has been jelling as a high-tech haven, in large measure because it has brains but to a greater extent because it has land and good freeways. Both Silicon Valley, about 30 miles to the south, and San Francisco, 30 miles to the west, are short of land. In the 1990s, BART (commute rail) was extended to Dublin.

At the start of 2001, Cisco, Commerce One and Oracle were committed to building giant complexes in "Digital Dublin." Then the economy tanked and the three, in one way or another, bailed out. On the plus side, Sybase (software) moved its headquarters and 900 employees from Emeryville to Dublin. Signs of the (modern) times: the Sybase facility includes a day-care center for employees' kids (also a gourmet cafeteria, a fitness center, a children's play-ground and a jogging track.).

Dublin, named by Irish pioneers, lagged behind San Ramon and Pleasanton. Up until about 1960, the town was no more than a farm hamlet under the jurisdiction of the county government. When the housing came, it followed a plan but residents soon became dissatisfied. The county had one vision, the residents another — an old story in California. In 1982, Dublin incorporated as a legal city and took control of its own planning. It revised its general plan and focused its energy on securing a diverse economy with a good base of high-tech and retail.

The initial housing followed middle-class tract lines, nothing fancy. As the prosperity of the region increased, homes stepped up in quality and size. The oldest housing, much of it spruced up and remodeled, is found on the valley floor near the freeway. As you move west into the hills, the homes become newer, wood-shake roofs give way to terra cotta or tile and at a certain point utility lines are placed underground. Some hill homes command great views of the valley and the Diablo hills.

In the 1990s, Dublin approved a plan to build thousands of homes and apartments on its east side — Dublin Ranch. This section, close to the BART station, set aside large parcels for high-tech firms, hotels and modern retail stores in a large mall.

Much of this work is under way. The mall, Hacienda Crossings, is up — Barnes and Noble bookstore, Pier I, Old Navy, Bed, Bath and Beyond, restaurants, etc. Safeway has built a giant store here and another in downtown Dublin. Wells Fargo has opened a banking complex. Target, Mervyn's, Ross, Marshalls can be found in the downtown. Stoneridge Mall, with a Macys and Nordstrom, is located a few miles to the south. There's a Costco and a Wal-Mart a few miles to the east. Pleasanton has a Trader Joe's. New apartments are available for rent, new homes (at Dublin Ranch) are being sold. By one estimate made in 2004, Dublin has approved plans for 11,000 homes and apartments, almost all of them to be built on the east side.

In the 1990s, Dublin schools split from Pleasanton and formed their own district. Scores follow demographics: in state rankings, Dublin is scoring in the 80th and 90th percentiles. A bond was passed to add classrooms and other amenities. The new housing is being taxed, often indirectly, to provide schools as the tracts are built. Four schools have been built in recent years; another elementary is to go up in 2007 or 2008.

Residents, aware of the need for construction funds, approved $184 million bond in late 2004. Earlier in the year, it turned down a measure to raise funds for school programs and operations. One big difference between the two efforts, the construction bond required 55 percent approval, the program measure, two-thirds, very hard to get. About 56 percent voted for the measure. Many school districts fail with the two-thirds requirement. When this happens, parents and school supporters try to raise the money to keep the programs.

Thanks to the bond, many of the schools are now being renovated. Among the major jobs: an overhaul of the high school and the addition of a math building, a science building, a sports center and a performing arts center.

Many activities for children. Tennis courts, bowling center, ice-skating rink, six parks, a swim center and a library. Summer water carnival. Movie complex with 20 screens and an IMAX (giant) screen. Soccer thrives. Nearby San Ramon has a roller-skating rink. Seniors center and community center. Adult schools offer variety of classes, many vocational or hobby oriented. Little theater. Heritage center. SPCA recently opened a large center that encourages adoptions. It puts the dogs through obedience training. Among new parks: Emerald Glen on east side: lighted tennis and basketball courts, baseball and softball diamonds, soccer fields, skate park. Fairgrounds in Pleasanton; many events, including — hoot mon! — the annual Scottish Festival. New, large library in the civic center complex. Recently, the library converted a room into a homework center where kids can get special help.

Dublin ties into a trail called Iron Horse that runs to Walnut Creek and beyond. It follows an abandoned rail track. Iron Horse has proved very popular; on weekends, people take to it by the hundreds.

About 230 cities and towns in this great nation allow the sale of fireworks for the Fourth of July. Dublin is one. For safety, Dublin directs the buyers to certain parks where they can fire away without setting the countryside ablaze.

If you have a local job, the commute is a snap. If you toil in Oakland or Berkeley, your nerves will grate but your sanity should remain intact. If you're heading for San Francisco and driving ... good luck. You're going to need it. The Bay Bridge is being rebuilt; chaos. In a few years, another BART station will open in Dublin. Interstate 680 to San Jose was widened in 2002; this helps the often miserable trek. Altamont Commute Express runs trains from Manteca to San Jose with a stop in Pleasanton.

Zero homicides in 2004, 2003 and 2002, one each in 2001 and 2000, zero in 1999, two in 1998, zero in 1997, 1996 and 1995, one in 1994, zero in 1993 and in 1992, two in 1991, zero in 1990, 1989, 1988, 1987.

Just east of town, two jails, one run by county, one by feds. The locals don't like them. The fed place is noted for its alumni, who include Patricia Hearst and Theodore Kaczynski, Unabomber. Dublin's population includes about 5,000 inmates. County wanted to build a juvenile detention center near county jail but residents said, forget it, and killed project. Also on the east side, Camp Parks, training ground for Army reservists.

In 1989, Dublin opened a civic center, a building that gives more substance to the idea of a downtown. But Dublin still wrestles with the criticism that it lacks an "identity." Its response: mild regret to indifference. Downtown being spruced up and public art encouraged. The state tally in 2005 showed 13,564 residential units: 7,600 single homes, 1,304 single attached, 4,632 apartments or condos, 28 mobile homes. Chamber of commerce (925) 828-6200.

• Thousands of homes are going up in the hills and valleys north of Dublin. Dougherty Road, which runs through Dublin, is being widened to handle the traffic from these master-planned communities. To see them yourself, drive Doughterty to Bollinger Canyon Road (San Ramon.)

• 2003 saw the opening of the BART line to San Francisco International Airport. The Dublin-Pleasanton line is the only one that goes directly to SFO.

• Spring in your step? Could be the rubberized sidewalks Dublin is installing on some of its streets. Supposedly it lasts longer than concrete.

• The Ikea project is supposed to include other large box stores. Location near Sybase on Hacienda Drive.

• Transit center going up near BART station — about 1,500 apartments, condos and townhouses, stores and offices; 12-acre park.

• School district is using some of the bond money to install wi-fi at the schools and in general upgrade technology and computers (300 to be purchased.)

• Not all is tract and condo and townhouse. In 2005, Dublin approved the construction 10 homes in the Victorian style of San Francisco. The town, in some locations, is also mixing apartments with stores.

Population by Age Groups in Alameda County

City or Area	Under 5	5-19	20-34	35-54	55+
Alameda	4,057	12,923	14,725	24,579	15,975
Albany	988	3,069	3,737	5,627	3,023
Berkeley	4,109	15,984	34,939	28,635	19,076
Castro Valley	3,266	11,603	9,586	19,424	13,413
Dublin	1,758	5,297	8,434	11,090	3,394
Emeryville	257	636	2,525	2,170	1,294
Fremont	15,137	41,823	46,463	67,437	32,553
Hayward	11,011	30,494	35,761	38,831	23,933
Livermore	5,650	16,622	14,461	25,178	11,434
Newark	3,062	9,736	9,806	12,998	6,869
Oakland	28,292	81,300	101,273	117,175	71,444
Piedmont	582	2,936	731	3,979	2,724
Pleasanton	4,359	14,821	10,262	23,738	10,474
San Leandro	5,032	14,332	16,580	24,191	19,317
San Lorenzo	1,336	4,741	3,909	6,712	5,200
Union City	4,870	15,644	15,283	20,416	10,656
County Total	98,378	293,865	341,818	449,224	260,456

Source: 2000 Census.

EMERYVILLE

● Dublin
Emeryville
● Fremont

SMALL BUT DYNAMIC. On the Bay near the Bay Bridge. One of the best commutes in the East Bay. Loaded with shops, restaurants. Many apartments and condos. Favorite town of young professionals and empty nesters. Population 8,261.

In 2001 and 2002, after years of success upon success, Emeryville took a few hits. Sybase, the large software firm, relocated to Dublin. When dot-coms flourished, many called Emeryville home. The world and Emeryville have far fewer dot-coms now.

On the other hand, Chiron (bio-tech) expanded, adding labs and offices and a garage with 1,000 spaces. Pixar, the creators of Shrek and Captain Nemo, also expanded. The animation studio, run by Steve Jobs of Apple fame, is headquartered in Emeryville.

In 2002, "Bay Street" opened: stores, restaurants, a movie complex of 16 screens, Barnes & Noble book store. This project includes or will include 65 stores, nine restaurants, 363 housing units and a luxury hotel. The town already has several.

The state tally in 2005 showed 5,094 residential units: 270 single homes, 329 single attached, 4,458 apartments or condos, 37 mobile homes. Over the next few years, the city intends to bring its housing total up to about 6,000 units. Most of the new units will be condos.

Other recent additions: an office tower, 16 stories, west of Interstate 80; two hotels, each 11 stories, and an IKEA, a giant furniture that draws mobs on weekends.

Emeryville has an Amtrak station and a freeway, Interstate 80, that bisects the town.

Emeryville was born 105 years ago when residents, fed up with the sluggishness of the county government, voted to incorporate themselves into a city. For income, the new city went in for heavy industry and later trucking, and fun, notably horse racing, minor league baseball and gambling. When Prohibition came, Emeryville blissfully ignored the law of the land and won the wrath of Earl Warren, then district attorney of Alameda County (later California governor and chief justice of the U.S. Supreme Court). Warren raided and fulminated and castigated, all apparently to little avail. World War II came and went, the race track closed but for decades after Emeryville was known as a good place for a shot and a beer and a card game.

Alameda County Single-Family Home Prices

City	Sales	Lowest	Median	Highest	Average
Alameda	132	$165,909	$711,500	$2,200,000	$761,123
Albany	35	238,000	690,000	1,065,000	693,948
Berkeley	228	100,000	761,500	4,409,500	841,663
Castro Valley	211	99,000	670,000	1,450,000	684,633
Dublin	141	250,000	785,000	1,975,000	820,951
Emeryville	66	50,000	500,000	675,000	482,137
Fremont	660	66,500	687,000	2,250,000	748,083
Hayward	613	31,000	565,727	2,106,818	574,367
Livermore	387	39,545	628,000	1,245,000	655,030
Newark	193	59,200	649,000	1,105,000	640,625
Oakland	1,252	31,500	500,000	5,910,000	604,973
Pleasanton	263	183,818	849,500	3,675,000	972,660
San Leandro	369	35,000	560,000	1,350,000	573,102
San Lorenzo	122	175,000	570,000	690,000	560,961
Union City	218	89,000	675,000	1,358,000	703,432

Source: DataQuick Information Systems, Inc., La Jolla, Calif. **Key:** Resale single-family detached housing sales from May 1, 2005 to July 31, 2005.

The forces of change, however, were at work. The Bay Bridge, built in the 1930s, and the freeways, built in the 1950s, elevated the value of Emeryville's location. Came the day when the city council approved the construction of Watergate, an apartment-condo complex that brought in the educated middle class. Within a few years, they voted out the Old Crowd and began to fix up Emeryville.

In the 1980s, high-tech and biotech discovered the town. Emeryville draws many of its brains from the UC-Berkeley crowd.

In the 1980s and 1990s, Emeryville reoriented its retail and amusements to its younger audience. Restaurants, a Trader Joe's and a Borders bookstore were opened. Waterfront trails were spruced up, bike lane added. Hotels were built, bringing in more restaurants. The new apartment complexes came with pools, workout rooms and saunas. The town has a marina — sailing, fishing, boating. Among remnants of the old days: a popular gambling (cards) called the Oaks.

Emeryville sits almost opposite the Golden Gate. Many residents and hotel guests have great views of San Francisco and the Bay. San Francisco is within 10 minutes, Berkeley and Oakland are next door. All three are loaded with things to do.

Served by Emery Unified School District, one elementary school, one middle, one high. Enrollment about 900. School rankings bounce all over but many land in the 30th to 50th percentile. Bond passed in 1995 to spend $8 million to improve the schools and buy them computers. In 2003, residents passed a parcel tax to fund educational needs.

Emeryville has many theft crimes — car thefts and shoplifting — but its serious crime is not as bad as found in other metropolitan cities. Nonetheless, be wary. The city is. The main housing complexes have hired security guards and installed devices and procedures to protect their residents. Emeryville has more officers per 1,000 residents than many other suburban cities and the small size of the town, 1.5 square miles, makes for a rapid response.

Zero homicides in 2003, one in 2002, three in 2001, zero in 2000 and 1999, three in 1998, zero in 1997 and 1996, one in 1995, two in 1994.

• Many of Emeryville's residential units can be found in just three complexes: Watergate, 1,247 condos, Pacific Park Plaza, 30 stories with 583 condos, and Emery Bay, 684 apartments.

• City has a small artists colony residing in live-work lofts.

• Restaurant trivia: in the 1940s, the posh Trader Vic's opened its very first restaurant in Emeryville.

• City runs free buses around town and to BART stations. Popular service, over 700,000 passengers a year.

• Summer fogs cool the air, winter fogs decrease visibility.

• Industrial buildings remain but they are steadily being pushed out by sleek and modern buildings.

Chamber of commerce (510) 652-5223.

FREMONT

Oakland

•Dublin

★ Fremont

BEDROOM HIGH-TECH CITY in south county. Population 210,445. School scores high. Almost every school is scoring above the 50th percentile and some are scoring in the 90th percentile, among the tops in the state. In 2002, passed a $157 million bond to renovate its schools.

Five homicides in 2004, two in 2003, zero in 2002 and 2001, three in 2000, one in 1999. The counts for previous years, 9, 4, 3, 2, 6, 4, 6, 2, 2, 2, 2, 1. Bicycle patrols in some neighborhoods.

Fremont rises from the Bay to the hills, which to a large extent have been spared housing. In winter, the hills turn green and snow sometimes caps Mission Peak. Streets clean. Homes kept in good repair. Trees plentiful, softening the lines of the housing. Fremont has been honored for planting many trees. The town has also done a good job on the little touches that at first you might miss then you notice: for example, the median strip along Mission Boulevard planted with shrubs, flowers and small trees.

Temperate climate. Breezes from the Bay yet warm enough for many homes to use solar heat.

Hard work and intelligent planning have helped Fremont but the city owes much of its good fortune to timing and fate.

First came the Indians, called Ohlones, then the Spanish, who built the mission in 1797 and passed on diseases that killed just about all the Indians. Fremont has a large Indian cemetery a short distance from the mission, which has been restored.

Then came the Americans who farmed and welcomed the railroad. In the early 20th century, Charlie Chaplin shot some silent films in the Niles neighborhood, which now celebrates a June festival of silent movies.

As the century progressed, five hamlets blossomed and in 1956, seeing development coming, they incorporated themselves into the City of Fremont, population 22,443. A big city. Fremont, in square miles, is almost double the size of San Francisco. Left as five villages, "Fremont" would have grown up disjointed and difficult to administer. Also by this time, planning for suburban cities was shedding its diapers and becoming more of a force. New cities are often more cleverly designed than old ones. Fremont officials established zones for homes, for apartments, for light industry, for shops and malls.

$15.95

McCormack's GUIDES

How California Schools Work

A PRACTICAL
GUIDE FOR
PARENTS

FROM THE EDITORS OF McCormack's Guides

www.mccormacks.com
1-800-222-3602

Meanwhile, across the Bay, reachable over the Dumbarton Bridge and Highway 237, and south to San Jose, Silicon Valley was coming to life and home prices on the Peninsula were rising. Many families looked east to Fremont.

By 1960, the population had jumped to 43,790 and then it soared, reaching 100,869 by 1970. In the 1970s, Fremont added about 32,000 residents and in the 1980s, about 41,000. By this time, the city was running out of land. In the 1990s, Fremont increased its population by 30,000.

In the 1960s and 1970s, housing tastes were changing. Garages went from one stall to two and three, bedrooms from three to four and five, stories from one to two. Lots shrunk. With both parents working, low-maintenance landscaping found favor over lawns.

Fremont has its very old housing, erected around the original towns. And it has its old suburban tracts, constructed just after World War II. But having built so many units after 1960, the city comes across as "new," particularly in the hills, along and above Mission Boulevard, and down near Interstate 880. The state in 2005 counted 71,237 residential units: single homes 42,182, single attached 7,181, multiples 21,118, mobile homes 756.

The old Fremont used to be considered blue-collar. It had a large auto plant that employed thousands. The plant is still there, General Motors-Toyota NUMMI, and it is still the city's largest employer, about 5,000 workers.

By and by, Silicon Valley also ran out space for plants and research facilities. Up to Fremont it came and built hundreds of high-tech firms, and later bio-tech firms. This wiped out the blue-collar image and turned Fremont into a Silicon Valley town. Needing highly skilled and educated workers, the new firms pushed the demographics further up the scale, which explains in part the high academic rankings.

In SATs, among Alameda County high schools, Mission San Jose High usually places first or second in math and among the top five in verbal. Every year only about three dozen California high schools crack the 600 mark in the math SAT. Mission San Jose High School is always in this elite group. Parents in this neighborhood, the richest in the city, are prickly about education. When the school board tried to change attendance boundaries of the schools serving the Mission San Jose neighborhood, parents said, no way, hired lawyers and petitioned to form their own school district. In 2001, the state rejected the petition and, meanwhile, the school board softened its reorganization plan.

Fremont also has a large community college, Ohlone, a big plus. Community colleges are loaded with activities and classes open to the public. In 2002, Ohlone won approval of a bond to build a campus in Newark and to renovate its Fremont facilities and add a student services building.

Activities plentiful. About 40 parks and playgrounds. Lake in middle of town. Large library, small neighborhood libraries. Symphony orchestra. Trails, bay wildlife refuge, historic farm. Annual arts festival draws about 350,000. Mission Days Festival. Festival of India. Celtic Festival. Performing arts center at Ohlone features touring shows. Ice-skating rink, in part a tribute to local girl who made good: Kristi Yamaguchi, winner of Olympic gold in figure skating. Skate park. City sponsors dozens of activities and classes, gymnastics, dance, cooking, singing, kiddie and toddler get togethers, jazzercize, etc. Usual kid sports, soccer, softball, football. New nine-hole golf course. Lagoon is being converted into a water recreation park. East Bay Regional Park District opened a swimming beach at its 450-acre Quarry Lakes Park, which has been stocked with fish.

Ohlone College runs summer programs for young children — sports, arts, drama, English, math, chess, computers and more.

University of California at Berkeley offers extension classes in town. Many of the classes are aimed at working professionals. Several other schools — Silicon Valley College, Northwestern Polytechnic — offer courses for working adults.

Fremont promotes ethnic harmony and throws a Heritage Festival. Churches and schools help with the getting along. Many residents are professionals who came in the immigration wave that started in the 1970s.

Commute better than most. Buses, BART (commute rail), freeways, bridge to Silicon Valley. Boulevards, almost all four-lane, crisscross the city and end usually at a freeway. Two freeways: Interstate 680 and Interstate 880. The latter used to be a real dog, always congested, but in recent years it has been widened and overpasses and exits have been added or renovated. The result: still a mutt. More people, more cars ... can't win.

If you're taking BART to Oakland or San Francisco, you have to rise about a half hour earlier than Berkeley residents and make the station by 7 a.m. On the plus side, Fremont being the beginning of the BART line, you're assured of a seat. The Altamont Commuter Express, trains from Stockton to San Jose, makes stops in Fremont and Santa Clara.

In 2000, Santa Clara County voters approved a sales tax increase that will raise money to extend BART to San Jose, and possibly beyond. When completed, the BART extension will make life easier for many commuters but the job is going to take probably decades. In the same year, Alameda voters extended a half-cent sales tax for transit projects.

- After years of arguing, Wal-Mart won permission to build a store at Osgood Road and Auto Mall Parkway. Store up. Another recent addition: a Target.

- Mountain lions occasionally spotted in the hills. Shy animals. No one attacked. Also spotted: the helmeted hang glider. The ridges seem ideal for this pursuit.

- The original towns were Niles, Centerville, Irvington, Mission San Jose and Warm Springs. As a way of building neighborhood cohesiveness, the city is restoring these old towns as business centers and gathering places (restaurants, cafes, a movie house or a theater).

- More stores. Pacific Commons, 800 acres near Interstate 80. Costco, Lowe's Home Improvement, Kohl's Department Store, Circuit City, Office Depot, Claim Jumper Restaurant, Starbucks, In-N-Out Burger, Linens N Things.

- Washington Medical Center is located near BART station.

- The Centerville and Irvington neighborhoods run year-round farmers markets.

- Fremont has an ordinance discouraging home construction in the hills.

- As land zoned for residential becomes scarce, the city has taken a closer look at some industrial parcels and switched them to housing. In recent years, this has led to projects bringing in over 500 townhouses and apartments.

- School district is losing enrollment. To even out attendance at the schools, the district assigns some students to schools outside their neighborhoods.

- Every year a group re-enacts a Civil War battle at Ardenwood Farm. Part of national movement to keep history alive.

- In 2005, the California School for the Deaf celebrated its 25th year in Fremont.

- Jager gets vested. Local veterinarian donated $1,600 to buy a bullet-proof vest for Jager, a canine cop with the police department. Said Jager's master, the German shepherd gets sent into dangerous situations; a vest makes sense.

Chamber of commerce (510) 795-2244.

HAYWARD

Oakland • Dublin
★ Hayward
• Fremont

EAST SHORE BEDROOM city, suburban, third-most populous in Alameda County, 146,027 residents. Good commute. Recently renovated many of its schools. Educational offerings include a community college and a California State University, both of which wave the flag for academics.

Following World War II, thousands of GIs, having sampled California sunshine on their way to the Pacific, migrated to the West Coast. Hayward and countless other suburbs were built for them. Practical and unpretentious, these towns were oriented around home, school, recreation and reasonable proximity to jobs. Home designs favored the three-bedroom, two-bath model.

Almost half the city's housing units were built between 1950 and 1970. The great majority of the homes and apartments were constructed on the flat or gently sloping land to the west of Mission and Foothill, two of the main boulevards.

Hayward ascends gradually from the Bay to the hills and east of Mission Boulevard soars into elevations that command sweeping views of San Francisco Bay. After 1970, Hayward, in its hills neighborhoods and near the university, moved upmarket with 4-6 bedroom homes. For the best of what Hayward offers, take a spin up Skyline Drive.

Hayward also has older, smaller housing around its downtown.

All this means a good housing mix with prices across the spectrum. Many people coming in at the low end are buying their first homes.

The state in 2005 counted 47,489 housing units, of which 23,666 were single homes, 3,548 single attached, 17,976 apartments and 2,299 mobile homes.

Around the downtown BART station and the civic center, the city has been encouraging "smart growth," in this instance townhouses, live-work lofts and condos. "Smart growth" tries to place people near transit centers and favors apartments and multiple units over single homes.

Amtrak has a station just west of the downtown. In recent years, Amtrak has started a commute schedule called the Capitol Corridor, trains from Silicon Valley to Sacramento.

Hayward has a second BART station near Mission Boulevard on the south side. BART also has a station in Castro Valley, within a short drive of North Hayward.

About 17 miles to Bay Bridge on Interstate 880, recently widened. About 10 miles to Peninsula via the Hayward-San Mateo Bridge, which in 2002 added a second span (it ties into the first at the San Mateo side.)

Quick shot to Livermore-Pleasanton over Interstate 580. About 15 miles to San Jose. AC Transit buses.

In the 1990s, the school district won money from the state to remove asbestos and remodel many of its schools and equip them for high tech. Local voters in 1997 gave the OK to continue a tax that paid for school landscaping, maintenance of playing fields and graffiti removal. Hayward runs several year-round schools. Academic rankings bounce all over the place. Several private schools, including a Catholic High School (Moreau).

Shopping malls follow freeways. The Southland Mall came to life with the construction of Interstate 880 and weakened Hayward's old town, about two miles to the east. The city and merchants have been tinkering for years to rejuvenate the downtown and have come up with antique stores, restaurants and shops. One of the two BART stations borders the downtown and this helps attract shoppers. New city hall and fire station. Old city hall sat astride the Hayward Fault. The building was abandoned.

The city is headquarters for Mervyn's Stores and has a small airport, warehouses and light industry down near Interstate 880. These businesses create local jobs, the ideal commute.

Nine homicides in 2004, eight in 2003, nine in 2002, 10 in 2001, nine in 2000, eleven in 1999. Counts for previous years are five, seven, twelve, twelve, twelve, eight, five, ten, four, six, eight, three, five. The hill sections have far fewer incidents of crime than the flatlands and some flatland sections are safer than others.

Many activities. Boys and Girls Club. Plays and events at the colleges, baseball, basketball, soccer, tennis, arts and crafts. Bowling alley. Big indoor swimming pool. Neighborhood and regional parks. Shoreline preserve. Lake Chabot. Japanese Gardens. Roller-skating rink. Libraries. Movies. Annual zucchini festival. Nine-hole golf course. Many classes at Chabot Community College and Cal State are open to public. Chamber of commerce (510) 537-2424.

• What's in a name? Plenty, think some at Cal State Hayward. They thought that the university would have wider appeal if its named was changed to California State University, East Bay. Hayward protested but the change was made.

• Hayward is building or recently built a 100-acre high-tech business park, 578 homes and a 25-acre sports park with lights for night games, baseball, soccer, softball. The project is located near the Bay.

LIVERMORE

Oakland Dublin
★ Livermore
● Fremont

BEDROOM, HIGH-TECH TOWN, population 80,723, that also grows grapes and fights development, often successfully, but still accepts a fair amount of change and new construction.

Home to Lawrence Livermore Lab, which has helped make the town a brainy place.

School rankings bounce around a bit but many are in the 80 and 90th percentile. The school district mixes parents across a diverse social spectrum, rural to suburban, low income to highly educated. The latter tend to produce high-scoring kids.

In 1999, in partnership with the city government, the school district passed a $150 million bond to renovate schools and make civic improvements. In 2001, the district opened another elementary on the east side, north of the freeway.

In 2004, however, short of money, the district closed two schools. This angered some parents who organized a campaign to turn one of the closed schools into a charter school. After every local agency rejected the parents, the state Dept. of Education agreed with them and the new school (Livermore Charter) opened in 2005. There's a lot of head scratching over this dispute. The money for the new school must come, in part, from the school district, which means that any savings from closing the two schools probably has been lost. Because charters encourage variety, Livermore is going to get something different in this new school.

In 2004, perhaps more sensitive to the plight of the schools, Livermore voters approved a parcel tax that restored programs cut or reduced in recent years and kept class sizes low.

Crime low. Zero homicides in 2004, 2003, 2002, 2001 and 2000, two in 1999 and 1998, zero in 1997 and 1996. Counts for previous years are two, one, one, zero, two, two and one.

Commute not as bad as might be thought because the region is loaded with jobs.

In and about Livermore are located 23 wineries, Wente the best known. Residents call Livermore the "Alameda Wine Country." Livermore is situated in a bowl called the Amador Valley. The city is frequently mentioned in connection to its western neighbors, Dublin and Pleasanton, and to a lesser extent, San Ramon.

The town was named after Robert Livermore, an English sailor who married into a Spanish-Mexican family and secured a grant of 44,000 acres. For much of its early history, Livermore crushed the grape and rounded up the cattle. It produced one celebrity, boxer Max Baer, who in 1934 won the heavyweight crown. He was called "the Livermore Larruper."

In 1952, as the Cold War was swinging into high gear, Dr. Edward Teller, father of the H-Bomb, persuaded the U.S. government to build the Lawrence Livermore Lab to do research on nuclear weapons and other defense-related projects. The town at that time had a population of about 7,000.

Homes followed to house the people who worked at the lab and its spinoffs. The freeway, Interstate 580, was gradually extended, making the commute from Livermore to the Bay Area much easier and tying Livermore into the regional economy. Many of its residents now work in other towns.

In the 1960s, Livermore built about 6,400 housing units, in the 1970s, about 6,000 units and in the 1980s, about 4,000 units. In the 1990s, housing starts rose to about 5,700 units (census 2000).

By any standards, this is good amount of housing in a fairly short time. Nonetheless, Livermore picked up a reputation for being anti-growth.

The Lawrence Lab is run by the University of California at Berkeley. Yes ... that Berkeley! The leader in free speech, environmentalism and a few other causes. The Livermore locals initially saw the lab as this bonanza that would boom the local economy and build homes over the valley and into the hills.

The UC people saw the vineyards and the open hills and the small-town qualities and said, no, no, no, NO! to the development plans. Basic cultural clash, the kind that happens when people from different galaxies meet.

But even without the Berkeley connection, the fights would have come. In the 1980s and 1990s, the whole region, including San Ramon, Dublin and Pleasanton, went high-tech and up-market, bringing in thousands of professionals with upscale ideas of slowing growth and protecting the countryside. The same fights that show up in Livermore broke out in the other towns, the main difference being intensity. Livermore tops the scale in this category.

The big job, fought over for decades, is the equivalent of a new city, on Livermore's north border: 12,500 homes, condos and apartments. In 2000, residents passed a measure restricting growth in the area but in 2005 a developer reworked the plan, threw in a lot civic goodies, and said, please pass it, please, please, please. No dice. Rejected.

Down through the years, however, the pro and anti groups learned somewhat to work together to the benefit of the town. Instead of ripping out the vineyards, ways were devised to protect them, about 3,500 acres, and blend in the housing. Much of the new housing and retail stores were built near Interstate 580. Livermore is forever trying to revive its downtown. It has had some success but removed from the freeway, the neighborhood will never be the vibrant center it once was. In some quarters this amounts to the end of the world, in others ... no big deal. And it's by no means a dead downtown. It has movies, restaurants, shops, a regional hospital, and a certain old-fashioned charm.

Like most towns, Livermore built to the demands of the times. When the times called for middle-class housing, that's what it built, standard three-bedroom tract models, especially around its downtown. In the 1980s, many people were taking the equity in their first homes and moving into something bigger and better.

Livermore went in this direction. Many of the new homes run to four-bedrooms, with walk-in closets in the master bedroom, large or gourmet kitchens, plenty of windows and natural light, living rooms oriented toward the television or entertainment center and modern wiring.

In the overall picture, there's a good amount of variety. This includes custom homes, some built near the downtown, others in the country. And it includes in the downtown, cottages and bungalows erected before 1950. On many of the older streets the trees have matured into leafy umbrellas that cast pleasing shadows for the hotter days.

The state in 2005 counted 29,002 residential units, of which 21,023 were detached single homes, 2,365 attached homes, 5,183 apartments or condos and 431 mobile homes.

Many new homes sell for $650,000 plus and some soar over $1 million. The resale market offers old homes for less but Livermore is no longer the affordable town it used to be. See profiles on Dublin and Pleasanton.

In 2002, the Lawrence Lab, which employs about 8,000, celebrated its 50th anniversary. With the end of the Cold War, there was talk of closing the Lab but after cutbacks, it won a contract to build a super laser, cost about $2 billion. Besides research into nuclear weapons (computer testing and modeling) and disposal of aging bombs, the lab does research on cancer detection, fusion energy and mapping the genetic code, developing stronger materials and stopping bio-terrorism. After Sept. 11, Americans took national security more seriously and if anything this only underscored the importance of the lab.

.Across the street is the Sandia National Lab, different outfit, approximately same mission, about 1,000 employees. Years ago, a newspaper reported that Livermore had one of the highest — if not the highest — concentrations of Ph.Ds in the world. This boast is hard to prove but the labs are crawling with scientists.

Lawrence Lab and Las Positas Community College run special programs for the kids. Lab also trains teachers. Las Positas, which attracts many adults, in 1996 opened a science-technology center.

Of the $150 million approved in the 1999 bond, $20 million went for a new library, $20 million for a seniors center, a teen center, and a swim center, and $110 million for schools. The school district is also gets building funds from the state. The library and a community center were opened in 2004. The town also has two branch libraries.

Livermore is attracting many professionals with young families. The school bond and the success of the 2004 measure that restored programs reflects the town's high interest in education. So did the school closure fight. Those parents, believing they were helping their kids education, fought and fought and refused to get discouraged.

BART station was opened in 1997 in nearby Dublin, a comfort to commuters, especially those traveling to San Francisco. Local buses and express buses to Silicon Valley job sites.

Interstate 680 has been widened south of Pleasanton, easing the commute for people working in Silicon Valley.

Altamont Commuter Express runs commute trains from Stockton to San Jose with stops in Livermore and Pleasanton. This is removing a little traffic from Interstate 680. Some residents are bothered by the train horns.

Even with these improvements, if you have a long commute, you will often find it a time-consuming drive. The Bay Bridge, the main route to San Francisco, is almost always backed up at commute hours. Many people now commute from the Central Valley and this is congesting Interstate 580.

Nonetheless, many Livermore residents have a short commute because they have local jobs. Besides the Lawrence Lab and Sandia, the region has attracted such high-tech or office firms as: Pac Bell, AT&T, ChevronTexaco, Hewlett-Packard, Oracle and Sybase.

Located on the east side of the coastal range, Livermore is warmer and drier than the shore cities of Alameda County but not as hot as the Central Valley, which is separated from Livermore by the Diablo range. Livermore and Pleasanton occasionally trap some of the smog that blows around the Bay Area but air quality in the region has been improving. Just east of Livermore is the Altamont Pass, site of a notorious rock concert of the 1970s. (Rolling Stones hired Hell's Angels for security; bedlam meets mayhem.) Windy. About 5,000 windmills, power generators. Many dislike windmills, eye-insulting bird killers. Plans afoot to tear down many of the small ones and replace them with fewer but larger and more powerful ones that supposedly will kill fewer birds.

To elaborate on the appearance, Livermore is suburban pleasant with a strong country atmosphere. Empty or almost empty hills still surround the city. Mt. Diablo rises to the northwest and in the winter takes on a mantle of snow. The homes are generally well-maintained, the streets clean, graffiti rare to the point of escaping notice. New police station, city hall renovated.

The freeway stores include a Costco, a Target, a Mervyn's, Home Depot, a Lowe's and a Wal-Mart. Dublin is to open an Ikea, giant furniture in a few years.

Usual recreation — baseball, soccer, activity classes, softball — much better than you'll find in many suburban cities. About 40 parks or play facilities. Three golf courses. Bowling alley. Annual rodeo. Large park, Del Valle, which has camping, boating, windsurfing and swimming. Equestrian events are popular. Thoroughbred ranches in hills. Plenty of horse and hiking trails. Camelot amusement center: video games, miniature golf, go-carts. Wine-country social life, of sorts, with an intellectual underpinning (the lab people). Livermore throws a harvest festival, a wine and honey festival and an arts festival. Wine museum. Skate park.

Dublin has a movie complex, 20 screens and an IMAX (giant) screen and a large bookstore. Pleasanton also has its big bookstore and a downtown popular with the restaurant crowd. And a giant mall with a Nordstroms and a Macys. Other goodies, a Trader Joe's.

In the 1950s, when the Lab arrived, Livermore and the region really were hicksville. Television, movies, small markets and a few greasy spoon restaurants — and that was it. Now ... a much different picture, not only for Livermore but for affluent suburbia. The giant supermarkets routinely field bakeries, delis, fish markets, pharmacies and banks. For the harried commuter and soccer parents all this means more convenient shopping. Starbucks and other coffee shops.

Local groups are not only staging plays but operas, a demanding art. The more ambitious productions draw on talent from the Bay Region. Many people and city officials are working to find ways to build a performing arts center in the downtown.

Livermore may remember 2004 as the year when the goofy and unexpected happened.

The pride of the town's main street was a tall flag pole, 99 years old and thought indestructible. Upon closer exam, the pole was revealed to be rotten and in danger of falling. Down it came and up went a new one.

The town celebrated the opening of the library by commissioning a mosiac fountain that included the names of famous artists, writers, musicians and scientists. Did you know that Einstein is spelled with two "n"s? The artist spelled it with one. She also misspelled Michelangelo, van Gogh and a few others. The media had a field day (but life goes on).

• BART in 2003 started direct service from Dublin to San Francisco International Airport. Another BART station is to be built in Dublin, on the Livermore border.

- For local medical attention, Valley Memorial Hospital and Kaiser clinics.

- Livermore runs many of its recreation programs through a park and recreation district, an agency separate from city hall. For information and a schedule of activities, (925) 373-5700.

- Livermore Airport, located to west of downtown. If moving near airport, check out noise, especially at night. Airport is home to about 600 planes, mostly small.

- Downtown has a small movie house. The city, which has been trying for years to enliven the downtown, has landed a 10-screen movie plex. Plans call for the building of about 2,000 apartments or condos in the downtown.

- Las Positas College in 2004 won a bond that will pay for renovations and new buildings.

- For Yosemite and the mountains and snow slopes, Livermore offers a quick getaway — three or four hours.

- New synagogue opened in 2004; serves families in Livermore, Pleasanton and Dublin.

- Lights, Camera, Action! Livermore has its own annual film festival, a weekend event that screens about 65 films and mixes in dinners and wine tastings.

Chamber of commerce (925) 447-1606.

NEWARK

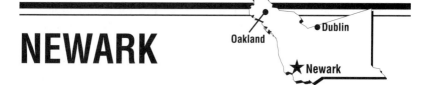

Oakland
•Dublin
★ Newark

SHORT OF LAND FOR HOMES, plants and business facilities, Silicon Valley has reached out to embrace cities that missed out on the initial waves of high-tech development.

Newark, population 43,708, was one of the last cities to join the Silicon family. In 1999, Sun Microsystems opened a large complex for offices, manufacturing and research. Hewlett-Packard and other firms had already set up plants in the town, spurring the construction of homes, condos and apartments.

The result: a city that blends the old with the new and fairly new, pays more attention to appearances, and offers housing that is attracting more high-tech professionals.

And a city more in touch, painfully, with the ups and downs of high tech. Sun has greatly reduced its work force at the Newark complex.

Served by Newark Unified School District, which passed an improvement bond in 1990 and a second one, for $66 million, in 1997. The money was spent to upgrade and repair the schools and equip them for high tech. In 2002, the high school opened a tech center and a new cafeteria. Among California schools, Newark schools historically have landed about the middle but as the city changes these numbers may rise. Scores often follow demographics; Newark, in many parts, is ascending into middle-class plus.

Ohlone Community College leases space for classes in Newark and in 2002 won a voter approval of a bond to build a large, well equipped campus, cost $100 million. To be located on Boyle Road near Mowry Avenue, the place will open about 2007. The City of Newark will help fund the college library on condition that it also serve the public. Washington Hospital, to train its medical students, will open a clinic at the new campus.

Zero homicides in 2004, one in 2003, zero in 2002 and 2001, three in 2000, zero in 1999 and 1998, two in 1997, five in 1996. The counts for the previous years are two, zero, zero, four, one, five, zero, zero. Overall crime rate low-medium.

In commuting, Newark falls into the category of, "not bad." The town borders I-880, one of the main freeways to San Jose and Silicon Valley. The Dumbarton Bridge, located just northwest of the city, leads directly to North Santa Clara County and, not coincidentally, to the large Sun Microsystems complex in Menlo Park. BART stations in nearby Fremont and Union City.

As for appearance, Newark, especially in its northeast section, has built neighborhoods and many homes that would fit very nicely into any upscale town. One development is built around a lake ringed by open space and trail.

The city has planted trees (about 15,000 of them) all over the place. Graffiti absent, homes and lawns generally well-maintained. In some sections, industry and housing live side by side, which some people may not like. The town works with the older industries to buffer them from residential areas.

Ten parks. City adjoins a large (29,000 acres) shore refuge and just over city limits is a regional park with historic farm. Newark is developing 28 acres into a sports complex. Fields have been laid and work completed on facility that includes teen center, gym and rooms for aerobics and day care. Town also has a seniors center. City hall runs activities for kids and adults. Fireworks sold locally on the Fourth of July. Farmers market.

Opened in 2004, a large indoor swimming complex that includes a lap pool, two water slides, a spa and a wheelchair-friendly pool.

In 1956, Fremont, seeing growth coming, incorporated itself as a legal city. What is now Newark was included in the original "Fremont" but a dispute arose over how "Fremont" would develop "Newark." The locals pulled out of the proposal and pushed through their own cityhood drive. Newark's suburban boom began about this time. About 1,500 housing units were built in the 1950s and 4,000 in the 1960s.

In the postwar era, the East Bay economy was built around large industrial plants, General Motors, Ford, Caterpillar Tractors, Peterbilt Trucks, and around San Francisco International Airport, easily reached by the Dumbarton or San Mateo bridges. Newark's initial housing was priced and designed to serve this blue-collar market, the standard three-bedroom home forming the backbone of the units built.

In the following years, many of the industrial plants were closed or reduced in size and a new type of job appeared: computer, high tech. Newark still has many residents working blue-collar jobs, and many outsiders probably still hold the image of Newark as a blue-collar town. But with the influx of white-collar workers and professionals, the housing and social mix has become more varied and the town has moved up the scale.

The state in 2005 counted 13,414 residential units, of which 9,205 were single detached homes, 1,238 single attached, 2,912 apartments and 59 mobile homes.

Large mall with a Macys, a Sears, and Penneys (tax revenue for civic amenities). Another hotel opened in 2002. The state is buying many of the salt ponds and returning them to marsh.

If you want to meet the town's business and civic leaders, break out the tie and tails or the flowing gown. Every September residents and business people celebrate Newark Days with a fair, a parade and a grand ball.

Home Price Sampler from Classified Ads

Alameda
•4BR/2BA, Victorian, $665,000
•5BR/3BA, new paint, $975,000

Berkeley
•3BR/2BA, office, $700,000
•3BR/2BA, blt. 1904, $895,000

Castro Valley
•3BR/2BA, brand new, $719,000
•3BR/2BA, near lake, $660,000

Dublin
•5BR/2.5BA, corner lot, $698,000
•4BR/2BA, hrdwd. flrs., $800,000
•4BR/2BA, upgrds., $660,000

Fremont
•3BR/2BA, nr. frwys., $630,000
•4BR/2BA, jacuzzi, $705,000
•4BR/2BA, remod., $660,000
•4BR/2.5BA, nr. sch., $735,000

Hayward
•3BR/1BA, garage, $580,000
•2BR/2BA, nr. park, $495,000
•3BR/2BA, upgrades, $735,000

Livermore
•3BR/2BA, vault. ceil., $565,000
•3BR/2BA, oak kitch., $767,000
•3BR/1BA, $530,000

Newark
•4BR/2.5BA, form. DR, $748,000
•3BR/2BA, new roof, $649,000

Oakland
•4BR/3BA, views, $725,000
•2BR/1BA, frplc., $470,000
•3BR/2.5BA, lndscpd., $829,000
•3BR/2BA, open flr. plan, $695,000

Pleasanton
•3BR/2BA, ranch style, $879,000
•4BR/2.5BA, nr. sch., $899,000
•4BR/3.5BA, brand new, $1.1 mil.

San Leandro
•3BR/2BA, hilltop, $660,000
•3BR/1BA, views, $489,000

San Lorenzo
•5BR/2.5BA, nr. park, $695,000
•3BR/3BA, $596,000

Union City
•4BR/2BA, fruit trees, $730,000
•4BR/2BA, cov. patio, $735,000
•3BR/2.5BA, hrdwd. flrs, $599,000

In Dumbarton, Scotland, stands a castle named Newark. Pioneering developer came from Scotland and remembered the old castle. Hence, Newark, one, it is estimated, of 29 Newarks around the planet..

Chamber of commerce (510) 744-1000.

• Newark High School in 2004 was turned into a "closed" campus. This means that students, unless given permission, were not allowed to leave the campus during the school day.

• Scheduled to open in 2006: a movie complex with 20 screens at the NewPark Mall.

• K-Mart closed. May be replaced by a Home Depot.

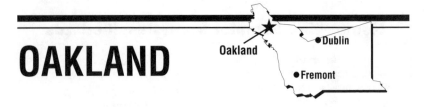

OAKLAND

LARGEST AND MOST POPULOUS (412,318 residents) city in county. Great commute. Many jobs. Dynamic and lively downtown. International airport. Largest shipping port in Northern Cal. Big-time sports.

Crime high in some neighborhoods. Scores low at many schools. School district went bankrupt and had to borrow $100 million from state.

In other words, a mixed bag. Many pluses, some minuses.

In 2003, after voters passed three bonds to renovate the schools and a new superintendent was brought in, class sizes were lowered and Oakland district seemed to be making progress. The people in charge, however, forgot to keep tabs on what they were spending and were forced to declare bankruptcy. Superintendent was fired and the state installed an experienced money person to run the show. Many fingers were pointed, many sighs heaved. In recent years, the district has seen its enrollment drop by about 6,000; this has forced the closure of several schools.

On the slightly bright side, many of the schools have been overhauled and some of the program improvements will remain. As for academics, many schools do score low but a fair number score at the middle and at the top. Financially, Oakland still supports its schools. In 2004, it passed a tax to raise salaries and maintain programs. Oakland in effect has two school systems: the public and the private, in the form of many private schools in Oakland and nearby communities. One study estimated that about 22 percent of the local school-age children attend private schools.

In 1999, homicides fell to their lowest number in 32 years but then began to rise and by 2002 and 2003 had people shaking their heads. In 2004, voters approved a tax to hire more cops. Other tactics were employed. Murders dropped.

In 2004, Oakland recorded 83 homicides. For the previous years are 109, 108, 84, 80, 60, 72, 99, 93, 138, 140, 154, 165, 149, 146, 129, 112, and 114.

Despite this, Oakland continues to add residents and many people will find it a pleasing home. Oakland is like many a big city. It has serious problems that residents try to ameliorate and it has neighborhoods with low crime and fairly high scores. The state in 2005 counted 161,022 residential units, of which 72,236 were single homes, 6,646 single-homes attached, 81,684 apartments or condos, 456 mobile homes.

Founded in 1852, Oakland grew quickly and by 1900 was the second biggest city in the Bay Area and the civic and business leader of the East Bay. In 1910, Oakland had 150,000 residents; in 1950, it counted 385,000. After 1950, Oakland lost residents to the suburbs, then gradually came back and in some ways surpassed its crossbay rival, San Francisco. That city is built on a peninsula; expensive and time consuming to reach by train and truck. Oakland put together a containerized port that shut down the San Francisco docks.

Being an old city, Oakland has plenty of old housing, ideal for immigrants and people starting up the housing ladder. Oakland also has a good deal of middle- and upper-income housing.

The city starts at the bay on flatlands then ascends into low and steep hills. Many homes have views of the bay and Golden Gate. In situations like this, often the cheaper housing is in the flatlands (next to the downtown) and the expensive housing in the hills. This generalization holds for Oakland but there are exceptions. Some low-income neighborhoods are built over hills and have great views. Some high-income neighborhoods were erected in the flatlands (around Lake Merritt).

Oakland borders Berkeley on its north side and in this section — Montclair, Hiller Highlands, Claremont, Rockridge — has become part of the university community. The Oakland hills, running the length of the city, favor upscale housing. The views are sweeping; the homes back up to regional parks; the crime is low.

Moving toward the flatlands, housing values, with exceptions, decline then rise at the waterfront where live-work lofts are being built. Many homes on the south side were built just after World War II for the veterans; here the three-bedroom home is favored.

Oakland is the government seat of Alameda County and the headquarters for the University of California system. Downtown has large federal complex (twin buildings, 18 stories). In recent years, the downtown has added two hotels and several office buildings, including a 20-story tower, and made efforts to land high-tech.

Moving down the shore to Hegenberger Road, Oakland has erected a sports complex that hosts the Athletics (baseball), the Warriors (basketball) and the Raiders (football).

Just across the freeway from the sports complex is Oakland International Airport, which specializes in cheap flights. Among its carriers, Southwest and Jet Blue (and more). The airport has improved its access roads and is expanding its terminals and is considered a success, about 13 million passengers a year. Many East Bay residents prefer Oakland over San Fran.

Among Oakland's cultural and recreational ornaments are a first-class museum specializing in California history, concerts, plays, ballets, a symphony orchestra, about five dozen parks, first-class restaurants, hotels, zoo, a convention center, marinas, ice skating rink. Concerts and shows in restored Paramount Theater or at the Coliseum. Victorian neighborhood preserved in downtown. Night life thrives around Jack London Square, which has one of best jazz clubs in the Bay Area, a bookstore, movies, restaurants and shops.

Lake Merritt and park in downtown. At almost any time during the day, residents and workers can be found walking and jogging or skating around lake. All the usual activities for kids and adults: softball, football, Little League, etc. Many enrichment classes offered through schools. Libraries. Several community colleges and four-year private colleges, including Mills, the women's college, and Holy Name. Fairyland, popular amusement park for kids, recently renovated. In 1999, after years of work and fund-raising, the Chabot Space and Science Center was reopened in the hills — state-of-art planetarium and large telescope. Berkeley and San Francisco and all they offer are within a few minutes drive or a BART ride.

Almost all the homicides take place in flatlands in the low-income neighborhoods. Many are drug related and this has called attention to failed drug prevention and prison efforts. If the figures were broken out, many of the hill neighborhoods — Montclair, Claremont, Hiller Highlands, Rockridge, the homes near the Oakland Zoo — probably would show low crime rates.

For suburban average, the neighborhoods above or east of Lake Merritt, including Trestle Glen, Temescal, the Dimond District would probably fall in this grouping.

These are generalizations. If you drive the poorer neighborhoods, you will see many homes with security doors and window bars but you will also find sections where the homes are well kept, the streets clean, the security devices less-frequently employed. In the poor neighborhoods, the law abiding are many, the criminal are few but unfortunately damaging. Oakland is a diverse and changing city; the demographics, the social chemistry, are always in flux. Whatever the neighborhood, however, the rules of big-city life apply: take care.

Excellent commute for many, with the exception of the Bay Bridge, which during peak hours tries everyone's nerves. Damaged in the 1989 quake, the east span of the bridge is to be replaced over the next five years. Traffic congestion may worsen. BART, which has stations all around Oakland, offers a convenient alternative to the bridge, and now runs down to San Francisco International Airport. Amtrak stations. Buses. Ferries to San Francisco.

Improvements costing about $1.4 billion are being made to the Oakland airport. Terminals and gates are to be added, cargo space expanded, garage built to more than double parking spaces, access roads improved. On the last job, the roads, it is much easier now to get to and from the freeway.

City also intends to build a monorail to carry people from BART station to airport. Another big job: overhaul of the port, new rail yard, deeper channels, new berths.

About $100 million is being spent to turn the land around the Fruitvale BART station into a "transit village" that will include housing, offices, a senior center, a child-care center, a library and a larger parking lot. Other BART station neighborhoods are also being improved.

Another big project: about 400 units in the hills, at the site of a quarry.

A city Mother Nature smiles on — lovely weather — and afflicts. The 1989 earthquake collapsed a double-deck stretch of Interstate 880 and a portion of the Bay Bridge, and seriously damaged many buildings in the downtown. Two years later, fueled by hot winds, a fire killed 25 in the hills and destroyed over 2,500 homes and apartments. Oakland bounced back. The Cypress was rebuilt to modern earthquake standards. The apartments and homes destroyed in the fire have been rebuilt.

Opposite the Golden Gate, Oakland catches the Pacific breezes and fogs and enjoys cool and balmy weather almost year round. The cool air discourages outdoor pools. Annual rain: flatlands, 18 inches; hills, 27.

• High-rise condos and senior housing around Lake Merritt.

• Oakland's mayor Jerry Brown, a former governor, is making noises about running for state office in 2006.

• Oakland has distinctive neighborhoods, some set off by freeways, some by housing and personal styles. Montclair is built over hills and ravines and is heavily wooded. It has its own shopping "downtown," a library, churches and community buildings. Highway 13 defines one border, Highway 24 another and two regional parks mark the other boundaries. The result: a sense of being a separate village and strong feeling of community. Lake Merritt is ringed with luxury apartment and retirement buildings. The Temescal and Rockridge section have cafes, restaurants, upscale shops. The Fruitvale neighborhood draws many immigrants. Many Asians have settled in downtown Oakland and this section is winning renown for its restaurants — Chinese, Vietnamese, Burmese, Korean, Cambodian, Thai, Indian.

• Oakland schools run diverse programs. One school, Lazear, operates under a charter that gives parents and teachers a great deal of influence. Another charter school follows a military regimen. Some schools follow year-round schedules.

• Kaiser hopes to build a large medical center near the downtown to replace the existing center. Ground breaking might start in 2008.

• Among new stores, a Whole Foods.

• Oakland Army Base, 170 acres, turned over to Oakland years ago has been ignored. In 2005, a film producer said it was interested in setting up operation at the base. City hall is studying the proposal. Chamber of commerce (510) 874-4800.

PIEDMONT

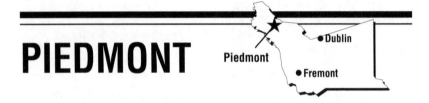

ONE OF THE WEALTHIEST and prettiest cities in the East Bay, Piedmont from its beginnings has attracted the boss, the broker, the heir, the heiress and the professional. But some things do change. Piedmont used to be a bastion of the Republican party but these days most voters call themselves Democrats.

Crime low, scores high, remodelings many. Piedmont is surrounded by Oakland; no room to grow. In 1960, the census counted 11,150 residents. In 2005, the state put the population at 11,055. Piedmont does build new homes but very few — according to the 2000 census, zero in the 1990s and only 31 in the 1980s. The state in 2005 counted 3,861 residential units, of which 3,784 were single detached homes, zero single attached, 69 apartments 8 mobiles.

Served by the Piedmont Unified School District, enrollment about 2,600. Academic rankings in the 90s, one of the highest scoring districts in the state. Piedmont High is one of the few Bay Area schools that every year scores over 600 in the math SAT. In the 1990s, Piedmont voters raised their taxes several times to improve and retain academic programs and renovate and add buildings. In 2001 and 2005, voters renewed parcel taxes to pay for class aides and sports, music and fine arts. In a town that prizes the old, the schools present the most modern face. Piedmont High graduates students into the most prestigious universities in the U.S. Several private and parochial schools in Oakland and Berkeley round out the educational offerings.

Every year the teens stage a bird-calling contest. Winners are sometimes invited on late-night shows (David Letterman) to sound off. In 2002, a group of choir students, many from Piedmont, visited Cuba where they found themselves feted by Fidel himself. The students said he was friendly and talkative, denounced the American media and praised Popeye, because he encouraged children to eat their vegetables. At that, one student broke into "I'm Popeye the sailor man ...." and others joined in, including the Cuban minister of culture.

One of lowest crime rates in East Bay. Zero homicides in 2004, 2003, 2002, 2001 and 2000, one in 1999 and zero between at least 1985 through 1998. Piedmont has its own police department and many homes subscribe to private security. In the 1999 homicide, wife was slain, husband arrested.

Commute generally good. Short drives to freeways that lead to the Bay Bridge, which on most days is congested. AC Transit buses to San Francisco and to East Bay cities. BART stations nearby. If you work in Oakland or Berkeley, the commute comes down to 10 to 15 minutes.

Piedmont, located almost opposite the Golden Gate, catches some of the fog that blows through the Gate. Not a place for outdoor pools. Here and there around town some impressive redwoods have taken hold, testament to the nourishing fog. But weakened by distance and sunlight, the fog lacks the thickness of the billows blowing into the western neighborhoods of San Francisco. By midday, Piedmont usually emerges into sunlight.

Lovely town. One park greets visitors with an edifice decorated by what looks like a Grecian urn. As symbolism goes, this kind of sums up Piedmont. Elegant. For the lucky residents, views of the Bay and Golden Gate. Homes exceptionally well-maintained. Kind of place where residents varnish the garage door. Variety of home styles, fair number of custom homes that allowed architects to show their stuff. Trees galore. Former mansion serves as city hall.

Lots to do, if not in town then nearby. Before-and-after school programs for kids, including computers, dance, music, camps. Soccer, basketball, flag football, etc. City and school district offer over 150 programs and activities for adults, from aerobics to flower arranging to yoga. Two golf courses nearby. All that Berkeley and Oakland have to offer. Theater, foreign movies, jazz clubs, first-class cuisine. San Francisco on most evenings can be reached within 20 minutes. Three universities nearby: Berkeley, Holy Names, Mills.

When the businessmen and their families of the 1800s tired of the bustle and grime and probably fog of San Francisco, their eyes drifted across the Bay to the farms and wooded hills of the East Bay. Gradually they purchased lots and built sometimes magnificent homes and by the turn of the century, Piedmont had about 1,000 residents. Cable cars, connecting the hills to the rail station, spurred development, The Great Earthquake of 1906 also helped, people fleeing for what was thought to be safer ground. About this time, the town became embroiled with Oakland in arguments over taxes, school construction, municipal services. Oakland probably could have smoothed some ruffled feathers but it ignored complaints and moved quickly to annex Piedmont. Some residents said, let's form our own city and did. Quickly Piedmont grew to its borders: by 1910, residents numbered 1,719, by 1920 the count went to 4,282, by 1930, to 9,333, close to what it is today.

Although opulent homes stand out, many smaller homes were also constructed, mostly on the west side. In the 1990 census, the three-bedroom home showed itself to be the most popular (36 percent of all units) followed by the four-bedroom (33 percent). Piedmont has maybe two dozen businesses and depends on Oakland, particularly Rockridge and Montclair neighborhoods, for food, stores, restaurants, services and a library.

Old towns, old laws, Piedmont prohibits keeping of lions, tigers, bears and rhinos. You can't wash your clothes on a public street. In modern times, laws were enacted to spare trees on sidewalks, ban gasoline leaf blowers and pooper-scoop the dogs. No chamber of commerce. City hall (510) 420-3040.

PLEASANTON

Oakland

• Dublin
★ Pleasanton
• Fremont

HIGH-TECH SUBURB located at the junction of two freeways. Crime low, school scores high, jobs plentiful. Home to many tech professionals. Well-kept town with many parks and amusements. Population 67,650.

In 2004, Pleasanton said goodbye to PeopleSoft, which employed about 3,000 in town, and was gobbled up by big, bad Oracle and Larry Ellison. The fear was that Larry would lock up the buildings, fire thousands and move the survivors across the Bay to Oracle headquarters in Redwood City. About 600 did get sacked but Oracle retained the Pleasanton campus and 2,300 employees and sold four buildings to Kaiser Medical, which is moving in about 1,000 "knowledge" workers. The result: at the worst, a wash, but some think it a plus. The town has stopped badmouthing Larry and every once in while, in a low voice, a few will actually praise him.

Its name inspired by a Civil War general, Pleasanton for most of its modern history slumbered in rural obscurity serving as a general store for local farmers and a refreshment station for travelers. After World War II, the nation and the state began constructing wide highways and these, combined with a large migration into California, created the suburbs. Being somewhat removed from the old cities, Pleasanton did not boom until the 1960s when Interstates 580 and 680 were built and intersected at Pleasanton. In 1960, the town counted about 1,200 homes and apartments and 4,200 residents.

About this time, several forces were at work that benefitted Pleasanton. In the 1950s, the University of California opened a large research lab at Livermore, the neighboring city, bringing in thousands of highly-educated people. The old cities were running out of space; the large firms began to move operations to the suburbs. Silicon Valley started to boom with the new technology.

Here was Pleasanton (and its neighboring towns): freeways, plenty of cheap land for housing and commerce, high-tech core of residents, educated population. And, credit where credit is due, a savvy city hall and civic leaders. By 1970, the population had risen to 18,328 and by 1980 to 35,160. This number increased to 50,553 by 1990. The 2000 census counted 63,654 residents. Pleasanton is running out of land and in recent years residents have voted to preserve open space and slow development.

By 1960, planners had a much better idea of how to build suburbia and buffer residential streets from traffic. In the 1960s and 1970s, many homeowners were taking their equity and buying up, creating demand for larger homes, two-story instead of one, four bedrooms instead of three. Pleasanton flowered in this market. It is an old town, incorporated in 1894, but a new suburb, filled with new or fairly new homes, many of them up-market.

Pleasanton channeled its high-tech and offices into a modern business park called Hacienda, which is situated near the freeway interchange. The place is loaded with firms. Also, service businesses and miscellaneous clean industries, including Safeway headquarters, the kind that cities do handstands for. Another business park is located on the south side of town. Hotels followed the businesses.

Also near the interchange is a regional mall called Stoneridge (Macys, Nordstrom). Near by are a Costco, a Wal-Mart and a Trader Joe's, the merchants of modern suburbia.

In the 1990s, BART (commuter rail) extended service to the Amador Valley and built a station at Dublin-Pleasanton, which made the town even more attractive to big business.

The result: a nice-looking suburb, attentive to and supportive of its schools, loaded with jobs, housing well-tended, ranging from old and small (pre 1960) to middle-class stalwart (three- and four-bedroom) to knockout, the gated Ruby Hill neighborhood. The lawns are mowed, the homes and apartments are in good repair, graffiti absent, streets clean. Some homes rise into the hills, affording views of countryside. Mt. Diablo to north. Still a good deal of open space at city's edge. Main Street, removed somewhat from the freeways, nonetheless appears to be thriving. The city has spruced up the street with trees and brick sidewalks and helped create a setting that nourishes restaurants, delis, bakeries, cafes and small shops. The old Pleasanton Hotel, now a restaurant, anchors one end of the restaurant row; a library and a park, the other end. County fairgrounds and office complex help the downtown with visitors and noon shoppers. On weekends, the restaurants and coffee shops and sidewalk cafes are filled with people at their leisure.

Served by Pleasanton Unified School District, which in two elections over the last 15 years has passed bonds worth $155 million and used the money to equip, build and renovate schools. The school board in 2000 raised fees on developers to help pay for the renovation and expansion of the town's two high schools, Foothill and Amador Valley. In 2002, Amador High built a library-media center and more classrooms. Foothill High built a pool and added classrooms.

Compared to other California schools, scores are running in the top 10 percent. SAT scores come in well above national and state averages. Community college in Livermore. UC Berkeley and Cal State Hayward and other universities offer classes in nearby towns. Pleasanton teachers are among the highest paid in Alameda County. Dublin, which recently raised salaries, also pays high. The point both are making — we're willing to pay for quality.

Overall crime rate low. Zero homicides in 2004, 2003, one in 2002, zero in 2001. One homicide in 2000, zero in 1999 and 1998, one in 1997, two in 1996. The counts for previous years are two, zero, zero, zero, one, two, two, two, zero, zero, zero.

Good to horrible commute, depending on destination and choice of vehicle. Local jobs are a snap. Freeways and wide arterials move traffic along. For about six years — it seemed forever — the state was rebuilding the interchange of freeways 580 and 680. In 2002, the job was finished. Hallelujah! Altamont Commuter Express (ACE), which began service in 1998, dispatches commute trains from Stockton to San Jose with stops in Tracy, Manteca, Livermore, Pleasanton, Fremont and Santa Clara. ACE recently added another train.

In 2003, BART extended its service to San Francisco International. One perk for Dublin-Pleasanton; its line goes directly to SFO; no transferring.

Trouble spots: Interstate 680. If you are commuting to San Jose and Silicon Valley, this freeway often grinds to halt near Fremont. The good news: another lane was added in 2002. Second spot: the Bay Bridge, which is now rebuilding its east span. This bridge, which leads to downtown San Francisco, simply carries too much traffic and at peak hours often backs up for more than a mile.

In 2000, Alameda County voters extended a sales tax for transportation and Santa Clara County passed one to bring BART to San Jose and make general improvements. Both taxes will fund a variety of projects throughout the two counties and bring some relief to commuters. But more people are coming in, bringing more cars, and inciting residents to vote against developments. The arguments and ballot battles have been going on for decades. See Livermore.

With all its stores and businesses, Pleasanton has a strong tax base. It has used a lot of this money to fund parks and recreation programs for kids and adults. Swim complex with four pools. Regional park with lake. Other regional and state parks nearby. One of the largest sports parks in Northern Cal: 24 multipurpose fields, basketball and volleyball courts, three play areas for kids, trails. Usual sports, soccer for kids perhaps the most popular. Soccer season kicks off with a parade down Main Street. There's also adult soccer.

About 30 neighborhood parks, teen dances and concerts, ice skating rink in Dublin. Roller rink in nearby San Ramon. Two high-school stadiums were fitted out with a new type of artificial turf, supposedly very close to real thing. In 2001, the city added another park, 24 acres, three soccer fields, roller hockey rink, climbing wall, water-play areas, garden. A middle school, located in Hacienda Business Park, shares its gym with the community. One of the high schools does the same with a performing arts center. Trails galore. Skateboard park. Pasta Festival. Pleasanton hosts the county fair, an annual celebration with horse racing and games and many events. The fairgrounds stay open year round and attract a variety of amusements, including Scottish games, dog shows, Octoberfest and hot-rod show. In 2002, the Women's United Soccer Assn. named two Contra Costa women the best soccer moms in the U.S. Interviewed by a reporter, both women said that Pleasanton had some of the best soccer fields in the region.

First-class shopping at Stoneridge Mall (Macys, Nordstrom). Good mix of restaurants, from fast food to tablecloth. Livermore and Pleasanton have two dozen wineries that down through the years have figured out ways to blend in with housing tracts. The wineries have encouraged residents to pay attention to wines and tastings and fine dining. Wente, the biggest vintner, sponsors musical events at its winery, which is bordered by a golf course.

Livermore-Pleasanton without the wineries would be attractive suburban towns. With the wineries they have become classy, attractive suburban towns. And a little more interesting and a little more fun.

Library. Senior Center. Driving range. Nine-holes of golf at fairgrounds, two private courses (one at Ruby Hill). Tennis park. Private exercise clubs. Barnes and Noble bookstore on one side of BART and a Borders on the other side, in Dublin. Many residents shop in Dublin, which has opened large discount stores and a movie complex, 21 screens, including giant IMAX screen. On the way in Dublin, an Ikea, the giant furniture store.

If you like swimming, this is the right side of Alameda County. West of the hills, the waterfront cities catch the cooling, sometimes cold, breezes coming through the Golden Gate On the east side, the hills block or tame the breezes, giving the Amador Valley a warmer climate but the valley bowl sometimes impedes circulation of the air, raising pollutant and pollen counts. Overall, however, mild and balmy and similar to what's found in Napa.

Kaiser clinics and ValleyCare Medical Center provide health care. In 2000, ValleyCare added a wing with 30 beds. The hospital contracts with Lucille Packard Children's Hospital to provide neonatal care.

If shopping for housing, start with the old downtown. As you move out, the homes will get newer and bigger. At Ruby Hill, which is gated, they jump way up the scale but for the most part modern Pleasanton was built for the middle and upper middle class (but these days you can pay in Pleasanton almost $1 million for a nice but not fancy tract home). The state in 2005 counted 25,253 residential units: 16,536 single detached homes, 2,742 single attached, 5,519 multiples and 456 mobiles. Chamber of commerce (925) 846-5858.

• Local bus agency, called WHEELS has expanded routes and hours of service along some routes.

• Traffic circles in the new subdivisions. Part of campaign of traffic calming. Slow down, smell roses, watch the road.

• BART to add another station just east of the existing one. About 1,800 apartments, condos and townhouses and stores and offices are being built near the BART station, on the Dublin side.

• Animal lovers are raising money to build a small shelter, 5,240 square feet, in Stanley Business Park.

• Some new homes are including mother-in-law units as part of the garage.

• Meandering paths around town. Canal path.

• Livermore airport on the east side. Pleasanton is concerned about noise from the aircraft.

• Opened in 2005, another golf course, public, 18-hole, par 72. Surrounded by 280 acres of open space, some of which has been turned to hiking and horse paths.

• On its south side, off Bernal Avenue, Pleasanton is building a large park that, according to initial plans, will include a cultural arts center, an amphitheater with 1,000 seats, eight playing fields, basketball courts and a teen center.

• Elementary enrollments are slipping but unevenly. School district plans to build another elementary near Ruby Hill but the project has been slowed by arguments over funding.

• In the late 1800s and early 1900s, small towns throughout California erected arches at the entrance to their downtowns, a showing of civic pride. In 1931, thanks to the efforts of the Women's Club, Pleasanton built its arch, cost $700. In 2005, the city council voted to renovate the arch, cost $35,000.

SAN LEANDRO

LOCATED JUST SOUTH of Oakland, on the BART (commute rail) line, served by two freeways, one of the better suburban commutes in Alameda County. Population 81,442.

Viewed as a good town to move up to. Good mix of housing and prices. Many of the residents work in Silicon Valley. First-class marina and waterfront with restaurants. School rankings low to middle to fairly high. In 1997, residents passed a $54 million bond to renovate all schools.

In the 1990s, San Leandro increased its housing stock by about 1,100 units and its population by 8,000 and in recent years has added about 800 apartments and townhouses.

San Leandro rises from the Bay to the hills and has many older neighborhoods, built just after World War II, two- and three-bedroom units. In the flatlands, near Interstate 880, the homes border industrial areas. Although San Leandro retains many blue-collar jobs, the town for some time has been moving into white-collar territory.

In the Sixties and Seventies, several industries pulled out of San Leandro, leaving large empty plants. The city rallied, sought new businesses and took care to keep up appearances and morale.

When the downtown was crippled by bypassing freeways and shopping plazas, the city pulled together and pumped money and planning into the section. The result: The downtown looks nice, attracts shoppers and gives the city a strong center. In recent years, this section and the east side have been landing restaurants.

When people describe San Leandro, two words frequently pop out: stable neighborhoods. The homes are old and plain but the paint is fresh, the lawns neat, the shrubs clipped. Drive the east side to see San Leandro at its best. Drive the west side to see some of the largest suburban lots of any city in the Bay Area. For a final perspective, drive the flatland thoroughfare of International Boulevard-14th Street-Hesperian through several towns. Even the old streets of San Leandro come across as clean and presentable. Graffiti painted over as soon as possible. City staffers are assigned to discourage blight, get people to clean up yards, get rid of junk cars. In 2004, the city council approved a plan to upgrade 14th Street and make if more pedestrian-shopper friendly.

State in 2005 counted 31,842 housing units: single homes, 19,415, single attached 2,028, multiples 9,495, mobile homes 904.

Near Interstate 880, large stores have opened, including a Costco and a Sportmart. Another mall has attracted clothing outlets, including a Nordstroms.

Nice waterfront: parks, a marina, two golf courses, restaurants. On sunny weekends, the waterfront attracts strollers, families, golfers, ball players, boaters — a lot of people. Well-stocked library. About 18 parks. Plenty of sports and activities for kids: baseball, soccer, swimming, day camp. Boys and Girls Club. Annual Cherry Festival celebrates local history. California State University, East Bay, and Chabot Community College are within 10-15 minutes.

Four homicides in 2004. In previous years: 3, 2, 1, 5, 3, 4, 5, 6, 4, 4, 5, 6, 4, 1, 2, 2 5, 1. In 2005, officer shot to death in traffic stop. Suspect arrested. Shocked town.

Good commute. Besides BART and the freeways, AC Transit buses carry people to San Francisco and East Bay cities. Near Oakland Airport but few noise problems (but check for self). Close to San Mateo and Bay bridges. Interstate 880, which partially collapsed in the 1989 earthquake, was reconnected in 1997 to the Bay Bridge. This has helped the drive commute but the bridge itself often jams. BART and I-580 are handy alternatives. I-880 recently widened in San Leandro and Hayward. In 2002, the San Mateo Bridge added, in effect, a second bridge. This helps people commuting to jobs around San Francisco International Airport.

Suburban cities inevitably grow old and in need of rejuvenation. San Leandro aggressively has tackled its problems and moved the city ahead. Good choice for young families who want to get in the housing market at a reasonable price (relative rest of Bay Area.) Chamber of commerce (510) 351-1481.

• San Leandro fields over 40,000 jobs. Among the major employers: Kraft General Foods, Incandescent, Albertson's, stores at Bay Fair Mall. City has a technology center and is trying to attract high-tech firms.

• Bay Fair Mall has a Target, a Macys and a movie complex, 16 screens.

• Safeway is remodeling, modernizing and expanding its supermarket.

• Auto mall at Marina Square. Generates $1 million a year in tax revenue.

• On its northwest side, San Leandro just about butts up against Oakland Airport. City hopes to build a business park in this area and serve airport firms.

• In 2004, Eden Hospital of Castro Valley purchased and took over the management of San Leandro Hospital.

• Kaiser is building a medical center in San Leandro, replacing Hayward facility.

SAN LORENZO

UNINCORPORATED NEIGHBORHOOD between San Leandro and Hayward west of Interstate 880. A member of the Hayward Park and Recreation District. Many activities. Park with lake, golf course. Playground-park at Del Rey School. Community swim center. Homeowners association works to keep appearances up.

Many well-kept lawns, an indication of community pride. Older residences. San Lorenzo got its great spurt just after World War II, when 1,300 homes were built. Many were later remodeled and expanded.

Some new homes are being added but San Lorenzo is fairly stable. Lost 558 residents in 1980s, added 1,911 in the 1990s. The 2000 census counted 21,898 residents.

Served by San Lorenzo Unified School District, enrollment about 12,000. In 2001, the district won a grant to equip just about every student in grades four to 12 with a lap top. San Lorenzo is within 10 to 15 minutes of Chabot Community College and Hayward State University.

In 2004, voters approved a $49 million bond to renovate every school in the San Lorenzo district.

Like other towns, becoming more ethnically diverse, many immigrants among the newcomers.

San Lorenzo is governed from Oakland by board of supervisors. Lacking its own city council, San Lorenzo rarely makes headlines and, indeed, the average East Bay resident would probably have difficulty locating the town. Still, it offers much in the way of affordable housing.

Good commute city. Short drive to Oakland and to Bay Bridge. BART stations in nearby San Leandro. Many jobs around Oakland airport.

Hayward airport borders San Lorenzo. Check out plane noise.

Chamber of Commerce (510) 351-1481

UNION CITY

BEDROOM TOWN in south county. Population 70,685. Many new homes, especially near Mission Boulevard in the hills and along Union City Boulevard in the flatlands near the shore. In the 1990s, the city built about 3,100 homes and apartments.

Many children. Schools enjoy strong community support. Three school bonds, for total $101 million, passed in last 15 or so years, the most recent in 1996. It paid for technological upgrades, improvements to facilities and a new school. Served by New Haven Unified School District.

Academic rankings, on statewide comparisons, land above and below the 50th percentile but elementary schools and Logan High have a reputation for hard work and close attention to academics. Logan sends many kids to top universities and boasts one of the top athletic programs in the state.

Logan, which has probably the largest enrollment of any high school in Northern Cal (about 4,000 students), has innovative student-union building. Place for kids to go after school, keep out of trouble: jukebox, video games, snack bar. School also stages an annual high-tech fair. The school's swimming pool is open to the community in summer months.

School board is wrestling with problem of enrollment at Logan High. Some members favor moving ninth graders to their own school. Other alternative: try for a bond to build a new high school. Or see if the state would put up the money. This would reduce Logan's enrollment to about 3,000.

Guy Emanuele, who retired in 1997, had been superintendent of the school district seemingly forever. He was one of the best schmoozers and administrators in education (top-down style, forceful; he made a lot of the decisions), close to parents and business and civic leaders. It's rare for a school district to win three bonds in short period. And at that time, bonds needed two-thirds approval; now they need 55 percent. Emanuele deserves some of the credit. He's also credited with saving art and science programs at a time when many districts were eliminating them. When he retired, the district named a school after him.

Voters in 1996 passed resolution to restrict development in the hills. Housing units number 19,783— single homes 12,678, single attached 2,379, multiples 3,823, mobile homes 903 (state tally, 2005).

One homicide each in 2004 and 2003, two in 2002, three in 2001. The counts for previous years are, 2, 2, 0, 0, 0, 3, 3, 1, 2, 1, 0. Overall crime rate about low-suburban average. Curfew for kids. If under 18, with reasonable exceptions, they have to be in by 10 p.m.

About 17 parks. Many sports, soccer, baseball, football, boxing club, softball. Seniors center. Every year the school district stages "Marching On," a dance-musical that gives about 2,000 kids a chance to show their stuff.

BART (commute rail) station. Union City is close to one freeway and bisected by another, the congested I-880, which has been widened in recent years but on many mornings and evenings just crawls along. If commuting to San Francisco, BART might be the best bet. One of these years, thanks to the recent approval of a tax increase in Santa Clara County, BART will be extended to San Jose. Union City is talking about creating a transit hub around its BART station. Around the hub: apartments, high-tech, shops; buses, Amtrak, Altamont Commuter Express.

The other freeway, I-680, is faster and on many days does a better job moving motorists. But in recent years it has become more traveled and is running into traffic snarls. Also nearby, the Dumbarton Bridge, which leads to Silicon Valley and Peninsula. AC Transit buses serve neighborhoods.

About 100 small manufacturing plants in Union City. Kaiser Permanente medical center. Many warehouses. City is trying to attract high-tech firms and is using redevelopment to boost Dyer business section, near I-880 and Alvarado-Niles Road. Dyer Triangle, also known as Union Landing, has a giant supermarket, Office Max, Wal-Mart, movie complex. Also, Borders Books, Lowe's Home Improvement Store, Michael's (Crafts), Kinkos Copies, Krispy Kreme Donuts and In 'N Out Burger.

Ethnic mix diverse and becoming more diverse. Schools and city are making efforts to help everyone get along. Another part of the mix: Union City is building middle and upper middle housing close to its low-income neighbor-hoods, one of the more effective and benevolent forms of integration. It brings kids of varied backgrounds together at an early age.

Gladioli used to grow row on row in Union City. The town song starts, "Meet me at the Union City station...."

A town with a little bang. City council voted to outlaw sale of fireworks. Residents voted to bring them back and back they are, for the Fourth of July. Local civic groups, to raise funds, sell the fireworks — supposedly safe. Chamber of commerce: (510) 471-3115.

• School district, with enrollment declining, may close two schools.

• High school offers classes in French, German, Tagalog, Punjabi and sign language.

• Chabot College offers evening classes at Logan High.

Chapter 4

Central Valley at a Glance

LOCATED EAST AND SOUTHEAST of Alameda County, San Joaquin, Stanislaus and Merced counties for most of their existence have been farm communities that served their immediate regions. This is becoming less the case as people seek lower-cost housing than the San Francisco region offers.

In the 1980s, the Bay Area cities filled their last big open areas and home prices rose sharply. About the same time, the state completed Interstate 5, which runs down the Central Valley, and improved the other freeways in the region, foremost Interstate 580.

Interstate 580 connects I-5 and indirectly Highway 99, the other major freeway serving the Central Valley, to the freeway networks of the Bay Area.

Also in the 1980s, the original "Silicon Valley," which had been confined to Santa Clara County, leapt its boundaries and opened research facilities, plants and office complexes in Fremont and in Livermore-Pleasanton-San Ramon. These openings moved thousands of jobs closer to the Central Valley.

There came the day when developers realized that some people in the Bay Region were willing to commute to the Central Valley — in exchange for lower home prices. First there was a trickle of buyers, then in the late 1980s and 1990s and early 2000s a river. Jobs multiplied in the 1990s and home prices kept rising, forcing more and more people to look to the Central Valley for housing.

Between 1980 and 2000, Merced County added 76,000 residents, San Joaquin 219,000 and Stanislaus 175,000 — a total 470,000. From 2000 to 2003, the three counties were among the five fastest growing counties in the state, averaging more than 10 percent growth apiece over the three-year period.

Home Prices in the Central Valley

In neighborhoods of Modesto-Ceres, new homes in 2005 were selling for less than $400,000. In the suburban way, pleasant: three bedrooms, two baths, at least one walk-in closet, large kitchen, modern wiring and design.

The same home transplanted to say Sunnyvale or San Ramon would go probably for about $700,000; transplanted to Palo Alto or Los Gatos or Saratoga, $800,000 or $900,000 or higher.

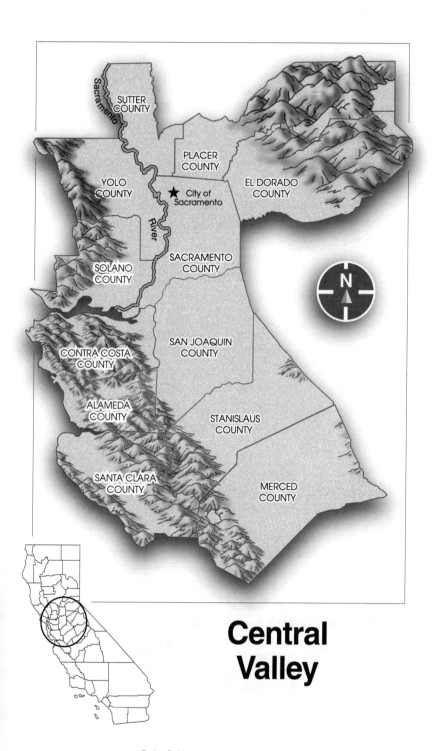

Central Valley

Central Valley Area Population

Merced County

City or Area	1990	2000	2005*
Atwater	22,282	23,113	26,693
Dos Palos	4,196	4,581	4,854
Gustine	3,931	4,698	5,311
Livingston	7,317	10,473	12,344
Los Baños	14,519	25,869	32,380
Merced	56,155	63,893	73,610
County Total	178,403	210,554	240,162

San Joaquin County

City or Area	1990	2000	2005*
Escalon	4,437	5,963	6,912
Lathrop	6,841	10,445	12,565
Lodi	51,874	56,999	62,467
Manteca	40,773	49,258	61,927
Ripon	7,455	10,146	13,241
Stockton	210,943	243,771	279,513
Tracy	33,558	56,929	78,307
County Total	480,628	563,598	653,333

Stanislaus County

City or Area	1990	2000	2005*
Ceres	26,413	34,609	38,813
Hughson	3,259	3,980	5,942
Modesto	164,746	188,856	207,634
Newman	4,158	7,093	9,134
Oakdale	11,978	15,503	17,439
Patterson	8,626	11,606	16,158
Riverbank	8,591	15,826	19,988
Turlock	42,224	55,810	67,009
Waterford	4,771	6,924	7,897
County Total	370,522	446,997	504,482

Source: 1990 Census, 2000 Census. *California Dept. of Finance, Jan. 1, 2005.

As for resale homes, in some Valley towns it's possible to buy mansions—two stories, five bedrooms, gourmet kitchens — for $400,000 to $500,000. It's also possible to purchase many homes for $200,000 to $300,000.

Endurable and Miserable — The Commute

If you work in Livermore, Dublin, Pleasanton or San Ramon and live in Tracy or Manteca, the commute is fairly short, 25 to 40 miles, mainly over Interstate 580. This freeway slows at peak hours but for the most part it moves the traffic along. It should be noted that many firms start their employees early and release them about 3 p.m. That's when traffic starts to swell.

People who move to Modesto-Ceres probably will find the commute to Livermore-Dublin endurable. Highway 132 from Modesto feeds into Interstate 580, a shortcut.

But if you work in Silicon Valley or San Francisco or the Peninsula (San Mateo-Palo Alto), the trek is long and wearying.

Distance is half the drawback. Many people will be driving 90 miles, one way, some over 100 miles.

Congestion is the other half. The Bay Area simply has more vehicles than it can handle.

If you commute to San Francisco, you have to brave the Bay Bridge, almost always congested and now undergoing the construction of new eastern span. Navigating the approaches to the Bay Bridge and getting over the bridge can take a half hour to 40 minutes.

If you work in Fremont or San Jose, Interstates 680 and 880 frequently congest long before you reach your destination (But both roads have been widened.) On bad days, it can take 45 minutes to drive from Pleasanton to San Jose, a distance of about 25 miles.

People who buy in Merced and Los Banos often use Highway 152, which winds over the Diablo range and drops into Gilroy, the southernmost city in Santa Clara County. Then it's a drive of 30 to 40 miles up Highway 101, which has just been widened, to the job centers of Silicon Valley. Hard slogging.

Alternatives

BART has extended its commute rail line to Dublin-Pleasanton. If you're working in San Francisco or Oakland, try BART.

The Altamont Express runs commute trains from Stockton to San Jose with stops in Manteca, Tracy, Livermore, Pleasanton, Fremont, Santa Clara and San Jose.

Many people are forming car and van pools to the major job centers.

Trains or carpools, the alternatives are still long and time-consuming. At the end of the train ride, you might have to hop in your car and drive another 30 to 50 miles.

For people who are thinking about buying in the Central Valley and commuting to San Francisco or San Mateo County or Fremont-Union City or San Jose-Silicon Valley, there are no magic tricks to make the commute short and easy.

A word of advice: try the drive or the commute before you buy the house or condo. For some people, the affordable and often very nice suburban house will be worth the pain. For others it won't. With the price of gas rising, fuel costs should be factored into any commute decision.

Greater Sacramento Central Valley

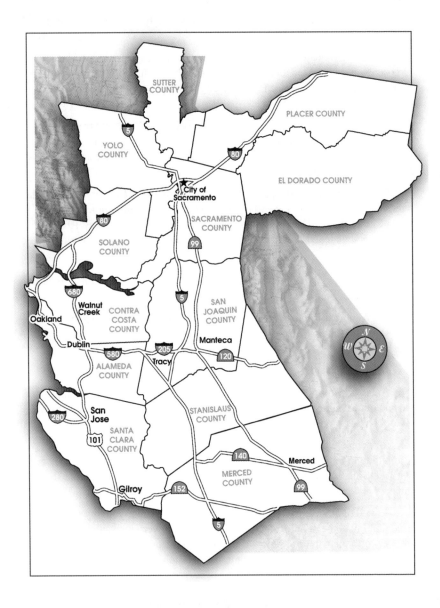

Central Valley Voter Registration

Merced County Voter Registration

City	Democrat	Republican	*NP
Atwater	4,448	5,204	1,083
Dos Palos	957	803	146
Gustine	1,193	756	228
Livingston	1,891	882	359
Los Banos	5,333	4,698	1,139
Merced	14,117	12,744	2,438
Unincorporated	14,120	14,916	3,019
Countywide	42,059	40,003	8,412

San Joaquin County Voter Registration

City	Democrat	Republican	*NP
Escalon	1,155	1,618	356
Lathrop	2,047	1,623	506
Lodi	8,602	14,814	2,634
Manteca	9,399	10,997	2,864
Ripon	1,602	3,643	672
Stockton	54,606	44,302	9,808
Tracy	11,303	12,188	4,160
Unincorporated	23,006	29,035	5,148
Countywide	111,719	118,220	26,148

Stanislaus County Voter Registration

City	Democrat	Republican	*NP
Ceres	7,197	5,532	1,494
Hughson	857	738	222
Modesto	38,225	36,022	9,433
Newman	1,440	818	344
Oakdale	3,013	3,024	799
Patterson	2,140	1,250	472
Riverbank	3,115	2,383	748
Turlock	11,334	10,889	2,728
Waterford	1,224	1,072	343

Source: California Secretary of State's office, 2004. **Key:** *NP (Non-partisan; declined to state any political party preference).

2004 Presidential Voting in Central Valley

Merced	Kerry	22,403	Bush*	29,968
San Joaquin	Kerry	74,868	Bush*	87,336
Stanislaus	Kerry	49,640	Bush*	70,981

Source: California Secretary of State's office. *Election winner.

Greater Sacramento

San Joaquin, Stanislaus and Merced counties have attracted very few high-tech firms.

Greater Sacramento has landed many firms, including Intel, Hewlett-Packard, Sun, Microsoft, Aerojet and the region has large office complexes, food processing sites and thousands of jobs in state and federal government agencies.

Many people living in Lodi-Stockton-Manteca and Modesto tap into the job market in and around Sacramento. If the commute to Silicon Valley turns you off, look to Sacramento or San Ramon-Livermore-Dublin-Pleasanton for a job.

Necessary definitions

The Central Valley covers the whole valley, from Redding to Bakersfield and the Grapevine.

The Central Valley is divided into two sections.

The Sacramento Valley refers to the land drained by the Sacramento River, generally from Stockton to Redding.

The San Joaquin Valley refers to the land drained by the San Joaquin River, from Stockton to Bakersfield.

Many people just use "Central Valley" to refer to the whole area and ignore the divisions. McCormack's Guides, for the title of this guide, chose Alameda-Central Valley because this acknowledges the connection between the two and, to us, seems the clearest way to identify the region.

Overview of San Joaquin, Stanislaus, Merced

Flat, with the exception of the western hills, which have few inhabitants.

Oriented more toward Highway 99 than Interstate 5, the better, faster, newer freeway.

Highway 99, which runs east of Interstate 5, follows the rail lines that in the 19th century spurred the development of the Central Valley. When the towns were built, they generally stayed close to or straddled the rail lines.

In the 1980s and 1990s, when the commute to the Bay Area blossomed, the new housing went into the established cities because they had the infrastructure — sewers, water, schools, etc. Little new housing has gone up along Interstate 5, consequently adding miles to the commute (but this is changing; more housing is coming to I-5).

San Joaquin, Stanislaus and Merced are oriented in recreation more toward Yosemite and the Sierra than toward the Bay and Pacific. If you like the mountains and skiing, hiking and camping, you'll find a lot to like in these counties.

The weather is California balmy but the summers are hotter than the Bay Area's and the winters a little chillier. In winter, skies are often overcast in the Central Valley. See weather chapter.

Air quality is an issue in the Central Valley. Residents blame Bay Area pollution blowing into valley. The Environmental Protection Agency is leaning hard on the valley to meet tough new standards.

Small-town atmosphere. If you like it, the Central Valley towns have it by the wagonload. Wide-open spaces. Farms start at the edge of many of the towns. Miles of cultivated fields and orchards. Mountains to the east. Your neighbor may wear a Stetson and it will not be out of place.

Games and amusements. Just about every town will field soccer, baseball, football, softball and basketball teams. Private groups have opened exercise and gymnastic places. Movies. Plays and art galleries are few, antique stores many.

Restaurants plentiful. White-tablecloth, haute-cuisine places scarce.

Variety. Some towns are small and have changed little over the last 50 years. Some towns have gone suburban in a mild way, others whole hog.

Convenient shopping. In some ways, the Central Valley stores outdo the stores in Silicon Valley. The Central Valley supermarkets tend to be new and gigantic and include bakeries, delis, pharmacies and fast-food diners. Great variety in offerings, including gourmet food such as glazed carrots and string beans in an almondine sauce. Good selection of wines. Almost every mid-sized town will have a Wal-Mart, a Home Depot, a Target or Big K, and a Staples or Office Club. A few of the big cities have regional malls, usually with a Sears and a Penneys, but the malls are often 40 or 50 years old.

School Scores

If you are coming from Silicon Valley, where scores are quite high, you might be shocked by scores in the Central Valley, often quite low.

Scores are heavily influenced by demographics. Central Valley schools educate many children from low-income farm families. To meet the needs of the higher-scoring kids, the schools, in many cases, have installed programs across the spectrum.

As more professionals move in, scores are rising. The new people tend to pay close attention to school and support academics. Some Tracy schools, on statewide comparisons, are scoring in the 70th percentile, the top 30 percent in the state.

It's possible to spin this to make it seem that scores don't matter, that everything will work out. The reality is that you have to get involved in the schools and push for the programs that benefit your children. Also, you may have to supply the intensity, the push for high achievement. It's not an impossible task; other parents have done it, but it takes work.

Transition

When Silicon Valley hit its first boom years, back in the 1940s and 1950s, the farms in Santa Clara County rapidly surrendered to industry and housing, and high-tech quickly found its voice in local government.

The Central Valley is still largely farm land. Miles upon miles of farm land. Even if cities gave developers a free hand — which they haven't — it would take decades for firms and houses to chew up the countryside.

Farms, ranches and food-processing plants generate the great majority of the local jobs. Farmers and people connected to agriculture sit on the city councils and school boards and regional agencies.

The high-tech newcomers are not the type people who say, whatever you give us, we will accept. Many are college-educated professionals. Many are young parents. A good deal of their energy will be going into the schools and to raising their families and to securing parks, playgrounds, playing fields and other amenities that modern parents want, indeed, expect. Almost inevitably, there will be fights over school and government allocations. Also over the pace of development and, probably, protecting the farm lands. The newcomers probably will bring with them a more aggressive Bay Area attitude toward protecting the environment. Political alignments probably will change. The Bay Area favors liberals and Democrats. The Central Valley, except for Sacramento, is more evenly divided between the parties.

Chances are good, however, that the locals will continue to staff the elective and administrative offices. Lacking local jobs, on the road so much, the newcomers will have little time for running for office. But the local leaders will have a new constituency.

Lest this sound hostile, the locals want a lot of what the newcomers are bringing in — money, energy, new ideas, more stores and a foot in the door for high tech.

The Central Valley wants high-tech. Every village from Tracy to Timbuktu wants high-tech. Sooner or later Silicon Valley will start building in the Central Valley because more and more the Central Valley has what Silicon Valley needs — an educated work force with high-tech credentials.

The Central Valley has five California State Universities: at Bakersfield, Chico, Fresno, Sacramento and Turlock (Stanislaus County).

But until 2005, it has only one University of California, at Davis, west of Sacramento. The state in 2005 opened a new University of California at Merced. This will help make the Central Valley a more attractive address.

The difference between a state university and a UC: the former, with few exceptions, tops out at the master's degree; the latter, at the Ph.D level and gets heavily involved in research.

These days, both state universities and UCs import people who are often pro-environment and anti-growth. But they also bring in people, especially the UCs, which are more research oriented, who know how to work high-tech and create and sustain high-tech jobs and businesses. In addition, the universities nourish the arts, enrich community life and in subtle ways wave the flag for education.

Merced County Fingertip Facts

• Population: 240,162, of whom 65 percent live in the county's six legal cities. In the 1990s, Merced added 32,151 residents and increased its population by 18 percent.

• Spanish explorers (1805-06) arrived in the region about the time of the feast day of Nuestra Señora de la Merced (Our Lady of Mercy) and named the river in her honor. Hence, the county name.

• Size of county, 2,007 square miles.

• Highest mountain, Laveaga Peak, 3,801 feet, in the Diablo Range on the west side.

• Average annual rain and temperatures. See San Joaquin Fingertip Facts in this chapter, and weather chapter.

• Most populous city, Merced, 73,610.

• County housing stock: Residential units totaled 77,138, of which 55,780 were single homes, 2,538 single attached, 13,245 apartments or condos, 5,575 mobiles (2005 tally).

• Ethnic makeup. 2000 Census: 85,585 Caucasians, 95,466 Hispanics, 14,321 Asian or Pacific Islanders, 8,064 African-Americans, 2,510 Native Americans and 396 Native Hawaiians or other Pacific Islanders.

• Trivia. When the Spanish-Mexicans explored the county, they camped in a slough filled with butterflies, one of which lodged itself in a soldier's ear. The Spanish for butterfly is mariposa. The explorers named several places in the region after the mariposa, including a creek.

• Merced is one of the most popular duck hunting regions in the U.S.

• In 2004, Merced recorded 16 homicides. The counts for previous years: 18, 18, 5, 6.

San Joaquin Fingertip Facts

• Population: 653,333, of whom 77 percent live in the county's seven legal cities. In the 1990s, the county added 82,970 residents, an increase of 17 percent.

• Origins of name. Spanish explorers about 1805 named local river after St. Joachim (Joaquin), the father of Jesus' mother, Mary.

Top 30 Baby Names

San Joaquin County		Stanislaus County		Merced County	
Boys	**Girls**	**Boys**	**Girls**	**Boys**	**Girls**
Jose	Emily	Daniel	Emily	Angel	Emily
Jacob	Isabella	Jose	Alexis	Adrian	Jessica
Angel	Ashley	David	Emma	David	Alondra
Anthony	Samantha	Jacob	Jasmine	Michael	Alexis
Andrew	Madison	Anthony	Madison	Daniel	Vanessa
Christopher	Alyssa	Adrian	Elizabeth	Isaac	Natalie
Daniel	Jessica	Angel	Isabella	Anthony	Elizabeth
Michael	Jasmine	Ethan	Jessica	Jose	Hailey
David	Elizabeh	Joshua	Natalie	Juan	Alyssa
Joseph	Natalie	Andrew	Alyssa	Alexander	Ashley
Juan	Jennifer	Luis	Ashley	Miguel	Isabella
Isaiah	Emma	Michael	Victoria	Gabriel	Samantha
Joshua	Sophia	Diego	Hannah	Jesus	Jasmine
Nicholas	Abigail	Joseph	Maria	Jacob	Jennifer
Luis	Alexis	Ryan	Mia	Joshua	Destiny
Matthew	Destiny	Alexander	Andrea	Brian	Madison
Jesus	Maria	Elijah	Hailey	Diego	Bianca
Gabriel	Ariana	Jesus	Alexa	Matthew	Emma
Julian	Daisy	Isaac	Grace	Andrew	Andrea
Christian	Stephanie	Matthew	Stephanie	Joseph	Angela
Alexander	Kayla	Christopher	Angelina	Brandon	Brianna
Brandon	Alondra	Jonathan	Abigail	Jonathan	Hannah
Ryan	Andrea	Carlos	Jennifer	Tyler	Mia
Carlos	Hailey	Dylan	Jocelyn	Christian	Stephanie
Jonathan	Juliana	Miguel	Samantha	Nathaniel	Victoria
Jordan	Michelle	Juan	Taylor	Aaron	Alexandra
Dylan	Sarah	Isaiah	Adriana	Alexis	Anahi
Elijah	Angelina	Logan	Alondra	Nathan	Ariana
Isaac	Brianna	Benjamin	Savannah	Carlos	Evelyn
Zachary	Chloe	Brian	Vanessa	Christopher	Isabel

Source: California Department of Health Services, 2004 birth records. Some names would move higher on the list if the state grouped essentially same names with slightly different spellings, for example, Sarah and Sara. But state computer goes by exact spellings.

- Highest peak, Mt. Boardman, 3,626 feet high, in the Diablo Range on the west side of the county.

- Average annual rain over 30 years: 12 inches. (Modesto 1950-1980). Same or close to 12 inches for Merced and Stanislaus.

- Average temperatures over 30 years: 61 degrees. Days temperature exceeded 90 degrees in an average year: 81. Days temperature fell below 32 degrees in average year: 21. (Modesto 1950-1980)

- Size of county: 3,326 square miles.

- Most populous city: Stockton, 279,513.

- County housing stock: 213,688 housing units, of which 152,435 are single detached homes, 11,283 single attached, 40,492 apartments or condos and 9,478 mobiles (2005 tally).

- Ethnic makeup. 2000 census: 267,002 Caucasians, 177,073 Hispanics, 64,283 Asians or Pacific Islanders, 37,689 African-Americans, 6,377 American Indians and 1,955 Native Hawaiians or other Pacific Islanders.

- County approved half-cent of sales tax for transit projects.

- Trivia. Although well inland, Stockton has a port that serves ocean vessels. They make their way to the city through a long ship channel carved through the Delta.

- In 2004 San Joaquin County had 55 homicides. The counts for previous years: 58, 59, 50 and 39. Most of the homicides take place in Stockton, 40 in 2004. The counts for previous years are 37, 36, 30, 32.

Stanislaus Fingertip Facts

- Population 504,482. About three-fourths of the residents live in the county's nine cities. In the 1990s, Stanislaus added 76,475 residents, an increase of 21 percent.

- Named after Indian educated by padres and given the name "Estanislao," after Polish St. Stanislaus. About 1827, Estanislao ran away from Mission San Jose, joined other Indians and became their leader. The Spanish-Mexican rancheros feared an uprising and sent out their troops. Before the Indians were subdued, several battles were fought, the largest at a river that was given the name of the Indian leader.

- Highest mountain, Stanislaus, 3,804 feet, on the west side in the Diablo Range.

- Size of county 1,521 square miles.

- Most populous city: Modesto, 207,634.

- County housing stock: 167,048 housing units, of which 124,093 are single homes, 7,159 single attached, 26,696 apartments or condo and 9,100 mobiles (2005 tally).

- Ethnic makeup, 2000 census: 256,001 Caucasians, 141,871 Hispanics, 18,848 Asians or Pacific Islanders, 11,521 African-Americans, 5,676 American Indians and 1,529 Native Hawaiians or other Pacific Islanders.

- Trivia: In 1933, just after Prohibition ended and alcohol again became legal, two brothers born and raised in Modesto started a winery. In their first year, the brothers sold wine at 50 cents a gallon, half the going price, and realized a profit of $34,000. And so was born the Gallo Winery, one of the world's giants, and headquartered in Modesto.

- In 2004 Stanislaus recorded 41 homicides. For previous years, 27, 15, 34, 16.

Population by Age Groups

Merced County

City or Area	Under 5	5-19	20-34	35-54	55+
Atwater	2,169	6,633	4,908	5,656	3,747
Dos Palos	390	1,327	830	1,172	862
Gustine	350	1,192	817	1,231	1,108
Livingston	1,000	3,380	2,435	2,343	1,315
Los Banos	2,422	7,428	5,094	6,920	4,005
Merced	5,860	18,591	13,812	15,590	10,040
County Total	18,693	61,069	42,883	53,248	34,661

San Joaquin County

City or Area	Under 5	5-19	20-34	35-54	55+
Escalon	375	1,654	907	1,818	1,209
Lathrop	919	3,029	2,113	3,073	1,311
Lodi	4,495	13,213	11,460	15,323	12,508
Manteca	3,716	13,425	9,215	14,900	8,002
Ripon	707	2,820	1,670	3,170	1,779
Stockton	20,977	66,847	51,310	62,374	42,272
Tracy	5,360	15,667	11,634	17,550	6,718
County Total	44,960	148,322	113,208	155,349	101,759

Stanislaus County

City or Area	Under 5	5-19	20-34	35-54	55+
Ceres	2,993	10,055	7,055	9,513	4,993
Hughson	291	1,168	735	1,121	665
Modesto	14,335	48,123	24,856	53,302	35,240
Newman	627	2,104	1,414	1,874	1,074
Oakdale	1,159	3,758	2,935	4,396	3,255
Patterson	1,061	3,545	2,420	3,077	1,503
Riverbank	1,445	4,436	3,946	4,343	2,222
Salida	1,336	3,456	2,990	3,454	1,324
Turlock	4,505	13,941	12,608	14,392	10,364
Waterford	574	2,187	1,350	1,931	882
County Total	35,582	117,517	90,909	123,169	79,820

Source: 2000 Census.

How Merced Residents Make Their Money

City or Town	MAN-PRO	SERV	SAL-OFF	FARM	CON	MANU-TRANS
Atwater	27%	16%	22%	6%	10%	19%
Dos Palos	19	14	28	11	14	14
Gustine	15	21	28	7	9	21
Livingston	12	15	18	18	8	30
Los Banos	27	17	22	5	13	16
Merced	27	18	25	4	10	16
Merced County	26	16	22	9	11	17

How Stanislaus Residents Earn Their Money

Occupation Profile by Percent of Population

City or Town	MAN-PRO	SERV	SAL-OFF	FARM	CON	MANU-TRANS
Ceres	19%	18%	26%	2%	12%	23%
Hughson	20	17	25	5	14	20
Modesto	28	16	28	1	11	16
Newman	24	13	21	10	12	20
Oakdale	25	17	25	2	13	19
Patterson	25	13	21	9	16	16
Riverbank	26	15	22	5	12	21
Turlock	30	15	25	4	8	18
Waterford	22	14	20	8	12	23
Stanislaus County	27	15	26	4	11	18

How San Joaquin Residents Make Their Money

City or Town	MAN-PRO	SERV	SAL-OFF	FARM	CON	MANU-TRANS
Escalon	24%	13%	32%	4%	10%	17%
Lathrop	22	16	25	2	15	21
Lodi	28	15	26	4	11	17
Manteca	25	14	29	2	13	18
Ripon	33	15	28	2	11	13
Stockton	27	16	28	4	9	17
Tracy	31	12	30	1	11	16
San Joaquin County	27	15	27	4	10	17

Source: 2000 Census. Figures are percent, rounded off, of working civilians over age 16. **Key**: MAN-PRO (managers, professionals); SERV (service); SAL-OFF (sales people, office workers); FARM (farming, fishing, forestry); CONSTRUCTION (building, maintenance, mining), MANU-TRANS (manufacturing, distribution, transportation).

Merced Education Level of Population Age 25 & Over

City or Town	ND	HS	SC	AA	BA	Grad
Atwater	13%	23%	27%	9%	8%	4%
Dos Palos	23	26	20	6	2	2
Delhi	16	28	20	4	5	1
Firebaugh	19	19	12	2	3	1
Gustine	17	25	23	4	7	2
Hilmar-Irwin	16	32	14	7	8	2
Le Grand	14	18	16	3	4	2
Livingston	16	17	10	4	5	1
Los Banos	15	28	26	6	7	3
Merced	13	23	24	8	9	5
Planada	10	13	12	2	1	0
Winton	15	22	16	6	5	1
Merced County	15	24	22	7	8	3

Stanislaus Education Level of Population Age 25 & Older

City or Town	ND	HS	SC	AA	BA	Grad
Ceres	19%	30%	23%	6%	6%	3%
Denair	14	31	29	7	7	3
Hughson	18	28	21	5	5	2
Modesto	15	25	26	8	11	5
Newman	15	27	24	5	6	4
Oakdale	17	33	26	6	7	3
Patterson	14	23	22	7	8	3
Riverbank	17	25	23	5	10	2
Turlock	15	25	21	5	13	6
Waterford	17	30	22	6	8	5
Stanislaus County	16	26	24	7	10	4

San Joaquin Education Level of Population Age 25 & Over

City or Town	ND	HS	SC	AA	BA	Grad
Escalon	13%	29%	28%	9%	8%	3%
Farmington	16	14	26	12	3	11
French Camp	24	26	14	4	3	3
Lathrop	16	32	25	7	9	2
Linden	7	24	33	12	17	4
Lodi	15	25	24	8	11	5
Lockeford	16	22	30	9	8	7
Manteca	15	32	28	7	8	3
Ripon	11	28	27	7	16	5
Stockton	16	22	23	8	11	5
Tracy	11	25	29	9	14	4
San Joaquin County	16	25	24	8	10	4

Source: 2000 Census. Figures are percent of population age 25 and older, rounded to the nearest whole number. Not shown are adults with less than a 9th grade education. **Key**: ND (high school, no diploma); HS (high school diploma or GED only, no college); SC (some college education); AA (associate degree); Bach. (bachelor's degree only); Grad (master's or higher degree).

Chapter **5a**

State School Rankings

HERE ARE COMPARISON RANKINGS from the 2005 STAR tests taken by almost every public-school student in California. This test is administered annually by the California Department of Education.

We have broken out the results in a way that makes comparisons between schools easy.

The rankings, based on the scores, range from 1 (the lowest) to 99 (the highest). A school that scores in the 20th percentile is landing in the bottom 20 percent of the state. A school that scores in the 95th percentile is placing among the top 5 percent of schools in the state.

These rankings should be considered rough measures of how the schools and their students are performing.

Many low- and middle-scoring schools have students who score high. Many high-scoring schools have students who land below the 25th percentile.

A few schools post average scores but turn out many high-scoring students. These schools often will have many students at the bottom and many at the top and few in the middle.

For more information, visit the school or go on the web and check out reports about individual schools. For more test results, go to www.star.cde.ca.gov. See also the school accountability reports.

To flesh out these scores, we are including in Chapter 5B a ranking system issued by the California Department of Education and in Chapter 7 the SAT scores, math and verbal, for the regular high schools. These scores and a chart that presents SAT scores by state will give you some idea of how local schools compare to schools nationwide.

Scores range from 1-99. A school scoring 75 has done better than 75 percent of other public schools in California.
Key: Eng (English), Ma (Math), Sci (Science).

Merced County

Atwater Elem. School Dist.

Bellevue Elem.

Grade	Eng	Ma	Sci
2	22	19	
3	35	21	
4	9	29	
5	23	56	25
6	19	20	

Colburn Elem.

Grade	Eng	Ma	Sci
2	37	26	
3	12	20	
4	17	15	
5	28	29	34
6	34	45	

Heller Elem.

Grade	Eng	Ma	Sci
2	48	45	
3	65	68	
4	51	51	
5	37	49	57
6	59	64	
7	66	61	
8	67		

Mitchell Elem.

Grade	Eng	Ma	Sci
2	33	34	
3	45	29	
4	49	41	
5	26	39	18
6	23	39	

Mitchell Int.

Grade	Eng	Ma	Sci
7	31	43	
8	27		

Olaeta Elem.

Grade	Eng	Ma	Sci
2	52	35	
3	55	52	
4	55	71	
5	43	56	35
6	26	47	

Shaffer Elem.

Grade	Eng	Ma	Sci
2	80	67	
3	53	61	
4	46	48	
5	31	34	33
6	20	36	

Wood Elem.

Grade	Eng	Ma	Sci
2	80	72	
3	31	49	
4	50	61	
5	60	50	48
6	62	79	

Ballico-Cressey Elem. School Dist.

Ballico Elem. (Ballico)

Grade	Eng	Ma	Sci
4	37	47	
5	48	28	36
6	47	27	
7	70	58	
8	54		

Cressey Elem. (Cressey)

Grade	Eng	Ma	Sci
2	27	16	
3	23	8	

Delhi Unified School Dist.

Delhi Educational Pk. Middle

Grade	Eng	Ma	Sci
7	35	43	
8	36		

Delhi High

Grade	Eng	Ma	Sci
9	49		
10	48		
11	66		

El Capitan Elem.

Grade	Eng	Ma	Sci
2	17	39	
3	12	17	
4	34	11	
5	40	62	30
6	24	25	

Harmony Elem.

Grade	Eng	Ma	Sci
2	8	4	
3	26	17	
4	36	12	
5	35	9	27

Schendel Elem.

Grade	Eng	Ma	Sci
2	23	8	
3	34	30	
4	29	11	
5	29	15	16
6	37	17	

Shattuck Cont. High

Grade	Eng	Ma	Sci
9	6		
10	6		
11	19		

Dos Palos Oro Loma Jt. Unif. Sch. Dist.

Bryant Middle (Dos Palos)

Grade	Eng	Ma	Sci
6	25	29	
7	45	48	
8	49		

Dos Palos Elem. (Dos Palos)

Grade	Eng	Ma	Sci
2	24	34	
3	36	47	
4	48	54	
5	20	12	29

Dos Palos High (Dos Palos)

Grade	Eng	Ma	Sci
9	59		
10	58		
11	58		

Marks Elem. (Dos Palos)

Grade	Eng	Ma	Sci
2	13	7	
3	32	18	
4	4	2	
5	10	11	10

Scores range from 1-99. A school scoring 75 has done better than 75 percent of other public schools in California.

Key: Eng (English), Ma (Math), Sci (Science).

Oro Loma Elem. (Firebaugh)

Grade	Eng	Ma	Sci
2	31	14	
3	7	6	
4	30	15	
5	27	14	50
6	56	69	
7	32	38	
8	45		

Westside High (S. Dos Palos)

Grade	Eng	Ma	Sci
9	8		
10	4		
11	40		

El Nido Elem. School Dist.
El Nido Elem.

Grade	Eng	Ma	Sci
2	40	44	
3	15	6	
4	31	49	
5	39	51	45
6	19	24	
7	58	47	
8	66		

Gustine Unified School Dist.
Gustine Elem.

Grade	Eng	Ma	Sci
2	40	33	
3	33	38	
4	45	63	
5	36	69	39

Gustine High

Grade	Eng	Ma	Sci
9	64		
10	48		
11	50		

Gustine Middle

Grade	Eng	Ma	Sci
6	37	36	
7	32	60	
8	35		

Pioneer High (Cont.)

Grade	Eng	Ma	Sci
11	40		

Romero Elem.

Grade	Eng	Ma	Sci
2	7	4	
3	5	15	
4	37	49	
5	17	48	17

Hilmar Unified School Dist.
Colony Alt. High

Grade	Eng	Ma	Sci
9	29		

Elim Elem.

Grade	Eng	Ma	Sci
2	54	47	
3	56	57	
4	47	50	
5	46	58	47

Hilmar High

Grade	Eng	Ma	Sci
9	67		
10	57		
11	68		

Hilmar Middle

Grade	Eng	Ma	Sci
6	35	43	
7	41	56	
8	65		

Irwin High (Cont.)

Grade	Eng	Ma	Sci
11	1		

Merquin Elem. (Stevinson)

Grade	Eng	Ma	Sci
2	9	12	
3	13	18	
4	21	14	
5	46	49	27

Le Grand Union Elem. School Dist.
Le Grand Elem.

Grade	Eng	Ma	Sci
2	35	7	
3	10	3	
4	21	11	
5	18	9	13
6	13	7	
7	45	85	
8	24		

Le Grand Union High School Dist.
Granada High

Grade	Eng	Ma	Sci
11	33		

Le Grand High

Grade	Eng	Ma	Sci
9	37		
10	50		
11	44		

Livingston Union Elem. School Dist.
Campus Park Elem.

Grade	Eng	Ma	Sci
2	32	41	
3	13	10	
4	32	56	
5	14	21	10

Livingston Middle

Grade	Eng	Ma	Sci
6	24	48	
7	32	45	
8	39		

Selma Herndon Elem.

Grade	Eng	Ma	Sci
2	24	14	
3	41	24	
4	24	14	
5	32	41	45

Yamato Colony Elem.

Grade	Eng	Ma	Sci
2	76	52	
3	49	31	
4	43	38	
5	37	47	47

Los Banos Unified School Dist.
Charleston Elem.

Grade	Eng	Ma	Sci
2	87	95	
3	53	80	
4	49	38	
5	52	63	58

Scores range from 1-99. A school scoring 75 has done better than 75 percent of other public schools in California.
Key: Eng (English), Ma (Math), Sci (Science).

Grade	Eng	Ma	Sci
Henry Miller Elem.			
2	22	26	
3	6	21	
4	30	50	
Lorena Falasco Elem.			
2	30	43	
3	39	28	
4	30	19	
5	46	39	38
Los Banos Elem.			
2	39	36	
3	34	41	
4	41	58	
Los Banos High			
9	44		
10	51		
11	53		
Los Banos Jr. High			
7	40	36	
8	38		
Miano Elem.			
2	27	33	
3	7	18	
4	42	58	
5	54	76	70
San Luis High (Cont.)			
11	13		
Volta Elem.			
2	81	61	
3	47	60	
4	52	37	
5	59	48	40
Westside Union Int.			
5	33	41	21
6	36	27	

McSwain Union Elem. School Dist.
McSwain Elem.

Grade	Eng	Ma	Sci
2	77	66	
3	68	68	
4	85	86	
5	75	67	82
6	76	75	
7	89	77	
8	70		

Merced City Elem. School Dist.
Burbank Elem.

Grade	Eng	Ma	Sci
2	42	23	
3	31	36	
4	10	9	
5	29	30	33
Chenoweth Elem.			
2	52	59	
3	36	38	
4	55	48	
5	68	71	63

Grade	Eng	Ma	Sci
Cruickshank Middle			
6	55	43	
7	61	61	
8	63		
Franklin Elem.			
2	45	30	
3	47	31	
4	34	37	
5	28	10	27
Fremont Char.			
2	31	25	
3	42	37	
4	49	27	
5	53	62	63
Givens Elem.			
2	27	22	
3	26	10	
4	49	55	
5	33	33	30
Gracey Elem.			
2	30	26	
3	32	42	
4	27	18	
5	26	23	20
Hoover Middle			
6	36	26	
7	35	27	
8	34		
Muir Elem.			
2	24	35	
3	20	27	
4	35	23	
5	8	18	12
Newcomer Language Academy			
2	1	1	
3	1	1	
4	1	2	
5	1	2	1
6	1	1	
7	1	1	
8	1		
Peterson Elem.			
2	39	15	
3	72	71	
4	62	44	
5	54	38	58
Reyes Elem.			
2	20	15	
3	49	41	
4	40	47	
5	13	26	15
Rivera Middle			
6	49	41	
7	52	42	
8	45		
Sheehy Elem			
2	58	78	
3	55	59	
4	48	52	
5	35	30	30

Scores range from 1-99. A school scoring 75 has done better than 75 percent of other public schools in California.

Key: Eng (English), Ma (Math), Sci (Science).

Grade	Eng	Ma	Sci
Stowell Elem.			
2	14	16	
3	16	37	
4	21	29	
5	15	59	22
Tenaya Middle			
6	32	26	
7	23	31	
8	18		
Wright Elem.			
2	40	31	
3	37	34	
4	39	27	
5	25	24	33

Merced River Union Elem. School Dist.

Grade	Eng	Ma	Sci
Hopeton Elem. (Snelling)			
2	63	58	
3	54	70	
Washington Elem. (Winton)			
4	37	47	
5	68	6	52
6	51	38	
7	22	44	
8	48		

Merced Union High School Dist.

Grade	Eng	Ma	Sci
Atwater High (Atwater)			
9	48		
10	51		
11	58		
Buhach High (Atwater)			
9	52		
10	59		
11	55		
Golden Valley High (Merced)			
9	51		
10	61		
11	56		
Independence High (Alt.) (Merced)			
9	22		
10	27		
11	25		
Livingston High (Livingston)			
9	62		
10	61		
11	68		
Merced High			
9	52		
10	60		
11	64		
Yosemite High (Cont.) (Merced)			
10	9		
11	17		

Plainsburg Union Elem. School Dist.

Grade	Eng	Ma	Sci
Plainsburg Elem. (Merced)			
7	53	41	

Planada Elem. School Dist.

Grade	Eng	Ma	Sci
Chavez Middle			
6	9	10	
7	17	22	
8	20		
Planada Elem.			
2	15	18	
3	4	13	
4	15	23	
5	10	26	15

Snelling-Merced Falls Elem. Sch. Dist.

Grade	Eng	Ma	Sci
Snelling-Merced Falls (Snelling)			
5	88	84	88

Weaver Union Elem. School Dist.

Grade	Eng	Ma	Sci
Pioneer Elem. (Merced)			
2	44	46	
3	43	67	
Weaver Elem. (Merced)			
4	43	47	
5	35	48	31
6	26	22	
7	25	34	
8	32		

Winton Elem. School Dist.

Grade	Eng	Ma	Sci
Crookham Elem.			
2	19	17	
3	17	12	
4	23	20	
5	14	7	6
Sparkes Elem.			
2	27	12	
3	25	20	
4	18	19	
5	12	14	8
Winton Middle			
6	15	19	
7	24	39	
8	32		

Scores range from 1-99. A school scoring 75 has done better than 75 percent of other public schools in California.
Key: Eng (English), Ma (Math), Sci (Science).

San Joaquin County

Banta Elem. School Dist.
Banta Elem. (Tracy)

Grade	Eng	Ma	Sci
2	13	29	
3	35	48	
4	60	75	
5	24	21	37
6	76	66	
7	52	80	
8	63		

Escalon Unified School Dist.
Collegeville Elem. (Stockton)

Grade	Eng	Ma	Sci
2	3	10	
3	26	18	
4	22	31	
5	57	82	97

Dent Elem. (Escalon)

Grade	Eng	Ma	Sci
2	53	32	
3	50	25	
4	55	58	
5	42	37	51

El Portal Middle (Escalon)

Grade	Eng	Ma	Sci
6	64	61	
7	64	63	
8	66		

Escalon High (Escalon)

Grade	Eng	Ma	Sci
9	70		
10	63		
11	72		

Escalon Unified Comm. Day (Escalon)

Grade	Eng	Ma	Sci
6	28	19	

Farmington Elem. (Farmington)

Grade	Eng	Ma	Sci
2	16	16	
3	44	57	
4	66	66	
5	44	58	68

Van Allen Elem. (Escalon)

Grade	Eng	Ma	Sci
2	37	37	
3	53	50	
4	70	79	
5	56	34	79

Vista High (Cont.) (Escalon)

Grade	Eng	Ma	Sci
11	7		

Holt Union Elem. School Dist.
Holt Elem. (Stockton)

Grade	Eng	Ma	Sci
2	44	9	
3	2	2	
4	4	6	
5	11	10	9
6	27	9	
7	15	23	
8	10		

Jefferson Elem. School Dist. (Tracy)
Hawkins Elem.

Grade	Eng	Ma	Sci
2	76	61	
3	85	85	
4	68	60	
5	77	66	67
6	72	60	
7	82	78	
8	71		

Jefferson Elem.

Grade	Eng	Ma	Sci
5	70	66	73
6	80	88	
7	74	76	
8	78		

Monticello Elem.

Grade	Eng	Ma	Sci
2	70	66	
3	74	71	
4	69	62	

Traina Elem.

Grade	Eng	Ma	Sci
2	69	69	
3	69	62	

Lammersville Elem. School Dist.
Lammersville Elem. (Tracy)

Grade	Eng	Ma	Sci
2	57	56	
3	69	59	
4	83	49	
5	70	74	88
6	72	74	
7	70	80	
8	69		

Wicklund Elem. (Mountain House)

Grade	Eng	Ma	Sci
2	77	57	
3	77	71	
4	86	88	
5	73	70	70
6	61	57	
7	79	68	
8	84		

Lincoln Unified School Dist. (Stockton)
Barron Elem.

Grade	Eng	Ma	Sci
2	60	63	
3	54	25	
4	64	55	
5	68	64	59
6	61	51	
7	75	69	
8	66		

Brookside Elem.

Grade	Eng	Ma	Sci
2	73	55	
3	85	76	
4	90	93	
5	84	93	86
6	88	84	
7	81	70	
8	87		

Scores range from 1-99. A school scoring 75 has done better than 75 percent of other public schools in California.
Key: Eng (English), Ma (Math), Sci (Science).

Grade	Eng	Ma	Sci
Colonial Heights			
2	59	70	
3	37	45	
4	38	34	
5	47	26	55
6	64	40	
7	45	38	
8	38		
Don Riggio Elem.			
2	14	20	
3	51	36	
4	49	43	
5	63	70	63
6	58	70	
7	57	49	
8	64		
Knoles Elem.			
2	39	21	
3	44	22	
4	41	31	
5	58	51	61
6	44	25	
7	41	36	
8	39		
Landeen Elem.			
2	71	81	
3	68	70	
4	77	80	
5	69	69	80
6	74	83	
7	72	80	
8	70		
Larsson High (Cont.)			
10	22		
11	26		
Lincoln Elem.			
2	56	41	
3	52	42	
4	38	56	
5	51	25	40
6	46	40	
Lincoln High			
9	67		
10	72		
11	76		
Sierra Middle			
7	52	42	
8	47		
Village Oaks Elem.			
2	27	17	
3	28	32	
4	32	37	
5	33	30	24
6	7	17	

Grade	Eng	Ma	Sci
Williams Elem.			
2	46	42	
3	15	18	
4	38	32	
5	50	68	48
6	36	47	
7	24	30	
8	32		24
Linden Unified School Dist.			
Glenwood Elem. (Stockton)			
2	55	65	
3	62	64	
4	67	42	
5	36	41	47
6	25	28	
7	59	56	
8	45		
Linden Elem. (Linden)			
2	37	28	
3	51	36	
4	48	46	
Linden High (Linden)			
9	59		
10	59		
11	65		
Waterloo Elem. (Stockton)			
5	55	37	32
6	43	41	
7	39	55	
8	60		
Waverly Elem. (Stockton)			
2	84	86	
3	68	69	
4	52	45	
5	56	41	55
6	40	36	
7	67	70	
8	65		
Lodi Unified School Dist.			
Ansel Adams Elem.			
2	29	30	
3	23	21	
4	23	28	
5	48	31	49
6	25	31	
Bear Creek High (Stockton)			
9	53		
10	62		
11	66		
Beckman Elem. (Lodi)			
2	17	18	
3	24	32	
4	33	29	
5	16	12	23
6	33	44	

Scores range from 1-99. A school scoring 75 has done better than 75 percent of other public schools in California.
Key: Eng (English), Ma (Math), Sci (Science).

Grade	Eng	Ma	Sci
Benjamin Holt College Prep. (Stockton)			
6	55	55	
7	68	71	
8	63		
9	70		
10	69		
Christa McAuliffe Middle			
7	36	44	
8	33		
Clairmont Elem.			
2	26	37	
3	19	35	
4	19	35	
5	25	25	32
6	41	54	
Creekside Elem. (Stockton)			
2	28	39	
3	28	21	
4	31	41	
5	29	19	23
6	39	36	
Davis Comm. Day (Stockton)			
4	10	19	
Davis Elem. (Stockton)			
2	39	30	
3	35	50	
4	51	47	
5	31	28	40
6	25	45	
Delta Sierra Middle (Stockton)			
7	20	18	
8	28		
Elkhorn Elem. (Lodi)			
4	99	99	
5	97	98	99
6	98	98	
7	99	99	
8	99		
Henderson Comm. Day (Lodi)			
7	6	11	
8	10		
Heritage Elem. (Lodi)			
2	9	7	
3	3	5	
Houston Elem. (Acampo)			
2	2	6	
3	22	10	
4	42	50	
5	44	61	54
6	65	48	
7	68	67	
8	57		
Joe Serna, Jr. Char.			
2	5	70	
3	8	42	
4	38	60	
5	17	12	21
6	12	10	

Grade	Eng	Ma	Sci
Lakewood Comm. Day (Lodi)			
4	12	22	
Lakewood Elem. (Lodi)			
2	70	52	
3	60	46	
4	44	42	
5	47	23	55
6	45	38	
Lawrence Elem. (Lodi)			
2	4	9	
3	40	41	
4	7	23	
5	5	9	13
6	5	6	
Liberty High (Cont.) (Lodi)			
10	9		
11	29		
Live Oak Elem. (Lodi)			
2	4	5	
3	4	4	
4	14	14	
5	3	4	3
6	17	38	
Lockeford Elem. (Lockeford)			
2	48	54	
3	41	59	
4	61	70	
5	50	55	46
6	61	56	
Lodi High (Lodi)			
9	67		
10	77		
11	74		
Lodi Middle (Lodi)			
7	37	44	
8	41		
Lodi Usd. Alt. Ctr.			
8	37		
9	43		
10	39		
11	33		
Lois E. Borchardt Elem.			
2	42	58	
3	38	53	
4	34	22	
5	31	46	48
6	35	37	
Middle College High (Stockton)			
9	97		
10	98		
11	96		
Millswood Middle			
7	49	48	
8	50		
Morada Middle (Stockton)			
7	26	40	
8	36		

Scores range from 1-99. A school scoring 75 has done better than 75 percent of other public schools in California.
Key: Eng (English), Ma (Math), Sci (Science).

Grade	Eng	Ma	Sci
Morgan Elem. (Stockton)			
2	34	36	
3	54	67	
4	50	42	
5	46	60	60
6	56	67	
Muir Elem. (Stockton)			
2	60	56	
3	54	66	
4	70	70	
5	72	76	64
6	65	77	
Needham Elem. (Lodi)			
4	5	21	
5	2	3	5
6	9	19	
Nichols Elem. (Lodi)			
2	25	25	
3	19	14	
4	24	8	
5	25	12	16
6	49	42	
Oakwood Elem. (Stockton)			
2	8	7	
3	31	26	
4	10	5	
5	12	8	23
6	14	23	
Parklane Elem. (Stockton)			
2	18	17	
3	8	5	
Plaza Robles Cont. High (Stockton)			
10	8		
11	10		
Reese Elem. (Lodi)			
2	66	65	
3	70	53	
4	52	36	
5	63	54	63
6	67	75	
River Oaks Char.			
2	60	68	
3	54	60	
4	56	74	
5	46	67	51
Sutherland Elem. (Stockton)			
4	6	5	
5	23	33	29
6	19	22	
Tokay Colony Elem. (Lodi)			
2	9	49	
3	44	56	
4	3	4	
5	74	69	65
6	38	55	
Tokay High (Lodi)			
9	56		
10	63		
11	71		

Grade	Eng	Ma	Sci
Turner Elem. (Lodi)			
2	10	26	
5	17	8	9
University Public Elem.			
2	84	92	
3	76	75	
4	84	79	
5	86	71	78
Victor Elem. (Victor)			
2	32	46	
3	28	53	
4	44	49	
5	21	7	14
6	42	35	
Vinewood Elem. (Lodi)			
2	40	52	
3	67	58	
4	82	78	
5	77	85	79
6	85	88	
Wagner-Holt Elem. (Stockton)			
2	15	14	
3	29	44	
4	20	15	
5	24	14	24
6	22	26	
Washington Elem. (Lodi)			
2	6	18	
3	19	53	
4	11	9	
5	24	45	23
6	32	36	
Westwood Elem. (Stockton)			
2	26	37	
3	28	40	
4	30	44	
5	29	48	42
6	15	18	

Manteca Unified School Dist.

Grade	Eng	Ma	Sci
Brockman Elem.			
2	63	55	
3	56	49	
4	69	73	
5	70	38	64
6	57	51	
7	42	38	
8	40		
Calla High (Cont.)			
10	2		
11	4		
Cowell Elem.			
2	55	63	
3	41	42	
4	58	54	
5	35	36	31
6	43	52	
7	52	50	
8	56		

Scores range from 1-99. A school scoring 75 has done better than 75 percent of other public schools in California.
Key: Eng (English), Ma (Math), Sci (Science).

Grade	Eng	Ma	Sci
East Union High			
9	59		
10	59		
11	66		
Elliott Elem.			
2	84	74	
3	69	67	
4	62	68	
5	53	30	52
6	61	55	
7	58	70	
8	71		
French Camp Elem. (French Camp)			
2	18	4	
3	24	29	
4	16	28	
5	21	11	16
6	35	37	
7	22	34	
8	40		
Golden West Elem.			
2	50	50	
3	48	45	
4	53	54	
5	46	34	32
6	59	61	
7	43	60	
8	39		
Great Valley Elem. (Stockton)			
2	47	27	
3	41	21	
4	48	40	
5	36	17	24
6	45	49	
7	28	29	
8	39		
Hafley Elem.			
2	58	60	
3	40	50	
4	54	58	
5	50	36	48
6	53	52	
7	44	43	
8	69		
Knodt Elem. (Stockton)			
2	37	17	
3	64	67	
4	50	48	
5	48	37	44
6	55	61	
7	50	38	
8	61		
Komure Elem.			
2	30	19	
3	34	17	
4	40	36	
5	50	40	45
6	41	42	
7	43	20	
8	40		

Grade	Eng	Ma	Sci
Lathrop Elem. (Lathrop)			
2	23	13	
3	39	30	
4	42	42	
5	36	42	42
6	27	29	
7	26	41	
8	48		
Lincoln Elem.			
2	46	15	
3	42	36	
4	43	39	
5	36	34	40
6	42	48	
7	49	55	
8	28		
Manteca Comm. Day (7-12)			
9	9		
10	15		
11	3		
Manteca High			
9	57		
10	62		
11	71		
McParland Elem.			
2	80	75	
3	64	59	
4	43	56	
5	57	62	64
6	61	60	
7	61	56	
8	69		
New Haven Elem.			
2	63	70	
3	71	88	
4	62	71	
5	61	60	45
6	49	59	
7	67	78	
8	73		
Nile Garden Elem.			
2	58	53	
3	63	64	
4	51	58	
5	70	67	56
6	62	46	
7	70	68	
8	67		
Sequoia Elem.			
2	51	55	
3	24	20	
4	19	7	
5	36	11	32
6	26	20	
7	53	35	
8	52		

Scores range from 1-99. A school scoring 75 has done better than 75 percent of other public schools in California.
Key: Eng (English), Ma (Math), Sci (Science).

Grade	Eng	Ma	Sci
Shasta Elem.			
2	63	47	
3	47	44	
4	49	57	
5	33	28	28
6	61	62	
7	33	33	
8	34		
Sierra High			
9	65		
10	78		
11	69		
Walter E. Woodward Elem.			
2	55	33	
3	49	45	
4	58	56	
5	54	16	44
6	49	47	
7	56	52	
8	73		
Weston Ranch High (Stockton)			
9	50		
10	54		
11	45		
Widmer Elem. (Lathrop)			
2	35	13	
3	53	49	
4	51	43	
5	54	29	52
6	37	54	
7	61	52	
8	55		
New Hope Elem. School Dist.			
New Hope Elem. (Thorton)			
2	65	51	
3	69	59	
4	47	5	
5	31	57	41
6	14	13	
7	47	49	
8	48		
New Jerusalem Elem. School Dist.			
Delta Char. High (Tracy)			
9	46		
10	38		
11	51		
New Jerusalem Char. (Tracy)			
4	19	23	
5	78	52	90
6	59	48	
7	63	42	
8	70		

Grade	Eng	Ma	Sci
New Jerusalem Elem. (Tracy)			
2	68	53	
3	63	72	
4	63	38	
5	74	83	52
6	54	47	
7	55	58	
8	35		
Oak View Union Elem. School Dist.			
Oak View Elem. (Acampo)			
2	82	78	
3	82	93	
4	63	72	
5	82	87	77
6	73	73	
7	88	94	
8	94		
Ripon Unified School Dist.			
Colony Oak Elem.			
2	82	79	
3	90	82	
4	79	78	
5	87	89	84
6	85	93	
7	80	76	
8	86		
Ripon Elem.			
2	60	56	
3	47	47	
4	61	64	
5	21	19	21
6	57	61	
7	48	47	
8	70		
Ripon High			
9	81		
10	81		
11	80		
Ripona Elem.			
2	55	54	
3	79	43	
4	69	76	
5	58	45	58
6	72	83	
7	87	72	
8	73		
Weston Elem.			
2	72	48	
3	57	23	
4	49	44	
5	66	72	67
6	69	78	
7	81	69	
8	92		

Scores range from 1-99. A school scoring 75 has done better than 75 percent of other public schools in California.
Key: Eng (English), Ma (Math), Sci (Science).

Grade	Eng	Ma	Sci
Stockton City Unified			
Adams Elem.			
2	25	25	
3	20	20	
4	31	50	
5	28	45	24
6	25	43	
August Elem.			
2	16	19	
3	29	57	
4	29	61	
5	43	59	36
6	22	45	
Bush Elem.			
2	38	41	
3	59	60	
4	44	27	
5	34	40	32
6	35	42	
Childrens Home of Stockton			
7	1	1	
8	5		
10	6		
11	11		
Cleveland Elem.			
2	16	18	
3	10	23	
4	4	14	
5	12	25	13
6	15	25	
District Special Ed.			
10	29		
11	34		
Dolores Huerta Elem.			
2	3	9	
3	22	42	
4	19	32	
5	4	21	9
6	30	37	
Edison High			
9	29		
10	36		
11	40		
El Dorado Elem.			
2	19	24	
3	20	41	
4	9	9	
5	17	11	10
6	20	21	
Elmwood Elem.			
2	11	44	
3	18	46	
4	29	53	
5	18	39	27
6	25	45	
Fillmore Elem.			
2	13	11	
3	20	56	
4	10	36	
5	13	24	38
6	8	23	

Grade	Eng	Ma	Sci
Franklin Sr. High			
9	28		
10	38		
11	37		
Fremont Middle			
7	9	23	
8	16		
Garfield Elem.			
2	7	5	
3	19	35	
4	3	12	
5	4	10	3
6	3	5	
Golden Valley Secondary Comm. Day			
7	4	5	
8	5		
9	5		
10	1		
Grant Elem.			
2	4	22	
3	4	10	
Grunsky Elem.			
2	19	41	
3	13	31	
4	4	9	
5	8	18	8
6	14	30	
Hamilton Middle			
7	22	35	
8	24	75	
Harrison Elem.			
2	10	11	
3	29	24	
4	18	20	
5	4	6	3
6	17	19	
Hazelton Elem.			
2	17	40	
3	13	33	
4	19	38	
5	35	59	41
6	33	50	
Hoover Elem.			
2	29	43	
3	16	36	
4	16	24	
5	18	35	23
6	21	55	
Institute of Business			
9	58		
10	54		
11	46		
James L. Urbani Elem.			
4	1	3	
5	1	2	1
6	2	3	
7	3	6	
8	4		

Order Guides at www.mccormacks.com

Scores range from 1-99. A school scoring 75 has done better than 75 percent of other public schools in California.

Key: Eng (English), Ma (Math), Sci (Science).

Grade	Eng	Ma	Sci
Kennedy Elem.			
2	13	20	
3	49	50	
4	12	5	
5	8	9	6
6	15	22	
King Elem.			
2	32	42	
3	18	40	
4	22	51	
5	7	28	15
6	25	38	
Kohl Open Elem.			
2	66	63	
3	52	28	
4	60	34	
5	56	17	39
6	46	29	
Madison Elem.			
2	20	23	
3	22	52	
4	10	29	
5	11	29	17
6	7	22	
Marshall Middle			
7	13	26	
8	20	67	
McKinley Elem.			
2	8	17	
3	25	39	
4	11	40	
5	6	24	15
6	11	27	
Monroe Elem.			
2	30	44	
3	22	36	
4	4	13	
5	6	16	4
6	9	28	
Montezuma Elem.			
2	3	10	
3	12	20	
4	9	18	
5	10	14	14
6	19	26	
Nightingale Elem.			
2	4	10	
3	6	6	
4	4	6	
5	3	5	4
6	7	10	
Pulliam Elem.			
2	24	45	
3	39	36	
4	24	34	
5	14	18	5
6	19	27	

Grade	Eng	Ma	Sci
Rio Calaveras Elem.			
2	72	84	
3	62	80	
4	62	83	
5	62	90	59
6	59	76	
7	57	80	
8	61		
Roosevelt Elem.			
2	29	30	
3	30	38	
4	8	13	
5	6	7	6
6	9	9	
San Joaquin Elem.			
2	43	54	
3	40	44	
4	45	48	
5	46	59	33
6	27	42	
Stagg Sr. High			
9	41		
10	51		
11	53		
Stockton Skill Elem.			
2	70	75	
3	65	81	
4	75	87	
5	60	65	43
6	48	62	
7	71	85	
8	58		
Stockton Unif. Alt./Cont.			
10	10		
11	12		
Taft Elem.			
2	21	40	
3	17	29	
4	25	15	
5	37	18	23
6	13	20	
Taylor Skills Elem.			
2	7	9	
3	5	7	
4	12	18	
5	12	17	8
6	18	23	
Tyler Skills Elem.			
2	37	59	
3	33	46	
4	33	28	
5	9	11	12
6	35	29	
Valenzuela Magnet Elem.			
2	42	54	
3	42	55	
4	43	67	
5	32	14	25
6	76	84	

Scores range from 1-99. A school scoring 75 has done better than 75 percent of other public schools in California.
Key: Eng (English), Ma (Math), Sci (Science).

Grade	Eng	Ma	Sci
Van Buren Elem.			
2	6	25	
3	8	28	
4	3	10	
5	21	26	34
6	13	40	
Victory Elem.			
2	10	10	
3	19	24	
4	28	37	
5	17	19	15
6	16	22	
Washington Elem.			
2	5	18	
3	10	21	
4	20	29	
5	20	20	6
6	11	13	
Weber Institute			
9	60		
10	48		
11	54		
Webster Middle			
7	14	21	
8	19		
Wilson Elem.			
2	27	34	
3	27	46	
4	18	12	
5	24	40	19
6	26	41	
Tracy Joint Unified School Dist.			
Art Freiler			
2	72	78	
3	68	70	
4	65	58	
5	74	70	74
6	70	61	
7	76	76	
8	79		
Bohn Elem.			
2	50	52	
3	55	51	
4	62	73	
5	48	39	43
Central Elem.			
2	19	19	
3	17	14	
4	15	18	
5	18	23	27
Clover Middle			
6	23	26	
7	36	29	
8	40		

Grade	Eng	Ma	Sci
Delta Island Elem. (Stockton)			
2	2	2	
3	4	11	
4	7	8	
5	8	8	11
6	7	3	
7	8	16	
8	52		
Discover Char.			
5	69	52	52
6	86	88	
7	84	77	
8	93		
Duncan-Russell Cont.			
11	21		
Excel High (Cont.)			
10	30		
Hirsch Elem.			
2	74	67	
3	67	60	
4	69	68	
5	62	69	52
Jacobson Elem.			
2	50	36	
3	25	29	
4	45	48	
5	43	38	37
McKinley Elem.			
2	25	23	
3	25	17	
4	40	39	
5	23	8	17
Millennium Char.			
9	86		
Monte Vista Middle			
6	39	36	
7	53	41	
8	50		
North Elem.			
2	56	52	
3	13	20	
4	24	32	
5	28	28	21
Poet-Christian Elem.			
2	46	24	
3	48	21	
4	64	43	
5	57	33	41
6	63	48	
7	50	23	
8	67		
Primary Char.			
2	51	66	
South/West Park Elem.			
2	39	55	
3	34	28	
4	33	38	
5	34	40	45

Scores range from 1-99. A school scoring 75 has done better than 75 percent of other public schools in California.
Key: Eng (English), Ma (Math), Sci (Science).

Grade	Eng	Ma	Sci	Grade	Eng	Ma	Sci
Success High (Cont.)							
10	39						
Tracy High							
9	57						
10	62						
11	49						
Villalovoz Elem.							
2	55	38					
3	41	28					
4	57	62					
5	56	49	67				
West High							
9	60						
10	67						
11	56						
Williams Middle							
6	61	54					
7	62	53					
8	55						
Willow Comm. Day							
10	32						

Scores range from 1-99. A school scoring 75 has done better than 75 percent of other public schools in California.
Key: Eng (English), Ma (Math), Sci (Science).

Stanislaus County

Grade	Eng	Ma	Sci

Ceres Unified School Dist.

Argus High (Cont.)

Grade	Eng	Ma	Sci
10	23		
11	25		

Blaker-Kinser Jr. High

Grade	Eng	Ma	Sci
7	47	48	
8	49		

Carroll Fowler Elem.

Grade	Eng	Ma	Sci
2	38	41	
3	36	17	
4	39	23	
5	32	14	38
6	45	48	

Caswell Elem.

Grade	Eng	Ma	Sci
2	22	10	
3	22	22	
4	16	10	
5	24	19	32
6	24	16	

Ceres High

Grade	Eng	Ma	Sci
9	61		
10	60		
11	59		

Don Pedro Elem.

Grade	Eng	Ma	Sci
2	29	16	
3	41	44	
4	32	37	
5	35	29	25
6	47	60	

Endeavor Alt. High

Grade	Eng	Ma	Sci
9	38		
10	54		
11	29		

Mae Hensley Jr. High

Grade	Eng	Ma	Sci
7	54	62	
8	46		

Parks Elem. (Modesto)

Grade	Eng	Ma	Sci
2	69	58	
3	51	62	
4	64	67	
5	65	62	56
6	68	76	

Vaughn Elem.

Grade	Eng	Ma	Sci
2	26	12	
3	50	62	
4	50	48	
5	64	57	49
6	47	55	

Westport Elem. (Modesto)

Grade	Eng	Ma	Sci
2	13	21	
3	28	45	
4	30	66	
5	34	46	22
6	35	46	

White Elem.

Grade	Eng	Ma	Sci
2	42	37	
3	27	24	
4	28	37	
5	29	22	50
6	36	46	

Whitmore Char.

Grade	Eng	Ma	Sci
8	63		

Whitmore Char. High

Grade	Eng	Ma	Sci
9	90		
10	86		

Whitmore Char. School

Grade	Eng	Ma	Sci
2	31	32	
3	51	53	
4	57	57	
5	67	27	43
6	38	51	
7	65	59	
8	87		

Chatom Union Elem. School Dist.

Chatom Elem. (Turlock)

Grade	Eng	Ma	Sci
2	48	36	
3	30	28	
4	28	24	
5	15	14	9

Mountain View Middle (Crows Landing)

Grade	Eng	Ma	Sci
6	44	29	
7	64	37	
8	37		

Denair Unified School Dist.

Denair Char. Academy

Grade	Eng	Ma	Sci
7	16	11	
8	13		
9	26		
10	30		
11	37		

Denair Elem.

Grade	Eng	Ma	Sci
2	45	26	
3	45	26	
4	66	35	
5	63	43	65

Denair High

Grade	Eng	Ma	Sci
9	72		
10	75		
11	78		

Denair Middle

Grade	Eng	Ma	Sci
6	48	35	
7	44	27	
8	65		

Scores range from 1-99. A school scoring 75 has done better than 75 percent of other public schools in California.
Key: Eng (English), Ma (Math), Sci (Science).

Empire Union Elem.

Capistrano Elem. (Modesto)

Grade	Eng	Ma	Sci
2	47	25	
3	49	55	
4	31	14	
5	46	68	61

Empire Elem. (Empire)

Grade	Eng	Ma	Sci
2	42	30	
3	34	29	
4	39	47	
5	28	27	24

Glick Middle

Grade	Eng	Ma	Sci
6	55	59	
7	63	46	
8	66		

Hughes Elem. (Modesto)

Grade	Eng	Ma	Sci
2	70	56	
3	59	58	
4	44	59	
5	63	67	57

Sipherd Elem. (Modesto)

Grade	Eng	Ma	Sci
2	63	49	
3	66	65	
4	70	68	
5	65	56	72

Stroud Elem. (Modesto)

Grade	Eng	Ma	Sci
2	62	35	
3	64	66	
4	65	58	
5	68	78	54

Teel Middle (Empire)

Grade	Eng	Ma	Sci
6	43	58	
7	46	34	
8	53		

Gratton Elem. School Dist.

Gratton Elem. (Denair)

Grade	Eng	Ma	Sci
3	62	61	
5	91	91	95
8	97		

Hart-Ransom Union Elem. School Dist.

Hart-Ransom Academic Char. (Modesto)

Grade	Eng	Ma	Sci
2	22	14	
3	64	32	
4	76	45	
5	64	45	66
6	72	58	
7	87	77	
8	75		

Hart-Ransom Elem. (Modesto)

Grade	Eng	Ma	Sci
2	53	45	
3	61	58	
4	61	69	
5	56	44	53
6	57	45	
7	71	62	
8	71		

Hickman Comm. Char. School Dist.

Hickman Char.

Grade	Eng	Ma	Sci
2	40	28	
3	60	18	
4	67	24	
5	75	35	81
6	84	58	
7	90	70	
8	95		

Hickman Elem.

Grade	Eng	Ma	Sci
2	54	49	
3	39	67	
4	67	67	
5	62	64	67

Hickman Middle

Grade	Eng	Ma	Sci
6	77	77	
7	88	88	
8	81		

Hughson Unified School Dist.

Fox Road Elem.

Grade	Eng	Ma	Sci
4	40	39	
5	49	54	53

Hughson Elem.

Grade	Eng	Ma	Sci
2	51	44	
3	54	60	

Hughson High

Grade	Eng	Ma	Sci
9	65		
10	77		
11	71		

Ross Middle

Grade	Eng	Ma	Sci
6	45	28	
7	40	27	
8	64		

Keyes Union Elem. School Dist.

Barbara Spratling Middle

Grade	Eng	Ma	Sci
6	47	35	
7	27	18	
8	42		

Gold Rush (Sonora)

Grade	Eng	Ma	Sci
7	39	15	
8	26		
9	50		
10	42		
11	56		

Keyes Elem. (Keyes)

Grade	Eng	Ma	Sci
2	5	2	
3	12	7	
4	14	7	
5	53	64	34

Keys To Learning Char. (Keyes)

Grade	Eng	Ma	Sci
2	8	3	
3	69	29	
4	75	28	
5	71	20	63
6	55	40	
7	58	35	
8	80		
9	76		

Scores range from 1-99. A school scoring 75 has done better than 75 percent of other public schools in California.
Key: Eng (English), Ma (Math), Sci (Science).

Grade	Eng	Ma	Sci	Grade	Eng	Ma	Sci
Summit Char. Academy (Modesto)				**Everett Elem.**			
2	51	80		2	67	86	
3	47	54		3	72	71	
4	42	28		4	56	59	
5	24	20	35	5	42	46	29
6	63	52		6	51	50	
7	88	71		**Fairview Elem.**			
8	62			2	17	34	
The California Char. School				3	21	33	
6	66	30		4	14	28	
University Char. (Modesto)				5	8	14	7
2	92	99		6	13	25	
3	86	93		**Franklin Elem.**			
4	92	92		2	24	31	
5	77	70	69	3	20	18	
6	62	57		4	8	9	
Knights Ferry Elem. School Dist.				5	13	13	9
Knights Ferry Elem.				6	16	11	
2	54	39		**Fremont Elem.**			
3	99	93		2	63	70	
4	90	39		3	67	47	
5	91	41	96	4	67	69	
6	90	74		5	60	57	53
7	97	92		6	57	65	
				Garrison Elem.			
Modesto City Elem. School Dist.				2	44	43	
Beard Elem.				3	32	30	
2	49	46		4	31	14	
3	51	39		5	44	49	41
4	64	29		6	34	30	
5	65	58	53	**Hanshaw Middle**			
6	43	42		7	22	24	
Bret Harte Elem.				8	33	99	
2	2	11		**Kirschen Elem.**			
3	3	4		2	8	9	
4	5	9		3	13	9	
5	5	6	3	4	19	11	
6	5	12		5	11	14	8
Burbank Elem.				6	16	19	
2	5	3		**La Loma Jr. High**			
3	8	8		7	64	50	
4	11	8		8	63		
5	13	8	11	**Lakewood Elem.**			
6	34	33		2	96	88	
El Vista Elem.				3	93	87	
2	15	12		4	90	89	
3	22	24		5	92	86	85
4	21	14		6	96	92	
5	29	25	28	**Marshall Elem.**			
6	18	26		2	17	19	
Enslen Elem.				3	5	10	
2	84	94		4	3	12	
3	88	92		5	10	28	5
4	65	62		6	8	16	
5	60	59	55	**Martone Elem.**			
6	86	71		2	27	16	
				3	48	47	
				4	56	65	
				5	61	72	56
				6	52	56	

Scores range from 1-99. A school scoring 75 has done better than 75 percent of other public schools in California.

Key: Eng (English), Ma (Math), Sci (Science).

Muir Elem.

Grade	Eng	Ma	Sci
2	71	68	
3	57	66	
4	35	32	
5	44	55	62
6	47	53	

Robertson Road Elem.

Grade	Eng	Ma	Sci
2	13	12	
3	13	19	
4	18	28	
5	10	11	10
6	6	8	

Roosevelt Jr. High

Grade	Eng	Ma	Sci
7	64	51	
8	74		

Rose Ave. Elem.

Grade	Eng	Ma	Sci
2	66	66	
3	67	65	
4	70	71	
5	62	57	53
6	72	53	

Shackelford Elem.

Grade	Eng	Ma	Sci
2	4	7	
3	13	13	
4	2	5	
5	12	11	4
6	7	7	

Sonoma Elem.

Grade	Eng	Ma	Sci
2	70	76	
3	91	90	
4	71	72	
5	85	87	74
6	91	96	

Tuolumne Elem.

Grade	Eng	Ma	Sci
2	7	21	
3	6	10	
4	17	28	
5	30	42	27
6	30	38	

Twain Jr. High

Grade	Eng	Ma	Sci
7	27	21	
8	34	91	

Wilson Elem.

Grade	Eng	Ma	Sci
2	41	45	
3	42	19	
4	16	12	
5	32	32	17
6	23	28	

Wright Elem.

Grade	Eng	Ma	Sci
2	4	25	
3	8	15	
4	11	30	
5	19	18	16
6	8	12	

Modesto City High

Beyer High

Grade	Eng	Ma	Sci
9	77		
10	82		
11	84		

Elliott Alt. Ed. Cntr.

Grade	Eng	Ma	Sci
7	4	6	
8	2		
9	14		
10	20		
11	14		

Grace M. Davis High

Grade	Eng	Ma	Sci
9	70		
10	80		
11	73		

Johansen High

Grade	Eng	Ma	Sci
9	69		
10	78		
11	77		

Modesto High

Grade	Eng	Ma	Sci
9	70		
10	77		
11	74		

Thomas Downey High

Grade	Eng	Ma	Sci
9	66		
10	68		
11	70		

Newman-Crows Landing Unif. Sch. Dist.

Bonita Elem. (Crows Landing)

Grade	Eng	Ma	Sci
2	82	55	
3	96	97	
4	68	76	
5	45	88	43

Hunt Elem.

Grade	Eng	Ma	Sci
2	31	45	
3	49	37	
4	54	71	
5	53	83	34

Orestimba High (Newman)

Grade	Eng	Ma	Sci
9	63		
10	69		
11	72		

Von Renner Elem. (Newman)

Grade	Eng	Ma	Sci
2	36	48	
3	48	59	
4	24	48	
5	19	49	25

Yolo Jr. High (Newman)

Grade	Eng	Ma	Sci
6	41	41	
7	57	38	
8	44		

Oakdale Joint Unified School Dist.

Cloverland Elem.

Grade	Eng	Ma	Sci
2	69	40	
3	65	63	
4	55	40	
5	54	43	61
6	61	52	

East Stanislaus High

Grade	Eng	Ma	Sci
11	30		

Scores range from 1-99. A school scoring 75 has done better than 75 percent of other public schools in California.
Key: Eng (English), Ma (Math), Sci (Science).

Grade	Eng	Ma	Sci
Fair Oaks Elem.			
2	48	36	
3	64	34	
4	76	61	
5	66	75	80
6	71	67	
Magnolia Elem.			
2	61	44	
3	71	67	
4	77	71	
5	56	42	65
6	67	68	
Oakdale Char.			
9	76		
10	91		
11	90		
Oakdale High			
9	76		
10	86		
11	85		
Oakdale Jr. High			
7	49	46	
8	62		
Valley Oak High (Alt.)			
10	32		
11	51		

Paradise Elem. School Dist.

Grade	Eng	Ma	Sci
Paradise Elem.			
2	56	60	
3	76	65	
4	84	98	
5	46	76	37
6	33	43	
7	47	47	
8	57		

Patterson Joint Unified School Dist.

Grade	Eng	Ma	Sci
Creekside Middle			
6	30	36	
7	33	39	
8	38		
Del Puerto High (Cont.)			
9	14		
10	16		
11	20		
Grayson Char. (Westley)			
2	3	13	
3	57	29	
4	31	52	
5	9	22	4
Las Palmas Elem.			
2	18	17	
3	33	13	
4	30	35	
5	52	47	39

Grade	Eng	Ma	Sci
Northmead Elem.			
2	42	24	
3	31	12	
4	37	21	
5	30	31	21
Patterson High			
9	55		
10	56		
11	63		

Riverbank Unified School Dist.

Grade	Eng	Ma	Sci
California Ave. Elem. (Riverbank)			
2	42	25	
3	33	47	
4	46	81	
5	41	88	48
Cardozo Middle (Riverbank)			
6	28	42	
7	43	33	
8	36		
Milnes Elem. (Modesto)			
3	6	8	
4	11	8	
5	32	21	29
Rio Altura Elem. (Riverbank)			
2	23	31	
3	23	22	
4	38	43	
5	34	53	42
Riverbank High (Riverbank)			
9	45		
10	46		
11	51		

Roberts Ferry Union Elem. School Dist.

Grade	Eng	Ma	Sci
Roberts Ferry Union Elem. (Waterford)			
2	58	52	
5	92	82	83
6	60	45	

Salida Union Elem. School Dist.

Grade	Eng	Ma	Sci
Dena Boer Elem.			
2	64	49	
3	51	36	
4	61	42	
5	56	21	53
Perkins Elem. (Modesto)			
2	56	53	
3	70	42	
4	64	59	
5	71	64	64
6	47	64	
Salida Elem.			
2	61	41	
3	45	35	
4	41	42	
5	60	81	75
6	34	40	

Scores range from 1-99. A school scoring 75 has done better than 75 percent of other public schools in California.
Key: Eng (English), Ma (Math), Sci (Science).

Grade	Eng	Ma	Sci
Salida Middle School			
6	54	37	
7	54	52	
8	68		
Sisk Elem.			
2	38	22	
3	69	42	
4	67	60	
5	63	55	58
Shiloh Elem. School Dist.			
Shiloh Elem. (Modesto)			
3	79	83	
4	41	45	
5	35	55	34
6	18	51	
7	69	68	
8	82		
Stanislaus Union Elem. School Dist.			
(Modesto)			
Baptist Elem.			
2	59	51	
3	48	44	
4	73	77	
5	80	79	80
6	67	63	
Chrysler Elem.			
2	38	24	
3	12	12	
4	20	25	
5	27	48	23
6	38	34	
Eisenhut Elem.			
2	51	6	
3	43	38	
4	43	46	
5	49	42	54
6	53	54	
Mary Lou Dieterich Elem.			
2	56	50	
3	54	56	
4	56	60	
5	38	57	40
6	68	73	
Muncy Elem.			
2	21	11	
3	29	19	
4	22	24	
5	33	14	38
6	52	29	
Prescott Sr. Elem.			
7	48	52	
8	58		
Stanislaus Elem.			
2	62	42	
3	64	79	
4	45	30	
5	60	36	56
6	68	71	

Grade	Eng	Ma	Sci
Sylvan Union Elem. School Dist.			
Brown Elem.			
2	59	36	
3	43	38	
4	51	43	
5	55	37	48
Freedom Elem.			
2	82	75	
3	77	61	
4	65	51	
5	71	58	67
Orchard Elem.			
2	57	55	
3	53	51	
4	65	47	
5	70	50	51
Sherwood Elem.			
2	89	80	
3	66	47	
4	67	55	
5	65	47	57
Somerset Middle			
6	81	73	
7	80	80	
8	78		
Standiford Elem.			
2	80	72	
3	77	78	
4	92	95	
5	86	83	89
Stockard Coffee Elem.			
2	67	50	
3	68	46	
4	59	41	
5	63	50	60
Sylvan Elem.			
2	63	56	
3	71	63	
4	73	60	
5	38	9	34
Ustach Middle			
6	51	51	
7	46	60	
8	54		
Woodrow Elem.			
2	74	67	
3	49	38	
4	51	54	
5	41	52	51
Turlock Unified School Dist.			
Brown Elem.			
2	62	47	
3	70	69	
4	67	53	
5	53	34	41
6	59	50	

Scores range from 1-99. A school scoring 75 has done better than 75 percent of other public schools in California.
Key: Eng (English), Ma (Math), Sci (Science).

Grade	Eng	Ma	Sci
Crowell Elem.			
2	47	42	
3	37	25	
4	65	62	
5	54	43	30
6	51	52	
Cunningham Elem.			
2	38	40	
3	19	9	
4	24	22	
5	25	11	22
6	10	8	
Dutcher Jr. High			
7	66	67	
8	62		
Dutcher Elem.			
2	74	77	
3	80	58	
4	84	65	
5	79	61	77
6	85	86	
Earl Elem.			
2	80	45	
3	61	39	
4	65	46	
5	59	24	33
6	58	49	
Freedom Alt. High			
10	37		
11	39		
John H. Pitman High			
9	64		
10	66		
11	75		
Julien Elem.			
2	54	44	
3	64	49	
4	55	48	
5	69	56	65
6	58	63	
Osborn Elem.			
2	7	11	
3	29	23	
4	42	39	
5	25	17	25
6	34	23	
Roselawn High (Cont.)			
10	32		
11	21		
Turlock High			
9	64		
10	68		
11	70		
Turlock Jr. High			
7	38	37	
8	48		

Grade	Eng	Ma	Sci
Wakefield Elem.			
2	10	10	
3	25	19	
4	15	16	
5	7	8	4
6	10	10	

Valley Home Joint Elem. School Dist.
Valley Home Elem.

Grade	Eng	Ma	Sci
2	78	74	
3	37	5	
4	67	58	
5	82	51	78
6	64	21	
7	76	44	
8	54		

Waterford Unified School Dist.
Connecting Waters Char.

Grade	Eng	Ma	Sci
2	18	12	
3	31	3	
4	38	8	
5	61	9	51
6	45	22	
7	46	22	
8	54		
9	31		
10	46		
11	39		
Moon Elem.			
2	49	50	
3	39	19	
4	35	26	
Waterford			
5	44	54	65
6	42	55	
7	36	58	
8	47		
Waterford High			
9	62		
10	71		
11	61		

Chapter 5b

State 1 to 10 Rankings

FOR EASE OF COMPREHENSION, the California Department of Education has worked out a system to rank schools by their test scores.

This system takes several forms, the simplest of which is a ranking of 1 to 10.

One is the lowest score, ten is the highest.

This chapter lists the rankings for just about every school in the county.

Keep in mind that this is a crude representation of how the schools are scoring. If you combine this data with the rankings in Chapter 5a and the SAT scores and other data in Chapter 7, you will have a more rounded picture of the scores at each school.

Nonetheless, the scores can still mislead. Almost every school, even those at the bottom, will graduate students who score at the top.

Almost every school with scores at the top will graduate kids who score at the bottom and the middle.

For a general discussion of scores and what they mean, read the chapter on How Public Schools Work.

Merced County

School	District	City/Town	Rank
Bellevue Elem.	Atwater Elem.	Atwater	2
Colburn Elem.	Atwater Elem.	Atwater	3
Heller Elem.	Atwater Elem.	Atwater	5
Mitchell Elem.	Atwater Elem.	Atwater	3
Olaeta Elem.	Atwater Elem.	Atwater	5
Shaffer Elem.	Atwater Elem.	Atwater	6
Wood Elem.	Atwater Elem.	Atwater	7
Mitchell Int.	Atwater Elem.	Atwater	4
Ballico Elem.	Ballico-Cressey Elem.	Ballico	6
El Capitan Elem.	Delhi Unified	Delhi	2
Schendel Elem.	Delhi Unified	Delhi	3
Dos Palos Elem.	Dos Palos Oro Loma Unif.	Dos Palos	3
Marks Elem.	Dos Palos Oro Loma Unif.	Dos Palos	1
Oro Loma Elem.	Dos Palos Oro Loma Unif.	Firebaugh	3
Bryant Middle	Dos Palos Oro Loma Unif.	Dos Palos	3
Dos Palos High	Dos Palos Oro Loma Unif.	Dos Palos	3
El Nido Elem.	El Nido Elem.	El Nido	3
Gustin Elem.	Gustine Unified	Gustine	3
Romero Elem.	Gustine Unified	Gustine	3
Gustine Middle	Gustine Unified	Gustine	4
Gustine High	Gustine Unified	Gustine	3
Elim Elem.	Hilmar Unified	Hilmar	6
Merquin Elem.	Hilmar Unified	Hilmar	4
Hilmar Middle	Hilmar Unified	Hilmar	7
Hilmar High	Hilmar Unified	Hilmar	5
Le Grand Elem.	Le Grand Union Elem.	Le Grand	1
Le Grand High	Le Grand Union High	Le Grand	2
Campus Park Elem.	Livingston Union Elem.	Livingston	2
Herndon Elem.	Livingston Union Elem.	Livingston	3
Yamato Colony Elem.	Livingston Union Elem.	Livingston	5
Livingston Middle	Livingston Union Elem.	Livingston	3
Charleston Elem.	Los Banos Unified	Los Banos	7
Miller Elem.	Los Banos Unified	Los Banos	1
Los Banos Elem.	Los Banos Unified	Los Banos	5
Miano Elem.	Los Banos Unified	Los Banos	4
Volta Elem.	Los Banos Unified	Los Banos	6

School	District	City/Town	Rank
Westside Union Int.	Los Banos Unified	Los Banos	3
Los Banos Jr. High	Los Banos Unified	Los Banos	3
Los Banos High	Los Banos Unified	Los Banos	4
McSwain Elem.	McSwain Union Elem.	Merced	8
Burbank Elem.	Merced City Elem.	Merced	2
Chenoweth Elem.	Merced City Elem.	Merced	6
Franklin Elem.	Merced City Elem.	Merced	4
Fremont Char.	Merced City Elem.	Merced	4
Givens Elem.	Merced City Elem.	Merced	3
Gracey Elem.	Merced City Elem.	Merced	3
Muir Elem.	Merced City Elem.	Merced	2
Peterson Elem.	Merced City Elem.	Merced	6
Reyes Elem.	Merced City Elem.	Merced	2
Sheehy Elem.	Merced City Elem.	Merced	3
Stowell Elem.	Merced City Elem.	Merced	2
Wright Elem.	Merced City Elem.	Merced	3
Cruickshank Middle	Merced City Elem.	Merced	5
Hoover Middle	Merced City Elem.	Merced	4
Rivera Middle	Merced City Elem.	Merced	5
Tenaya Middle	Merced City Elem.	Merced	2
Washington Elem.	Merced River Union Elem.	Winton	6
Atwater High	Merced Union High	Atwater	4
Buhach Colony High	Merced Union High	Atwater	5
Golden Valley High	Merced Union High	Merced	5
Livingston High	Merced Union High	Livingston	6
Merced High	Merced Union High	Merced	6
Planada Elem.	Planada Elem.	Planada	1
Chavez Middle	Planada Elem.	Planada	1
Pioneer Elem.	Weaver Union Elem.	Merced	6
Weaver Elem.	Weaver Union Elem.	Merced	4
Crookham Elem.	Winton Elem.	Winton	2
Sparkes Elem.	Winton Elem.	Winton	1
Winton Middle	Winton Elem.	Winton	4

San Joaquin County

School	District	City/Town	Rank
Banta Elem.	Banta Elem.	Tracy	5
Collegeville Elem.	Escalon Unified	Stockton	5
Dent Elem.	Escalon Unified	Escalon	6
Van Allen Elem.	Escalon Unified	Escalon	7
El Portal Middle	Escalon Unified	Escalon	7
Escalon High	Escalon Unified	Escalon	5
Holt Elem.	Holt Union Elem.	Stockton	1
Hawkins Elem.	Jefferson Elem.	Tracy	8
Monticello Elem.	Jefferson Elem.	Tracy	8
Jefferson Elem.	Jefferson Elem.	Tracy	8
Lammersville Elem.	Lammersville Elem.	Tracy	7
Barron Elem.	Lincoln Unified	Stockton	6
Brookside Elem.	Lincoln Unified	Stockton	9
Colonial Hts. Elem.	Lincoln Unified	Stockton	5
Don Riggio Sch.	Lincoln Unified	Stockton	5
Knoles Elem.	Lincoln Unified	Stockton	3
Landeen Elem.	Lincoln Unified	Stockton	7
Lincoln Elem.	Lincoln Unified	Stockton	5
Village Oaks Elem.	Lincoln Unified	Stockton	1
Williams Elem.	Lincoln Unified	Stockton	3
Sierra Middle	Lincoln Unified	Stockton	5
Lincoln High	Lincoln Unified	Stockton	6
Glenwood Elem.	Linden Unified	Stockton	6
Linden Elem.	Linden Unified	Linden	4
Waverly Elem.	Linden Unified	Stockton	6
Waterloo Elem.	Linden Unified	Stockton	6
Linden High	Linden Unified	Linden	5
Beckman Elem.	Lodi Unified	Lodi	3
Borchardt Elem.	Lodi Unified	Lodi	6
Clairmont Elem.	Lodi Unified	Stockton	4
Creekside Elem.	Lodi Unified	Stockton	4
Davis Elem.	Lodi Unified	Stockton	5
Heritage Elem.	Lodi Unified	Lodi	1
Houston Elem.	Lodi Unified	Acampo	5
Joe Serna Jr. Char.	Lodi Unified	Lodi	3
Lakewood Elem.	Lodi Unified	Lodi	6

School	District	City/Town	Rank
Lawrence Elem.	Lodi Unified	Lodi	1
Live Oak Elem.	Lodi Unified	Lodi	2
Lockeford Elem.	Lodi Unified	Lockeford	7
Morgan Elem.	Lodi Unified	Stockton	6
Muir Elem.	Lodi Unified	Stockton	8
Needham Elem.	Lodi Unified	Lodi	1
Nichols Elem.	Lodi Unified	Lodi	3
Oakwood Elem.	Lodi Unified	Stockton	1
Parklane Elem.	Lodi Unified	Stockton	1
Reese Elem.	Lodi Unified	Lodi	7
River Oaks Char.	Lodi Unified	Stockton	4
Sutherland Elem.	Lodi Unified	Stockton	2
University Public Char.	Lodi Unified	Stockton	8
Victor Elem.	Lodi Unified	Victor	5
Vinewood Elem.	Lodi Unified	Lodi	8
Wagner-Holt Elem.	Lodi Unified	Stockton	3
Washington Elem.	Lodi Unified	Lodi	3
Westwood Elem.	Lodi Unified	Stockton	3
Holt College Prep.	Lodi Unified	Stockton	7
Delta Sierra Middle	Lodi Unified	Stockton	3
Elkhorn Elem.	Lodi Unified	Lodi	10
Lodi Middle	Lodi Unified	Lodi	4
Morada Middle	Lodi Unified	Stockton	3
Woodbridge Middle	Lodi Unified	Woodbridge	4
Bear Creek High	Lodi Unified	Stockton	5
Lodi High	Lodi Unified	Lodi	6
Middle College High	Lodi Unified	Stockton	10
Tokay High	Lodi Unified	Lodi	6
Brockman Elem.	Manteca Unified	Manteca	6
Cowell Elem.	Manteca Unified	Manteca	5
Elliott Elem.	Manteca Unified	Manteca	7
French Camp Elem.	Manteca Unified	French Camp	3
Golden West Elem.	Manteca Unified	Manteca	6
Great Valley Elem.	Manteca Unified	Stockton	5
Hafley Elem.	Manteca Unified	Manteca	4
Knodt Elem.	Manteca Unified	Stockton	5
Komure Elem.	Manteca Unified	Stockton	4
Lathrop Elem.	Manteca Unified	Lathrop	4

School	District	City/Town	Rank
Lincoln Elem.	Manteca Unified	Manteca	3
McParland Elem.	Manteca Unified	Manteca	7
New Haven Elem.	Manteca Unified	Manteca	6
Nile Garden Elem.	Manteca Unified	Manteca	6
Sequoia Elem.	Manteca Unified	Manteca	2
Shasta Elem.	Manteca Unified	Manteca	4
Widmer Elem.	Manteca Unified	Lathrop	4
East Union High	Manteca Unified	Manteca	3
Manteca High	Manteca Unified	Manteca	4
Sierra High	Manteca Unified	Manteca	6
Weston Ranch High	Manteca Unified	Stockton	2
New Hope Elem.	New Hope Elem.	Thorton	2
New Jerusalem Elem.	New Jerusalem Elem.	Tracy	6
Oak View Elem.	Oak View Union Elem.	Acampo	8
Colony Oak Elem.	Ripon Unified	Ripon	9
Ripon Elem.	Ripon Unified	Ripon	6
Ripona Elem.	Ripon Unified	Ripon	8
Weston Elem.	Ripon Unified	Ripon	8
Ripon High	Ripon Unified	Ripon	7
Adams Elem.	Stockton City Unified	Stockton	3
August Elem.	Stockton City Unified	Stockton	4
Bush Elem.	Stockton City Unified	Stockton	6
Cleveland Elem.	Stockton City Unified	Stockton	3
El Dorado Elem.	Stockton City Unified	Stockton	2
Elmwood Elem.	Stockton City Unified	Stockton	3
Fillmore Elem.	Stockton City Unified	Stockton	2
Garfield Elem.	Stockton City Unified	Stockton	1
Grant Elem.	Stockton City Unified	Stockton	1
Grunsky Elem.	Stockton City Unified	Stockton	1
Harrison Elem.	Stockton City Unified	Stockton	2
Hazelton Elem.	Stockton City Unified	Stockton	4
Hoover Elem.	Stockton City Unified	Stockton	2
Huerta Elem.	Stockton City Unified	Stockton	2
Kennedy Elem.	Stockton City Unified	Stockton	3
King Elem.	Stockton City Unified	Stockton	2
Kohl Open Elem.	Stockton City Unified	Stockton	6
Madison Elem.	Stockton City Unified	Stockton	2
McKinley Elem.	Stockton City Unified	Stockton	1

School	District	City/Town	Rank
Monroe Elem.	Stockton City Unified	Stockton	2
Montezuma Elem.	Stockton City Unified	Stockton	1
Nightingale Elem.	Stockton City Unified	Stockton	1
Pulliam Elem.	Stockton City Unified	Stockton	3
Rio Calaveras Elem.	Stockton City Unified	Stockton	7
Roosevelt Elem.	Stockton City Unified	Stockton	2
San Joaquin Elem.	Stockton City Unified	Stockton	6
Stockton Skills Elem.	Stockton City Unified	Stockton	7
Taft Elem.	Stockton City Unified	Stockton	2
Taylor Skills Elem.	Stockton City Unified	Stockton	2
Tyler Skills Elem.	Stockton City Unified	Stockton	4
Valenzuela Elem.	Stockton City Unified	Stockton	5
Van Buren Elem.	Stockton City Unified	Stockton	2
Victory Elem.	Stockton City Unified	Stockton	3
Washington Elem.	Stockton City Unified	Stockton	2
Wilson Elem.	Stockton City Unified	Stockton	3
Fremont Middle	Stockton City Unified	Stockton	1
Hamilton Middle	Stockton City Unified	Stockton	2
Marshall Middle	Stockton City Unified	Stockton	2
Urbani Char.	Stockton City Unified	Stockton	1
Webster Middle	Stockton City Unified	Stockton	1
Edison Sr. High	Stockton City Unified	Stockton	2
Franklin Sr. High	Stockton City Unified	Stockton	1
Inst. Of Business	Stockton City Unified	Stockton	3
Stagg Sr. High	Stockton City Unified	Stockton	3
Weber Inst.	Stockton City Unified	Stockton	2
Bohn Elem.	Tracy Jt. Unified	Tracy	6
Central Elem.	Tracy Jt. Unified	Tracy	2
Delta Island Elem.	Tracy Jt. Unified	Stockton	1
Freiler Elem.	Tracy Jt. Unified	Tracy	7
Hirsch Elem.	Tracy Jt. Unified	Tracy	8
Jacobson Elem.	Tracy Jt. Unified	Tracy	5
McKinley Elem.	Tracy Jt. Unified	Tracy	4
North Elem.	Tracy Jt. Unified	Tracy	4
Poet-Christian Elem.	Tracy Jt. Unified	Tracy	6
South/West Park Elem.	Tracy Jt. Unified	Tracy	3
Villalovoz Elem.	Tracy Jt. Unified	Tracy	7
Clover Middle	Tracy Jt. Unified	Tracy	4

School	District	City/Town	Rank
Discovery Charter	Tracy Jt. Unified	Tracy	9
Monte Vista Middle	Tracy Jt. Unified	Tracy	4
Williams Middle	Tracy Jt. Unified	Tracy	5
Tracy High	Tracy Jt. Unified	Tracy	6
West High	Tracy Jt. Unified	Tracy	5

Stanislaus County

School	District	City/Town	Rank
Carroll Fowler Elem.	Ceres Unified	Ceres	4
Caswell Elem.	Ceres Unified	Ceres	4
Don Pedro Elem.	Ceres Unified	Ceres	5
Vaughn Elem.	Ceres Unified	Ceres	7
Virginia Parks Elem.	Ceres Unified	Ceres	8
Westport Elem.	Ceres Unified	Ceres	4
White Elem.	Ceres Unified	Ceres	4
Whitmore Charter	Ceres Unified	Ceres	5
Blaker-Kinser Jr. High	Ceres Unified	Ceres	6
Mae Hensley Jr. High	Ceres Unified	Ceres	5
Ceres High	Ceres Unified	Ceres	4
Chatom Elem.	Chatom Union Elem.	Turlock	3
Mountain View Middle	Chatom Union Elem.	Crows Landing	2
Denair Elem.	Denair Unified	Denair	6
Denair Middle	Denair Unified	Denair	7
Denair High	Denair Unified	Denair	5
Capistrano Elem.	Empire Union Elem.	Modesto	4
Empire Elem.	Empire Union Elem.	Empire	4
Hughes Elem.	Empire Union Elem.	Modesto	8
Sipherd Elem.	Empire Union Elem.	Modesto	7
Stroud Elem.	Empire Union Elem.	Modesto	7
Glick Middle	Empire Union Elem.	Modesto	6
Teel Middle	Empire Union Elem.	Empire	5
Hart-Ransom Academic Char.	Hart-Ransom Union Elem.	Modesto	7
Hart-Ransom Elem.	Hart-Ransom Union Elem.	Modesto	7
Hickman Charter	Hickman Comm. Char.	Hickman	6
Hickman Elem.	Hickman Comm. Char.	Hickman	6
Hickman Middle	Hickman Comm. Char.	Hickman	9
Fox Road Elem.	Hughson Unified	Hughson	4
Hughson Elem.	Hughson Unified	Hughson	6
Ross Elem.	Hughson Unified	Hughson	6
Hughson High	Hughson Unified	Hughson	7
Keyes Elem.	Keyes Union Elem.	Keyes	2
Keys to Learning Char.	Keyes Union Elem.	Keyes	4
Summit Char. Acad.	Keyes Union Elem.	Modesto	4
University Charter	Keyes Union Elem.	Modesto	9

School	District	City/Town	Rank
Spratling Middle	Keyes Union Elem.	Keyes	3
Gold Rush Home Study Char.	Keyes Union Elem.	Sonora	3
Beard Elem.	Modesto City Elem.	Modesto	6
Bret Harte Elem.	Modesto City Elem.	Modesto	1
Burbank Elem.	Modesto City Elem.	Modesto	2
El Vista Elem.	Modesto City Elem.	Modesto	3
Enslen Elem.	Modesto City Elem.	Modesto	8
Everett Elem.	Modesto City Elem.	Modesto	7
Fairview Elem.	Modesto City Elem.	Modesto	2
Franklin Elem.	Modesto City Elem.	Modesto	2
Fremont Elem.	Modesto City Elem.	Modesto	6
Garrison Elem.	Modesto City Elem.	Modesto	4
Kirschen Elem.	Modesto City Elem.	Modesto	2
Lakewood Elem.	Modesto City Elem.	Modesto	9
Marshall Elem.	Modesto City Elem.	Modesto	1
Martone Elem.	Modesto City Elem.	Modesto	7
Muir Elem.	Modesto City Elem.	Modesto	4
Robertson Road Elem.	Modesto City Elem.	Modesto	1
Rose Ave. Elem.	Modesto City Elem.	Modesto	8
Shackelford Elem.	Modesto City Elem.	Modesto	1
Sonoma Elem.	Modesto City Elem.	Modesto	9
Tuolumne Elem.	Modesto City Elem.	Modesto	3
Wilson Elem.	Modesto City Elem.	Modesto	3
Wright Elem.	Modesto City Elem.	Modesto	1
Hanshaw Middle	Modesto City Elem.	Modesto	3
La Loma Jr. High	Modesto City Elem.	Modesto	7
Roosevelt Jr. High	Modesto City Elem.	Modesto	6
Twain Jr. High	Modesto City Elem.	Modesto	4
Beyer High	Modesto City High	Modesto	9
Davis High	Modesto City High	Modesto	7
Johansen High	Modesto City High	Modesto	7
Modesto High	Modesto City High	Modesto	7
Thomas Downey High	Modesto City High	Modesto	5
Hunt Elem.	Newman-Crows Lndng Unif.	Newman	4
Von Renner Elem.	Newman-Crows Lndng Unif.	Newman	3
Yolo Middle	Newman-Crows Lndng Unif.	Newman	5
Orestima High	Newman-Crows Lndng Unif.	Newman	4
Cloverland Elem.	Oakdale Jt. Unified	Oakdale	7

School	District	City/Town	Rank
Fair Oaks Elem.	Oakdale Jt. Unified	Oakdale	8
Magnolia Elem.	Oakdale Jt. Unified	Oakdale	7
Oakdale Jr. High	Oakdale Jt. Unified	Oakdale	6
Oakdale High	Oakdale Jt. Unified	Oakdale	8
Grayson Charter	Patterson Jt. Unified	Westley	1
Las Palmas Elem.	Patterson Jt. Unified	Patterson	5
Northmead Elem.	Patterson Jt. Unified	Patterson	4
Creekside Middle	Patterson Jt. Unified	Patterson	4
Patterson High	Patterson Jt. Unified	Patterson	4
California Ave. Elem.	Riverbank Unified	Riverbank	5
Rio Altura Elem.	Riverbank Unified	Riverbank	3
Cardozo Middle	Riverbank Unified	Riverbank	4
Riverbank High	Riverbank Unified	Riverbank	2
Dena Boer Elem.	Salida Union Elem.	Salida	6
Perkins Elem.	Salida Union Elem.	Modesto	7
Salida Elem.	Salida Union Elem.	Salida	6
Sisk Elem.	Salida Union Elem.	Salida	7
Salida Middle	Salida Union Elem.	Salida	7
Shiloh Elem.	Shiloh Elem.	Modesto	6
Baptist Elem.	Stanislaus Union Elem.	Modesto	7
Chrysler Elem.	Stanislaus Union Elem.	Modesto	4
Eisenhut Elem.	Stanislaus Union Elem.	Modesto	5
Muncy Elem.	Stanislaus Union Elem.	Modesto	4
Stanislaus Elem.	Stanislaus Union Elem.	Modesto	7
Prescott Sr. Elem.	Stanislaus Union Elem.	Modesto	7
Brown Elem.	Sylvan Union Elem.	Modesto	6
Coffee Elem.	Sylvan Union Elem.	Modesto	8
Freedom Elem.	Sylvan Union Elem.	Modesto	7
Orchard Elem.	Sylvan Union Elem.	Modesto	7
Sherwood Elem.	Sylvan Union Elem.	Modesto	8
Standiford Elem.	Sylvan Union Elem.	Modesto	9
Sylvan Elem.	Sylvan Union Elem.	Modesto	8
Woodrow Elem.	Sylvan Union Elem.	Modesto	7
Somerset Middle	Sylvan Union Elem.	Modesto	8
Ustach Elem.	Sylvan Union Elem.	Modesto	6
Brown Elem.	Turlock Jt. Elem.	Turlock	7
Crowell Elem.	Turlock Jt. Elem.	Turlock	6
Cunningham Elem.	Turlock Jt. Elem.	Turlock	3

School	District	City/Town	Rank
Dutcher Elem.	Turlock Jt. Elem.	Turlock	9
Earl Elem.	Turlock Jt. Elem.	Turlock	6
Julien Elem.	Turlock Jt. Elem.	Turlock	7
Osborn Elem.	Turlock Jt. Elem.	Turlock	3
Wakefield Elem.	Turlock Jt. Elem.	Turlock	1
Dutcher Middle	Turlock Jt. Elem.	Turlock	7
Turlock Jr. High	Turlock Jt. Elem.	Turlock	5
Pitman High	Turlock Jt. Union High	Turlock	6
Turlock High	Turlock Jt. Union High	Turlock	4
Valley Home Elem.	Valley Home Jt. Elem.	Valley Home	7
Moon Elem.	Waterford Unified	Waterford	3
Waterford Middle	Waterford Unified	Waterford	4
Waterford High	Waterford Unified	Waterford	4

$15.95

McCormack's GUIDES

How California Schools Work

A PRACTICAL
GUIDE FOR
PARENTS

FROM THE EDITORS OF McCormack's Guides

www.mccormacks.com
1-800-222-3602

Chapter 6

City & Town Profiles

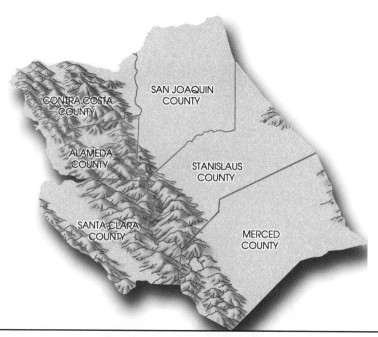

CONTRA COSTA
COUNTY

SAN JOAQUIN
COUNTY

ALAMEDA
COUNTY

STANISLAUS
COUNTY

SANTA CLARA
COUNTY

MERCED
COUNTY

INDEX TO PROFILES

Before you move ... buy

$13⁹⁵
SINGLE COPY
VOLUME DISCOUNTS

McCormack's Guides are published for:

- ALAMEDA-CENTRAL VALLEY • CONTRA COSTA-SOLANO
- SANTA CLARA-SANTA CRUZ-SILICON VALLEY
- SAN FRANCISCO-SAN MATEO-MARIN-SONOMA
- SAN DIEGO • ORANGE COUNTY • GREATER SACRAMENTO

Available in e-book format at www.mccormacks.com:

LOS ANGELES • RIVERSIDE • SANTA BARBARA • SAN BERNARDINO • VENTURA

Also from McCormack's Guides:
How California Schools Work

www.mccormacks.com
1•800•222•3602

ATWATER

LOCATED ON HIGHWAY 99 in Merced County just north of the City of Merced. Farm town that for decades also served as a military town. Now going suburban.

Castle Air Force Base was closed in 1995 and is being turned to other uses, including a federal prison (about 1,600 inmates). The base also houses a variety of firms and includes an air museum.

Atwater should also benefit from the University of California that opened in 2005 in Merced.

Home construction, stagnant after the base closed, has revived.

Family town. Many kids. Median age is 29. Children under 18 comprise 35 percent of Atwater. Those over 55 make up 16 percent.

Small town, compact, three miles from east to west, and north to south. Population 26,693. Atwater started the 1950s with about 3,000 people. By 1960, the population had soared to 7,300 and by 1970 to 11,600. Over the next two decades, the city doubled its population to 22,300. When the air base closed, many people who worked or served at the base departed. The population leveled out, then came back, newcomers taking the place of those who left. In the 1990s, the town erected 1,500 residential units, almost all of them single-detached homes.

These numbers will give you a good idea of Atwater's housing stock. Most of its homes and apartments were erected between 1960 and 1990. The old town is situated near the freeway and the rail lines. As you drive north and cross Juniper Avenue, the housing becomes newer and newer.

More new housing is going up next to the base and on the edge of the town. Some new homes are stepping up to two-story, three-car garage, four-six bedroom.

Sharp differences between the small and old and faded housing in and near the downtown and the new housing but this adds to the pricing variety. Some infilling with new homes.

Atwater, for the most part, built for the middle class and for the military. The streets are clean, the homes well maintained. Little jumps up the scale although the north side has some large and handsome homes. Typical American suburban. Water tank atop tower announces in large letters, Atwater. Cannon in front of the memorial building.

In 2005, the town counted 8,784 housing units, of which 5,871 were single homes, 584 single-attached, 1,822 condos or apartments and 507 mobile homes. "Active adult" community with three and four-bedroom villas. Among new businesses, a drug-general store and a supermarket.

City officials predict that by 2020, Atwater's population will grow to 39,000. Located near the UC Merced campus, Atwater is expected to benefit from the growth the university will encourage.

Highway 99 borders the town on the south, near the train tracks. Check out the train whistles and noise; some will find them soothing, some annoying.

One homicide in 2004, two in 2003, zero in 2002, one in 2001, zero in 2000, three in 1999. The counts for the previous years are 2, 2, 0, 0 and 1.

Education by the Atwater Elementary School District, enrollment about 5,000. On state rankings, scores bounce all over, many below the 50th percentile, several schools in the 50th to 70th percentile. Teens move up to Atwater High, in the Merced High School District. Scores at Atwater High land in the 50th percentile. Voters approved an $11 million bond issue in 2004 for new elementary classrooms and renovations. High school district also has approved construction bond.

One Catholic, two Christian schools. Community college about six miles down Highway 99, in City of Merced.

For the Bay Area commute, Atwater is a long drive to Silicon Valley and to San Francisco (130 miles). The city and the region are putting their energy into converting Castle into a business-industrial park and besides the prison have landed some industrial firms.

The old airbase also contains an aviation museum with about 43 planes dating back to World War II. Impressive and worth a visit.

About a dozen parks. One golf course. One park has small zoo and train. Skate park. City recreation department offers dance aerobics, co-ed softball, men's basketball, volleyball, tennis. Many sports-activities for the kids. Public swimming at high-school pool. Driving range a few miles outside of town. High school has large playing fields used by the community.

Chamber of commerce (209) 358-4251.

• Atwater is annexing land with the intention of building about 2,000 housing units. Local school districts and other agencies have sued Atwater to force it to prove that it can handle this growth. In 2005, developers agreed to put up more money for schools.

CERES

FARM-TOWN SUBURB located between Modesto and Turlock and so close to Modesto that it almost seems part of that city. Doubled its population over the last 20 years and now counts 38,813 residents.

For the most part, Ceres is building for middle class but some streets jump way up the scale into opulence. Drive the streets around Park Elementary School (Payne Avenue) on the north side. Another pleasing neighborhood: west of freeway, around Blaker-Kinser School. On the south side, many low-income neighborhoods. With in-filling and general construction, Ceres is moving toward a more rounded community — low, middle and high.

When the railroad came to the region and a depot was built, the town followed. A pioneer woman was given the honor of naming the village. She decided on Ceres, the Roman goddess of agriculture — most appropriate. For the next 100 years or so, Ceres, incorporated as a city in 1918, tilled the fields and orchards until suburbia crept in, about the 1970s. In that decade, the population went from 6,000 to 13,000. These numbers tell this story: old downtown bordered by cottages and bungalows, then the first suburban tracts, then as you move up, more modern tracts. It's not quite that neat because Ceres has filled in with modern housing parcels that were skipped in the initial development. In 2005, the town tallied 11,865 units — 9,142 single homes, 343 single-attached, 1,668 condos or apartments, 712 mobiles. Under 18 years, 34 percent of town; over 55 years, 14 percent. Family town. Loads of playmates.

Ceres Unified School District also serves part of Modesto. Scores a mix but many about the 50th percentile, a few higher. Bond passed in 2001 to build another high school; it opened in 2005 for ninth and tenth graders.

Highway 99 splits the town. The old town has its charms, among them a large clock, but commerce has shifted to other parts of Ceres. Wal-Mart on Mitchell Road. Regional airport and food processing plants north of town. For commuters to the East Bay, Ceres is probably an endurable drive. Highway 132, a few miles to the north, cuts over to I-580.

Two homicides in 2004, zero in 2003, two in 2002, zero in 2001, 2000 and 1999. Counts for previous years is 1, 0, 0, 1 and 0.

Half-dozen parks, including a giant along river near airport. Parks and schools are built as the homes come in. Golf course. Driving range. Library. Usual sports. Many soccer fields. Chamber of commerce (209) 537-2601.

DOS PALOS

SMALL FARM TOWN in Merced County. Population 4,854. Surrounded by miles of fields. Located southeast of Los Baños, off of Highway 33.

Outside the commute reach of the Bay Area and Sacramento. Between 1970 and 1990, Dos Palos increased its population by 1,700. But in the 1990s, the town added only 259 residents. In 2005, the town, a legal city, tallied 1,584 housing units, of which 1,364 were single homes, 55 single-attached, 126 condos or apartments and 39 mobile homes. Median age is 30. Under 18 years makes up 35 percent of population; over 55 years, 19 percent. Lot of kids. Family town. More homes going up and with them arguments over how fast town should grow.

Education by Dos Palos-Oro Loma Unified School District, enrollment 2,700. Many scores land below the 40th percentile. Branch campus of Merced Community College. In 2002, voters passed $4.4 million bond to renovate schools.

Zero homicides in 2003, 2002, 2001, 2000 and 1999. Town has own police department. Some bars on windows in adjacent South Dos Palos.

In 1891, German immigrants founded the Dos Palos Colony, taking the name from an 1840s survey that took note of two tall trees. Residents call themselves "Dos Palosans." Sounds Spanish but has a German accent: Dache Palosians. In the early 20th century, the farms grew rice and cotton. Dos Palos celebrates its past with annual Cotton Festival. Quaint town that in many places looks its age. Many old buildings. Residential streets generally well maintained.

Dos Palos, energetic in pursuit of its interests, has five parks, twice the state average in park acreage per resident. City rec department sponsors aerobics, T-ball, baseball, basketball, flag football, soccer, softball, street dances, swimming. Library. Post office. Dos Palos has its own city flag. Police station. Movies. Wal-mart. Town measures about 20 blocks east to west and 15 blocks north to south. Kids walk to school. Friday night high school football a big event. Some games draw 3,000 fans; championship games up to 7,000.

Many people moving into Dos Palos supposedly are Los Baños residents going back to small-town life. No chamber of commerce.

ESCALON

SMALL TOURIST, farm town in San Joaquin County. Well known to many Bay Area residents because it straddles Highway 120, the road to Yosemite. Population 6,912.

Since 1970, Escalon has been adding 800 to 1,300 people a decade. In the 1990s, Escalon erected about 500 housing units, most of them single detached homes. The city now limits how many units can be built each year. Median age of residents is 36. Children and teens under 18 years make up 31 percent of town; over 55 years, 20 percent. Family town. In 2005, the town tallied 2,399 housing units, of which 1,993 were single homes, 20 single-attached, 251 condos or apartments and 135 mobile homes.

Escalon is about 12 miles east of Manteca, a popular Bay Area commute town. But these are long miles, over a two-lane road. Still, some people probably commute to the Bay Area or to Livermore-Pleasanton-San Ramon. Another possibility: retirement living. Escalon is close to the Sierra. In drive miles, Oakland 65, San Francisco 82, Sacramento 55.

Zero homicides in 2003, 2002, 2001, 2000, and 1999. Crime rate low.

Education by the Escalon Unified School District, enrollment 3,200. On a state comparison, scores are landing in the 50th to 80th percentile. In 2002, voters approved a bond to build a performing arts center and library at the high school and gym at the middle school.

Town calls itself "Land of peaches and cream" and is sprucing up its downtown with landscaping, brick sidewalks and decorative lights. One problem: Main Street is a few blocks away from the major commercial routes through town. Streets lined with trees. City council is trying to put together an industrial center that would not route trucks through town.

Golf course. Library built with brick. Half-dozen parks. Museum. Community center. Usual sports, baseball, soccer, softball, etc. Also horseback riding, cycling and fishing. Community pool. Annual park fete with walk-run race. Escalon Times hits the stands every Wednesday. More restaurants opening.

Packing houses are the main employers, generally seasonal work. Fruit and vegetable stands for the travelers who want country freshness. Trains rumble through town. Chamber of commerce (209) 838-2793.

GUSTINE

SMALL FARM TOWN, population 5,311, located at junction of Highways 33 and 140, eight miles east of Interstate 5, which by today's standards makes it commute endurable to Alameda County and — a longer haul, over Highway 152 — to Gilroy and Silicon Valley. Many kids, young families.

In the 1990s, Gustine added about 175 single homes and increased its population by 500. The town is steadily, if slowly, adding tract homes, some of them two-story, 4-6 bedrooms, a departure for Gustine, which has favored two- and three-bedroom homes. New homes on the outskirts. Gustine measures about 13 blocks in each direction. You can get the hang of the town quickly.

Where Gustine stands, there once was a rail stop called Cottonwood Switch. About 1907, the New Era Creamery concluded that if it built a creamery at the switch, a town would blossom. So it purchased the land from a rancher named Miller, sold 80 lots and lo and behold, a town. Miller's daughter Gussie had died young. The town was named in her memory. In 1915, Gustine incorporated as a legal city. By 1950, Gustine claimed 2,000 residents and since then it has added a couple hundred each decade. The exceptions were the 1980s when its population jumped by 800 and the last decade, also up 800. In 2005, the town counted 1,983 housing units, of which 1,622 were single homes, 30 single-attached, 203 condos or apartments and 128 mobile homes. Trains still running. Bells and whistles. Zero homicides in 2003, 2002, 2001 and 2000.

Old town, a mix of cottages and bungalows and wide streets shaded by full trees. Then the tract styles of modern suburbia. Diners, shops, saloons, pizza parlor, video rentals in downtown. Old movie house converted into an antiques place. The first McDonald's opened in 2002. Many of the older businesses have been gutted and refitted as modern stores.

Education by Gustine Unified School District, two elementaries, a middle and a high. The elementaries, on a state comparison, are scoring below the 30th percentile, the middle above and below the 30th percentile, the high school about the 60th percentile. Catholic elementary school.

Four parks, one with a pool and bandstand. Library. Playing fields at schools. Town museum. Usual sports. Chamber of commerce (209) 854-6975.

• Small-town, we forget-you-not. Little veterans memorial. Red, white and blue flowers, plastic fabric, but the ground is neatly and respectfully kept. Inscription: "They gave up their tomorrow so we could have our today."

HUGHSON

SMALL FARM TOWN in Stanislaus County. Population 5,942. Located about 10 miles east of Modesto and removed from freeways, Hughson for a long time was overlooked by suburbia but in the last few years the inevitable pulled into town. Most of the new housing is going up on the north side.

Median age of residents is 31. Under 18 years make up 33 percent of town; over 55 years, 18 percent. Many kids; family burg. In the 1990s, Hughson added about 700 people.

In 2005, the town counted 1,836 housing units, of which 1,481 were single homes, 65 single-attached, 201 condos or apartments and 89 mobiles. The new homes are often much bigger — four bedrooms , two-story — than the rest of the town's offerings.

Education by Hughson Unified School District, one school, K-3; second, 4-5; third, 6-8; and high school, total enrollment 2,050. School rankings, state comparison, pretty good, many above the 60th percentile. Orchards border the high school, which draws students from Hughson and from small school districts in the region.

In 2004, the district won voter approval of a bond to renovate and build schools.

Zero homicides between 1996 and 2003. Town contracts with the sheriff for police protection. Station in town.

Older housing a mix of cottages and bungalows that gradually move into suburban tract, some of which was built decades ago. For old and well done, drive 7th Street. Church with bell tower, restaurants, medical offices, antique stores. For shopping, Modesto has department and discount stores. Seniors housing complex opened in 2002.

For about 10 years, Hughson was unable to build much housing because its sewer treatment and water supply were inadequate. Improvements have been made to both, clearing the way for more construction.

Two parks. Library. Town swimming pool. Many driveways are decorated with basketball hoops. Hiking-jogging trail along the canal on the north side. Non-profit arboretum, 13 acres donated by a lover of plants. Annual Fruit and Nut Festival.

Burlington Northern Santa Fe line runs along the west side of town. Santa Fe Avenue leads up to Modesto.

LATHROP

SMALL TOWN LOCATED OFF OF INTERSTATE 5 between Stockton and Manteca. Population 12,565. Half new town, half old. Market willing, Lathrop will build thousands of homes on its south side. Lots of kids. Family town.

Several years ago, Lathrop annexed 7,000 acres on its south to build 13,000 residential units, a business park and retail-commercial centers. Officials expect Lathrop's population to quadruple by 2025. Community demographics will likely change.

In 2005, city opened a library and new city hall, hired a new police chief, spruced up the entrances to town and announced a crackdown on code violations. Lot of energy!

In the 1990s, Lathrop built about 1,000 homes, most in a handsome subdivision to the north of Lathrop Road, a main thoroughfare. Next door is a neighborhood of older homes, many over 50 years old. To the south mixing continues but in a different way. A block of very old homes will give way to new homes, then to homes built in 1950s and 1960s, followed by homes built in the last 20 years. New homes north off Lathrop Road are a mix of one and two story, two-car and three-car garages. Streets are clean, the homes in good care. The homes on the south side, new and old, also show good care. The old homes on the north are a bit disheveled here and there. Lathrop did not incorporate until 1989. With cityhood, Lathrop appears to be exerting tighter planning controls. In 2005, the town counted 3,498 housing units, of which 2,980 were single homes, 63 single-attached, 104 condos or apartments and 351 mobile homes. Mix of stores; Home Depot. The proximity of the freeways takes some pain out of the commute. Lathrop's internal traffic gets interrupted by trains. City is building an overpass over one main road.

Children attend Manteca Unified district schools. Sample rankings, state comparison, Lathrop Elementary, 30th to 50th percentile. New elementary school (Widmer). Teens attend Manteca high schools. District is buying land for more schools.

City runs activities for kids and adults. Boys and Girls Club. Several town festivals. New skate park.

Zero homicides in 2004, 2003, 2002, 2001, 2000, 1999. Sharpe Army Depot, outside Lathrop, employs about 1,200. Chamber of commerce (209) 858-4486.

LIVINGSTON

FARM TOWN that straddles Highway 99. Population 12,344. Old housing and the downtown are located south of the highway, much of the new housing to the north.

Median age of residents is 25. Under 18 years make up 38 percent of town; over 55 years, 13 percent. Another Valley town with scads of kids.

Livingston got its start in 1871 when the Central Pacific erected a rail bridge over the Merced River. A town followed. Livingston, named after a 19th century explorer of Africa, is growing but retains its small-town flavor. In the 1990s, the town increased its housing stock by 800 units and its population by 3,300.

Children attend the schools of the Livingston Elementary District, then move up to Livingston High, located in town but part of the Merced High School District. The elementary district enrolls about 2,400 students, the high school 1,100.

Scores in the elementary schools, state comparison, land generally below the 30th percentile. The high school scores in the 40th to 60th percentile. Nice-looking high school. Brick buildings. Pleasingly landscaped. Front lawn planted with trees and grass; inviting for lunch.

Highway 99 and a rail line pinch off the downtown from the rest of Livingston. The downtown has its shops and government buildings — city hall, library, community center, rec center, museum. And at its periphery, the downtown has some new housing. But clearly the downtown has not taken hold as a vibrant center, a problem not only for Livingston but for many towns. Old downtowns, built around the rail depot, have trouble adjusting to suburbia, which generally places shopping at freeway exits.

About a half dozen parks, including large sports park. Yamboree Festival with Sweet Potato Bake-Off at Memorial Park. Merced County grows a lot of yams. Livingston calls itself the "Sweet Potato Capital of California." Annual Sikh parade. Lighted soccer field. Town swimming pool. Typical sports.

Zero homicides in 2004, 2003, one in 2002, zero in 2001, one each in 2000 and 1999. Zero in 1998. Police headquarters is one of newest buildings in the downtown — tile roof, blue walls, lots of blue.

In 2005, Livingston tallied 2,874 housing units, of which 2,247 were single homes, 80 single-attached, 511 condos or apartments and 36 mobile homes. Bungalows and cottages near the old town. The rest runs to suburban models. The older housing, in parts, looks somewhat faded, the new, quite presentable and sometimes large (four-bedroom). Nothing fancy.

To the west of Livingston is a bit of fancy, the Hilmar Cheese Company in the hamlet of Hilmar. The company designed its plant along the lines of a Swiss chalet with turrets and, for contrast, planted the lawn with palm trees. Viewing room allows you to see how cheese is made. Store will sell you cheeses. Farmers in the region also raise grapes and chickens. Two of the largest firms in Livingston are Foster Poultry Farms, about 3,900 employees, and Gallo Vineyards, 1,000 employees.

Livingston anticipates that much of its growth will come from the suburban spillover.

Rare for a small town, Livingston supplies its own power.

Chamber of commerce (209) 394-8600.

Home Price Sampler from Classified Ads

Merced County
Atwater
•4BR/2BA, patio, $420,000
•4BR/3BA, gated, $450,000
Livingston
•4BR/3BA, near frwy., $410,000
•2BR/1BA, fixer, $265,000
Merced
•4BR/2.5BA, jacuzzi, $510,000
•3BR/2BA, pool, $439,000
•3BR/2BA, new appl., $278,000

San Joaquin County
Escalon
•4BR/3BA, 4 car gar., $520,000
•3BR/2BA, den, $505,000
Lathrop
•4BR/2.5BA, huge bckyrd., $455,000
•2BR/1BA, $265,000
Lodi
•3BR/2BA, garden, $369,000
•3BR/2BA, new tile, $400,000
Manteca
•3BR/2BA, remod. kit., $380,000
•4BR/2BA, pantry, $490,000
Ripon
•4BR/3BA, pool, $699,000
•4BR/3BA, cul-de-sac, $649,000

Stockton
•5BR/3.5BA, 2 story, $650,000
•3BR/2BA, open flr. plan, $419,000
Tracy
•4BR/1BA, nr. schs., $410,000
•2BR/1BA, garage, $365,000

Stanislaus County
Ceres
•4BR/3BA, nice comm., $460,000
•4BR/2.5BA, new crpt., $375,000
Modesto
•3BR/2.5BA, vault. ceil., $390,000
•4BR/3BA, upgrades, $435,000
Oakdale
•3BR/2BA, pond, $395,000
•5BR/3BA, loft, $550,000
Newman
•4BR/3BA, tri level, $490,000
•5BR/3BA, brand new, $600,000
Patterson
•3BR/2BA, starter, $350,000
•3BR/2BA, craftsman style, $440,000
Turlock
•3BR/2BA, $369,000
•3BR/2BA, spa, $415,000

LODI

ONE OF THE PRETTIEST OLD-NEW TOWNS in California. Population 62,467. Great job of preserving and invigorating its downtown. Crime low-middling. School rankings a mix but some fairly high. The Lodi school district serves the region and parts of Stockton, and has structured its schools in an unusual way.

Lodi, located in San Joaquin County, straddles Highway 99. Interstate 5 is about six miles to the west. In driving miles, the city is about 90 miles east of San Francisco and 35 miles south of Sacramento.

Established as a village in 1869, Lodi was originally called Mokelumne Station, for nearby Mokelumne River But when other towns came up with similar names, residents changed name to Lodi. Local lore suggests that people were influenced by a popular race horse. Credence Clearwater Revival made the town mildly famous with the lyric, "Oh, Lord, stuck in Lodi again."

If you're shopping for a home or apartment, getting stuck in Lodi would not be a bad choice.

A rail depot and a supply town for a farming region, Lodi incorporated as a legal city in 1906 and by 1940 had a population of 11,000. In the 1940s, Lodi increased its population by 2,700 and in the 1950s got its first injection of modern suburbia, 6,500 more residents.

In the 1960s and 1970s, Lodi increased its population, by 13,000, and in the 1980s went all out for development, taking on another 16,000 residents. In the 1990s, Lodi boosted its housing stock by about 2,700 units and its number of residents by 6,000.

In 2005, the town tallied 22,762 housing units, of which 14,572 were single homes, 1,464 single-attached, 6,262 condos or apartments and 464 mobile homes. Median age of residents is 34. Kids under 18 comprise 28 percent of town; over 55 years, 22 percent. Rounded demographics.

The growth numbers suggest a development pattern that shows up in many farm towns. Village turns into hamlet, then to town, then to regional city, development boosted by the railroad, around which the town is designed. Enter suburbia, oriented around the car. Freeways pull the traffic to the access ramps. Small shops in downtown can't compete against large supermarkets, malls and discount stores, which are located at the freeway ramps.

Downtowns die despite efforts of residents to preserve past and inject some life into fading business sector. Lodi somehow beat the odds. It has an old-style, yet vibrant downtown, a mix of specialty stores, restaurants, coffee and antique shops, half dozen bookstores, insurance and lawyer offices and so on. The old street lights and much of the old town atmosphere have been retained or restored. Nothing is falling down or looking like it's on its last legs.

Just as important, the neighborhoods around the downtown did not fall into ruin. The neighborhoods to the north and the south are actually low-income sections. The cottages and bungalow are old and in places show their age but many have been repaired and kept in reasonably good shape.

The neighborhood to the immediate east is old and upscale, meticulous care, tall and full trees, groomed lawns, homes in great condition, a lovely area Some older neighborhoods being rejuvenated by influx of young families.

Many old towns try to pull this off; many fail. Because it's hard. It takes energy, dedication, money, code enforcement, patience, cleverness and the willingness to work through the inevitable disagreements. And time, a long time. It's something that you always have to work at. For strangers moving into Lodi, the fact that the town has pulled this off suggests stability and interest in beauty, charm and a friendly town life (if you're not visitor friendly, few people will shop the downtown.)

Highway 99 runs down the east side of the downtown and this helps. Downtown shoppers have quick access to the freeway. Lodi does have its large stores — Target, Wal-Mart, Staples — but they are located on Kettleman Lane, on the southwest side, about two miles from the freeway. More stores are on the way in this section.

The downtown is still served by railroad, which sustains warehouses and food processing plants. In 2002, Amtrak started service to Lodi.

Moving out from the old town, suburban tract homes present themselves. The further you move out, the newer they get. On its south side, Lodi built for the middle class, generally three-bedroom homes. On the west side, three-bedroom homes can also be found but this section also includes four-bedroom and larger homes and the quality notches up. One neighborhood near Kettleman Lane approaches executive class, large homes with custom touches.

One homicide in 2004, 2003, four in 2002, one in 2001, zero in 2000, 1999 and 1998. Counts for previous years are zero, three, three, two and two.

Children attend schools in the Lodi Unified District, enrollment about 26,000. Lodi has schools that score way below the 50th percentile but it also has schools that land in the middle and a few in the 70th and 80th percentiles. The scores reflect the demographics of the town and region: low, middle and high income.

In Stockton, the Lodi district runs a gifted school, Elkhorn, grades three to eight, enrollment about 300. On state comparisons, the school, which is open to all high-I.Q. kids in the Lodi district, scores in the 99th percentile, one of the very tops in the state. Many schools run gifted programs, very few districts operate an entire school for gifted students. They often arouse the enmity and jealously of those excluded and are perceived as the prep school for the college bound. School districts reluctantly embrace them because, usually, parents of the high scoring are vocal and active and argue that the other schools do not meet the needs of their children. This is one way to satisfy diverse interests.

In 2002, Lodi voters approved a $109 million school bond to renovate and build schools and upgrade their facilities (better wiring, etc.). In recent years, the district has built in Lodi two elementaries and a middle school. About a half-dozen schools run on a year-round schedule, which the district is phasing out (2006).

In amusements and civic ornaments, Lodi does unusually well. Every neighborhood is equipped with a large park. The city boasts 26 parks, a lot for a city this size. The Mokelumne River feeds water into Lake Lodi — swimming, boating, fishing. Nature trail along river. Japanese garden. One park has swimming pools and a slide. Another roller hockey. Soccer, baseball, cheerleading, gymnastics, tumbling, football, softball — some of the sports and activities. Ballet, modeling, tap dance, manners for kids. After-school programs. Mother's Day Breakfast, Father's Day Lunch. Library with summer reading program. Performing arts center. Wine country. About 10 wineries in the region. Among local or regional festivals: Spring wine show, Cabaret Concert Series, Grape Festival and Harvest Fair, Asparagus Festival, Italian Festa, Cherry Blossom Festival, and — why not? — the Sandhill Crane Festival. Street fairs. Mucho dolce vita!

Community center. Seniors center. Skating rink. Nature center. Snake zoo (serpentarium), museum. Farmers market. Golf course. Orchards, vineyards and cultivated fields at city's edge. For the barbecue set, a meat firm specializing in hot dogs moved to area in 2002.

The drawbacks: while it's a very long way to the Bay Area, the Sacramento commute is a painful but endurable drive in Highway 99. If you want to live in a charming town, complete with a clock tower, the drive may be worth it. Dial-a-Ride buses transport residents around town.

Chamber of commerce (209) 367-7840.

Miscellaneous:

• Wal-Mart wants to build a giant store. Many opposed; matter in courts.

LOS BAÑOS

ONE OF THE KEY TOWNS if you are commuting to Santa Clara County. Los Baños is split by Highway 152, which snakes over the Diablo Range and drops into Gilroy, the southernmost town in Santa Clara County. In driving distance, Los Baños, 75-80 miles to San Jose, is one of the closest Merced County towns to Silicon Valley. Old timers use the Spanish pronunciation — Los Ban Yos. Newcomers vary between the correct pronunciation and Los Ban os.

Los Baños is a mix of old and new. Much of the new is very new. When home prices soared in Silicon Valley in the 1990s, Los Baños, which was already attracting commuters, became much more popular.

Los Baños started the 1990s with 14,519 residents and finished with 25,869, an increase of about 78 percent. The state in its 2005 estimate put the population at 32,380; the town keeps growing. In the 1990s, the city increased its housing stock by about 3,000 units, almost every one a single detached home.

But there are bumps in the road. Voters have twice rejected bonds to build schools, the second ballot in 2005 falling short by less than 1 percent. No doubt another try will be made. In the meantime, developers are putting up the money to build some schools and other housing projects are being delayed until funds show up.

In 2005, the state counted 10,039 housing units, of which 8,271 were single homes, 263 single-attached, 1,228 condos or apartments and 277 mobile homes.

Los Baños has a meandering past. A Spanish padre, pleased and refreshed by the clear waters of the local ponds, gave the region its name, which translates "The Baths." In the late 1800s, when pioneers were settling the area, Gustave Kreyenhagen, from Germany, opened a general store, the only one in the region. He soon concluded that he would do more business if he moved three miles east to a road junction. Move he did, taking his building with him. Then the people who owned the land fenced it off, including the roads. Kreyenhagen, who was also the postmaster, moved again, 12 miles to the west, and opened a store with a post office, address Los Baños. A small town grew up around the store-post office. In 1889, the railroad arrived, its line running five miles to the east. Kreyenhagen and apparently just about everyone else in town packed up Los Baños and moved it to the rail line.

Los Baños purred along as a farm town until about 1980, when the population took off. This said, it remains a farm town at heart. Step outside the new subdivisions and the crops are planted row upon row, for miles.

Education by the Los Baños Unified School District, enrollment about 7,500 and growing. Academic rankings generally fall below the 40th percentile but probably will rise as the town becomes more suburban middle class. One school is already scoring in the 70th and 80th percentiles. The district passed a bond in 1995 to build a junior high. Merced Community College runs a branch campus in Los Baños. One Catholic school, one Seventh-Day Adventist.

Library, about 30 parks and playgrounds, including large sports park on north side and a fairgrounds park. As the new neighborhoods come in, the city is inserting small parks. Usual sports. One of the pluses of an old city is that it has had time to build its parks and develop its sports and recreation programs. Skate park. Almost every park has a jungle gym; new homes usually mean young families and many kids.

Yosemite close by. Many large parks in the region. Town museum.

Shopping center with Wal-Mart. Los Baños also has a medical center and a variety of stores and restaurants, including a Starbucks.

As for the housing, it is handsomely done but not fancy in the styles of modern suburbia: recessed lighting, walk-in closets, large kitchens, living rooms designed around entertainment (TV-video) centers, tile roofs, creamy stucco sides. Most of the new stuff is found on the outskirts. Los Baños has been building suburbia for about 30 years and offers some variety in housing styles. Some of the new homes have three-car garages.

Cottages, bungalows and older housing can be found around downtown, near Seventh Street and Pacheco Boulevard. Some of the older homes show their age. The older streets are lined with trees. The new tracts, in many instances, pop two or three small trees on the front lawn and that's it. Very little in way of professional landscaping; do-it-yourself town.

Rail line goes through center of town. Small airport on the west side. Check out noise.

Zero homicides in 2004, 003, 2002, 2001, 2000, and one in 1999. Counts for previous years are 1, 2, 0, 1 and 0. Los Baños has its own police department.

The future: Highway 152 is being widened and improved piece by piece but the commute is still going to be a horror. But for many an endurable horror.

Chamber of commerce (209) 826-2495.

MANTECA

BEDROOM COMMUNITY located 25-30 miles east of Livermore in San Joaquin County. Population 61,927. Frequently mentioned in the same breath as Tracy, as in the commute to "Tracy-Manteca." Many new homes, more on the way.

Manteca is about 10 miles east of Tracy. As I-580 pulls east out of Tracy, it disappears into Interstate 5 and spins off Highway 120, the main road to Manteca (about five miles to the downtown.) Mileage figures are approximations. One part of Manteca, empty now, comes within a few miles of Tracy.

Both Tracy and Manteca caught their suburban growth about the same time, mainly the 1980s and the 1990s. Both are reasonable commutes to Livermore-Pleasanton-Dublin-San Ramon, an area that has many high-tech businesses.

Homes in Manteca probably sell for a little less than homes in Tracy. The extra commute miles account for the difference. In housing styles, both embraced suburban models, three and four bedrooms, one and two stories. A few streets in Manteca jump way up scale, mansions.

In the 1980s, Manteca built about 3,300 single homes and 1,400 apartments or condos. In the 1990s, the city pretty much stayed with single homes, building 2,300 of them and about 250 apartments or condos (state figures).

In 2005, the state tallied 20,697 housing units, of which 15,569 were single homes, 739 single attached, 3,520 multiples, and 869 mobiles.

Suburbia continues to boom but there's a lot of country feeling. Orchards and farms on the outskirts. Food processing plants located in the region.

As the town has grown, it has added necessities, amenities and stores, including Wal-Mart, Mervyns and Home Depot. Doctors Hospital-Manteca. Kaiser Permanente, 8.2 million members strong, purchased St. Dominic's hospital. Manteca is also building business parks, the better to diversify the local economy and create local jobs. Among the biggest, Spreckels with about 1 million square feet. The town has some electronic firms and hopes to attract more high-tech.

City is spending $3.5 million for downtown facelift and in a variety of ways is trying to revive the section and make it more attractive for shoppers.

Two homicides each in 2004, 2003 and 2002, one in 2001, two in 2000, zero in 1999 and 1998. The counts for the previous years are three, three, two, zero, one, three, one, one, two, five, two and two. Curfew to discourage juvenile crime. Overall crime rate is low.

Manteca Unified School District enrolls about 21,600 students and includes students from Lathrop, French Camp and communities near Stockton, demographically a real mix. Scores range from the 30th to the 70th percentile (state comparison). Many schools are new (eight opened since 1994). In 2004 voters approved a $66 million bond for new elementary, middle and high schools plus repairs and renovations of existing campuses. In 2005, the district was purchasing more land. But in some neighborhoods, enrollments are slipping. This might force changes in attendance boundaries.

About three dozen parks. Every neighborhood has at least one park and most have several. Some are linear parks, good for jogging and strolling. Public golf course. Many activities for kids and adults — bowling, soccer, basketball, baseball, gymnastics, softball. Three public swimming pools. Boys and Girls Club. Garden club. Seniors center. Great Pumpkin Festival. Farmers market. Delta nearby: fishing, boating, swimming. Yosemite and ski slopes a few hours to the east. Just outside city limits, vines and orchards and food stands, fresh produce.

Fellow by the name of Joshua Cowell owned much of the downtown in the late 1800s. At that time, the town was called Cowell Station. Cowell had a brother who owned a lot of land south of Tracy at a place also called Cowell Station. When the railroad came to region, the rail men and the local farmers decided to call Joshua's holdings Monteca, which is Spanish for sweet butter. When the railroad issued its first tickets, it spelled the name Manteca — Spanish for lard. This could happen only in the Untied Stotes.

Altamont Commuter Express runs commute trains from Stockton to Pleasanton to San Jose, with a stop in Manteca. Good way to beat the freeway traffic, which is getting congested.

Residents are muttering about tighter restrictions on pace of development. Many homes coming to region, including thousands at Lathrop.

City and sewage capacity are limiting new housing to about 850 units a year. Manteca is prodding developers to put in more playing fields, street lights and walking trails, and improve designs (example, fewer garage doors facing street). Developers pay fees — bill passed to home buyers — to add cops and schools. Chamber of commerce (209) 823-6121.

• St. Paul Methodist Church is building a labyrinth, a "quiet prayer walk."

• Highway 90-Highway 120, a bottleneck, is being overhauled.

• City in 2005 gave OK to construction of sports complex with six playing fields, volleyball courts, indoor soccer and skating, two restaurants.

MERCED

LARGEST AND MOST POPULOUS CITY in Merced County. In 2005, bursting with pride, Merced opened a University of California campus — a big deal.

UCs are research and educational institutions and usually — not always — increase the property values and prosperity of their home towns and regions. They also bring in plays, dance, the arts, a multitude of cultural activities and interesting and sometimes argumentative people who don't hesitate to stand up for their values. Merced is a quiet and conservative town. Should be interesting.

Population 73,610. Well-developed old town, in some parts charming. Merced also has many new homes. In the last two decades, the town has increased its population by about 75 percent.

Roads and rails and proximity to Yosemite and the Mother Lode (gold) made Merced the foremost city in the county. It came into existence when the railroad (Central Pacific) laid down its line and simply by this action dictated the location of a town. Santa Fe later routed its line through Merced. Complementing the rails, three highways — 99, 140, 59 — meet in Merced.

In 1900, the city counted 2,000 residents, in 1950, it tallied 15,000. Between 1950 and 1970, Merced added only 7,500 residents. Then it took off. In the 1970s, its population shot up by 14,000; in the 1980s, by 20,000. In the 1990s, Merced built 3,300 housing units, most of them single homes, and increased its population by 7,200. Median age of residents is 28. Kids under 18 comprise 35 percent of town; over 55 years, 15 percent. Young families like new and affordable housing. Merced has many young families.

Although people commute from Merced, it probably will not turn into a commute city to the Bay Area. Too long a haul. Interstate 5 is a good 30 miles to the west. Highway 99, the other main route, angles east as it travels down the Central Valley. San Jose is 115 miles to the west, San Francisco 128 miles to the northwest. San Ramon or Dublin or Pleasanton or Livermore — these cities are do-able for people with a good grip on their sanity.

Merced built out from its downtown. The oldest homes are in the center. A short distance out, modern suburbia, circa 1950, starts to kick in, then the 1960s and 1970s housing. The newest homes can generally be found on the periphery. Merced Community College is located on the north side, a nice plus for the town. Community colleges offer classes and activities for a low fee. It's easy to tap into the schedules and use their facilities. Merced is the seat of the county, where most of the courts and administrative offices are located. When you combine the community college with the county government with city hall with the school district (and now with the UC), government becomes a major and reliable employer, a good foundation for the city's economy. Tourism (Yosemite) and the farms of the region also pump in the dollars.

Before air conditioning, valley towns planted their own air conditioning, shade trees. They line many of the streets in the older part of town and please the eye. Merced has its rundown blocks but many of the older streets are well-maintained. The new housing follows tract designs and offers a mix of three- and four-bedroom homes. In 2005, the city counted 24,757 housing units: 15,218 single homes, 944 single-attached, 7,887 condos or apartments and 708 mobile homes.

Merced is a rounded town; it does a better job on stores and services than the smaller cities in the region. It has a mall (Sears, Penneys) near Highway 99 and it has the large discount stores, including a Wal-Mart, a Costco and a Circuit City. Also a Target, a Lowe's, a Home Depot, Barnes and Noble and Mervyns.

Many of these stores take business from the downtown, which the city has spruced up with street lights and brick crosswalks. Old movie house built in the Spanish Revival style, the Merced, has been divided into multiple screens. New movie house and shops recently opened. Main Street is just four blocks north of Highway 99 and this helps. Farmers' market. Mix of restaurants, fast food to white table cloth — Mandarin, Thai, Hunan, Japanese, Mexican, Italian; steak and seafood. Delis, coffee and espresso places; Starbucks. Government employees also help sustain the downtown, which has historic buildings. These include the Tioga Hotel and a courthouse designed in 1875 in the Italianate style. Amtrak station.

Twelve homicides in 2004, seven in 2003, six in 2002. Counts for the previous years are 2, 3, 5, 5, 5, 3, 2 and 3.

Children attend schools of Merced Elementary District then move up to the Merced High School District. Many of the elementary schools are scoring below the 40th percentile. Merced High and Golden Valley High score in the 50th and 60th percentiles. Both the high school and the elementary district have passed renovation-construction bonds. In 2005, another elementary school was under construction. The elementary district won a grant of $1,145,000 to help the kids become better readers.

Library, about two dozen parks and playgrounds. Usual sports and activities. Zoo. Youth sports complex. Three public pools. Tennis courts. Bike trails. Farm museum. Lake Yosemite to the east of town; boating, swimming, fishing, canoeing, skiing. About 85 miles to Yosemite, a drive of 1.5 hours. First-class skiing in winter. County fair. City rec department sponsors activities.

Mercy Hospital and county medical center. Fairly large airport on the west side. Check out plane noise and train whistles. Farms start right at the city's border. Plenty of fruits and fresh vegetables. Chamber of commerce (209) 384-7092.

• Merced Airport expanding to handle increases in business air travel.

• The university isd situated on the northeast side of town — looks raw, buildings popping up in the corn fields. The first class started with 1,000 students. Campus one day to hold 20,000. Plans call for construction of a large community around the campus.

• Downtown Merced, south of Highway 99, favors 1950s and 1960s tract housing, a few let go, many well maintained, low to middle income. Some fixing up. Wide streets give feel of spaciousness. Fairgrounds.

Downtown, north of Highway 99, runs to much older homes, cottages and bungalows, historic, a fair number renovated into offices but most still used as homes. Streets lined with shade trees. Close to restaurants, coffee shops and downtown ornaments. As you move north (toward Applegate Park and Bear Creek Road), the homes grow into large 1960s plus ranchers, professionally landscaped, a handsome and somewhat hidden neighborhood.

• In many towns, the freeways get routed well away from — and kill — the downtown. In Merced, Highway 99 flows right through it, with the result that the downtown has managed to attract some large stores, foremost the Costco. This brings in shoppers and street traffic that helps the other stores. One impediment: the trains sometime tie up traffic.

• New suburbia takes over north of the downtown, about Olive Avenue, and at the edges. Middle and upper-middle homes, many running to two stories, four to six bedrooms. If you want space, these homes, for a California reasonable price, deliver. Here and there some clusters of homes take a leap up market. Merced also has pockets of unincorporated land that run to country relaxed; little or no code enforcement.

• Plenty of room for more homes. Continuous building. The new subdivisions will not show up on some maps but development signs will be posted around town.

• UCs, as engines of local prosperity, are tricky devils. They provide thousands of jobs and through their purchases pump millions into their communities. Some UCs — Irvine, San Diego — have enormously benefitted their home towns and counties. But UCs also bring in people who are often anti-growth or have aesthetic feelings that make construction difficult and expensive. UC Santa Cruz is perhaps the best example. At least one UC made a mess of planning — Santa Barbara and its tacky (but affordable) student quarter, Isla Vista. Will Merced and the county government, which politically controls the land around the UC, do it right? Tune in.

MODESTO

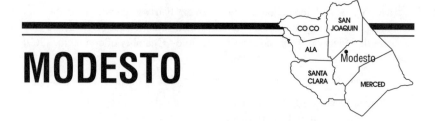

LARGEST CITY IN STANISLAUS COUNTY and one of the most popular destinations for Bay Area commuters. Population 207,634. Many new homes and more on the way. Modesto has its luxury homes but the great majority of its housing is priced for the middle class.

In 2001, voters passed bonds to build more high schools and renovate elementary schools. Modesto is also upgrading its schools; for example, adding math and science wings.

Salida, about 13,000 people, is an unincorporated community on the northwest side of Modesto. More on Salida after Modesto.

Modesto school rankings low, middle and high. Behind these scores is a city that demographically is divided between rural and modern suburban but moving toward the latter.

Half-dozen elementary school districts: Modesto Elementary, about 18,500 students, Empire, 4,000, Hart-Ransom, 1,000 students, Paradise, 200, Stanislaus, 3,300, and Sylvan Elementary, 7,700 students. All advance their students, at the ninth grade, to the schools of the Modesto high school district, 15,000.

These districts have either passed bonds or imposed developer fees or both to finance the construction of new schools. More schools will be opened as homes are built and some schools might be closed. Or their attendance zones might be changed. Tracts built about 20 years came with a lot of students. The students have moved on, their parents, in many instances, have stayed put and stopped having children — declining enrollments.

Many schools run year-round schedules, a way to handle crowding. Check schools before you buy; these schedules sometimes make child care difficult.

Modesto homicides: Nineteen in 2004. For previous years: 17, 5, 17, 3, 5, 6, 17, 12, 13 and 12. For a middle-class suburb, Americana, 19 is a little high.

Driving distances: 90 miles to San Francisco, 75 to Sacramento, 40-50 miles to Livermore-Pleasanton, 75 plus miles to Silicon Valley cities. Highway 99 divides the town and leads up to Manteca, I-5 and Stockton. Highway 132 shortcuts across the valley floor to Interstate 580. If you work in the East Bay, an endurable commute; if Fremont-San Jose, pushing it; if Mountain View, or San Francisco, psychiatric help may be in order but probably many do it.

The town came to life in the 1870s when the Southern Pacific steamed in and built a depot. The rail people wanted to name the town Ralston, after one of the fabulous speculators of the era, William Ralston. He declined the honor, an act of modesty. Modesto is Spanish for modest. In 1875, Ralston's bank failed. He often swam in San Francisco Bay. His body was recovered, a suspected suicide but he may have accidentally drowned.

Modesto thrived as an agricultural center and greeted 1900 with about 2,000 residents. By 1930, the city had blossomed to almost 14,000 residents. In the 1930s, after Prohibition ended, Julio and Ernest Gallo, brothers who had learned their craft in their father's vineyard, brought out their first vintage and founded one of the most successful wine companies in the world. Gallo is headquartered in Modesto and has done much for the prosperity of the region.

Modesto hit 1950 with 17,389 residents and began a period of rapid growth. By 1960, population had doubled to 36,585 and by 1970, it had reached 61,712. By 1980, the number of residents stood at 106,963. The 1990 census counted 164,730 people. In the 1990s, Modesto added about 6,800 residential units and increased its population by 24,000. Median age of residents is 33. Kids under 18 make up 30 percent of residents. Translation: family town In 2005, the city counted 72,615 housing units, 51,090 single homes, 4,010 single-attached, 15,524 condos or apartments and 1,991 mobiles.

Before suburbia kicked in, Modesto was a compact city with a downtown bordered by low, middle and high-income neighborhoods. As the tracts arrived, they were appended to the existing housing. The farther you move out from the downtown, the newer it gets — with exceptions. Much of the land west of Highway 99, and close to the downtown, did not develop until the 1980s.

The first post World War II tracts followed the standard models of the 1950s and 1960s — three-bedroom, two bath, family room. About the 1970s, many homes notched up to a second story and a fourth bedroom. Lot sizes shrunk. In the 1990s, a market for large, opulent homes blossomed. Modesto has some on its north side. If you want small and modest and old, Modesto can deliver. If you want old affluence and new affluence, it's there. The downtown has some lovely streets.

Modesto is the Stanislaus county seat and its downtown houses city, county, state and federal agencies with thousands of workers. Highway 99 splits the downtown. Many private firms have downtown offices. Helps support restaurants, shops. The downtown has a hospital and medical offices and a high-rise hotel near a movie complex. But if strong, the downtown is not as dominant as it used to be. The downtown is on the west side, much of the housing was built toward the east. With the housing came large neighborhood shopping centers. About five miles north of the downtown, along Highway 99, a regional mall (Vintage Faire) was built and beyond the mall the large discount stores — Costco, Wal-Mart, Home Depot, etc. — were erected.

Kaiser Permanente has expanded its medical facilities and on the north side is building a $500 million medical center with the first phase to open in 2007.

Modesto has a night life, gourmet restaurants, delis and coffee shops, giant bookstores (Borders and a Barnes and Noble), a Trader Joe's and a lot to do. Two large community college campuses and an airport with shuttle flights to San Francisco International. All neighborhoods have at least one park (which often adjoins a school). Skate park. Four golf courses. Some parks have swimming pools. Little theater, musicals, opera, jazz concerts, ballet, children's theater. Usual sports — soccer, softball, football, baseball, etc.— and many activities for kids and adults. Yosemite, King's Canyon, winter skiing within two to three hours. Chamber of commerce (209) 577-5757.

• In the downtown an iron arch with electric lights proclaims: "Modesto: Water, Wealth, Contentment, Health." That nostalgic classic, "American Graffiti" was shot in Modesto.

• Under construction in 2005: the Gallo Center for the Arts. Includes two theaters: one 1,200 seats, the other, 400. Plays, symphoies, musicals, cultural,business, and community events. Scheduled to open in 2007.

• Another high school is opening on the north side.

• Modesto is criss-crossed with four-lane arterials that help greatly with getting around the town. The big problem is getting over to Interstate 580, the road to the jobs of the Bay Area. Many improvements have been made to the region's roads but they have been somewhat nullified by the addition of more vehicles. Most people take Highway 132, one lane in each direction with occasional turnouts. If Highway 132 moves, fine. If it gets a fender bender or a major accident, not fine. One consolation: a barbecue stand has opened along the highway. If you're late and don't feel like cooking, you have options.

•Salida, pronounced sa lie da, is split by Highway 99. Almost all the old housing is located west of the highway, almost all the new, east of the highway. The exceptions, as usual in these towns, is the periphery. Some new or fairly new homes have been built on the west side, next to farm fields. On the east (new) side, construction started probably in late 1960s and has not stopped. Drive Sisk Road and the Sun Ridge and Colony tracts, which were built as planned communities maintained to some extent by the homeowner associa-tions. Well kept. Many two-story homes. Playing fields at Sisk Elementary School. Large Christian high school. Stores and coffee at the freeway along with a small amusement park (many video games.) On the west side, off of Broadway, a small downtown with a library, post office and a variety of stores. Some small homes blend into the tract models, two and three bedrooms, of the 1960s and 1950s and with in-filling — always going on — later models. Elementary schools run by the Salida district, kindergarten to 8th. Most of the kids move up to Davis High School in Modesto.

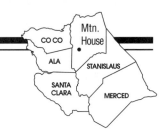

MOUNTAIN HOUSE

NEW TOWN in San Joaquin County, built from scratch, on Alameda County border, near Tracy. First homes offered in 2003. Master-planned community. Special attention paid to moving traffic quickly to freeways. Plans calls for 16,000 housing units, 44,000 people, over 20-40 years. Includes 12 schools, shopping centers, parks, recreational facilities and commercial space. Development has own wastewater treatment. Homes are wired for high-speed internet.

The Bay Area is separated from the Central Valley by a range of hills and mountains, notched by the Altamont Pass. Interstate 580 travels through the Altamont. When home prices soared in the Bay Area and buildable land became scarce, developers took to the Central Valley, foremost to Tracy, the first town east of the Altamont Pass. Over the past 20 years, Tracy and many Central Valley towns boomed with residential construction. Mountain House is located just before Tracy, a big reason why it is expected to blossom quickly. Compared to the other Central Valley towns, Mountain House has the shortest commute to the East Bay and Silicon Valley.

Take I-580 to I-205 to the San Joaquin county line and look north for signs to Mountain House Road. Alameda County has a Mountain House school district and some maps will show Mountain House in Alameda County. Wrong.

Education by Lammersville Elementary District, which opened its first Mountain House school in 2004. New high school planned. Teens attend West High in Tracy, scores about the 50th percentile. Scores should increase as demographics change.

• Fire station opened in 2005. Eau-de-bovine (cow stink) abated. Low water pressure elevated. Start up problems.

• Small convenience store to be followed, once enough people have settled in, by a supermarket and a community swim center.

• Delta Community College to open a branch campus in Mountain House but as of late 2005, Tracy was trying to detour campus into its bailiwick.

• Developers have rules for aesthetics, including acceptable varieties of flowers in gardens. Local press scoffed at list, which excludes daffodils.

• Windmills in abundance in the nearby hills.

NEWMAN

FARM TOWN ADDING HOUSING. In the 1990s, Newman erected about 830 homes, not a lot but an increase of 38 percent in its housing stock. Population 9,134. Zero homicides between 2003 and 1999.

Located in Stanislaus County about five miles east of Interstate 5, which would seem to make Newman commute friendly. But it's too far south to be a good commute to the Bay Area, too far north to be good for Highway 152 and Silicon Valley. But, as arduous as the commutes are, some people are making them. The saving aspect is Interstate 5. It rarely congests and the CHP cuts slack, even on the 70 mph speed limit. In 2005, the town counted 2,756 housing units, of which 2,292 were single homes, 76 single-attached, 362 condos or apartments and 26 mobile homes. Median age 29. Kids under 18 make up 35 percent of Newman; over 55 years, 15 percent. Family town.

The old town, laid out on a grid, includes a library, a museum with farm implements, three of the town's five parks and municipal court. Highway 33, two-lanes, splits the town, running parallel to the train tracks (active). South of the downtown is a modern shopping center: Nob Hill Market, Rite Aid, deli, bakery. In 2001, Newman ripped up its downtown to make it more pedestrian oriented. Flower planters, benches, better lighting, slanted parking, new storm drains, landscaping, old-fashioned clock. Movie house converted into play house. In 2005, it staged "Grease." Translation: a town with energy. Chamber of commerce (209) 862-1000. Food processing plants — cheeses, turkeys, tomatoes — supply local jobs.

Most of the new housing has been erected east of the railroad tracks, around Barrington Park. Older tracts on the southwest side of town. Some pretty bungalows and small homes near the downtown. Shade trees. Retail stores now moving closer to new subdivisions.

City runs activities for kids and adults. Soccer, baseball, etc. Usual sports. Playing fields at schools. Annual fall festival. Farmers market. On summer days, moms fill the plastic wading pools on the lawn and let the kids frolic. High school has a plunge open to residents. The charms of a small town.

Children attend schools in the Newman-Crows Land Unified School District. In 2000, bond passed to build and renovate schools. New middle school; old one converted to elementary. Orestimba High, on state rankings, scores in the 60th percentile.

OAKDALE

SHIPPING-FARMING TOWN that's building commuter housing, a lot of it upscale. Straddles one of the main roads to Yosemite. Mountains in the background. Pretty setting. Population 17,439. State is building a bypass around town; this will cut traffic on local streets.

Oakdale came to life in the 1870s when the railroad arrived and over the next 100 years ambled along in rural obscurity, the population slowly rising. About 1980, the pace quickened and over the past 20 years Oakdale has increased its numbers by about 75 percent. Family town with retirees. In 2005, the town tallied 6,419 housing units: 4,803 single homes, 207 single-attached, 1,198 condos or apartments, 211 mobiles. Two homicides in 2004, zero in 2003 and 2002, one in 2001, 2000, 1999, 1998. Then zero, zero.

The oldest housing can be found in the downtown, which is laid out on a grid and bisected by Yosemite Avenue, the main thoroughfare, and by railroad tracks. Many shade trees, the homes small and modest but kept in good repair. As you move away from the downtown, suburban designs, some dating from the 1950s and 1960s, show themselves. Modern suburbia can be found along Maag Avenue in gentle hills on the east side, and on the west side of town. Just east of town is a golf course-country club and a neighborhood of ranchettes and custom mansions. Downtown overhauled. Old buildings gutted and converted to new uses; historic look retained. New stores, ice cream parlor and restaurants. Nicely done. In 2004 and 2005, Oakdale on its west side was erecting a large master-planned tract that jumped way up-market, well-appointed homes running 2,800 sf and higher. You could almost hear the town's demographics notching up (and this often raises school scores).

Annual rodeo. Cowboy museum. Stanislaus River borders the north side and forms little lakes to the east and west of Oakdale. Around the lakes large parks have been built. About 12 local parks, including sports park. Golf course. Library. Museum. Usual sports and activities, soccer, baseball, etc. Farmers' market. Annual antique show. Community pool. Movies. Two hours to Yosemite. Hershey plant. Annual chocolate festival. Food plants and business park. New business park. Small airport east of town. Local buses.

Oakdale Unified School District. In 2002, voters approved a $20 million bond to build elementary school, add classrooms and upgrade high school. On state rankings, high school is scoring in top 25th percentile. Chamber of commerce (209) 847-2244.

PATTERSON

HALF FARM TOWN, HALF SUBURB. Old town laid out in an interesting way. Population 16,158. Located in Stanislaus County about three miles east of Interstate 5. Popular with commuters to Bay Area.

In Patterson, five minutes and you're on the freeway and, if your luck holds, whizzing to work. Other valley towns have to drive long distances to the key freeways.

Patterson starkly illustrates the rapidly changing nature of many Valley towns. Almost all the new tracts are being built on west side. The new stuff is so spanking, shiny new that it makes old Patterson look like a different town.

In 1909, Thomas Patterson, nephew of pioneer, decided to build one of the first planned towns in California. For his inspiration, he chose Washington D.C. Patterson's main streets spoke out from a downtown hub or circle, within which are the town hall, a museum, a library, churches, a park and stores. Streets have been planted with palm, eucalyptus and sycamore. Patterson has stayed with roundabouts or traffic circles; it has six.

One of the town main streets is Las Palmas Avenue. It is lined on both sides with thick, old and half dead (in appearance) palm trees. When Las Palmas hits the city limits on the east side, the palms keep going for miles. The town, in its new subdivisions, has tried to stay with the palm motif.

In many ways, a typical farm town going suburb, Patterson nonetheless has a quirky kind of charm. It's different.

In the 1990s, Patterson built 560 single homes and increased its population by 2,300. And it's been building ever since.

Although suburbia is on the march, Patterson retains much of its farming and calls itself "The Apricot Capital of the World."

In 2005, the town counted 4,484 housing units, of which 3,952 were single homes, 190 single-attached, 214 condos or apartments and 128 mobiles. Median age of residents is 28. Kids under 18 make up 36 percent of town; over 55 years, 13 percent. Family burg; lot of kids.

Highway 33 and the railroad splits the town. East of the highway the housing runs to farm cottages and suburbia. In the center, the bungalows and cottages of the early 20th century. Moving west, more modern housing and at the west edge the new tracts, with many of the with streets named after birds, eagle, osprey, swan, etc.

Also new stores, supermarket, deli, bakery, mix of stores, some restaurants. And two large new schools with fields and facilities shared by the community. Another elementary is to be built.

Housing is aimed at middle and middle plus. Homes are big (two story, four bedrooms) but not fancy. Landscaping left to homeowners. Clean. Maintenance by homeowner association. Sidewalks for evening strolls.

Zero homicides in 2004, 2003, 2002, 2001 and 2000, three in 1999. Overall crime rate low. Protection by sheriff's deputies; substation in town.

Education by Patterson Unified School District, enrollment 4,000. Scores are landing generally in the 30th to 50th percentile. These scores should come up as the town turns more suburban. In 1996, district passed a $3 million bond to upgrade schools. Catholic school enrolls about 200.

Three community parks, two neighborhood parks. More coming with new homes. Tot lots. Rec department runs sports and activities for kids and adults. Among offerings soccer, basketball, arts and crafts, gymnastics, coed volleyball for adults. Chamber of commerce fax number: (209) 892-2821.

• Long's Drug stores building a giant warehouse near freeway. Will employ 375-400. Open in 2006.

• At the freeway, Patterson has a grand collection of fast-food joints (and gas stations and at least one hotel). The restaurants were built for I-5 travelers but can be enjoyed by all.

RIPON

SMALL TOWN MOVING from farming to suburbia. Population 13,241. Ripon has been building custom upscale homes near golf courses on its east and west sides. This has pushed up its demographics and its school scores. Zero homicides in 2004, one in 2003, zero from 2002 to 1999.

Between 2000 and 2004, the town increased its population by 17 percent. The city, partially bordered by the Stanislaus River, is limiting home construction to about 215 units a year and zoning for high-quality homes. Downtown streets have older small homes, well maintained and shaded by many trees. Highway 99 splits Ripon, which is located between Modesto and Manteca. This makes for an endurable commute to Livermore-Pleasanton. In the 1990s, Ripon, a San Joaquin County city, increased its population by 3,000 and erected 1,000 housing units, almost all single homes.

The downtown has kept much of the old-town flavor — shops, hardware, plumbing, appliances, drug store, an athletic club, restaurants and sandwich-diners. The city, through redevelopment, has installed decorative lights and sidewalks. Modern shopping center with supermarket near city hall.

The Stanislaus River winds around the south and east sides of Ripon. At each side, golf courses surrounded by custom homes have been developed. About six parks. Skate park. Community center. Seniors center. Programs for kids and adults. City is building 60-acre sports park with nine soccer fields, two baseball diamonds, four softball fields and a dog run.

In 2005, the town tallied 4,371 housing units, of which 3,759 were single homes, 136 single-attached, 467 condos or apartments and 9 mobile homes. Median age of residents is 34. Kids under 18 make up 32 percent of town; over 55 years, 18 percent. Family town.

Education by the Ripon Unified School District, enrollment 2,600. Academic rankings, on a state comparison, are landing in the 70th to 90th percentile. School superintendent credits good job by teachers, small classes and small schools. In 2002, voters approved a $10 million bond to build another elementary school and renovate the high school. Ripon has a large Christian school with a stadium.

Man from Ripon, England, immigrated to a place in Wisconsin and called it Ripon. A man from Ripon, Wisconsin, came to California and named his new home Ripon. How riponly logical! Chamber of commerce (209) 599-7519.

RIVERBANK

LOCATED ABOUT THREE MILES NORTH of Modesto on the banks of the Stanislaus River. Population 19,988. Riverbank's history can be told through its downtown names: Atchinson Street, Topeka Street, Sante Fe Street. The town started as a ferry station, then blossomed as rail depot and farm town. Trains still roll through the heart of Riverbank.

Incorporated as a city in 1922, Riverbank grew slowly and by 1980 counted 5,695 inhabitants. In the 1980s, it added about 2,800 residents and in the last decade, about 6,000. In the 1990s, Riverbank built about 1,800 single homes. The north side of town overlooks the Stanislaus. In this section, on the west side, Riverbank has encouraged custom and upscale tract housing. Directly south of Patterson Road, also on the west side, is modern tract aimed at the middle market. The oldest housing is located south of the downtown: Cottages and small homes, some showing their age, sidewalks on one side of some streets and not on the other side. New homes where lots have been in-filled. Former military depot has been converted into a business park. Food processing plants near rail lines. Zero homicides in 2004, 2003, 2002 and 2001, one in 2000, zero in 1999. Commuters can pick up Highway 120 at Escalon, about five miles to the north. Green trolleys run people around town.

Downtown has lovely wide streets. Del Rio movie house turned into restaurant. New movie complex. Community center. Library. Museum. Antique stores. In 2005, Riverbank tallied 4,999 single homes, 185 single-attached, 362 condos or apartments and 289 mobiles. Kids under 18 make up a third of the town. That's a lot. About 1,500 homes to go up on southwest side.

Riverbank school district: three elementaries, one middle, one high, total enrollment 3,200. Two schools score above 50th percentile, two below, one about middle (state rankings). Scores suggest a town in transition, moving from farm to farm-suburban. Improvements made to high school. Riverbank voters turned down $14 million school bond in 2003; got 63 percent, needed 67. Money was found to improve high school. Developers and homebuyers are being squeezed for money. Some children attend schools in the Sylvan district and move up to Beyer High School.

Annual Cheese and Wine Expo. Public pool. Community gym. Community center. Rec. department sponsors games, events, crafts, other activities. Nine parks, including a big one along the river. Soccer, softball, basketball, etc. Many amusements in region. Chamber of Commerce (209) 869-4541.

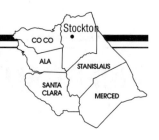

STOCKTON

LARGEST CITY IN SAN JOAQUIN COUNTY and county seat. Population 279,513. Old city with a good many new homes and more under construction. Crime high in some sections. School scores low in some sections.

Diverse city — low, middle and high income. Changing demographics, getting livelier. New homes bring in young families. Median age of residents is 30. Kids under 18 make up 32 percent of city, a lot. Home to University of the Pacific, San Joaquin Delta College and a branch campus of a California State University.

Highway 99 runs down Stockton's east side, Interstate 5, the west side. In the downtown, Highway 4 joins the two. Freeways make Stockton a commute city to Sacramento and to the Bay Area. The Altamont Commuter Express runs trains from Stockton to Livermore-Pleasanton and Santa Clara-San Jose. Amtrak. In driving miles, it's 45 to Sacramento and 83 to San Francisco, and 40-50 miles to the job centers of Livermore-Pleasanton-Dublin-San Ramon.

Stockton is a regional commercial center — thousands of jobs. City has a deep-water port, connected to Sacramento estuary, San Francisco Bay and the Pacific. Many farm products and goods from the Central Valley are shipped from the port. The city also has a large commercial airport. Union Pacific and Burlington Northern-Santa Fe run through Stockton.

One of California's oldest cities, Stockton first was supply center-jumping-off point for gold fields. About 10,000 residents by 1870 (double the population of Los Angeles); economy turned to farming. Benjamin Holt of Stockton invented the tread tractor, well suited to work the marshy Delta fields (and propel tanks). In 1900, Stockton claimed 17,500 residents.

Stockton's modern boom started in 1940s war years. By 1950, city boasted 71,000 residents, 110,000 by 1970. Between 1970 and 1990, the city just about doubled its inhabitants. In the 1990s, Stockton increased its population by 33,000 and built about 13,000 housing units.

Homes were built to the styles of their times: in the 1940s, homes ran to two bedrooms, in the 1950s to 1970s to three bedrooms. After the 1970s, larger homes, some four bedrooms; later, three-car garages, showed up.

As region prospered, people took their equity and moved up, creating a resale market. Older post war homes turned into low-income housing and, in the way of cities, into rundown housing in some sections. This brought the city social problems, which it is addressing. If you want to get into the housing market for under $150,000, Stockton can oblige. But the exchange might be a neighborhood with crime problems. Forty homicides in 2004. The counts for previous years are 37, 36, 30, 30, 32, 27, 45, 46, 42 and 44.

Mix of housing styles and prices helped Stockton and the region create a diverse and energetic economy. Middle- and upper-income neighborhoods can be found on the west side of town. Some are built around lagoons. Thousands of homes are going up around the city (but mostly on the outskirts.) In pricing, the homes are aimed the middle class.

Near the downtown, Stockton has lovely old neighborhoods with streets lined with trees. Homes may be cottages, bungalows or the occasional Victorian-Queen Anne.

As the San Joaquin county seat, Stockton has many government buildings in its downtown and on its periphery. Also in the downtown, a convention center, a large library, museums, office buildings, banks. The downtown has some elegant fountains. Yacht harbor at the edge of the downtown. Some of the downtown buildings are being gutted and modernized. In 2005, Stockton counted 91,725 housing units, of which 58,146 were single homes, 6,592 single-attached, 25,699 condos or apartments and 1,288 mobile homes.

Stockton children are educated by several school districts. The largest are Stockton Unified, 39,000 students, and Lodi Unified, which serves the north part of Stockton. Other school districts serving the Stockton area include Lincoln Unified, 9,000 students, Linden Unified, 2,500, and Holt Elementary, about 200.

With few exceptions, scores in the Stockton district fall below the 50th percentile. Scores in the Lodi district are also low but not as low, and the district runs an elementary school in Stockton for high-I.Q. students. This school, Elkhorn, scores at top of the state rankings. Lincoln schools score from the 30th to the 80th percentile; Linden schools, the 30th to the 60th percentile.

City does very well in parks and rec. Soccer, baseball, basketball, gymnastics, softball, dance. Winter ice skating. Swim complexes. New baseball stadium and events center (see following). About 50 parks. Ten golf courses. Many activities and classes for children, adults and the elderly. The community college and the University of the Pacific sponsor a variety of musical and cultural activities. The 49ers train at Stockton. Half-dozen theater groups. Small theater. Children's Museum. Wildlife museum. Pioneer museum. Four libraries. On the Delta: boating, fishing, swimming, water skiing. Movie complexes. Sears, Penneys, Macys, big-box Wal-Mart, Costco, Home Depot, Borders, Gottschalks, Barnes and Noble, Target, Dillards, Trader Joe's.

• Between the 2000 census and 2005, Stockton increased its population by about 15 percent or 36,000 people.

• In 2004 Stockton was named an All America City by the National Civic League, the second time it has been so honored in the past five years.

• In 2004, after a two-year, $6 million renovation, the Fox California Bob Hope Theater reopened in downtown. The job included an elaborate mosaic lobby floor.

• In 2005, Stockton was completing work on an arena, 10,000 seats, that will be used for minor league hockey, soccer and football.

• In 2005, Stocktop opened a baseball stadium, the home field for the Stockton Ports, a Triple A minor team.

• Annual Asparagus Festival in April draws 100,000-plus who manage to eat 27,000 pounds of deep-fried asparagus.

• The number of "stretch" commuters travelling from Stockton to San Francisco every day increased by 104 percent from 1990 to 2000. Stretch commuters are people traveling more than 50 miles to work. Some start out as early as 4:30 a.m. and on bad days spend three hours getting to the job.

• In 2004, Lincoln School District won voter approval of $40 million in bonds to upgrade 12 campuses.

• Stockton planners are employing a "villages" concept, creating discrete communities within the city with their own mix of housing types, parks, schools and some shops.

Chamber of commerce (209) 547-2770.

TRACY

LOCATED ON INTERSTATE 580, Tracy is the second community to greet eastbound commuters once they descend from the Altamont Pass and enter the San Joaquin Valley. Its crime is low, its school scores fairly high and probably rising. Its population, 78,307.

Family town. Loads of playmates. But as new subdivisions mature, the number of school-age children is slipping. In 2000, kids under 18 make up 34 percent of the town. In 2005, an informal survey put the percentage at 28. Tracy's school districts serve communities beyond the city's borders. These communities are growing, creating a demand for new schools, which are being built.

Tracy is about 20 miles from Livermore and 25-30 miles from Pleasanton-San Ramon, a fairly easy commute on Interstate 580. Up over the Altamont Pass down into the Amador Valley and you're in Livermore.

For San Francisco and Silicon Valley commuters, the drive is 60-80 miles. Many people make this commute but it's long, tiring and frequently congested.

In 2005, a survey showed that 42 percent of the all residents worked in Alameda County, 21 percent in Santa Clara County (Silicon Valley).

If you are looking at housing in the Central Valley, Tracy is a good town to begin your search. It retains a lot of its small-town character and offers a good choice of modern suburban housing. And it will give you a good idea of what you will find in other Valley towns: the flat terrain, the mountains to the west and distant east, the "youth" of these towns, even though many started long ago as farm communities. They are attracting many young families and this has pushed them into activities for children and families. In old cities with many empty nesters, Halloween attracts few trick or treaters. In these towns, Halloween fills the street with kids and parents.

As late as 1980, Tracy counted only 18,000 residents and much of its commercial activity was still centered in its downtown. In the 1980s, the city increased its population by 15,000 and in the 1990s by 23,371.

The timing is important. The U.S. came out of World War II fearing the return of the Depression. The first postwar housing was small and timid — two bedrooms, one story, flat or sloping roofs, one tree in the front yard. As time passed and the country became more confident, developers became more adventuresome. Homes moved up to three bedrooms, then four, added second story and expanded the garage. Lots shrank; with both spouses working, lawn care became a chore. Inside appointments became more comfortable: lights were recessed, walk-in closets made their appearance, living rooms were oriented toward the entertainment center, which was often spotted next to the fireplace. Kitchens grew bigger and added "islands." In the bathroom, the tubs and showers were made soothing and relaxing.

Perhaps just as important, city planners advanced their knowledge. Instead of piecemeal development, planners favored bringing master-planned projects that from their inception recognized the reality of cars. The old towns were often oriented around the rail depot.

The new developments erected walls around the housing tracts to shunt arterial traffic away from residential streets and built arterials to move vehicles quickly to freeway access points.

The new Tracy — and the new Modesto, Manteca, etc. — blossoming as late as they did, caught the wave of modern suburbia. Many people will find the housing pleasant. And the prices, compared to the Bay Area's, affordable, although prices have gone up. At times in 2005, the median price for homes in Tracy was $495,000.

At the same time, old town intrudes pleasantly, connects Tracy with past. Many old buildings house coffee shops, restaurants, antique stores, boutiques.

In 2005, the town tallied 24,174 housing units, of which 19,892 were single homes, 1,015 single-attached, 2,791 condos or apartments and 476 mobile homes. Like every town in Central California, Tracy favors the single-detached homes.

In the 1990s, Tracy opened a regional mall near Interstate 580 — Gottschalks, JC Penney, Target, Ross, Sears, Old Navy, many small shops and a movie complex with 14 screens. Home Depot, Costco, Wal-Mart, Barnes and Noble. Also in the 1990s, along the freeway, Tracy opened an outlet mall, a favorite endeavor of cities. Malls and stores levy sales taxes, which help fund city activities.

When the new neighborhoods are built, the parks go in with the housing and they are usually placed next to the schools. The schools also function as neighborhood-activity centers for adults and families. Usual sports, soccer the most popular. But also baseball, basketball, gymnastics. City rec department offers a variety of activities. Skate park. Town pool. City and the school district went partners on a swim center at West High School; to be used by students and public. Teen center. Delta close by; fishing, boating, water sports. Library. Boys and Girls Club. Farmers' market. If you pack the kids up by 7 a.m., you can be in Yosemite by 10 a.m. The same for the ski slopes, maybe faster.

Two homicides in 2004, 2003 and 2002, zero in 2001 and 2000, and one in each of 1999 and 1998, three in 1997, zero in 1996 and 1995, two in 1994, zero in 1993. The counts for the previous years are one, zero, two, zero, one, zero, and zero.

The largest school district is Tracy Unified, enrollment 16,000. Not too long ago many schools in Tracy scored below the 50th percentile. Now many are scoring at and above the 50th percentile and a few in the 80th percentile. As Tracy becomes more middle class, scores should rise.

Tracy has been building schools as the population increases, much of the funding coming from developer fees (which are passed to homebuyers.) Two recent efforts at bond elections failed. To save money, several elementaries are running on year-round schedules.

Highway 580 in the Livermore-Pleasanton area slows and sometimes crawls but generally it manages to move. At Pleasanton-Dublin, the inter-change to I-680 south was rebuilt, fairly successfully eliminating the mess there. Beyond Pleasanton, going toward San Jose, congestion, but some relief arrived in 2003 with the opening of extra lane for high-occupancy vehicles. Altamont Commuter Express runs commute trains from Stockton to San Jose, with stops at Tracy, Pleasanton, Fremont and Santa Clara. Tracy has many local or regional jobs: warehouse-distribution centers, government facilities. Airport to south of town. Transit Center in Tracy.

The town celebrates past with Dry Bean Festival, draws 60,000 — car show, live entertainment, the Princess and Little Sprout Pageant, Best Bean Dish Contest, a 5K and 10K run and arts, crafts and food vendors, and endless jokes on the gassy powers of the bean. Chamber of commerce (209) 835-2131.

• Downtown is being overhauled. To be built or renovated: transit center, city hall, old movie house to cultural arts center, fire station. Also lights, trees, more parking, street improvements. Town hopes the job brings in restaurants, specialty shops, more stores.

• Survey done in 2005. About two of every three Tracy residents moved to the town in the last five years.

• Under discussion at city hall: an aquatics center.

• Slow growth measure passed in 2000. Limits construction to an average 600 units per year. Arguments continue, some involving whether to push the 600 units upscale or make them affordable.

• Soon to be under construction, a third high school for Tracy Unified. The school, funded by developers' fees, is scheduled to open in 2008. The district is trying to find money to overhaul Tracy High School.

TURLOCK

COLLEGE TOWN LOCATED ON HIGHWAY 99 in Stanislaus County. Population 67,009. Mix of old, fairly new and new housing. Some lovely old neighborhoods.

Median age of residents is 31. Kids under 18 make up 30 percent of Turlock; a good number, over 55 years, 19 percent.

For commuters to the Bay Area, a do-able job but tiring. Turlock lies about 10 miles south of Modesto and the Highway 132 shortcut to Interstate 580. On some nights, those last 10 miles can seem like 50.

Incorporated as city in 1908, Turlock, rooted in farming, grew slowly and by 1950 counted 6,200 inhabitants. In the 1950s, California State University opened a campus in the town and the population picked up and by 1970 Turlock tallied 14,000 residents. In the 1970s, the population just about doubled, rising to 26,000, and in the 1980s, Turlock took another big leap, adding 16,000 residents.

In the 1990s, Turlock built 4,000 housing units, the great majority of them single homes, and increased its population by 13,586.

In other words, a lot of new housing, most of it priced for the middle class, three- and four-bedroom homes, one and two stories, a few neighborhoods in appointments and landscaping jumping a little up the scale. Some of the homes erected in the 1950s and 1960s are showing their age but the new stuff is well done in the manner of modern suburbia. Many of the apartment complexes were placed near the university, on the north side.

Old Turlock has a housing pattern that shows up in many valley cities — downtown surrounded by diverse neighborhoods, everything close-in. When people got around by horse and foot, they did not want to travel great distances for groceries or schools or churches. The towns had their poor, middle and rich neighborhoods, housing sizes varying in each sector. Air conditioning did not come along until almost 1950. In the old days, people kept cool by planting shade trees.

Turlock has some lovely streets just north of its downtown, small, medium and large homes, some quite large, bungalows and mansions, big lots, trees, trees, trees. And a feeling of stability and order that the new subdivisions, no matter how pretty, cannot match. It's like the homes were handed down from generation to generation and, inevitably, this influences impressions of the town. Turlock seems to care about its housing and appearances and preserving its history. New homes developments also going in east and north of city. Prices in new developments lower than areas closer to Sacramento or Bay Area. Middle and upper middle class homes, away from traffic, kid friendly.

This said, the downtown is struggling. Turlock has built a large mall on Highway 99, northeast of the downtown — Wal-Mart, Home Depot, etc. — and it, not the downtown, is Turlock's shopping center. Other big stores include a Target, Pennys, Sears, Costco, Borders Books.

To revitalize the downtown, the city has installed brick sidewalks and old-fashioned benches and lamp posts and planted more trees. Turlock got Highway 99 routed around the downtown but it allowed a "Business 99," Golden Gate Boulevard, which brings a lot of traffic into the neighborhood. The downtown will survive, probably as a restaurant, small-shop sector, quaint and pleasing to stroll.

In 2005, the city counted 22,581 housing units, of which 15,566 were single homes, 961 single-attached, 5,450 condos or apartments and 604 mobiles. More tracts are going up.

Two schools districts, Turlock Elementary and Turlock High, educate the children but as they are run by the same people, they should be considered one. Total enrollment, about 13,500. Both districts have passed bonds to build and renovate schools.

Elementary scores bounce all over, from the teens to the 90s, and reflect the town's jumbled demographics. Scores at Turlock High are landing in the 60s and 70s. The university boosts educational values and through its extension offers many classes open to the public. About 8,000 students attend the university.

About a dozen parks, many of them large and fitted with sports fields. Two public pools. Jogging trails along the irrigation canals. One or two hours to Sierra and mountain streams and lake and Yosemite. Usual sports: soccer, baseball, gymnastics, etc. Fitness centers. Dance studio. Library. Senior center. Movie complex. Turf club. Golf and country club. Arts center, large auditorium, university facilities. Turlock or the university stages art shows, musicals, plays, cultural events. Name acts, such as Anne Murray, play the auditorium. Skate park. Fairground hosts many events, including Skandi-Fest, an annual Scandinavian Folk Festival: folk music and dancing, horse show, arts and crafts, food.

Four homicides in 2004 and 2003, zero in 2002, two in 2001, one in 2000. Counts for previous years are 3, 7, 1, 4, 3 and 2.

Emanuel Medical Center is one of Turlock's largest employers, about 1,100 people. Food-processing plants in commercial section. Foster Farms employs 1,500. Turlock is famous for its turkeys. Chamber of commerce (209) 632-2221.

WATERFORD

LOCATED ABOUT 10 MILES east of Modesto, on the Tuolumne River. Split by Highway 132, one of the roads to the Gold Country and Yosemite. Population 7,897.

Over the last 10 years, Waterford has increased its population by about 45 percent, adding about 2,200 residents and 600 single homes but it remains a small, compact city but one that is taking a big leap up the scale. On its south side, near river, a large gated development was under construction in 2005.

In 2005, the town counted 2,330 housing units, of which 1,894 were single homes, 64 single-attached, 343 condos or apartments and 29 mobile homes.

Family town. Median age of residents is 29. Kids under 18 make up 36 percent of Waterford; over 55 years, 13 percent.

Three schools, all part of the Waterford school district, enrollment about 1,800. The two elementary schools are scoring in the 20th and 30th percentiles (state rankings). Waterford opened its own high school in 2002. The school includes a library, a science wing and a performing arts building.

Zero homicides in 2003 and 2002, one in 2001, zero in 2000 and 1999. Overall crime rate is very low.

Although the suburban look is coming in, Waterford still comes across as a quiet Valley town. In the summer, the kids put on their bathing suits and stroll through the lawn sprinklers or head down to the river. One big park. Usual sports, soccer, baseball.

Waterford is built over gentle hills and bluffs. A nursery has been planted near the river. Downtown has a bank, pharmacy, medical office, hardware store, new post office, pizza parlor, donut shop and shops that cater to tourists (rafts, jet ski rentals, etc.), and a Christian school. Out the outskirts, there's a large supermarket with a deli. Waterford sits at the edge of the Sierra and catches some of the traffic heading for the lakes and the resorts.

Farming fuels the economy of the town and region. Among the crops, tomatoes and jalapeños. Orchards start at the city limits. For the caffeinites, an espresso cafe. Chamber of commerce (209) 874-2328.

Chapter 7

How Public Schools Work

SCORES MEASURE academic success but they have their shortcomings. Some students know the material but are not adept at taking tests and some tests are so poorly designed that they fail to assess what has been taught. The rankings in the previous chapters do not break out students as individuals. A basic exam tests the least the children should know, not the most. Scores cannot assess goodness, kindness or wisdom or predict how helpful students will be to society.

There are other legitimate criticisms of probably every test given to California school children. Nonetheless, the tests probably give a fairly accurate picture of how the schools are doing academically. Students who do well in elementary school generally do well in high school and score high on the SAT and go on to succeed in college. With exceptions, the scores correlate with teacher assessments and so on. The exceptions cannot be ignored. A student who does poorly in one educational arrangement may thrive in another. This guide addresses patterns, not individuals.

When your children attend a school with high test scores, they are not assured of success. These schools have their failures. Neither can you be certain that your children will get the best teachers or the right programs. Other schools with lower scores might do better on these points. What you can be certain of is that your children are entering a setting that has proven successful for many students.

The main problem with making sense out of scores concerns what is called socioeconomics, a theory educators love, hate and widely believe.

Socioeconomics

In its crudest form, socioeconomics means rich kids score high, middle-class kids score about the middle and poor kids score low. Not all the time, not predictably by individual. Many children from poor and middle-class homes succeed in school and attend the best colleges. But as a general rule socioeconomics enjoys much statistical support.

Compare the rankings in the preceding chapter with income by cities. Piedmont, rich, high scores; parts of Oakland, poor, low; Union City and San

Scholastic Aptitude Test (SAT) Scores

High School	Enrollment*	% Tested	Verbal	Math
Alameda High	410	70	527	561
Albany High	213	77	549	602
Amador Valley High	475	60	550	589
American High	387	55	503	530
Arroyo High	364	44	472	509
Berkeley High	686	69	569	586
Castlemont Senior High	NA	NA	NA	NA
Castro Valley High	526	61	530	566
Dublin High	275	50	519	553
Emery High	44	30	399	412
Encinal High	266	47	441	478
Foothill High	495	69	550	576
Fremont Senior High	104	62	362	416
Granada High	446	41	534	569
Hayward High	493	31	471	480
Irvington High	356	66	529	591
James Logan High	805	55	476	512
Kennedy (John F.) High	309	41	495	549
Livermore High	448	46	539	541
McClymonds Senior High	92	37	377	392
Mission San Jose High	461	89	591	640
Mt. Eden High	500	30	445	473
Newark Memorial High	515	34	465	495
Oakland Senior High	340	59	397	457
Oakland Technical Senior High	274	63	437	474
Piedmont High	224	87	615	631
San Leandro High	510	41	474	510
San Lorenzo High	324	40	416	457
Skyline Senior High	354	66	457	485
Tennyson High	479	27	416	450
Washington High	429	55	509	539

Source: California Department of Education, 2004 tests. SAT scores are greatly influenced by who and how many take the test. The state education department has been pushing schools to have more students take the SAT. A school that has more marginal students taking the test will, by one line of reasoning, be doing a good job, but the scores are likely to be lower. *Senior class enrollment.

Leandro, middle-class towns, middling or middle-plus scores. SAT scores reflect the basic test scores.

Oakland School District has some of the lowest scoring schools in the state and some of the highest. All the teachers are paid the same. All are recruited by the same agency and all, presumably, meet the standards of the district.

Why the difference in scores? The background of the children is different. Montclair and adjoining neighborhoods are home to many professionals and people affiliated with the University of California. Academic culture strong. Scores high.

Scholastic Aptitude Test (SAT) Scores
Merced, San Joaquin, Stanislaus Counties

High School	Senior Class	% Tested	Verbal	Math
Atwater (Atwater)	390	24	454	463
Bear Creek (Stockton)	521	26	453	500
Beyer (Modesto)	685	39	514	519
Buhach Colony (Atwater)	300	30	450	471
Ceres (Ceres)	483	21	476	485
Davis (Modesto)	657	27	486	495
Denair (Denair)	98	24	471	471
Dos Palos (Dos Palos)	156	31	431	469
East Union (Manteca)	453	38	456	482
Edison (Stockton)	521	25	392	427
Escalon(Escalon)	214	34	497	499
Franklin (Stockton)	557	27	424	422
Golden Valley (Merced)	471	28	448	465
Gustine (Gustine)	115	32	482	480
Hilmar (Hilmar)	157	27	488	497
Hughson (Hughson)	185	28	488	495
Johansen (Modesto)	601	21	517	527
Le Grand (Le Grand)	116	24	369	422
Lincoln (Stockton)	551	33	505	526
Linden (Linden)	155	35	475	486
Livingston (Livingston)	250	25	436	438
Lodi (Lodi)	515	32	522	541
Los Banos (Los Banos)	380	29	479	470
Manteca (Manteca)	311	29	509	508
Merced (Merced)	526	30	454	469
Modesto (Modesto)	609	26	511	523
Oakdale (Oakdale)	337	30	515	518
Orestimba (Newman)	122	30	441	462
Patterson (Patterson)	206	31	465	447
Ripon (Ripon)	173	26	496	501
Riverbank (Riverbank)	195	19	506	526
Sierra (Manteca)	408	38	467	483
Stagg (Stockton)	598	23	443	469
Tokay (Lodi)	565	26	478	510
Tracy (Tracy)	435	31	498	507
Turlock (Turlock)	821	26	502	518
West (Tracy)	562	40	479	498

Source: California Department of Education, 2004 tests. **Note**: SAT scores are greatly influenced by who and how many take the test. The state education department has been pushing schools to have more students take the SAT. A school that has more marginal students taking the test will, by one line of reasoning, be doing a good job, but the scores are likely to be lower.

Oakland flatlands have many poor students, many welfare families. Academic push weak. Scores low.

The flatlands also have many minority children but to define achievement by ethnicity distorts the picture. Many middle-class towns or neighborhoods have high numbers of students from the same ethnic groups. Scores are much higher, sometimes very high.

National Scholastic Aptitude Test (SAT) Scores

State	*Tested (%)	Verbal	Math
Alabama	10	560	553
Alaska	53	518	514
Arizona	32	523	524
Arkansas	6	569	555
California	**49**	**501**	**519**
Colorado	27	554	553
Connecticut	85	515	515
Delaware	73	500	499
Dist. of Columbia	77	489	476
Florida	67	499	499
Georgia	73	494	493
Hawaii	60	487	514
Idaho	20	540	539
Illinois	10	585	597
Indiana	64	501	506
Iowa	5	593	602
Kansas	9	584	585
Kentucky	12	559	557
Louisiana	8	564	561
Maine	76	505	501
Maryland	68	511	515
Massachusetts	85	518	523
Michigan	11	563	573
Minnesota	10	587	593
Mississippi	5	562	547
Missouri	8	587	585
Montana	29	537	539
Nebraska	8	569	576
Nevada	40	507	514
New Hampshire	80	522	521
New Jersey	83	501	514
New Mexico	14	554	543
New York	87	497	510
North Carolina	70	499	507
North Dakota	5	582	601
Ohio	28	538	542
Oklahoma	7	569	566
Oregon	56	527	528
Pennsylvania	74	501	502
Rhode Island	72	503	502
South Carolina	62	491	495
South Dakota	5	594	597
Tennessee	16	567	557
Texas	52	493	499
Utah	7	565	556
Vermont	66	516	512
Virginia	71	515	509
Washington	52	528	531
West Virginia	19	524	514
Wisconsin	7	587	596
Wyoming	12	551	546
Nationwide	**48**	**508**	**518**

Source: California Dept. of Education, 2004 tests. *Percentage of class taking the test.

The difference: probably family stability and a host of other social influences. The same socioeconomic patterns show up around the Bay Area, the country and in other countries.

The federal study, "Japanese Education Today," notes a "solid correlation between poverty and poor school performance...."

Family and Culture

In its refined form, socioeconomics moves away from the buck and toward culture and family influence.

The towns with the highest number of college educated are generally also the towns with the highest scores. If your mom or dad attended college, chances are you will attend college or do well at school because in a thousand ways while you were growing up they and their milieu pushed you in this direction. Emphasis on "chances are." Nothing is certain when dealing with human beings.

What if mom and dad never got beyond the third grade? Or can't even speak English?

Historically, many poor and immigrant children have succeeded at school because their parents badgered, bullied and encouraged them every step of the way and made sacrifices so they would succeed. Asian kids are the latest example of poor kids succeeding but earlier generations could point to the children of peasant Europeans and Blacks risen from slavery.

Does it make a difference if the child is English proficient? Or the parents rich? Individual differences will always count. Immigrant children unfamiliar with English will have more difficulties with literature and language-proficient courses than native-born children. They will need extra or special help in schools.

Nonetheless, the home-school correlation retains much validity: The stronger the educational support the child receives at home, the better he or she will do at school. Simply reading daily to young children supposedly works wonders, studies indicate.

The Socioeconomic flaw

If you carry the logic of socioeconomics too far, you may conclude that schools and teachers and teaching methods don't matter: Students succeed or fail according to their family or societal backgrounds.

Just not the case! No matter how dedicated or well-intentioned the parent, if the teacher is grossly inept the child probably will learn little. If material or textbooks are out-of-date or inaccurate, what the student learns will be useless or damaging. Conversely, if the teacher is dedicated and knowledgeable, if the material is well-presented and appropriate, what the child comes away with will be helpful and, to society, more likely to be beneficial.

California College Admissions of Public School Graduates

High School	UC	CSU	CC
Alameda	85	65	199
Albany	63	21	61
Amador Valley (Pleasanton)	47	84	186
American (Fremont)	38	71	150
Arroyo (Livermore)	30	90	142
Berkeley	109	74	214
Castlemont (Oakland)	6	17	90
Castro Valley	68	97	250
Dublin	18	37	133
Emery (Emeryville)	2	2	17
Encinal (Alameda)	27	31	127
Foothill (Pleasanton)	64	71	155
Fremont (Oakland)	12	24	111
Granada (Livermore)	38	46	227
Hayward	23	44	185
Irvington (Fremont)	71	48	115
Kennedy (Fremont)	26	29	92
Livermore	28	52	228
Logan (Union City)	81	164	320
McClymonds (Oakland)	4	9	34
Mission San Jose (Fremont)	177	69	76
Mt. Eden (Hayward)	28	50	165
Newark Mem.	18	66	185
Oakland	53	48	195
Oakland Tech	38	33	149
Piedmont	50	12	17
San Leandro	39	71	193
San Lorenzo	24	41	113
Skyline (Oakland)	53	45	195
Tennyson (Hayward)	29	37	147
Washington (Fremont)	47	74	172

Source: California Department of Education. The chart lists the local public high schools and shows how many students they advanced in the year 2004 into California public colleges and universities. The state does not track graduates enrolling in private or out-of-state colleges. Continuation schools not included. **Key:** UC (University of California system); CSU (Cal State system); CC (Community Colleges).

The late Albert Shanker, president of the American Federation of Teachers, one of the largest teachers' unions in the nation, argued that U.S. students would improve remarkably if schools refused to tolerate disruptive behavior, if national or state academic standards were adopted, if external agencies (not the schools themselves) tested students and if colleges and employers, in admissions and hiring, rewarded academic achievement and penalized failure. These four reforms do little or nothing to address socioeconomics but many educators believe they have merit.

California College Admissions of Public School Graduates

Merced, San Joaquin, Stanislaus Counties

High School	UC	CSU	CC
Atwater (Atwater)	14	36	NA
Bear Creek (Stockton)	17	22	130
Beyer (Modesto)	31	97	281
Buhach Colony (Atwater)	5	36	NA
Ceres (Ceres)	9	49	10
Davis (Modesto)	22	54	246
Delhi	1	14	NA
Denair (Denair)	0	15	20
Dos Palos (Dos Palos)	3	12	7
Downey (Modesto)	7	35	78
East Union (Manteca)	14	42	140
Edison (Stockton)	10	24	139
Escalon (Escalon)	5	28	45
Franklin (Stockton)	19	29	145
Golden Valley (Merced)	19	42	7
Gustine (Gustine)	2	18	10
Hilmar (Hilmar)	4	23	28
Hughson (Hughson)	4	20	51
Johansen (Modesto)	21	32	210
Le Grand (Le Grand)	1	14	NA
Lincoln (Stockton)	23	46	172
Linden (Linden)	3	10	46
Livingston (Livingston)	15	18	24
Lodi (Lodi)	16	32	111
Los Baños (Los Baños)	9	37	29
Manteca (Manteca)	10	33	107
Merced (Merced)	17	35	26
Middle College (Stockton)	1	1	NA
Modesto (Modesto)	28	47	154
Oakdale (Oakdale)	19	28	107
Orestimba (Newman)	3	18	31
Patterson (Patterson)	4	22	74
Ripon (Ripon)	1	18	61
Riverbank (Riverbank)	5	18	53
Sierra (Manteca)	9	53	91
Stagg (Stockton)	16	16	145
Tokay (Lodi)	15	43	157
Tracy (Tracy)	18	32	122
Turlock (Turlock)	23	72	224
Waterford	2	10	NA
West (Tracy)	20	49	184

Source: Calif. Dept. of Education. Chart lists local public high schools and shows how many students they advanced in the year 2004 into California public colleges and universities. State does not track graduates enrolling in private or out-of-state colleges. Continuation schools not included. **Key:** UC (University of California system); CSU (Cal State system) CC (Community Colleges). NA (Not available).

Admittedly, however, this is a contentious area. Theories abound as to what is wrong with our schools and what should be done to fix them.

Where the Confusion Enters

It's very difficult, if not impossible, to separate the influence of home and schools. To be fair to parents, some experts argue that friends and peer groups exercise greater influence than the home.

When scores go up, often principals or superintendents credit this or that instructional program or extra efforts by teachers.

But the scores may have risen because mom and dad cracked down on excessive TV. Or a city with old and faded low-income housing (low scores) approved a high-end development. The new residents are more middle class, more demographically inclined to push their kids academically.

One last joker-in-the-deck, mobility. Johnny is doing great at his school, which has low to middling scores, but programs that seem to be working. And his family is doing better. Mom has a job, Dad a promotion. What does the family do? It moves. Happens all the time in the U.S.A. and this also makes precise interpretation of scores difficult.

Basic Instruction-Ability Grouping

California and American schools attempt to meet the needs of students by providing a good basic education and by addressing individual and subgroup needs by special classes and ability grouping.

In the first six years in an average school, children receive some special help according to ability but for the most part they share the same class experiences and get the same instruction.

About the seventh grade, students are divided into classes for low achievers, middling students and high achievers, or low-middle and advanced — tracking. Texts, homework and expectations are different for each group. The high achievers are on the college track, the low, the vocational.

Pressured by the state, some schools are curtailing this practice, but many schools retain accelerated English and math classes for advanced seventh- and eighth-graders. Parents can always request a transfer from one group to another (whether they can get it is another matter). The reality often is, however, that remedial and middle children can't keep pace with the high achievers.

In the last 40 years or so, schools introduced into the early grades special programs aimed at low achievers or children with learning difficulties. Although they vary greatly, these programs typically pull the children out of class for instruction in small groups then return them to the regular class.

Many schools also pull out gifted (high I.Q.) students and a few cluster them in their own classes. Some schools offer "gifted" classes after the regular program.

How Average Schools Succeed

So many local students attend the University of California and California State universities that public and private high schools must of necessity teach classes demanded by these institutions.

Almost all high schools will also offer general education classes in math and English but these will not be as tough as the prep courses and will not be recognized by the state universities. And usually the school will teach some trades so those inclined can secure jobs upon graduation.

Can a school with mediocre or even low basic scores field a successful college prep program? With comprehensive programs, the answer is yes.

College Track

Freshmen attending a California State University, a public community college or a University of California (Berkeley, Los Angeles, San Diego, Davis, Riverside, etc.) are asked to identify their high schools. In this way and others, the state finds out how many students the individual high schools are advancing to college.

The college admissions chart breaks out the high schools in Alameda County and shows how many students from each school went on to the public colleges.

UCs generally restrict themselves to the top 13 percent in the state. CSUs (Cal States) take the top third.

Every school on the chart is graduating kids into college but obviously some are more successful at it than others. Does this mean that the "lesser" schools have awful teachers or misguided programs? We have no idea. It simply may be socioeconomics at work.

Parents with college ambitions for their children should find out as much as possible about prospective schools and their programs and make sure that their kids get into the college-track classes.

Where does the chart mislead?

Students who qualify for a Cal State or even a UC often take their freshman and sophomore years at a community college. It's cheaper and closer to home.

To secure a more diverse student mix, the UCs have lowered their admission scores, a practice that has critics and supporters. The numbers mentioned above and listed in the accompanying chart do not consist of the top students as defined by tests and grade point. In 2004, the UCs raised their admission scores but the last word has not been said on this matter.

But socioeconomics does not sweep the field. Not every student from a high-scoring school goes on to college. Many students from low- and middle-income towns come through.

UCs Chosen by Public School Graduates

High School	Berk	Dav	Irv	UCLA	Riv	SD	SB	SC	Total
Alameda	11	38	1	11	3	4	6	11	85
Albany	11	20	3	4	3	6	4	12	63
Amador Valley	13	14	1	2	2	5	8	2	47
American	9	13	8	3	1	1	0	3	38
Arroyo	5	4	2	1	0	8	6	4	30
Berkeley	28	12	2	13	5	5	11	33	109
Castlemont	3	1	0	0	1	0	1	0	6
Castro Valley	9	33	5	6	5	5	4	1	68
Dublin	9	3	0	3	1	0	1	1	18
Emery	2	0	0	0	0	0	0	0	2
Encinal	8	6	0	3	2	0	2	6	27
Foothill	10	17	2	5	4	7	11	8	64
Fremont	3	8	0	0	0	1	0	0	12
Granada	4	16	0	4	0	8	4	2	38
Hayward	6	7	1	2	3	1	2	1	23
Irvington	13	19	12	2	6	6	8	5	71
Kennedy	6	6	3	1	3	1	3	3	26
Livermore	5	9	0	1	1	3	5	4	28
Logan, James	14	30	1	3	5	7	12	9	81
McClymonds	4	0	0	0	0	0	0	0	4
Mission S.J.	37	37	19	19	13	36	6	10	177
Mt. Eden	2	11	0	4	1	6	2	2	28
Newark Mem.	3	4	0	0	1	3	5	2	18
Oakland	17	25	0	6	1	1	0	3	53
Oakland Tech.	8	18	1	3	0	3	0	5	38
Piedmont	7	9	2	6	2	6	2	16	50
San Leandro	11	16	0	2	3	0	2	5	39
San Lorenzo	4	10	0	4	0	3	1	2	24
Skyline	8	19	1	6	3	4	5	7	53
Tennyson	3	15	0	7	1	0	2	1	29
Washington	8	10	2	3	2	9	7	6	47

Source: California Dept. of Education. The chart shows the University of California choices by 2004 local public high school graduates. The state does not track graduates enrolling in private or out-of-state colleges. Continuation schools not included in list. **Key**: Berk (Berkeley), Dav (Davis), Irv (Irvine), Riv (Riverside), SD (San Diego), SB (Santa Barbara), SC (Santa Cruz).

The chart does not track private colleges. It doesn't tell us how many local students went to Mills College or the University of San Francisco or Stanford or Harvard. Or public colleges out of the state.

Many college students drop out. These numbers are not included.

The chart does confirm the influence of socioeconomics: The rich towns, the educated towns or neighborhoods, send more kids to the UCs than the poorer ones. Berkeley High School and Mission San Jose (affluent neighbhorhood) send the most students to the University of California. Skyline

UCs Chosen by Public School Grads

Merced County

High School	Berk	Davis	Irv	UCLA	Riv	SD	SB	SC	Total
Atwater	2	0	0	2	0	2	7	1	14
Buhach Colony	0	1	0	0	0	0	2	2	5
Dos Palos	0	0	0	2	0	0	1	0	3
Golden Valley	3	1	0	0	2	6	5	2	19
Gustine	0	0	0	0	0	0	1	1	2
Hilmar	1	3	0	0	0	0	0	0	4
Le Grand	0	0	0	0	0	0	1	0	1
Livingston	1	12	1	0	1	0	0	0	15
Los Baños	1	2	0	1	1	1	2	1	9
Merced	2	8	0	1	0	0	5	0	17

San Joaquin County

High School	Berk	Davis	Irv	UCLA	Riv	SD	SB	SC	Total
Bear Creek	2	5	0	2	2	5	1	0	17
East Union	0	3	2	3	0	0	5	1	14
Edison	1	5	1	1	0	0	1	1	10
Escalon	0	1	1	1	0	0	1	1	5
Franklin	2	12	0	2	1	0	2	0	19
Lincoln	2	6	9	1	0	3	1	1	23
Linden	1	1	0	0	0	0	1	0	3
Lodi	2	5	0	2	0	0	7	0	16
Manteca	0	6	0	0	0	0	3	1	10
Ripon	0	0	0	0	0	0	0	1	1
Sierra	0	4	0	1	0	1	2	1	9
Stagg	1	7	0	1	0	2	3	2	16
Tokay	0	6	0	1	0	2	5	1	15
Tracy	0	4	2	1	1	3	6	1	18
West	3	5	1	0	1	4	5	1	20

Stanislaus County

High School	Berk	Davis	Irv	UCLA	Riv	SD	SB	SC	Total
Beyer	1	12	0	3	3	4	4	4	31
Ceres	1	4	2	0	0	0	2	0	9
Denair	NA	NA	NA	NA	NA	NA	NA	NA	NA
Davis	5	4	0	0	1	4	6	2	22
Downey (Thomas)	0	0	0	0	0	1	4	2	7
Hughson	0	1	1	1	0	0	0	1	4
Johansen	5	11	0	0	0	3	0	2	21
Modesto	6	10	0	3	0	3	5	1	28
Oakdale	1	5	2	0	0	2	6	3	19
Orestimba	0	1	0	0	0	0	2	0	3
Patterson	2	1	0	0	0	0	1	0	4
Riverbank	1	1	0	0	0	1	2	0	5
Turlock	0	7	3	1	0	4	6	2	23

Source: California Dept. of Education. The chart shows the University of California choices by local public high school graduates of 2004. The state does not track graduates enrolling in private or out-of-state colleges. Continuation schools not included in list. **Key**: Berk (Berkeley), Irv (Irvine), Riv (Riverside), SD (San Diego), SB (Santa Barbara), SC (Santa Cruz). NA (Not available).

High is located in the well-to-do neighborhoods of Oakland. Piedmont, a small school district, does proportionately quite well.

But socioeconomics does not sweep the field. Not every student from a high-scoring school goes on to college. Many students from low- and middle-income towns come through.

Dissatisfaction

If high schools can deliver on college education and train students for vocations, why are so many people dissatisfied with public schools? These schools can cite other accomplishments: Textbooks and curriculums have been improved, the dropout rate has been decreased and proficiency tests have been adopted to force high school students to meet minimum academic standards.

Yet almost every year or so, some group releases a study showing many California children are scoring below expectations or doing poorly as compared to Japanese or European children.

The California system is expensive, over $55 billion annually just for the K-12 system, three fourths from the state, one fourth from the feds.

Comparisons between countries are tricky. If Japanese or European high school students fail or do poorly on their tests, they are often denied admission to college. Those who do well, however, are marked not only for college but the higher-paying jobs. Our system gives second and third chances and allows easy admission to colleges, but bears down on students during college and after they graduate. Then they have to prove themselves at work to get ahead, and this forces many to return to college or get training. Their system pressures teenagers; ours pressures young adults. Some studies suggest that by age 30 the differences even out.

As intriguing as this theory is, many parents and teachers would feel much better if the learning curve showed a sharper rise for the high-school scholars and, of course, our top universities — Cal, Stanford, Harvard — demand top scores for admission.

Registering For School

To get into kindergarten, your child must turn five before Dec. 3 of the year he or she enters the grade.

For first grade, your child must be six before Dec. 3. If he is six on Dec. 4, if she is a mature Jan. 6 birthday girl, speak to the school. There may be some wiggle room. In 2000, the state changed the law to allow schools to admit children who turn six before Sept. 2. But to take advantage of this law, a school must offer pre-kindergarten instruction. Many don't. Talk to the school.

For registration, you are required to show proof of immunization for polio, diphtheria, hepatitis B, tetanus, pertussis (whooping cough), measles, rubella and mumps. If the kid is seven or older, you can skip mumps and whooping cough. New law: continuing students entering the seventh grade must show proof of being immunized against hepatitis B.

Register Early

Just because you enroll your child first does not necessarily mean that you will get your first choice of schools or teachers.

But in some school districts first-come does mean first-served. Enrollment and transfer policies change from year to year in some districts, depending on the number of children enrolled and the space available. When new schools are opened, attendance boundaries are often changed.

Even if the school district says, "There's plenty of time to register," do it as soon as possible. If a dispute arises over attendance — the school might get an unexpected influx of students — early registration might give you a leg up in any negotiations. Persistence sometimes helps in trying for transfers.

Choosing the "Right" School

Almost all public schools have attendance zones, usually the immediate neighborhood. The school comes with the neighborhood; often you have no choice. Your address determines your school.

Always call the school district to find out what school your children will be attending. Sometimes school districts change attendance boundaries and do not inform local Realtors. Sometimes crowding forces kids out of their neighborhood schools. It's always good to go to the first source.

Just say something like, "I'm Mrs. Jones and we're thinking about moving into 1234 Main Street. What school will my six-year-old attend?"

Ask what elementary school your child will attend and what middle school and high school.

Keep in mind that although a district scores high, not all the schools in the district may score high. In some districts, scores vary widely.

Several districts may serve one town, another reason to nail down your school of attendance.

Transfers

If you don't like your neighborhood school, you can request a transfer to another school in the district or to a school outside the district. But the school won't provide transportation.

Transfers to schools inside the district are easier to get than transfers outside the district. New laws supposedly make it easier to transfer children to other districts. In reality, the more popular (high scoring) districts and schools, lacking space, rarely — very rarely — accept "outside" students. This is a changing picture. New federal laws supposedly make it easier to transfer out of schools that do not meet academic standards.

A few parents use the address of a friend or relative to smuggle their child into a high-scoring school or district. Some districts make an effort to ferret out these students and give them the boot.

If your child has a special problem that may demand your attention, speak to the school administrators about a transfer to a school close to your job. If your child's ethnicity adds some diversity to a school or district, it might bend its rules. Never hurts to ask.

Does A Different School Make A Difference?

This may sound like a dumb question but it pays to understand the thinking behind choosing one school or school district over another.

Researching an earlier edition, we contacted a school district (not in this county) that refused to give us test results. This stuff is public information. In so many words, the school administrator said, look, our scores are lousy because our demographics are awful: low income, parents poorly educated, etc. But our programs and staff are great. I'm not giving out the scores because parents will get the wrong idea about our district and keep their kids out of our schools (He later changed his mind and gave us the scores.)

Second story, while working as a reporter, one of our editors covered a large urban school district and heard about a principal who was considered top notch. An interview was set up and the fellow seemed as good as his reputation: friendly, hard working, supportive of his staff, a great role model for his students, many of whom he knew by their first names. But scores at the school were running in the 10th to 20th percentiles, very low.

The reason: the old failing of demographics, weak academic push from home or neighborhood, perhaps indifferent or damaging parents, and so on. This stuff is actually complicated. Some parents do their best but the kid gets diverted by friends or buys into anti-academics.

Although neither person said this, the clear implication was that if the demographics were different, scores would be much higher. And they're probably right. If these schools got an influx of middle- and upper middle-class children, their scores would dramatically increase.

Why don't schools tell this to the public, to parents? Probably because socioeconomics is difficult to explain. Teachers want to work with parents, not alienate them with accusations of neglect. Some educators argue that even with poor socioeconomics, teachers should be able to do an effective job — controversy. Socioeconomics focuses attention on the problems of home and society to the possible detriment of schools (which also need help and funds). School, after all, is a limited activity: about six hours a day, about 180 teaching days a year.

When you strip away the fluff, schools seem to be saying that they are in the business of schools, not in reforming the larger society, and that they should be held accountable only for what they can influence: the children during the school day, on school grounds.

For these reasons — this is our opinion — many teachers and school administrators think that scores mislead and that parents often pay too much attention to scores and not enough to programs and the background and training of personnel. This is not to say that teachers ignore scores and measurements of accomplishment. They would love to see their students succeed. And schools find tests useful to determine whether their programs need changes.

No matter how low the scores, if you, as a parent, go into any school, and ask — can my child get a good education here — you will be told, probably invariably, often enthusiastically, yes. First, there's the obvious reason: if the principal said no, his or her staff and bosses would be upset and angry. Second, by the reasoning common to public schools, "yes" means that the principal believes that the school and its teachers have the knowledge, training and dedication to turn out accomplished students. And the programs. Schools stress programs.

Is all this valid? Yes. Programs and training are important. Many schools with middling scores do turn out students that attend the best universities.

But this approach has its skeptics. Many parents and educators believe that schools must be judged by their scores, that scores are the true test of quality.

Some parents fear that if their child or children are placed in classes with low-achieving or even middle-achieving children they will not try as hard as they would if their friends or classmates were more academic, or that in some situations their children will be enticed into mischief. In some inner-city districts, the children, for misguided reasons, pressure each other not to do well in school.

Some parents do not believe that a school with many low-scoring students can do justice to its few middle- and high-scoring students. To meet the needs of the majority, instruction might have to be slowed for everyone.

Discipline is another problem. Teachers in low-scoring schools might have to spend more time on problem kids than teachers in high-scoring schools.

There's much more but basically it comes down to the belief that schools do not stand alone, that they and their students are influenced by the values of parents, of classmates and of the immediate neighborhood.

To continue this logic, schools and school districts are different from one another and for this reason it pays to move into a neighborhood with high-scoring schools or one with at least middling-plus scores. Or to somehow secure a transfer to one of the schools in these neighborhoods.

Community College Transfers

ALTHOUGH PRIMARILY skills and training schools, community colleges are a major source of students for the University of California and for the California State universities.

The students usually take their freshman and sophomore classes at a community college, then transfer to a university.

Community colleges are cheap and often conveniently located. Many community colleges have worked out transfer agreements with local state universities and with the UCs.

The data below show how many students each sector advances.

Alameda County

Student Sector	Graduates	To UC	To CSU
Public High School	12,153	1,679	1,897
Community Colleges	NA	604	1,260

Merced County

Student Sector	Graduates	To UC	To CSU
Public High Schools	3,466	90	286
Community Colleges		16	231

San Joaquin County

Student Sector	Graduates	To UC	To CSU
Public High Schools	6,289	198	479
Community Colleges		93	495

Stanislaus County

Student Sector	Graduates	To UC	To CSU
Public High Schools	6,188	178	518
Community Colleges		60	459

UC, CSU Transfers by Community College Campus

Community College	To UC	To CSU
College of Alameda	56	86
Chabot College	135	395
Laney College	126	188
Las Positas College	82	225
Merced College (Merced County)	16	231
Merritt College	26	74
Modesto Junior College (Stanislaus County)	60	459
Ohlone College	107	249
San Joaquin Delta College (San Joaquin County)	93	495
Vista College	72	43

Source: California Postsecondary Education Commission, Student Profile, 2004. **Note:** Enrolling students counted in 2003-2004 by UCs and CSUs. NA, not available.

To an unknown extent, the marketplace has reinforced this belief. It rewards neighborhoods and towns with high-scoring schools by increasing the value (the price) of their homes.

Woven into all this is the suspicion, held by many in California, that public schools have failed to dismiss incompetent teachers and have become inflexible and unable to address problems. California for decades has been wracked by arguments over the power of the teachers' union, and over testing and teaching methods, and curriculum.

The parents who seem to do best at this business find out as much as possible about the schools, make decisions or compromises based on good information and work with the schools and teachers to advance their children's interests. Each school should be publishing an "accountability report." Ask for it.

Year-Round Schools

Year-round schools are used by many districts, especially in fast-growing towns, as a way to handle rapidly increasing enrollments. Schedules, called "tracks," vary by district but all students attend a full academic year.

Traditional holidays are observed. One group may start in summer, one in late summer and so on. A typical pattern is 12 weeks on, four weeks off. One track is always off, allowing another track to use its class space. Some school districts run a "year-round" program called modified traditional: two months summer vacation, three two-week breaks in the school year.

Families with several children on different tracks are sometimes forced to do quite a bit of juggling for vacation and child care. A new game is being played: how to get the tracks you want. Call your school for information.

High School Graduates College Choice By County

County	UC	CSU	CC
Alameda	1,679	1,898	5,203
Alpine	0	0	0
Amador	13	40	91
Butte	75	246	730
Calaveras	19	54	68
Colusa	7	36	73
Contra Costa	1,078	1,222	2,217
Del Norte	9	18	60
El Dorado	131	190	615
Fresno	320	1,247	1,175
Glenn	4	60	126
Humboldt	62	161	437
Imperial	82	133	1,595
Inyo	13	15	60
Kern	263	906	2,461
Kings	36	88	241
Lake	12	52	184
Lassen	6	13	103
Los Angeles	7,113	9,713	28,916
Madera	25	131	55
Marin	345	299	323
Mariposa	5	6	20
Mendocino	32	102	372
Merced	90	286	151
Modoc	5	6	30
Mono	4	17	36
Monterey	254	421	1,355
Napa	90	137	202
Nevada	49	100	338
Orange	2,937	3,060	15,172
Placer	223	434	1,365
Plumas	6	10	64
Riverside	1,056	1,402	4,661
Sacramento	882	1,398	5,178
San Benito	24	61	229
San Bernardino	959	1,821	5,805
San Diego	2,020	3,061	9,197
San Francisco	1,093	813	1,353
San Joaquin	217	524	2,008
San Luis Obispo	148	295	1,120
San Mateo	707	638	1,733
Santa Barbara	306	256	1,680
Santa Clara	2,226	2,182	4,185
Santa Cruz	234	298	969
Shasta	42	146	98
Sierra	2	7	10
Siskiyou	12	28	163
Solano	242	423	1,395
Sonoma	332	469	2,058
Stanislaus	187	553	1,642

High School Graduates Choice of School By County

County	UC	CSU	CC
Sutter	42	99	496
Tehama	14	61	83
Trinity	6	7	23
Tulare	134	395	1,537
Tuolumne	12	34	145
Ventura	541	656	4,193
Yolo	204	192	578
Yuba	9	47	278

Source: California Postsecondary Education Commission, 2004. Number of public and private high-school students moving up as freshmen to a UC or a California State University.

Ability Grouping

Ask about the school's advancement or grouping policy or gifted classes.

Without getting into the pros and cons of these practices, schools often tiptoe around them because they upset some parents and frankly because some children have to be slighted. Say the ideal in a middle school is three levels of math: low, middle and high. But funds will allow only two levels. So low is combined with middle or middle with high. If you know the school is making compromises, you might choose to pay for tutoring to bridge the gap.

Miscellaneous

- For much of the 1990s, California, in a tough economy, pulled the purse strings tight against school spending. Teacher salaries fell behind what was paid in other states. Programs were cut. Quality, many believe, suffered. In the late 1990s, the economy came roaring back and pushed billions of extra dollars into the state treasury.

- Teacher salaries were raised (tops in U.S), class sizes in the first three grades were lowered (to 20-1), programs were restored.

- Going into 2005, California has burned through its surplus and is saddled with a large deficit. We are entering another era of stingy spending that is spilling into cuts for education.

- On the positive side, several years ago voters dropped the approval vote for local bonds for school construction from two-thirds of ballots cast to 55 percent. School districts that had lost several bond elections went back to the voters and won approval. On the state level, voters in 2002 and 2004 approved construction bonds worth $24 billion. Many school districts have become skilled at squeezing developers for building costs.

- The contradiction: after decades of neglect, California is renovating thousands of its schools and building more. The state in 2004 settled a law suit that will inject more fixing-up money into the poorest and most rundown schools. At the same time, school districts are finding it harder to come up with operational funds — salaries, programs, books, etc. Extra operational money generally requires a two-thirds vote; hard to win. Many school districts have turned to parental and community fund raising to come up with operational money. This often amounts to a parental tax, usually collected by a "foundation" run by the parents.

- What if you or your neighborhood can't afford voluntary fees? Shop for bargains. Community colleges, in the summer, often run academic programs for children. Local tutors might work with small groups. Specific tutoring, say just in math, might be used to get the student over the rough spots. For information on tutors, look in the Yellow Pages under "Tutoring."

- In 2003, Oakland district, perhaps betting on the dotcom economy to supply funding, was forced into bankruptcy. The state loaned the district $100 million and put its own administrator in charge of the district.

- Private vs. public. A complex battle, it boils down to one side saying public schools are the best and fairest way to educate all children versus the other side saying public education is inefficient and will never reform until it has meaningful competition. The state has allowed over 560 schools to restructure their programs according to local needs — an effort at eliminating unnecessary rules. These institutions are called charter schools.

- Oakland district is losing students and with many arguments closing schools. Some of the losses come from demographics — fewer kids. Some because charter schools have siphoned students out of the neighborhood schools, especially the low-scoring ones. When schools are closed, attendance boundaries are changed.

- Once tenured, teachers are almost impossible to fire, which opens schools to accusations of coddling incompetents. If your child gets a sour teacher, request a transfer. Better still, become active in the PTA or talk to other parents and try to identify the best teachers. Then ask for them..

- Courts and school districts have sorted out Proposition 227, which curtailed non-English instruction in public schools. Parents can request a waiver, which under certain conditions allows instruction in the native language.

- Busing. School districts can charge and several do. Some low-income and special education kids ride free.

- Uniforms. Schools have the discretion to require uniforms, an effort to discourage gang colors and get the kids to pay more attention to school than to how they look. "Uniforms" are generally interpreted to mean modest dress; for example, dark pants and shirts for boys, plaid skirts and light blouse for girls.

- Closed campus vs. open campus. The former stops the students from leaving at lunch or at any time during the school day. The latter allows the kids to leave. Kids love open, parents love closed.

- Grad night. Not too many years ago, graduating seniors would whoop it up on grad night and some would drink and then drive and get injured or killed. At many high schools now, parents stage a grad night party at the school, load it with games, raffles and prizes, and lock the kids in until dawn. A lot of work but it keeps the darlings healthy.

- T-P. California tradition. Your son or daughter joins a school team and it wins a few games or the cheerleaders win some prize — any excuse will do — and some parent will drive the kids around and they will fling toilet paper over your house, car, trees and shrubs. Damn nuisance but the kids love it.

- The number of teaching days has been increased, from about 172 to 180 but some of these days are coming at the expense of preparation time for teachers.

- Open Houses, Parents Nights. One study, done at Stanford, concluded that if parents will attend these events, the students, or at least some of them, will be impressed enough to pay more attention to school.

- Rather than lug around books, lunches, gym gear, etc., students these days are using rolling suitcases similar to carry-on luggage. "They help your back," said one student. The outfits seem to be particularly popular in schools that have done away with lockers.

- Special education. Sore point in California education. When the feds and the state passed laws requiring schools to meet the special needs of students, they promised funding that never materialized. This forced school districts to take money from their regular programs and fund the special programs. Arguments and lawsuits followed accusing school districts of shorting special ed kids. The state is now offering more money for these programs.

- More kids are being pushed into algebra, not only in high school but in the seventh and eighth grades. New law requires all students to take algebra before graduating from high school.

- Exit exam. Starting in 2006, students must pass an exit exam to receive a high school diploma. To get the kids prepared, all of them must take the exam by their sophomore year. If they fail, the high school will offer extra help.

- California quietly but steadily has been setting standards as to what students should know at any grade level. If schools and students don't measure up to the standards, they risk, in ways that are still being worked out, the displeasure of the California Department of Education. Tests are being developed to see how thoroughly the students are mastering the required subjects.

- Social promotion, the practice of moving students up to the next grade, even if they have failed the current grade, is being discouraged. Schools are now required to hold back failing students and offer them tutoring and special instruction. If schools follow guidelines and the student is still failing, he or she can be held back but parents have right to appeal decision.

- Low scores in many Central Valley schools. Scores follow demographics and as many children in the Valley come from low-income families, the scores reflect this. But the region is now attracting many middle and upper middle students and they are pushing scores up. Tracy is a good example of what is happening. Its modern scores have risen noticeably. Many schools are trying to educate children across the spectrum — an often difficult task.

- The Calif. Dept. of Education recently named the below schools "Distinguished." This means the state thinks they are well run.

  • American High, Irvington High, Hopkins Junior High – Fremont

  • Amador Valley High, Foothill High, Harvest Park Middle,

Pleasanton Middle – Pleasanton

  • In Merced County, Hilmar Middle – Hilmar

  • In Stanislaus County, Blaker-Kinser Junior High – Ceres, Davis High, Somerset Middle – Modesto, Dutcher Middle – Turlock.

In 2005, National Blue Ribbons were awarded to:

  • Earhart Elementary, Alameda

  • John Muir Elementary, Berkeley

  • Palomares Elementary, Castro Valley

  • Henry P. Mohr Elementary, Pleasanton

SAT Test Scores By County 2004

County	Enroll.	% Tested	Verbal	Math
Alameda	13,522	48	504	537
Alpine	3	33	NA	NA
Amador	476	31	520	506
Butte	2,688	26	503	517
Calaveras	556	30	526	531
Colusa	337	26	449	454
Contra Costa	11,834	41	530	548
Del Norte	589	14	511	517
El Dorado	2,348	33	538	556
Fresno	11,569	29	468	487
Glenn	463	25	465	478
Humboldt	1,651	30	537	543
Imperial	2,257	27	449	459
Inyo	257	37	500	500
Kern	11,057	22	481	494
Kings	1,746	18	474	476
Lake	740	22	512	509
Lassen	579	18	477	486
Los Angeles	94,377	40	473	499
Madera	1,683	18	477	497
Marin	2,031	59	557	561
Mariposa	200	23	531	544
Mendocino	1,194	32	508	523
Merced	3,700	23	453	464
Modoc	190	29	466	466
Mono	170	44	522	500
Monterey	4,487	32	463	473
Napa	1,463	32	515	527
Nevada	2,275	18	551	548
Orange	32,337	40	523	557
Placer	4,657	33	522	539
Plumas	245	33	505	491
Riverside	21,643	31	474	489
Sacramento	15,080	30	495	512
San Benito	646	32	495	504
San Bernardino	24,828	27	475	489
San Diego	31,968	40	508	524
San Francisco	4,376	58	471	536
San Joaquin	8,645	24	472	491
San Luis Obispo	3,100	32	537	539
San Mateo	6,023	45	513	541
Santa Barbara	4,505	32	529	543
Santa Clara	17,231	47	528	565
Santa Cruz	2,891	36	519	531
Shasta	2,470	21	517	526
Sierra	70	40	514	501
Siskiyou	517	24	508	524
Solano	5,109	32	489	510
Sonoma	5,249	34	538	546

(Continued on next page)

(Continued from previous page)

SAT Test Scores By County 2004

County	Enroll.	% Tested	Verbal	Math
Stanislaus	7,210	21	499	507
Sutter	1,203	23	496	530
Tehama	806	18	512	512
Trinity	199	23	567	571
Tulare	5,772	23	462	478
Tuolumne	608	26	533	526
Ventura	10,317	31	528	543
Yolo	2,064	39	536	561
Yuba	983	18	461	486
Statewide:	395,194	35	496	519

Source: California Dept. of Education, 2004 School year.

School Districts in Alameda County

Note: Sunol Glen elementary students attend Foothill High School in the Pleasanton District.

School Accountability Report Card

Want more information about a particular school or school district?

Every public school and district in the state is required by law to issue an annual School Accountability Report Card. The everyday name is the SARC report or the SARC card (pronounced SARK).

Many schools have posted their SARCS on their web sites. If you don't know the name of the neighborhood school, start with the school district. Here are the phone numbers of the districts and the towns they serve.

Alameda County

Alameda City Unified School District
(510) 337-7060

Albany Unified School District
(510) 558-3750

Berkeley Unified School District
(510) 644-6348

Castro Valley Unified School District
(510) 537-3000

Dublin Unified School District
(925) 828-2551

Emery Unified Sch. Dist. (Emeryville)
(510) 601-4000

Fremont Unified School District
(510) 657-2350

Hayward Unified School District
(510) 784-2600

Livermore Valley Joint Unified School District (925) 606-3200

Mountain House Elementary School District (209) 835-2283

New Haven Unified Sch. Dist. (Union City) (510) 471-1100

Newark Unified School District
(510) 794-2141

Oakland Unified School District
(510) 879-8100

Piedmont City Unified School District
(510) 594-2600

Pleasanton Unified School District
(925) 462-5500

San Leandro Unified School District
(510) 667-3500

San Lorenzo Unified School District
(510) 317-4600

Sunol Glen Unified School District
(925) 862-2217

Merced County

Atwater Elementary School District (Atwater) (209) 357-6100

Ballico-Cressey Elementary School District (Ballico, Cressey) (209) 632-5371

Delhi Unified School District (Delhi)
(209) 668-6130

Dos Palos Oro-Loma Joint Unified School District (Dos Palos, Firebaugh) (209) 392-6101

El Nido Elementary School District (El Nido) (209) 385-8420

Gustine Unified School District (Gustine, Santa Nella) (209) 854-3784

Hilmar Unified School District (Hilmar, Stevinson) (209) 667-5701

Le Grand Union Elementary School District (Le Grand) (209) 389-4515

Le Grand Union High School District (Le Grand, Planada) (209) 389-9403

Livingston Union School District (Livingston) (209) 394-5400

Los Banos Unified School District (Los Banos) (209) 826-3801

McSwain Union Elementary School District (Merced) (209) 723-7877

Merced City Elementary School District (Merced) (209) 385-6600

Merced River Union Elementary School District (Snelling, Winton) (209) 722-4581

Merced Union High School District (Atwater, Livingston, Merced) (209) 385-6412

San Joaquin County

Banta Elementary School District
(Tracy) (209) 835-0171

Escalon Unified School District
(Escalon, Farmington, Stockton)
(209) 462-2346

Holt Union Elementary School
District (Stockton) (209) 463-2590

Jefferson Elementary School District
(Tracy) (209) 836-3388

Lammersville Elementary School
District (Tracy) (209) 835-0138

Lincoln Unified School District
(Stockton) (209) 953-8700

Linden Unified School District
(Linden, Stockton) (209) 887-3894

Lodi Unified School District
(Acampo, Clements, Lockeford, Lodi,
Stockton, Victor, Woodbridge)
(209) 331-7000

Manteca Unified School District
(Manteca) (209) 825-3200

New Hope Elementary School District
(Lodi, Thornton) (209) 794-2376

New Jerusalem Elementary School
District (Tracy) (209) 835-2597

Oak View Union Elementary School
District (Acampo) (209) 368-0636

Ripon Unified School District (Ripon)
(209) 599-2131

Stockton Unified School District
(Stockton) (209) 933-7000

Tracy Joint Unified School District
(Tracy) (209) 830-3200

Stanislaus County

Ceres Unified School District (Ceres,
Modesto) (209) 538-0141

Chatom Union Elementary School
District (Crows Landing, Turlock)
(209) 664-8505

Denair Unified School District
(Denair) (209) 632-7514

Empire Union School District
(Empire, Modesto) (209) 521-2800

Gratton Elementary School District
(Denair) (209) 632-0505

Hart-Ranson Union School District
(Modesto) (209) 523-9996

Hickman Elementary School District
(Hickman) (209) 874-1816

Hughson Unified School District
(Hughson) (209) 883-4428

Keyes Union Elementary School
District (Keyes) (209) 669-2921

Knights Ferry Elementary School
District (Knights Ferry) (209) 881-3382

La Grange Elementary School District
(La Grange) (209) 853-2132

Modesto City School District
(Modesto) (209) 576-4011

Newman-Crows Landing Unified
School District (Crows Landing,
Newman) (209) 862-2933

Oakdale Joint Unified School District
(Oakdale) (209) 848-4884

Paradise Elementary School District
(Modesto) (209) 524-0184

Patterson Joint Unified School
District (Patterson) (209) 892-3700

Riverbank Unified School District
(Riverbank, Modesto) (209) 869-2538

Roberts Ferry Union Elementary
School District (Waterford) (209)
874-2331

Salida Union School District
(Modesto, Salida) (209) 545-0339

Shiloh Elementary School District
(Modesto) (209) 522-2261

Stanislaus Union Elementary School
District (Modesto) (209) 529-9546

Sylvan Union Elementary School
District (Modesto) (209) 574-5000

Turlock Joint Elementary School
District (Turlock) (209) 667-0645

Valley Home Joint Elementary School
District (Valley Home) (209) 847-0117

Waterford Unified School District
(Waterford) (209) 874-1809

Chapter 8

Private Schools

ALTHOUGH PRIVATE SCHOOLS often enjoy a better reputation than public, they are not without problems. The typical private or parochial school is funded way below its public school counterpart. In size, facilities and playing fields, and in programs, public schools usually far outstrip private schools. Private school teachers earn less than public school teachers.

"Typical" has to be emphasized. Some private schools are well-equipped, offer exceptional programs, pay their teachers competitively and limit class sizes to fewer than 15 students. Private schools vary widely in funding. But even when "typical," private schools enjoy certain advantages over public schools.

The Advantages

Public schools must accept all students, have almost no power to dismiss incompetent teachers and are at the mercy of their neighborhoods for the quality of students — the socioeconomic correlation. The unruly often cannot be expelled or effectively disciplined.

Much has been said about the ability of private schools to rid themselves of problem children and screen them out in the first place. But tuition, even when modest, probably does more than anything else to assure private schools quality students.

Parents who pay extra for their child's education and often agree to work closely with the school are, usually, demanding parents. The result: fewer discipline problems, fewer distractions in the class, more of a willingness to learn.

When you place your child in a good private school, you are, to a large extent, buying him or her scholastic classmates. They may not be the smartest children — many private schools accept children of varying ability — but generally they will have someone at home breathing down their necks to succeed in academics.

The same attitude, a reflection of family values, is found in the high-achieving public schools. When a child in one of these schools or a private school turns to his left and right, he will see and later talk to children who read

California College Admissions of Private School Graduates

High School	UC	CSU	CC
Apostolic Christian	1	8	NA
Arrowsmith	3	0	1
Beacon	1	0	NA
Bishop O'Dowd	70	48	27
Calvary Baptist	1	0	3
Chinese Christian	22	0	6
College Prep.	20	2	5
Fremont Christian	8	5	2
Head-Royce	18	0	2
Holy Names	14	11	15
Maybeck	7	5	3
Moreau	41	69	44
Patten Acad.	1	2	7
Redwood Christian	1	14	20
St. Elizabeth	1	4	31
St. Joseph ND	12	26	41
St. Mary's	36	36	11
Valley Christian	14	2	19

Source: California Dept. of Education. The chart tracks California public colleges or universities, and high school graduates from private schools. It shows how many students from these high schools enrolled as college freshmen in fall 2004. The state does not track graduates enrolling in private colleges or out-of-state colleges. **Note**: Small or family schools not included in list. **Key**: UC (University of California system); CSU (Cal State system); CC (Community Colleges).

books and newspapers. A child in a low-achieving school, public or private, will talk to classmates who watch a lot of television and rarely read.

(These are, necessarily, broad generalizations. Much depends on whom the children pick for friends. High-achieving students certainly watch television but, studies show, much less than low-achieving students. Many critics contend that even high-scoring schools are graduating students poorly prepared for college.)

The Quality of Teaching

Do private schools have better teachers than public schools? Impossible to tell. Both sectors sing the praises of their teachers (Cont.).

San Joaquin County

High Schools	UC	CSU	CC
Lodi Academy	1	0	9
Ripon Christian	3	19	15
St. Mary's High	15	25	52

Stanislaus County

High Schools	UC	CSU	CC
Central Catholic High	8	26	47
Modesto Adventist Acad.	1	1	2
Turlock Chrstian Jr./Sr. High	0	8	6

Source: California Dept. of Education. The chart tracks California public colleges or universities and high school graduates from private schools. It shows how many students from these high schools enrolled as college freshmen in fall 2004. The state does not track graduates enrolling in private colleges or out-of-state colleges. **Note**: Small or family schools not included in list. **Key:** UC (University of California system); CSU (Cal State system); CC (Community Colleges).

UCs Chosen by Private School Graduates

School	Berk	Davis	Irv	UCLA	RIV	SD	SB	SC	Total
Arrowsmith	0	1	0	0	1	0	1	0	3
Beacon	0	0	0	0	0	0	0	1	1
Bishop O'Dowd	8	14	2	7	3	9	7	20	70
Calvary Baptist	0	0	0	0	1	0	0	0	1
Chinese Christian	1	6	3	4	2	6	0	0	22
College Prep.	6	2	0	4	0	2	1	5	20
Fremont Christian	3	2	1	1	0	1	0	0	8
Head-Royce	3	7	1	4	0	0	2	1	18
Holy Names	4	4	0	1	1	0	1	3	14
Maybeck	0	0	0	0	0	1	1	5	7
Moreau	10	11	1	5	3	2	0	9	41
Patten Academy	0	1	0	0	0	0	0	0	1
Redwood Christian	1	0	0	0	0	0	0	0	1
St. Elizabeth	1	0	0	0	0	0	0	0	1
St. Joseph ND	4	1	2	0	1	0	3	1	12
St. Mary's	12	5	0	3	5	1	2	8	36
Valley Christian	2	2	2	2	1	2	2	1	14

Source: California Dept. of Education. The chart shows how many students from these private schools enrolled as UC freshmen in fall 2004. **Key**: Berk (Berkeley), Irv (Irvine), Riv (Riverside), SD (San Diego), SB (Santa Barbara), SC (Santa Cruz).

San Joaquin County

High Sch.	Berk	Davis	Irv	UCLA	Riv	SD	SB	SC	Total
Lodi Academy	0	0	0	0	0	0	1	0	1
Ripon Christian	1	0	1	0	0	1	0	0	3
St. Mary's High	2	5	1	0	1	3	2	1	15

Stanislaus County

High Sch.	Berk	Davis	Irv	UCLA	Riv	SD	SB	SC	Total
Central Catholic	0	5	0	0	0	0	2	1	8
Modesto Adventist	0	1	0	0	0	0	0	0	1

Source: California Dept. of Education. The chart tracks the Universities of California and high school graduates from private schools. It shows how many students from these schools enrolled as UC freshmen in fall 2004. The state does not track graduates enrolling in private colleges or out-of-state colleges. **Key**: Berk (Berkeley), Irv (Irvine), Riv (Riverside), SD (San Diego), SB (Santa Barbara), SC (Santa Cruz).

Profile of Catholic Schools

THE LARGEST PRIVATE school system in Alameda County,
Catholic schools enroll 12,261 students — 8,582 elementary, 3,679
high school (2002-2003 school year).

The following is based on interviews with Catholic educators and
includes information from the diocese.

- 37 elementary schools, kindergarten through eighth, six high schools,
  one kindergarten (Mission San Jose, Fremont).

- All races, creeds welcome. But where schools are full, preference is
  given to Catholic children from families active in parish, and
  siblings. After that, to active Catholics unable to get into own parish
  schools.

  High schools recruit regionally for students. Admissions tests but
  many accept average students. Standards vary by school.

- School system includes both Alameda and Contra Costa County.
  Contra Costa enrolls 5,699 elementary students, 2,303 secondary.

- Why parents send kids to Catholic schools. Results of survey:
  academics, discipline, religion, safety. Order changes by parish. What
  happens in public schools affects enrollment in Catholic schools, said
  one educator.

  "Parents are looking for safe, positive environment," said another.

- Curriculum. Elementary schools cover same basic subjects as public
  schools but weave in religious-moral viewpoint. "Philosophy based
  in Jesus Christ. Religious values are integral to learning experience."
  State textbooks often used. Each school picks texts.

  High school instruction, although varied, is greatly influenced by
  requirements of University of California.

  Educators advise parents to approach high schools as they would any
  educational institution: ask about grades, what percentage of students
  go on to college, whether school is accredited.

- Non-Catholics. Same instruction as Catholics, including history of
  Church and scripture. Attend Mass but not required to take sacra-
  ments. "We don't try to convert them," said one nun.

- Corporal punishment. Thing of past. Stress positive discipline, name
  on board, detention, probation.

(Continued on page 224)

Catholic Schools

(Continued from page 223)

- Few expulsions. Try to work with kid, parents to solve problems. Elementary expulsions usually have to be approved by diocese. Often parents withdraw child before he or she can be expelled.

- Class sizes. Maximum 35, minimum 25. A few higher and lower. Average about 30, somewhat smaller for high schools because of special classes, e.g., French. Would like smaller classes but point out that with well-behaved students, teachers can accomplish a lot. Matter of economics. If parents wanted smaller classes, they would have to pay more.

  "We want to keep affordable prices so all people can choose us, not just rich."

- Tuition assistance often available.

- Schedule. Similar to public schools. 180 teaching days, 8:30 a.m. to 3 p.m.

- Ability grouping. In elementary grades (K-8) not done by class. Some grouping within classes, advanced children working at one level, slow children at another. Tutoring after class.

  All high schools run prep programs, tend to attract prep students, but will accept remedial students if they have remedial instruction. Admission standards vary by high school.

  Scores also vary by school — socioeconomics. Suburban Catholic schools tend to score higher than city schools.

- Report cards. At least four a year, plus results of state tests. Parents are expected to attend conferences, back-to-school nights.

- Teacher quality. Hired for competence and commitment to Catholic educational philosophy. No restriction in hiring non-Catholics but the system tends to attract Catholic teachers. "No trouble in attracting high-quality applicants."

- Uniforms. Yes, generally skirts, blouses for girls, collared shirts, trousers for boys. High schoolers have more sartorial discretion.

- Extended care. Many schools offer before- and after-school care. Ask.

- Drugs. "We're not immune to dangers of the larger society," said one educator. Schools try to work with kids.

Catholic Schools

- Extracurricular activities. Although small, schools try to offer variety of activities, sports, arts, music. At elementary school, much depends on work of parents. "Parents are expected to do a lot."

High schools offer good variety: music, band, arts, intramural sports, many club activities, cycling, golf.

Catholic high schools usually field very competitive football and basketball teams. "They help build school pride."

More information, admissions, call school directly. For list of schools, call education office at diocese,(510) 628-2154. See also directory at end of this chapter.

(Continued from page 221)

Private schools, compared to public, have much more freedom to dismiss teachers but this can be abused. The private schools themselves advise parents to avoid schools with excessive teacher turnover.

Although most can't pay as much as public schools, private institutions claim to attract people fed up with the limitations of public schools, particularly the restrictions on disciplining and ejecting unruly children. Some proponents argue that private schools attract teachers "who really want to teach."

Religion and Private Schools

Some private schools are as secular as any public institution. But many are religion-oriented and talk in depth about religion or ethics, or teach a specific creed. Or possibly they teach values within a framework of western civilization or some other philosophy.

Public schools teach the history of major religions and touch on the basic tenets of each, and try to inculcate in the children a respect for all religions.

It's hard, if not impossible, however, for public schools to talk about values within a framework of religion or a system of ethics. Often, it's difficult for them to talk about values. Some people argue that this is a major failing.

Many religious schools accept students of different religions or no religion. Some schools offer these students broad courses in religion — less dogma. Ask about the program.

Money

Private-school parents pay taxes for public schools and they pay tuition. Public-school parents pay taxes but not tuition. Big difference.

Ethnic Diversity

Many private schools are integrated and the great majority of private-school principals — the editor knows no exceptions — welcome minorities. Some principals fret over tuition, believing that it keeps many poor students out of private schools. Money, or lack of it, weighs heavily on private schools. Scholarships, however, are awarded, adjustments made, family rates offered.

What's in Alameda County

Alameda County has hundreds of private schools. Many are one-family schools, mother and father teaching their own children at home. A support network that supplies books and materials has grown up for these people.

Some regular private schools have low teacher-pupil ratios, fewer than 15 students per teacher, occasionally around 10 to 1. Public school classes usually go 25 to 30 per teacher, sometimes higher. Class sizes in Catholic schools run close to the public-school ratio, and in the lower grades higher (See Catholic schools profile). Catholic schools, nonetheless, are the most popular, a reflection in part of the high number of Catholics in East Bay.

Private schools in both counties come in great variety, Christian, Jewish, Montessori, Carden (schools with different teaching approaches), prep schools, schools that emphasize language or music, boarding and day schools, schools that allow informal dress, schools that require uniforms.

Susan Vogel has written "Private High Schools of the San Francisco Bay Area." (1999) Check with bookstores or call (415) 267-5978.

Choosing a Private School

1. Inspect the grounds, the school's buildings, ask plenty of questions. "I would make myself a real pest," advised one private school official. The good schools welcome this kind of attention.

2. Choose a school with a philosophy congenial to your own and your child's. Carden schools emphasize structure. Montessori schools, while somewhat structured, encourage individual initiative and independence.

   Ask whether the school is accredited. Private schools are free to run almost any program they like, to set any standards they like, which may sound enticing but in some aspects might hurt the schools. A few bad ones spoil the reputation of the good.

   Many private schools sign up for inspections by independent agencies, such as the Western Association of Schools and Colleges and the California Association of Independent Schools. These agencies try to make sure that schools meet their own goals. Some good schools do not seek accreditation.

3. Get all details about tuition carefully explained. How is it to be paid? Are there extra fees? Book costs? Is there a refund if the student is withdrawn or dropped from the school?

4. Progress reports. Parent conferences. How often are they scheduled?

5. What are the entrance requirements? When must they be met?

    Although many schools use entrance tests, often they are employed to place the child in an academic program, not exclude him from the school.

6. For prep schools, what percentage of the students go on to college and to what colleges?

7. How are discipline problems handled?

8. What are the teacher qualifications? What is the teacher turnover rate?

9. How sound financially is the school? How long has it been in existence? There is nothing wrong per se with new schools. But you want a school that has the wherewithal to do the job.

10. Do parents have to work at functions? Are they required to "volunteer"?

11. Don't choose in haste but don't wait until the last minute. Some schools fill quickly, some fill certain classes quickly. If you can, call the school the year before your child is to enter, early in the year.

12. Don't assume that because your child attends a private school you can expect everything will go all right, that neither the school nor the student needs your attention. The quality of private schools in California varies widely.

Directory of Private Schools

The directory contains the most current information available at press time.

In California, tuition ranges widely in private schools. Many Catholic elementaries charge from about $2,500 to $3,000 plus. Catholic high schools run $6,500 to $7,500.

Some non-denominational schools with low pupil-teacher ratios charge over $12,000.

Don't let the numbers scare you from calling. Some schools offer scholarships. Discounts are often given for siblings. If strapped, ask about financial help.

Day care costs extra.

Alameda County

Alameda

Alameda Christian, 2226 Pacific Ave., (510) 523-1000, Enroll: 93, K-8th.

Children's Learning Ctr., 1910 Central Ave., (510) 769-7100, Enroll: 47, 4th-12th.

Chinese Christian Schs.- Alameda, 1801 N. Loop Rd., (510) 522-0200, Enroll: 86, K-5th.

Peter Pan Acad., 3171 Mecartney Rd., (510) 523-4080, Enroll: 51, K-5th.

Rising Star Montessori Sch., 1421 High St., (510) 865-4536, Enroll: 100, K-5th.

St. Barnabas Elem. Sch., 1400 Sixth St., (510) 521-0595, Enroll: 141, K-8.

St. Joseph Elem. Sch., 1910 San Antonio Ave., (510) 522-4457, Enroll: 307, K-8.

St. Joseph Notre Dame High Sch., 1011 Chestnut St., (510) 523-1526, Enroll: 520, 9th-12th.

St. Philip Neri Elem. Sch., 1335 High St., (510) 521-0787, Enroll: 278, K-8.

Berkeley

Academy, 2722 Benvenue Ave., (510) 549-0605, Enroll: 114, K-8th.

Arrowsmith Acad., 2300 Bancroft Way, (510) 540-0440, Enroll: 126, 9th-12th.

Berkeley Montessori, 2030 Francisco St., (510) 849-8340, Enroll: 213, K-8.

Berkwood Hedge, 1809 Bancroft Way, (510) 883-6990, Enroll: 98, K-5th.

Black Pine Circle, 2027 Seventh St., (510) 845-0876, Enroll: 217, K-8th.

Crowden, 1475 Rose St., (510) 559-6910, Enroll: 84, 4th-9th.

Ecole Bilingue de Berkeley, 1009 Heinz Ave., (510) 549-3867, Enroll: 423, K-8th.

Maybeck High Sch., 2362 Bancroft Way, (510) 841-8489, Enroll: 96, 9th-12th.

Montessori Family Sch., 1850 Scenic Ave., (510) 848-2322, Enroll: 135, Presch.-6th.

School of the Madeleine, 1225 Milvia St., (510) 526-4744, Enroll: 286, K-8.

Shelton's Primary Ed. Ctr., 3339 Martin Luther King, Jr. Way, (510) 652-6132, Enroll: 79, K-5th.

St. Joseph the Worker Elem. Sch., 2125 Jefferson Ave., (510) 845-6266, Enroll: 121, K-8th.

St. Mary's College High, 1294 Albina Ave. Peralta Park, (510) 526-9242, Enroll: 630, 9th-12th.

Via Ctr., 2126 Sixth St., (510) 848-1616, Enroll: 25, K-12th.

Walden Center Elem., 2446 McKinley Ave., (510) 841-7248, Enroll: 86, K-6th.

Castro Valley

Camelot, 2330 Pomar Vista, (510) 481-1304, Enroll: 100, K-5th.

HIS Acad., 6694 Crow Canyon Rd., (925) 513-3179, Enroll: 100, 1-12th.

Our Lady of Grace Sch., 19920 Anita Ave., (510) 581-3155, Enroll: 285, K-8th.

Redwood Christian Sch., 19300 Redwood Rd., (510) 537-4288, Enroll: 347, K-6th.

Redwood Christian Sch. Crossroads Campus, 20600 John Dr., (510) 537-4277, Enroll: 188, K-6th.

Dublin

Quarry Lane Sch., 6363 Tassajara Rd., (925) 829-8000, Enroll: 182, K-8th.

St. Philip Lutheran Sch., 8850 Davona Dr., (925) 829-3857, Enroll: 140, K-8.

St. Raymond Sch., 11557 Shannon Ave, (925) 828-4064, Enroll: 297, K-8th.

Valley Christian Elem., 7508 Inspiration Dr., (925) 560-6270, Enroll: 707, K-6.

Valley Christian Jr.-Sr. High, 7500 Inspiration Dr., (925) 560-6250, Enroll: 552, 7th-12th.

Emeryville

Pacific Rim Int'l, 5521 Doyle St., (510) 601-1500, Enroll: 25, K-6th.

Fremont

Alsion Mid. High, 155 Washington Blvd., (510) 445-1127, Enroll: 27, 7th-9th.

Bethel Christian Acad., 36060 Fremont Blvd., (510) 795-1234, Enroll: 53, K-8th.

Christian Community, 39700 Mission Blvd., (510) 651-5437, Enroll: 4054, K-8th.

Dominican Kindergarten, 43326 Mission Blvd., (510) 657-2468, Enroll: 32, K.

Fremont Christian Sch., 4760 Thornton Ave., (510) 744-2200, Enroll: 1,176, K-12th.

Holy Spirit Elem. School, 3930 Parish Ave., (510) 793-3553, Enroll: 298, K-8th.

Montessori School of Fremont, 155 Washington Blvd., (510) 490-1993, Enroll: 118, K-6th.

New Horizons Sch., 2550 Peralta Blvd., (510) 791-5683, Enroll: 120, 1-6th.

Our Lady of Guadalupe Sch., 40374 Fremont Blvd., (510) 657-1674, Enroll: 242, K-8th.

Peace Terrace Acad., 33330 Peace Terrace, (510) 477-9946, Enroll: 70, K-8th.

Prince of Peace Lutheran, 38451 Fremont Blvd., (510) 797-8186, Enroll: 178, K-8th.

Seneca Center, 40950 Chapel Way, (510) 226-6180, Enroll: 56, K-12th.

St. Joseph Elem. Sch., 43222 Mission Blvd., (510) 656-6525, Enroll: 286, 1st-8th.

Stellar Acad. for Dyslexics, 5301 Curtis St., (510) 687-1490, Enroll: 33, K-8th.

Hayward

All Saints, 22870 Second St., (510) 582-1910, Enroll: 280, K-8th.

American Heritage Christian, 425 Gresel St., (510) 471-1010, Enroll: 117, K-12th.

Lea's Christian Sch., 26236 Adrian Ave., (510) 785-2477, Enroll: 78, K-4.

Montessori Children's House of Hayward, 166 W. Harder Rd., (510) 782-4427, Enroll: 36, 1st-3rd.

Moreau Catholic High Sch., 27170 Mission Blvd., (510) 881-4300, Enroll: 1,029, 9th-12th.

St. Bede Catholic Sch., 26910 Patrick Ave., (510) 782-3444, Enroll: 265, K-8th.

St. Clement Catholic Sch., 790 Calhoun St., (510) 538-5885, Enroll: 301, K-8th.

St. Joachim's Elem., 21250 Hesperian Blvd., (510) 783-3177, Enroll: 301, K-8th.

Woodroe Woods Sch., 22502 Woodroe Ave., (510) 582-3273, Enroll: 170, K-2nd.

Livermore

Celebration Acad., 1135 Bluebell Dr., (925) 277-4313, Enroll: 48, K-12th.

Our Savior's Lutheran, 1385 S. Livermore Ave., (925) 447-2082 Enroll: 365, K-8th.

Sonrise Christian Acad., 164 North L St., (925) 373-2161, Enroll: 38, K-8th.

St. Michael Elem., 345 Church St., (925) 447-1888, Enroll: 317, K-8th.

Sunset Christian Sch., 2200 Arroyo Rd., (925) 243-0972, Enroll: 39, K-4th.

Valley Montessori School, 1273 N. Livermore Ave., (925) 455-8021, Enroll: 463, K-8th.

Newark

Bay Area Baptist Acad., 38517 Birch St., (510) 797-8882, Enroll: 36, K-12th.

Challenger, 35487 Dumbarton Ct., (510) 739-0300, Enroll: 635, K-8th.

Challenger, 39600 Cedar Blvd., (510) 770-1771, Enroll: 60, K.

St. Edward Parish, 5788 Thornton Ave., (510) 793-7242, Enroll: 305, K-8th.

Oakland

Acts Christian Acad., 1034 66th Ave., (510) 568-3333, Enroll: 197, K-8th.

Agnes Mem. Christian Acad., 2372 Int'l Blvd., (510) 533-1101, Enroll: 55, K-12.

Archway, 250 41st St., (510) 547-4747, Enroll: 85, K-8th.

Atherton Academy, 8030 Atherton St., (510) 562-0381, Enroll: 105, 2nd-8th.

Aurora Sch., 40 Dulwich Rd., (510) 428-2606, Enroll: 115, K-5th.

Beacon Day Sch., 2101 Livingston St., (510) 436-4466 Enroll: 219, K-8th.

Bentley Sch., One Hiller Dr., (510) 843-2512, Enroll: 352, K-8th.

Bishop O'Dowd High, 9500 Stearns Ave., (510) 577-9100, Enroll: 1,092, 9th-12th.

Candell's College Prep. Acad., 6969 Sunkist Dr., (510) 632-1110, Enroll: 36, K-12th.

Clara Mohammed, 1652 47th Ave., (510) 436-7755, Enroll: 64, K-10th.

College Prep., 6100 Broadway, (510) 652-0111, Enroll: 327, 9th-12th.

Comm. Sch of the East Bay, 215 Ridgeway, (510) 649-0505, Enroll: 57, 7th-8th.

Fred Finch Oakland Hills Acad., 3800 Coolidge Ave., (510) 482-2244 , Enroll: 48, 6th-12th Spec. Ed..

Golden Gate Acad., 3800 Mountain Blvd., (510) 531-0110, Enroll: 113, 1st-12th.

GRADES K-8
St. Michael's School
Quality Catholic Education Since 1913

- Positive Christian Atmosphere
- Emphasis on Basic Academic Skills
- Enrichment in Music, Drama, Art
- Motor Development Classes
- Instruction in Computers
- Departmentalized Classes for Grades 6-8
- Before & After School Care Available

447-1888
345 Church Street
Livermore

Growing Light Montessori, 4700 Lincoln Ave., (510) 336-9897, Enroll: 38, K-4th.

Head-Royce Sch., 4315 Lincoln Ave., (510) 531-1300, Enroll: 752, K-12th.

Herbert Guice Christian Acad., 6925 International Blvd, (510) 729-0330, Enroll: 804, K-4th.

Holy Names High Sch., 4660 Harbord Dr., (510) 450-1110, Enroll: 277, 9th-12th.

Ile Omode Elem., 8924 Holly St., (510) 632-8230, Enroll: 32, K-6th.

Julia Morgan Sch. for Girls, 3510 Mountain Blvd., (510) 436-1400, Enroll: 146, 6th-8th.

Lincoln Child Center, 4368 Lincoln Ave., (510) 531-3111, Enroll: 78, K-10th.

Mills College Children's Sch., 5000 MacArthur Blvd., (510) 430-2118, Enroll: 47, K-5th.

Montessori Casa Dei Bambini, 281 Santa Clara Ave., (510) 836-4313, Enroll: 38, K-6th.

Muhammad University of Islam, 5277 Foothill Blvd., (510) 436-0206, Enroll: 96, K-12th.

Northern Light Sch., 4500 Redwood Rd., (510) 530-9366, Enroll: 107, K-8.

Park Day, Inc., 370 43rd St., (510) 653-0317, Enroll: 229, K-6th.

Patten Acad. of Christian Ed., 2433 Coolidge Ave., (510) 533-8300, Enroll: 198, K-12th.

Pentecostal Way of Truth Acad., 1575 Seventh St., (510) 625-2002, Enroll: 40, K-12th.

Raskob Day, 3520 Mountain Blvd., (510) 436-1275, Enroll: 62, 4th-8th.

Redwood Day Sch., 3245 Sheffield Ave., (510) 534-0800, Enroll: 273, K-8th.

Renaissance Sch., 3668 Diamond Ave., (510) 531-8566, Enroll: 36, K-7th.

Spectrum Ctr., 6325 Camden St., (510) 729-6384, Enroll: 98, K-12th.

St. Andrew Missionary Baptist Private Sch., 2624 West St., (510) 465-8023, Enroll: 195, K-12th.

St. Anthony Year Round Sch., 1500 East 15th St., (510) 534-3334, Enroll: 165, K-8th.

St. Bernard, 1630 62nd Ave., (510) 632-6323, Enroll: 141, K-8th.

St. Elizabeth Elem., 1516 33rd Ave., (510) 532-7392, Enroll: 442, K-8th.
St. Elizabeth High Sch., 1530 34th Ave., (510) 532-8947, Enroll: 574, 9th-12th.
St. Jarlath Elem. Sch., 2634 Pleasant St., (510) 532-4387, Enroll: 214, K-8th.
St. Lawrence O'Toole Elem., 3695 High St., (510) 530-0266, Enroll: 262, K-8th.
St. Leo Elem. Sch., 4238 Howe St., (510) 654-7828, Enroll: 248, K-8th.
St. Martin De Porres, 1630 10th St., (510) 832-1757, Enroll: 45, 6th-8th.
St. Martin De Porres, 675 41st St., (510) 652-2220, Enroll: 96, K-8th.
St. Paul's Episcopal Sch., 116 Montecito Ave., (510) 287-9600, Enroll: 297, K-8th.
St. Theresa Elem. Sch., 4850 Clarewood Dr., (510) 547-3146, Enroll: 281, K-8.
St. Vincent's Day Home, 1086 8th St., (510) 832-8324, Enroll: 48, K.

Piedmont
Corpus Christi Elem., One Estates Dr., (510) 530-4056, Enroll: 284, K-8th.
Zion Lutheran Elem. Sch., 5201 Park Blvd., (510) 530-7909, Enroll: 175, K-8th.

Pleasanton
Carden-West, 4466-A Black Ave., (925) 484-6060, Enroll: 205, K-5th.
Hacienda Sch., 3800 Stoneridge Dr., (925) 485-5750, Enroll: 75, K-8th.

San Leandro
Assumption Elem., 1851 136th Ave., (510) 357-8772, Enroll: 297, K-8th.
Candell's College Prep., 7309 Greenly, (510) 632-1110, Enroll: 42, K-12th.
Chinese Christian Sch., 750 Fargo Ave., (510) 351-4957, Enroll: 807, K-12th.
Community Christian, 562 Lewelling Blvd., (510) 351-3684, Enroll: 233, K-12th.
Eagle Acad., 3969 Carmel, (510) 928-9771, Enroll: 60, 1st-12th.
Montessori Sch. of San Leandro, 16292 Foothill Blvd., (510) 278-1115, Enroll: 52, 1st-6th.
Principled Acad., 2305 Washington Ave., (510) 351-6400, Enroll: 85, K-8th.

Head-Royce School

4315 Lincoln Avenue Oakland, CA 94602

A K-12 independent, college preparatory school, fully accredited with 118 years of excellence!

Outstanding academic and co-curricular programs

Commitment to scholarship, citizenship and diversity

Financial Aid Available

Admissions Office: 510/531-1300, x2113
www.headroyce.org

Seneca Center, 2275 Arlington Dr., (510) 481-1222, Enroll: 108, 1st-12th.
St. Felicitas Elem., 1650 Manor Blvd., (510) 357-2530, Enroll: 260, K-8th.
St. Leander, 451 Davis St., (510) 351-4144, Enroll: 260, K-8th.
STARS High, 2050 Fairmont Dr., (510) 678-5591, Enroll: 31, 5th-12th.

San Lorenzo
Calvary Lutheran Elem., 17200 Via Magdalena, (510) 278-2598, Enroll: 168, K-8th.
Challenger, 2005 Via Barrett, (510) 431-8690, Enroll: 68, K-3rd.
Redwood Christian Jr./Sr., 1000 Paseo Grande, (510) 317-8990, Enroll: 460, 7th-12th.
St. John Elem., 270 E. Lewelling Blvd., (510) 276-6632, Enroll: 270, K-8th.

Union City
Our Lady of the Rosary Sch., 678 B St., (510) 471-3765, Enroll: 176, K-8th.
Purple Lotus Buddhist, 33615 9th St., (510) 429-8808, Enroll: 41, 1st-12th.
Learning Universe, 4312 Dyer St., (510) 471-1774, Enroll: 90, K-6th.

Union City Christian Acad., 33700 Alvarado-Niles Rd., (510) 489-0394, Enroll: 127, K-12th.

Merced County
Atwater
Landmark Christian, 1925 Olive Ave., (209) 358-0790, Enroll: 34, K-12th.

St. Anthony, 1801 Winton Way, (209) 358-3341, Enroll: 129, K-8th.

Gustine
Our Lady of Miracles, 370 Linden Ave., (209) 854-3180, Enroll: 170, K-8th.

Livingston
Longview Mennonite, 12725 W. Longview Ave., (209) 394-7912, Enroll: 59, K-10th.

Merismos Christian, 10480 W. Liberty Ave., (209) 394-4742, Enroll: 26, K-12th.

Los Baños
Cornerstone Christian Acad., 221 N. Santa Clara St., (209) 826-8633, Enroll: 48, K-12th.

Los Banos Adventist, 404 Overland Rd., (209) 827-4624, Enroll: 45, K-8th.

Our Lady of Fatima, 1625 Center Ave., (209) 826-2709, Enroll: 205, K-8th.

Merced
Cal. Charter Acad. Sch., 2745 East Highway 140, (209) 722-6331, Enroll: 70, K-8th.

Central Valley Christian, 2457 Man O' War Ct., (209) 722-7799, Enroll: 93, K-12th.

Faith Christian, 1233 Parsons Ave., (209) 723-3316, Enroll: 27, K-8th.

Gospel Defenders Christian Acad., 2909 N. Beachwood Dr., (209) 723-6136, Enroll: 45, 1st-12th.

Harvest Christian, 161 E. 16th, (209) 384-0770, Enroll: 31, K-12th.

Joseph Novack Acad., 2025 E. Santa Fe, (209) 724-0323, Enroll: 34, K-12th.

Merced Christian, 3312 North G St., (209) 384-1940, Enroll: 187, K-9th.

Our Lady of Mercy, 1400 E. 27th St., (209) 722-7496, Enroll: 312, K-8th.

St. Luke's Episcopal, 350 W. Yosemite Ave., (209) 723-3907, Enroll: 79, K-5th.

St. Paul's Lutheran, 2916 N. McKee Rd., (209) 383-3302, Enroll: 96, K-5th.

Stone Ridge Christian High Sch., 500 Buena Vista Dr., (209) 386-0322, Enroll: 75, 9th-12th.

Winton
Evergreen Christian, 5935 Winton Way, (209) 357-3000, Enroll: 52, K-8th.

Grace Mennonite, 7200 N. Central Ave., (209) 358-0452, Enroll: 65 , K-10th.

San Joaquin County
Acampo
Mokelumne River Elem., 18950 N. Highway 99, (209) 368-7271, Enroll: 363, K-12th.

Lodi
Century Christian Schls., 550 W. Century Blvd., (209) 334-3230, Enroll: 323, K-8th.

Jim Elliot Christian High, 2695 W. Vine St., (209) 368-2800, Enroll: 198, 9th-12th.

Lodi Acad., 1230 S. Central Ave., (209) 368-2781, Enroll: 145, 9th-12th.

Lodi Seventh-Day Adventist Elem., 1240 S. Central Ave., (209) 368-5341, Enroll: 224, K-8th.

North Valley Sch., 12755 N. Highway 88, (209) 340-5800, Enroll: 75, K-12th.

St. Anne Elem., 200 S. Pleasant Ave., (209) 333-7580, Enroll: 264, K-8th.

St. Peter Evangelical Lutheran, 2400 Oxford Way, (209) 333-2225, Enroll: 195, K-8th.

Zion Middle, 105 S. Ham Ln., (209) 369-1910, Enroll: 85, 6th-8th.

Manteca
Christian Worship Ctr. Acad., 786 Button Ave., (209) 239-4702, Enroll: 32, K-2nd.

Manteca Christian, 486 Button Ave., (209) 239-3436, Enroll: 152, K-8th.

Plumfield Christian Acad., 444 Argonaut St., (209) 823-2655, Enroll: 130, K-8th.

St. Anthony's, 323 N. Fremont Ave., (209) 823-4513, Enroll: 270, K-8th.

Ripon
Ripon Christian, 435 N. Maple Ave., (209) 599-2155, Enroll: 806, K-12th.

St. Thomas Aquinas Acad., 319 3rd St., (209) 599-0665, Enroll: 68, K-12th.

Stockton

Annunciation, 1110 N. Lincoln St., (209) 444-4000, Enroll: 293, K-8th.

Carden School of Stockton, 1200 W. Hammer Ln., (209) 478-8135, Enroll: 80, K-8th.

Children's Home of Stockton, 430 N. Pilgrim St., (209) 466-0853, Enroll: 108, K-12th.

Cragmart Acad., 7273 Murray Dr., No. 6, (209) 476-1675, Enroll: 36, 1st-12th.

Inner City Christian Acad., 640 N. Center St., (209) 469-0312, Enroll: 31, K-12th.

Life Training Acad., 7405 Murray Dr. B, (209) 952-9473, Enroll: 89, K-12th.

Merryhill Sch., 4811 Riverbrook Dr., (209) 477-9005, Enroll: 301, K-8th.

New Harvest Christian Sch., 1950 E. Cherokee Rd., (209) 467-0283, Enroll: 38, K-12th.

Oakbrooke Private, Five W. Swain, (209) 478-1455, Enroll: 50, K-8th.

Presentation Elem., 1635 W. Benjamin Holt Dr., (209) 472-2140, Enroll: 284, K-8th.

Samuel Hancock Christian, 1610 E. Main St., (209) 943-0353, Enroll: 34, K-12th.

Sierra Christian Elem., 4368 N. Sutter St., (209) 941-2877, Enroll: 133, K-8th.

St. George's Primary and Senior Elem., 144 W. Fifth St., (209) 463-1540, Enroll: 209, K-8th.

St. Gertrude, 1701 E. Main St., (209) 941-0301, Enroll: 198, K-8th.

St. Luke's Catholic Elem., 4005 N. Sutter St., (209) 464-0801, Enroll: 279, K-8th.

St. Mary's High, 5648 N. El Dorado St., (209) 957-3340, Enroll: 1,124, 9th-12th.

Stockton Baptist, 5480 N. Highway 99, (209) 931-6101, Enroll: 55, K-12th.

Stockton Christian, 9021 N. West Ln., (209) 957-3043, Enroll: 415, K-12th.

Trinity Lutheran, 444 N. American St., (209) 464-0895, Enroll: 80, K-8th.

Twin Oaks Acad., 8800 Thornton Rd., (209) 473-1720, Enroll: 55, 1st-12th.

United Christian Schls., 915 Rose Marie Ln., (209) 954-7650, Enroll: 137, 9th-12th.

United Christian Schls. 2111 Quail Lakes Dr., (209) 954-7651, Enroll: 677, K-8th.

Write Start Learning Center, 4453 Precissi Ln., (209) 956-5437, Enroll: 109, K-6th.

Tracy

Bella Vista Christian Acad., 1635 Chester Dr., (209) 835-7438, Enroll: 105, K-4th.

Montessori Elem. Sch., 100 S. Tracy Blvd., (209) 833-3458, Enroll: 94, K-4th.

St. Bernard's Cath. Elem., 165 W. Eaton Ave., (209) 835-4560, Enroll: 268, K-8th.

Tracy Seventh-Day Adventist Elem., 126 W. 21st St., (209) 835-6607, Enroll: 51, K-8th.

True Vine Christian Acad., 711 W. Carlton, (209) 833-6239, Enroll: 35, K-5th.

Victory Christian Acad., 1195 W. 11th St., (209) 835-8777, Enroll: 43, K-12th.

West Valley Christian Acad., 1790 Sequoia Blvd., (209) 832-4072, Enroll: 360, K-6th.

Stanislaus County

Ceres

Hearthstone Christian Sch., 2735 5th St., (209) 537-4507, Enroll: 28, 1st-12th.

Modesto Adventist Acad., 2020 Academy Place, (209) 537-4521, Enroll: 306, K-12th.

Denair

Providence Christian Acad., 15307 E. Keyes Rd., (209) 874-2523, Enroll: 153, K-12th.

Reyn Franca, 4033 Main St., (209) 668-8594, Enroll: 45, K-12th.

Hughson

Hughson Christian, 1519 Tully Rd., (209) 883-2874, Enroll: 40, K-8th.

Modesto

Big Valley Christian, 4040 Tully Rd., #D, (209) 527-3481, Enroll: 953, K-11th.

Brethren Heritage, 3549 North Dakota Ave., (209) 543-7860, Enroll: 99, K-12th.

Calvary Temple Christian, 1601 Coffee Rd., (209) 529-7154, Enroll: 250, K-12th.

Central Catholic High, 200 S. Carpenter Rd., (209) 524-9611, Enroll: 448, 9th-12th.

Covenant Christian Acad., 2355 Millcreek Dr., (209) 537-3992, Enroll: 52, K-12th.

Grace Lutheran, 617 W. Orangeburg Ave., (209) 529-1800, Enroll: 89, K-8th.

Heritage Christian, 812 Thieman Rd., (209) 545-9009, Enroll: 41, K-12th.

Kirk Baucher, 918 Sierra Dr., (209) 523-4573, Enroll: 67, 3rd-10th.

Modesto Christian Elem., 3200 Tully Rd., (209) 529-5510, Enroll: 248, K-4th.

Modesto Christian High Sch., 5755 Sisk Rd., (209) 529-5510, Enroll: 309, 9th-12th.

Modesto Christian Mid. Sch., 5901 Sisk Rd., (209) 529-5510, Enroll: 165, 5th-8th.

New Harvest Christian Sch., 1360 Lone Palm Ave., (209) 527-0336, Enroll: 41, K-12th.

Orangeburg Christian Elem., 313 E. Orangeburg Ave., (209) 577-2576, Enroll: 200, K-8th.

Our Lady of Fatima, 501 W. Granger Ave., (209) 524-4170, Enroll: 245, K-8th.

Sierra View Christian, 5307 Tully Rd., (209) 538-7758, Enroll: 85, K-12th.

Small World Christian Elem., 1024 Sixth St., (209) 523-4388, Enroll: 62, K-3rd.

St. Peter Lutheran Sch., 3461 Merle Ave., (209) 551-4963, Enroll: 34, K-9th.

St. Stanislaus Sch., 1416 Maze Blvd., (209) 524-9036, Enroll: 284, K-8th.

Wood Colony Brethren, 2524 Finney Rd., (209) 544-9227, Enroll: 126, K-12th.

Oakdale

East Valley Education Center, 490 S. Fifth St., (209) 848-1834, Enroll: 37, 6th-12th.

Foster-Moore Oakdale SDA, 1501 Magnolia St., (209) 847-3711, Enroll: 39, K-8th.

Patterson

Berean Christian Sch., 650 W. Las Palmas Ave., (209) 892-5965, Enroll: 31, 1st-12th.

Sacred Heart, 505 M St., (209) 892-3544, Enroll: 211, K-8th.

West Valley Christian, 561 Clover Ave., (209) 892-3277, Enroll: 27, 1st-12th.

Riverbank

Riverbank Christian Acad., 6600 Claus Rd., (209) 869-4916, Enroll: 28, K-12th.

Turlock

Northview Christian, 200 North Ave., (209) 634-8083, Enroll: 67, K-8th.

Sacred Heart Elem., 1225 Cooper Ave., (209) 634-7787, Enroll: 272, K-8th.

Stanislaus Acad., 2513 Youngstown Rd., (209) 667-6415, Enroll: 49, 5th-12th.

Turlock Christian, 1360 N. Johnson Rd., (209) 632-6250, Enroll: 300, K-6th.

Turlock Christian Jr./Sr. High, Monte Vista at Berkeley, (209) 632-2337, Enroll: 250, 7th-12th.

Valley Oaks, 441 W. Linwood Ave., (209) 667-9667, Enroll: 54, 1st-8th.

BUY 10 OR MORE & SAVE!

*If you order 10 or more books of any mix, price drops by about 50 percent.
1-800-222-3602. Or fill out form and send with check to:
McCormack's Guides, P.O. Box 190, Martinez, CA 94553. Or fax
order to (925) 228-7223. To order online go to www.mccormacks.com*

1-800-222-3602

Next to title, write in number of copies ordered:

No.	McCormack's Guide	Single	Bulk
____	Alameda & Central Valley 2006	$13.95	.$6.25
____	Contra Costa & Solano 2006	$13.95	.$6.25
____	Orange County 2006	$13.95	.$6.25
____	Greater Sacramento 2006	$13.95	.$6.25
____	San Diego County 2006.	$13.95	.$6.25
____	San Francisco, San Mateo, Marin, Sonoma 2006	.$13.95	.$6.25
____	Santa Clara & Santa Cruz 2006	.$13.95	.$6.25
____	How California Schools Work	$15.95	.$6.25

Subtotal $ _____

CA sales tax (8.25%) _____

Shipping* _____

Total Amount of Order $ _____

**For orders of 10 or more, shipping is 60 cents per book. For orders of
fewer than 10, shipping is $4.50 for first book, $1.50 per book thereafter.*

Circle one: Check/Visa/MC/Am.Exp. or Bill Us

Card No. _____ Exp. Date _____

Name _____

Company _____

Address _____

City _____ State _____ Zip _____

Phone: (_____) _____ Fax (_____) _____

*The following guides are available online at www.mccormacks.com:
Los Angeles County 2006, Riverside County 2006, Ventura County 2006,
San Bernardino County 2006 and Santa Barbara County 2006.*

☐ **Check here to receive advertising information**

Chapter **9**

Infant-Baby Care

FOR LICENSING, California divides child-care facilities into several categories:
- Small family: up to 6 children in the providers' home.
- Large family: 7-12 children in the provider's home.
- Nursery Schools or Child-Care centers.
  A child is considered an infant from birth to age 2.

Individual sitters are not licensed and neither are people whom parents arrange for informally to take care of their children but if a person is clearly in the business of child care from more than one family he or she should be licensed. Each of the three categories has restrictions. For example, the small-family provider with six children cannot have more than three under age 2.

In everyday reality, many of the larger facilities tend to limit enrollments to children over age 2, and some have even higher age limits or a requirement that the child be toilet-trained.

The state and its local umbrella agencies maintain referral lists of local infant-care and day-care providers. All you have to do is call and they will send a list of the licensed providers and suggestions on how to make a wise choice. For a list of family-care providers, call BANANAS at (510) 658-0381 (Oakland) or the 4C's of Alameda County (Southern Alameda) at (510) 582-2182 or Child Care Links (Livermore-Dublin-Pleasanton) at (925) 455-0417.

Here's some advice from one licensing agency:
- Plan ahead. Give yourself one month for searching and screening.
- Contact the appropriate agencies for referrals.
- Once you have identified potential caregivers, phone them to find out about their services and policies. For those that meet your needs, schedule a time to visit while children are present.
- At the site, watch how the children play and interact with one another.
- Contact other parents using the programs. Ask if they are satisfied with the care and if their children are happy and well-cared-for.
- Select the program that best meet your needs. "Trust your feelings and your instincts."

This is a bare-bones approach. The referral centers can supply you with more information. To get you started, we are listing here the names of the infant centers in the county. For older children, see next chapter.

Alameda County

Alameda

Alameda Tiny Tots, 3300 Bridgeview Isle, (510) 521-8025

College of Alameda Children's Ctr., 555 Atlantic Ave., (510) 748-2381

ICRI of Alameda CCCtr., 2001 Santa Clara Ave., (510) 522-3194

Island H.S. Cal-Safe Program, 2437 Eagle Ave., (510) 748-4024

KinderCare, 2155 N. Loop Rd., (510) 521-3227

Little Seeds Children's Ctr., 2055 Santa Clara Ave., (510) 865-5900

Peter Pan Presch., 3171 McCarthy Rd., (510) 523-5050

Peter Pan Presch., 2100 Mariner Square Dr., (510) 521-2750

Wee Care Presch. & CC, 2133 Central Ave., (510) 523-7858

Berkeley

Aquatic Park Ctr., 830 Heinz Ave., (510) 843-2273

Berkeley YMCA Early Head Start, 1450 6th St., (510) 558-2110

BUSD-Vera Casey Parent Child, 2246 Martin Luther King, Jr. Way, (510) 644-6954

Cedar Street CC, 2138 Cedar St., (510) 549-3989

Child Ed. Ctr., 1222 University Ave., (510) 528-1414

Cornerstone Children's Ctr., 2407 Dana St., (510) 848-6252

Model Sch. Compre. Humanistic Lrng. Ctr., 2330 Prince St., (510) 549-2711

St. John's CC Prog., 2717 Garber St., (510) 549-9342

UCB-Anna Head Children's Ctr., 2537 Haste St., (510) 642-1960

UCB-Clark Kerr Inf. Ctr., 2601 Warring St., (510) 642-9795

UCB-Inf./Toddler Ctr., 2340 Durant Ave., (510) 642-1123

Woolly Mammoth CC & Presch., 2314 Bancroft Way, (510) 548-4779

Castro Valley

Camelot Sch., 2330 Pomar Vista, (510) 481-1304

His Growing Grove, 2490 Grove Way, (510) 581-5088

Lil' Sunflowers CDCtr., 20875 Chester St., (510) 881-0378

Dublin

KinderCare, 11925 Amador Valley Ct., (925) 875-0400

La Petite Acad., 5000 Hacienda Ave., (925) 236-7203

My Space To Grow, 7197 Amador Valley Blvd., (925) 829-4063

Resurrection Luth. Inf. Care Ctr., 7557 Amador Valley Blvd., (925) 828-2122

Emeryville

Emeryville CDCtr., 1220 53rd St., (510) 596-4343

Siebel Children's Ctr., 2100 Powell St., (510) 788-4780

Fremont

Children's Galaxy, 34735 Ardenwood Blvd., (510) 793-1696

Kidango-Delaine Eastin CDCtr., 584 Brown Rd., (510) 490-5570

Kidango-Fremont Ad. Sch. Child Dev. Sch., 4700 Calaveras Ave., (510) 494-9601

Kidango-Marie Kaiser Ctr., 4457 Seneca Park Ave., (510) 226-8130

Kidango-Rix Inf. Ctr., 43100 Isle Royal St., (510) 656-3949

Kidango-Washington Hospital, 2000 Mowry Ave., (510) 731-3400

KinderCare, 32710 Falcon Dr., (510) 324-3569

KinderCare, 38700 Paseo Padre Pkwy., (510) 796-0888

Montessori Children's Ctr., 33170 Lake Mead Dr., (510) 489-7511

Hayward

Chabot College Children's Ctr., 25555 Hesperian Blvd., (510) 723-6684

Cherubim's Children's Ctr., 30540 Mission Blvd., (510) 471-7713

Early Childhood Ed. Ctr., 25800 Carlos Bee Blvd., (510) 885-2480

Eden Youth CCCtr., 680 W. Tennyson Rd., (510) 782-6084
ESP-A Special Place CCCtr., 27305 Huntwood Ave., (510) 782-6635
His Kids, 26221 Gading Rd., (510) 786-3641
Li'l Angels at Ruus, 28924 Ruus Rd., (510) 670-9007
S. Alameda Co. Head Start-Eden Youth, 680 W. Tennyson Rd., (510) 782-6207

Livermore

Cape, Inc.-Jackson Ctr., 560 Jackson Ave., (925) 443-0220
Kidango-Marylin Inf. Dev. Ctr., 800 Marylin Ave., (925) 371-6376
Kidango-Owl's Landing CDCtr., 860 Hermann Ave., (925) 744-9280
Kidango-Pepper Tree Sch., 714 Junction Ave., (925) 447-0264
KinderCare, 4655 Lassen Rd., (925) 455-1560
Laboratory Employee Children's Ctr., 1401 Almond Ave., (925) 373-0865
New Horizons Nursery Sch.-Inf. Prog., 405 E. Jack London Blvd., (925) 455-6082
Trinity DCCtr., 557 Olivina Ave., (925) 449-5683
Valley Montessori Sch., 1273 N. Livermore Ave., (925) 455-8021

Newark

Kidango-Rushin Inf. Dev. Ctr., 36120 Rushin Blvd., (510) 793-5562

Oakland

AOCS-Brookdale Ctr., 3021 Brookdale Ave., (510) 261-1077
AOCS-Hedco Inf./Toddler Ctr., 2929 Coolidge Ave., (510) 261-1076
Booth Memorial Inf./Toddler Prog., 2794 Garden St., (510) 535-5088
First Step Children's Ctr., 111 Fairmount Ave., (510) 238-0882
Four C's CDCtr., 756 21st St.. (510) 272-0669
Kidango-Chestnut Ctr., 1058 W. Grand Ave., (510) 989-1111
Laney College Children's Ctr., 900 Fallon St., (510) 464-3104
Little Stars Presch., 169 14th St., (510) 286-9800
Merritt College Children's Ctr., 12500 Campus Dr., (510) 531-4911
Mills College Children's Sch., Mills College Campus, (510) 430-2118
PCDCI-Frank G. Mar Ctr., 274 12th St., (510) 835-9236
Sequoyah Comm. Toddler Ctr., 4292 Keller Ave., (510) 632-3481
Small Trans Depot-Honey Bee, 111 Grand Ave., (510) 286-5130
Spanish Speaking-Fruitvale Parent Child Ctr., 1266 26th Ave., (510) 535-6112
Spanish Speaking-Thurgood Marshall Early Headstart, 1117 10th St., (510) 836-0543

Alameda County Births — History & Projections

1980s		1990s		2000s	
Year	Births	Year	Births	Year	Births
1981	17,984	1991	23,252	2001	22,029
1982	18,220	1992	22,678	2002	21,802
1983	18,466	1993	21,919	2003	21,574
1984	19,255	1994	21,387	2004	21,829
1985	19,624	1995	20,941	2005	22,040
1986	20,127	1996	20,668	2006	22,252
1987	20,957	1997	20,766	2007	22,500
1988	21,862	1998	20,933	2008	22,773
1989	22,419	1999	20,547	2009	23,054
1990	23,285	2000	22,164	2010	23,331

Source: California Dept. of Finance, Demographic Research Unit. Projections start in 2004.

Supporting Future Growth, 5909 Camden St., (510) 567-8362

Up & Coming Inf. Dev. Ctr., 4143 MacArthur Blvd., (510) 531-9130

YWCA of Oakland-Alice St., 250 17th St., (510) 836-4117

Pleasanton

Hacienda CDCtr., 4671 Chabot Dr., (925) 463-2885

KinderCare, 3760 Brockton Dr., (925) 846-1240

La Petite Acad., 5725 Valley Ave., (925) 277-0626

Quarry Lane Sch., 3750 Boulder St., (925) 846-9400

YMCA-Pleasanton Child Dev. Prog., 4665 Bernal Ave., (510) 451-8039

San Leandro

Davis St. CDCtr., 580 Joaquin Ave., (510) 635-0536

Heaven Sent, 301 Dowling Blvd., (510) 568-0402

ICRI Early Childhood Ctr., 13305 Doolittle Dr., (510) 357-1588

Union City

Kidango-Decoto Inf. Ctr., 600 G St., (510) 744-9280

Kidango-Logan Inf. Dev. Ctr., 33821 Syracuse Ave., (510) 441-1841

Merced County

Atwater

Atwater Migrant CD & Inf. Ctr., 9200 W. Westside Blvd., (209) 357-7382

Le Grand

Planada Migrant CD & Inf. Ctr., 8880 E. Gerard Ave., (209) 382-1036

Los Baños

Los Banos Migrant CD & Inf. Ctr., 16570 S. Mercy Springs Rd., (209) 826-7521

Merced

Buhach Discovery Ctr., 2606 N. Buhach St., (209) 358-0177

Family CDCtr., 401 Lesher, (209) 525-4937

Family CDCtr., 1422 W. 6th St., (209) 723-7952

Merced College CDCtr., 3600 M St., (209) 384-6245

MUHSD CDCtr., 1900 G St., (209) 385-6440

South Dos Palos

South Dos Palos Migrant CD & Inf. Ctr., 22380 S. 7th St., (209) 392-2722

San Joaquin County

French Camp

Artesi II Migrant Inf. CCCtr., 777 W. Mathews Rd., (209) 983-0655

Artesi III Migrant Inf. CDCtr., 333 W. Mathews Rd., (209) 982-0520

Lodi

Adelita Migrant Child Inf. Dev. Ctr., 14320 E. Harney Ln., (209) 368-2087

Live Oak Sch. Head Start, 5099 E. Bear Creek Rd., (209) 331-7943

Lodi Day Nursery Sch., 760 S. Ham Ln., (209) 334-6884

Manteca

Creative Kids, 115 S. Powers Ave., (209) 825-5437

Hansel & Gretel DCCtr., 1014 W. Center St., (209) 823-6525

Mountain House

Wickland CDC, 300 E. Legacy, (408) 371-9900

Stockton

A Child's Smile Acad., 6 W. Main St., (209) 463-6220

Calif. St. Early Head Start, 425 N. California St., (209) 467-3424

Connie Romena Head Start Ctr., 2295 E. Fremont St., (209) 462-7153

Council For The Spanish Speaking, 106 Hammertown Dr., (209) 957-9435

Creative CC, 1700 Porter Way, (209) 477-5063

Creative CC, 1105 N. Sacramento St., (209) 939-9270

Creative CC-Univ., 1105 N. Sacramento St., (209) 478-2346

Creative CC-Eden Square, 17 E. Poplar, (209) 462-2282

Creative Head Start, 7505 Tam O'Shanter, (209) 956-2686

Franklin High Early Head Start, 300 Gertrude, (209) 467-0463

Garden of Eden DCCtr., 405 Pine St., (209) 474-6648

Kiddie Kingdom Presch., 1121 S. Oro Ave., (209) 462-3730

Kids Junction, 6311 Pacific Ave., (209) 951-5437

KinderCare, 7801 Mariners Dr., (209) 477-3723

Latin American Club Head Start, 548 S. Wilson Way, (209) 463-5616

Merryhill School, 7204 Shoreline Dr., (209) 474-0518

Miz B's Presch., 2220 W. Alpine, (209) 942-3514

San Joaquin Delta College CDCtr., 5151 Pacific Ave., (209) 954-5700

Write-Start Lrng. Ctr., 4453 Precissi Ln., (209) 956-5437

Tracy

KinderCare, 265 W. Grantline Rd., (209) 835-9247

Little Country CC, 1820 W. Grantline Rd., (209) 833-7882

McKinley Village CDCtr., 2105-2123 Tracy Blvd., (209) 832-7844

Tender Loving Care #2, Defense Depot, S. Chrisman Rd., (209) 832-8686

Stanislaus County

Ceres

Kiddie Kingdom DCCtr., 3900 Morgan Rd., (209) 537-8944

Walter Thompson CDCtr., 2003 Glenda Way, (209) 537-9032

Empire

Pearlene Reese CDCtr., 5124 South Ave., (209) 529-2322

Modesto

Centenary Christian Presch., 1911 Toyon Ave., (209) 522-7091

Children's Crisis Ctr.1, 133 Downey Ave., (209) 577-0138

Children's Crisis Ctr., 1244 Fiori Ave., (209) 577-0138

Childtime, 2320 Floyd Ave., (209) 551-0255

Childtime, 3912 Honey Creek, (209) 545-1664

Emanuel Lutheran DC, 324 College Ave., (209) 523-4531

Greenoak Christian Presch., 1308 Coffee Rd., (209) 529-3000

Inf. & Toddler CDCtr., 2201 Blue Gum, (209) 575-6972

KinderCare, 2825 W. Rumble Rd., (209) 529-1995

KinderCare, 1237 Oakdale Rd., (209) 521-5351

Merryhill Sch., 133 E. Roseburg Ave., (209) 527-2310

My Pride & Joy, 4825 Stratos Dr., (209) 548-9111

Tender Hearts CCCtr., 2118 Woodland Ave., (209) 527-7995

Trinity Nursery Sch., 1600 Carver Rd., (209) 578-5625

Newman

Starkids, 151 S. Hwy. 33, (209) 862-4227

Oakdale

Children's Crisis Ctr., 246 W. F St., (209) 577-0138

Patterson

Del Puerto CDCtr., 640 M St., (209) 892-1610

Patterson House of Children, 650 N. 2nd, (209) 892-2759

SCCICA-Patterson-Inf., 421 Franquette, (209) 892-8130

Turlock

A Special Place, 2490 N. Walnut, (209) 667-0322

CA State Univ. CDCtr., 801 W. Monte Vista, (209) 667-3036

Covenant Park Children's Campus, Laurel & High Sts., (209) 667-7622

TLC Ed. Acad., 1620 Colorado Ave., (209) 667-0668

Turlock CDCtr., 400 N. Kilroy Rd., (209) 669-6374

Turlock Christian Sch.., 2006 E. Tuolumne Rd., (209) 669-2192

Waterford

Byron F. Todd Christian Sch., 116 E St., (209) 874-2145

Westley

Westley CDC, 601 Livingston Cir., (209) 894-5194

Chapter 10

Day Care

SEE THE PRECEDING chapter on baby care for more information. For insights on how to pick a day-care center or provider, here is some advice offered by a person who runs a day-care center.

- Ask about age restrictions. Many centers and family-care providers will not take care of children under age two or not toilet trained. See previous chapter for infant centers.

- Give the center or home a visual check. Is it clean? In good condition or in need of repairs? Is there a plan for repairs when needed?

- Find out if the person in charge is the owner or a hired manager. Nothing wrong with the latter but you should know who is setting policy and who has the final say on matters.

- Ask about the qualifications of the people who will be working directly with your child. How long have they worked in day care? Training? Education? Many community colleges now offer training in early childhood and after-school care.

- What philosophy or approach does the center use? The Piaget approach believes children move through three stages and by exploring the child will naturally move through them. The job of the teacher is to provide activities appropriate to the right stage. For example, from age 2-7, many children master drawing and language; from 7-11, they begin to think logically. For the younger child art and sorting and language games would be appropriate; multiplication would not.

  Montessori believes that if given the right materials and placed in the right setting, children will learn pretty much by themselves through trial and error. Montessorians employ specific toys for teaching.

  Traditional emphasizes structure and repetition.

  These descriptions are oversimplified and do not do justice to these approaches or others. Our only purpose here is to point out that day-care providers vary in methods and thinking, and in choosing a center, you also choose a distinct philosophy of education.

- For family day-care providers. Some set up a small preschool setting in the home. Often your child will be welcomed into the family as an extended member. Is this what you want?

- Discipline. Johnny throws a snit. How is it handled? Does the provider have a method or a plan? Do you agree with it?

- Tuition. How much? When it is due? Penalty for picking up child late? Penalty for paying late?

- Hours of operation. If you have to be on the road at 5:30 a.m. and the day-care center doesn't open until 6, you may have to look elsewhere or make different arrangements. Some centers limit their hours of operation, e.g., 10 hours.

- Holidays. For family providers, when will the family take a vacation or not be available? For the centers, winter breaks? Summer vacations?

- Communication. Ask how you will be kept informed about progress and problems. Regular meetings? Notes? Calls? Newsletters?

- Classes-Tips for parents. Opportunities to socialize with other parents? Activities for whole family?

- Field trips and classes. Outside activities. Your son and daughter play soccer, an activity outside the day-care center. How will they get to practice? What's offered on site? Gymnastics? Dance?

- Siestas. How much sleep will the children get? When do they nap? Does this fit in with your child's schedule?

- Activities. What are they? How much time on them? Goals?

- Diapers, bottles, cribs, formula, extra clothes. Who supplies what?

- Food, lunches. What does the center serve? What snacks are available?

Remember, day-care centers and providers are in business. The people who staff and manage these facilities and homes may have the best intentions toward the children but if they can't make a profit or meet payrolls, they will fail or be unable to provide quality care. Even "nonprofits" must be run in a businesslike way or they won't survive. Some centers may offer a rich array of services but for fees beyond your budget. You have to decide the trade-offs.

For licensing, the state divides child care into several categories, including infant, licensed family, child-care centers, and school-age centers for older children. The previous chapter lists the infant providers. This chapter will list the large day-care centers, for both preschool and school-age children.

For a list of family-care providers, call BANANAS at (510) 658-0381 (Oakland) or the 4C's of Alameda County (Southern Alameda) at (510) 582-2182 or Child Care Links (Livermore-Dublin-Pleasanton) at (925) 455-0417.

Alameda

ABC Presch., 1525 Bay St., (510) 521-6488

Alameda CCCtr., 2001 Santa Clara Ave., (510) 522-3194

Alameda Head Start-Angela Aguilera, 1901 3rd St., (510) 865-4500

Alameda Head Start-Esperanza, 1901 3rd St., (510) 865-4500

Alameda Head Start-Redwood Ctr., 1700 Santa Clara Ave., (510) 865-4862

Alameda Head Start-Sue Matheson, 1980 3rd St., (510) 865-0108

Alameda Head Start-Washington, 825 Taylor Ave., (510) 748-4007

Alameda Head Start-Woodstock, 1900 3rd St., (510) 748-4012

Alameda Tiny Tots, 3300 Bridgeview Isle, (510) 521-8025

AUSD- Woodstock CDCtr., 190 Singleton, (510) 748-4001

Bayside Montessori Assoc., 1523 Willow St., (510) 865-6255

Child Unique Montessori Sch., 2212 Pacific Ave., (510) 521-1030

Child Unique Montessori Sch., 2226 Encinal Ave., (510) 521-9227

College of Alameda Children's Ctr., 555 Atlantic Ave., (510) 748-2381

Garner Presch. Lrng. Ctr., 2275 N. Loop Rd., (510) 769-5437

Girls Inc.-Edison Activity Ctr., 2700 Buena Vista Ave., (510) 769-1975

Girls Inc.-Lum Activity Ctr., 1801 Sandcreek Way., (510) 522-4729

Girls Inc.-Otis Activity Ctr., 3010 Fillmore St., (510) 523-6510

Girls Inc.-Paden Activity Ctr., 444 Central Ave., (510) 523-6977

Golden House CCCtr., 1545 Morton St., (510) 865-3468

Home Sweet Home CCCtr., 2750 Todd St., (510) 748-4314

ICRI of Alameda CCCtr., 2001 Santa Clara Ave., (510) 522-3194

Kiddie Kampus Coop. Play Sch., 1711 2nd St., (510) 521-1218

KinderCare, 2155 N. Loop Rd., (510) 521-3227

Montessori of Alameda-Daycare, 1247 Park Ave., (510) 521-2354

Our Children's Cottage, 770 Santa Clara Ave., (510) 865-4536

Peter Pan Presch., 1510 Encinal Ave., (510) 523-5050

Peter Pan Presch., 2100 Mariner Square Dr., (510) 521-2750

Peter Pan Presch. & DC, 3171 Mecartney Rd., (510) 523-4080

Rising Star Sch., 1421 High St., (510) 865-4536

Seedling Child Montessori Sch., 3183 McCartney Rd., (510) 521-5846

Son-Light Presch., 1910 Santa Clara Ave., (510) 865-6367

Sugar & Spice, 2238 Mariner Sq., (510) 865-1055

Wee Care Presch. & CC, 2133 Central Ave., (510) 523-7858

Albany

Albany Children's Ctr., 1140 9th St., (510) 525-2800

Albany Presch., 850 Masonic Ave., (510) 527-6403

Bay Area Kinder Stube, 842 Key Route Blvd., (510) 525-3105

Berkeley Chinese Sch., 720 Jackson St., (510) 525-9666

Bright Star Montessori Sch., 720 Jackson St., (510) 559-6530

Kid's Club YMCA-Albany Library, 1216 Solano Ave., (510) 524-9737

Little Village Presch., 919 Talbot Ave. (510) 528-4401

Wheezles and Sneezles, 1108 San Pablo Ave., (510) 526-7425

Berkeley

ALA/CCCtr. for Dev. Disabled, 1300 Rose St., (510) 527-2550

Aquatic Park Sch., 830 Heinz Ave., (510) 843-2273

Bahia Sch. Age Prog., 1718 8th St., (510) 524-7300

Berkeley Hills Nursery Sch., 1161 Sterling Ave., (510) 849-1216

Berkeley Montessori Sch., 2030 Francisco St., (510) 849-8341

Berkeley Youth Alt. Presch. & CD Prog., 1255 Allston Way, (510) 845-9010

Berkeley-Richmond Jewish Comm. Ctr., 1414 Walnut St., (510) 848-0237

BUSD-Columbus Montessori Presch., 920 Allston Way, (510) 644-8812

BUSD- Franklin State Presch., 1460 8th St., (510) 644-6339

BUSD-Hopkins, 1810 Hopkins St., (510) 644-6405

BUSD-King Children's Ctr., 1939 Ward St., (510) 644-6358

Cedar Creek Montessori, 1600 Sacramento St., (510) 525-1377

Cedar Street CCCtr., 2138 Cedar St., (510) 549-3989

Centro Vida Bilingual CCCtr., 1000 Camelia St., (510) 525-1463

Child Ed. Ctr., 1222 University Ave., (510) 528-1414

Children's Comm. Ctr., 1140 Walnut St., (510) 526-9739

Cornerstone Children's Ctr., 2407 Dana St., (510) 848-6252

Claremont Day Nurseries, 2845 Woolsey Ave., (510) 654-2511

Color Me Children Presch., 1141 Bancroft Way, (510) 548-6423

Congregation Beth El, 2301 Vine St., (510) 848-3988

Congregation Beth Israel-Gan Shalom, 2230-32 Jefferson St., (510) 848-3298

Dandelion Nursery Sch., 941 The Alameda, (510) 526-1735

Duck's Nest, 1411 4th St., (510) 527-2331

Ecole Bilingue de Berkeley, 2830 10th St., (510) 549-3867

Ephesian Children's Ctr., 1907 Harmon Ave., (510) 653-2984

Garden Day Montessori, 1332 Parker St., (510) 649-9110

Gay Austin Sch., 1611 Hopkins St., (510) 526-2815

Griffin Nursery Sch., 2410 Prince St., (510) 845-2025

Hearts Leap Presch., 2638 College Ave., (510) 549-1422

Hopkins Street CCCtr., 1910 Hopkins St., (510) 524-1352

I Can Before and After Sch., 515 58th St., (510) 644-8204

Kids' Club YMCA-Hillside, 1581 Leroy Ave., (510) 644-3152

Kids in Motion, 2955 Claremont Ave., (510) 549-9247

McGee's Farm Presch., 2214 Grant St., (510) 849-3593

Model Sch. Compre. Humanistic Lrng. Ctr., 2330 Prince St., (510) 549-2711

Montessori Family Sch., 1850 Scenic Ave., (510) 848-2322

Monteverde Sch., 2727 College Ave., (510) 848-3313

Mulberry Sch., 207 Alvarado Rd., (510) 540-5778

Mustard Seed Presch., 1640 Hopkins St., (510) 527-6627

New School of Berkeley, 1606 Bonita Ave., (510) 548-9165

New School of Berkeley-Sch. Age, 1924 Cedar St., (510) 548-9165

NIA House Lrng. Ctr., 2234 9th St., (510) 845-6099

Progressive Christian DCCtr., 1728 Alcatraz Ave., (510) 654-6686

Rose Street Comm. CCCtr., 1226 Rose St., (510) 524-4271

Shelton's Primary Ed. Ctr., 3339 Martin Luther King Jr. Way, (510) 652-6132

Snuggery, 2008 McGee Ave., (510) 548-9121

St. John's CCCtr., 2717 Garber St., (510) 549-9342

Step One Sch., 499 Spruce St., (510) 527-9021

UCB-After Sch. Prog., 2601 Warring St., (510) 642-8442

UCB-Anna Head Children's Ctr., 2537 Haste St., (510) 642-3239

UCB-Clark Kerr Campus Children's Ctr., 2900 Dwight Way., (510) 642-5527

UCB-Girton Hall CCCtr., UC Berkeley Central Campus, (510) 642-5677

UCB-Harold E. Jones Child Study Ctr., 2425 Atherton St., (510) 643-5449

Via Nova Children's Sch., 3032 Martin Luther King Jr. Way, (510) 848-6682

Woolly Mammoth CC & Presch., 2314 Bancroft Way, (510) 548-4779

YMCA Head Start, 1227 Bancroft Way, (510) 845-1213

YMCA Head Start-6th St., 1450 6th St., (510) 558-2110

YMCA Head Start-Berkeley Adult Sch., 1222 University Ave., (510) 841-4152

YMCA Head Start-Ocean View, 1422 San Pablo Ave., (510) 559-2090

YMCA Head Start-Sacramento, 3155 Sacramento St., (510) 547-6683

YMCA Head Start-S. YMCA, 2901 California St., (510) 848-9092

YMCA Head Start-W. YMCA 1,2,3,4, 2009 10th St., (510) 848-9092

Castro Valley

Aahl's ABC Presch. & DC, 20135 San Miguel Ave., (510) 581-5577

Adventure Time-Jensen Ranch, 20001 Carson Ln., (510) 728-9933

Bright World Presch., 20613 Stanton Ave., (510) 581-1580

Camelot Sch.-Valley View Campus, 2330 Pomar Vista, (510) 481-1304

Creative Beginnings Presch., 20121 Santa Maria Ave., (510) 581-5990

CVUSD-Marshall State Presch., 20111 Marshall St., (510) 537-5933

First Baptist Presch.- A Kids Kingdom, 18550 Redwood Rd., (510) 889-8800

Growing Years Day Camp, 20166 Wisteria Ave., (510) 733-0848

Growing Years Presch., 20320 Anita Ave., (510) 581-3731

Happiness Hill Presch., 20600 John Dr., (510) 537-0773

His Growing Grove, 2490 Grove Way, (510) 581-6203

Kids Care Plus-Cyn. Mid. Sch., 19600 Cull Canyon Rd., (510) 538-8351

Kids Care Plus-Stanton, 2644 Somerset Ave., (510) 733-0775

Lil' Sunflowers CD Prog., 20875 Chester St., (510) 881-0378

Montessori of Castro Valley, 19234 Lake Chabot Rd., (510) 582-9413

Montessori Sch. at Five Canyons, 22781 Canyon Ct., (510) 581-3729

Redwood Forest Presch., 19200 Redwood Rd., (510) 537-0222

Rise 'N Shine Presch., 20104 Center St., (510) 582-9136

R-Kids Ext. Day Ctr., 4779 Heyer Ave., (510) 329-7344

Saybrook Lrng. Ctr., 20375 Wisteria St., (510) 581-2340

YMCA-Y-Kids-Marshall, 20111 Marshall St., (510) 581-4996

YMCA-Y-Kids-Castro Valley, 20185 San Miguel Ave., (510) 881-4458

Dublin

Creative Playschool, 6837 Amador Valley Blvd., (925) 803-4035

Fountainhead Montessori Sch., 6901 York Dr., (925) 820-1343

John Knox Coop. Presch., 7421 Amarillo Rd., (925) 828-2887

Joy Presch. & DCCtr., 7421 Amarillo Rd., (925) 829-3233

Kidango-Arroyo Vista Presch., 6700 Dougherty Rd., (925) 560-0669

KinderCare, 11925 Amador Valley Ct., (925) 875-0400

La Petite Acad., 3 Sybase Dr., (925) 236-7203

Little Kids Lrng. Ctr., 11760 Dublin Blvd., (925) 828-2081

Love and Care Presch., 8010 Hollanda Ln., (925) 828-1170

Montessori Plus, 7234-40 San Ramon Rd. (925) 829-1321

My Space To Grow, 7197 Amador Valley Blvd., (925) 829-4063

Resurrection Lutheran Presch., 7557-A Amador Valley Blvd., (925) 829-5487

St. Philip Presch., 8850 Davona Dr., (925) 829-3857

Tot's University, 7890 Oxbow Ln., (925) 833-9002

Valley Christian Presch. & DC, 7504 Inspiration Dr., (925) 560-6235

Emeryville

Berkeley YMCA-Head Start, 1220 53rd St., (510) 653-2619

Berkeley YMCA-Head Start, 4727 San Pablo Ave., (510) 655-6936

Emeryville CDCtr., 1220 53rd St., (510) 596-4343

Pacific Rim Int'l. Sch., 5521 Doyle St., (510) 601-1500

Siebel Children's Ctr., 2100 Powell St., (510) 788-4780

Fremont

A Child's Hideaway, 37531 Fremont Blvd., (510) 792-8415

A Child's Hideaway, 45150 Grimmer, (510) 656-3218

ABC Magic Moments, 2367 Jackson St., (510) 656-3722

Adventure Time-Ardenwood, 33945 Emilia Ln., (510) 797-6280

Adventure Time-Brookvale, 3400 Nicolet Ave., (510) 797-5180

Adventure Time-Glenmoor, 4620 Mattos Dr., (510) 744-0772

Adventure Time-Maloney, 38700 Logan Dr., (510) 797-5373

Adventure Time-Mattos, 37944 Farwell, (510) 713-2158

Adventure Time-Mission San Jose, 43545 Bryant St., (510) 490-7874

Adventure Time-Niles, 37141 2nd St., (510) 797-4806

Adventure Time-Parkmont, 2601 Parkside Dr., (510) 713-2011

Adventure Time-Vallejo Mill, 38569 Canyon Heights Dr., (510) 658-7412

Adventure Time-Warwick, 3375 Warwick Rd., (510) 797-6122

Bay Area CC-Azeveda, 39450 Royal Palm Dr., (510) 651-7041

Bay Area CC-Brier/Glankler, 39201 Sundale Dr., (510) 657-8392

Bay Area CC-Gomes, 577 Lemos Ln., (510) 490-4222

Bay Area CC-Millard, 5200 Valpey Park Dr., (510) 683-8810

Bay Area CC-Olivera, 4180 Alder Ave., (510) 797-8613

Bay Area CC-Patterson, 35521 Cabrillo Dr., (510) 797-9145

Centerville Presby. Nursery Sch., 4360 Central Ave., (510) 797-6757

Children's Galaxy, 34735 Ardenwood Blvd., (510) 793-1696

Christian Comm. Presch., 39700 Mission Blvd., (510) 651-5437

Creative Life School, 40155 Blacow Rd., (510) 656-9955

Evangelical Free Church-Little Lamb Ministries, 505 Driscoll Rd., (510) 656-1359

Fremont Christian Presch., 4760 Thornton Ave., (510) 744-2260

Fremont Christian Presch., 38495 Fremont Blvd., (510) 405-5010

Fremont Congregational Nursery Sch., 38255 Blacow Rd., (510) 793-3999

FUSD-Alvirda Hyman Lrng. Ctr., 4700 Calaveras Ave., (510) 797-0128

FUSD-Blacow State Presch., 40404 Sundale Dr., (510) 353-9728

FUSD-Cabrillo State Presch., 36700 San Pedro Dr., (510) 792-3015

FUSD-Durham Presch., 40292 Leslie St., (510) 656-6360

FUSD-Glankler State Presch., 39207 Sundale Dr., (510) 651-3902

FUSD-Grimmer State Presch., 43030 Newport Dr., (510) 668-1543

Gan Sameach Nursery Sch., 42000 Paseo Padre Pkwy., (510) 651-5833

Happy Bear Forest Children's Lrng. Ctr., 39600 Mission Blvd., (510) 793-2327

Harvest Christian Presch. & DC, 4360 Hansen Ave., (510) 713-8748

Holy Spirit Presch., 3930 Parish Ave., (510) 793-2013

Kidango-Carlson, 1301 Mowry Ave., (510) 742-1226

Kidango-Delaine Eastin, 584 Brown Rd., (510) 490-5570

Kidango-Fremont Adult Sch., 4700 Calaveras Ave., (510) 494-9601

Kidango-Grace Draper, 255 H St., (510) 797-2732

Kidango-Ohlone College, 43600 Mission Blvd., (510) 659-6000

Kidango-Rix Ctr., 43100 Isle Royal St., (510) 656-3949

Kidango-Sharon Jones, 4700 Calaveras Ave., (510) 494-9601

Kidango-Washington Hospital, 2000 Mowry Ave., (510) 608-3288

Kiddie Kare, 2450 Durham Rd., (510) 226-7723

Kiddo Land Lrng. Ctr., 46280 Briar Place, (510) 490-7311

Kids Wonderland, 4343 Stevenson Blvd., (510) 651-0515

KinderCare, 32710 Falcon Dr., (510) 324-3569

KinderCare, 38700 Paseo Padre Pkwy., (510) 796-0888

Learning Tree CCCtr., 34050 Paseo Padre Pkwy., (510) 791-6161

Little Mud Puddle's DCCtr., 34072 Fremont Blvd., (510) 791-6158

Monarch Christian Presch., 38895 Mission Blvd., (510) 494-1221

Montessori Children's Ctr., 33170 Lake Mead Dr., (510) 489-7511

Montessori Sch. of Centerville, 4209 Baine Ave., (510) 797-9944

Montessori Sch. of Fremont, 155 Washington Blvd., (510) 490-0919

Montessori Sch. of Fremont Children's House, 1901 Washington Blvd., (510) 490-1727

One-Two-Three Lrng. Ctr., 46280 Briar Pl., (510) 490-7311

Our Savior Lutheran Presch. & K, 858 Washington Blvd., (510) 657-9269

Parkmont Sch., 4727 Calaveras Ave., (510) 791-2222

Precious Time Christian Presch., 33350 Peace Terr., (510) 429-3990

Rainbow Kids Presch. & Ext. DC, 38000 Camden St., (510) 797-2222

Scribbles Lrng. Ctr., 38660 Lexington St., (510) 797-9944

Shining Star Montessori, 4047 Alder Ave., (510) 573-2232

Simon's Presch. & DCCtr., 39614 Sundale Dr., (510) 659-0656

Sunshine Kids Presch., 47832 Warm Springs Blvd., (510) 445-0222

YMCA of the East Bay-Blacow, 40404 Sundale Dr., (510) 659-4051

YMCA-Y-Kids-Chadbourne, 801 Plymouth Ave., (510) 656-7243

YMCA-Y-Kids-Durham, 40292 Leslie St., (510) 683-9107

YMCA-Y-Kids-Weibel, 45135 S. Grimmer Blvd., (510) 683-9167

Hayward

Camelot Sch., 21753 Vallejo St., (510) 581-5125

Chabot College Children's Ctr., 25555 Hesperian Blvd., (510) 723-6684

Cherubim's Children's Ctr., 30540 Mission Blvd., (510) 471-7713

Children's Choice Educare, 185 West Harder Rd., (510) 887-3025

Circle Time Nursery Sch., 26555 Gading Rd., (510) 887-1885

CSUH- Early Childhood Ed. Ctr., 25800 Carlos Bee Blvd., (510) 885-2480

Eden Youth Ctr. CCCtr., 680 W. Tennyson Rd., (510) 887-1146

Elmhurst DC & Presch., 380 Elmhurst St., (510) 786-1289

ESP-A Special Place CCCtr., 27305 Huntwood Ave., (510) 782-6635

Fairview Hills Presch., 2841 Ramagnolo Ave., (510) 581-0604

Head Start-Darwin, 2560 Darwin St., (510) 264-9252

Head Start-Eden, 951 Palisade St., (510) 728-4923

Head Start-Glassbrook, 925 Schafer Rd., (510) 732-6628

His Kids, 26221 Gading Rd., (510) 786-3641

HUSD Child Dev.-Bowman, 520 Jefferson, (510) 582-1743

HUSD Child Dev.-Burbank, 353 B St., (510) 582-1675

HUSD Child Dev.-Cherryland, 585 Willow Ave., (510) 582-1737

HUSD Child Dev.- Helen Turner, 23640 Reed Way, (510) 783-3793

HUSD Child Dev.-Muir, 24823 Soto Rd., (510) 582-1792

HUSD Child Dev.-Palma Ceia, 27679 Melbourne Ave., (510) 293-9822

HUSD Child Dev.-Shepherd, 27211 Tyrrell Ave., (510) 783-1182

Kidango-Glen Berry CDCtr., 625 Berry Ave., (510) 728-0649

Kidango-Hillview Crest CDCtr., 31410 Wheelon Ave., (510) 324-3499

Lea's Christian Sch.-CCCtr., 26236 Adrian Ave., (510) 785-2477

Lil' Angels At Ruus, 28924 Ruus Rd., (510) 670-9007

Montessori Children's House, 26236 Adrian Ave., (510) 782-4427

State Presch. at Royal Sunset, 20450 Royal Ave., (510) 317-4412

Woodroe Woods Sch., 22502 Woodroe Ave., (510) 582-3273

YMCA-Y-Kids-Strobridge, 21400 Bedford Dr., (510) 538-7459

Livermore

Ark Presch. & CC, 4161 East Ave., (925) 447-8279

Beth Emek Presch., 1886 College Ave., (925) 443-1689

Bess Platt Presch., 543 Sonoma Ave., (925) 443-3434

CAPE-Jackson Ctr., 560 Jackson Ave., (925) 443-0220

CAPE-Wm. Ormand III Early Ed. Ctr., 800 Marylin Ave., (925) 443-3434

CAPE-Leahy Ctr., 3203 Leahy Way, (925) 443-3434

Celebration Lrng. Ctr., 1135 Bluebell Dr., (925) 245-1252

Christian World CCCtr., 3820 East Ave., (925) 455-5551

Comm. Sch. Age Prog., 2200 Arroyo Rd., (925) 447-0227

Creative Playschool, 676-690 N. L St., (925) 294-9955

Happyland CCCtr., 5800 East Ave., #208, (925) 245-9521

Holy Cross Lutheran Nursery Sch., 1020 Mocho St., (925) 447-1864

Kidango-Owl's Landing CDCtr., 860 Hermann Ave., (925) 744-9280

Kidango-Pepper Tree Sch., 714 Junction Ave., (925) 447-0264

KinderCare, 4655 Lassen Rd., (925) 455-1560

Kinderkirk Nursery Sch., 2020 5th St., (925) 455-0793

Kinderkirk Nursery Sch., 945 Concannon Blvd., (925) 915-5567

Laboratory Employee Children's Ctr., 1401 Almond Ave., (925) 373-0865

Little Rascals Lrng. Ctr., 1893 N. Vasco Rd., (925) 373-8988

Livermore Play Sch., 5261 East Ave., (925) 447-6042

LARPD-Jackson, 554 Jackson Ave., (925) 373-5732

LARPD-Marylin, 800 Marylin Ave., (925) 373-5733

LARPD-Michell, 1001 Elaine Ave., (925) 373-5780

LARPD-Portola, 2451 Portola Ave., (925) 373-5734

LARPD-Rancho, 401 Jack London Blvd., (925) 373-5781

LARPD-Smith, 391 Ontario Dr., (925) 373-5735

LARPD-Sunset, 1671 Frankfurt Way, (925) 373-5736

New Horizons Nursery Sch., 405 E. Jack London Blvd., (925) 455-6082

Our Savior Lutheran Early CDCtr., 1385 S. Livermore Ave., (925) 443-0124

R Skool Presch., 1836 B St., (510) 581-4926

Razan's Wonderland, 949 Central Ave., (925) 449-4999

St. Bartholomew's Episcopal CCCtr., 678 Enos Way, (925) 373-9564

Storyland Presch. & CCCtr., 2486 East Ave., (925) 449-1531

Sunset Christian Sch. & Presch., 2200 Arroyo Rd., (925) 443-5594

Trinity DCCtr., 557 Olivina Ave., (925) 449-5683

Valley Montessori Sch., 460 N. Livermore Ave., (925) 455-8021

Wee Care, 359 Jensen St., (925) 443-9977

Newark

Birch Grove Presch., 6020 Robertson Ave., (510) 792-1759

Challenger Sch., 35487 Dumbarton Ct., (510) 739-0300

Challenger Sch., 39600 Cedar Blvd., (510) 770-1771

Diversity Children's Ctr., 37371 Filbert St., (510) 797-7190

Head Start-Ash, 37365 Ash St., (510) 796-9511

Head Start-Whiteford, 35725 Cedar Blvd., (510) 791-1966

Kidango-Newark, 36120 Ruschin Dr., (510) 794-9186

King's Kids Presch., 38325 Cedar Blvd., (510) 791-8555

Montessori Sch. of Newark, 35660 Cedar Blvd., (510) 792-4546

Newark Comm. Ctr. Annex, 35501 Cedar Blvd., (510) 742-4437

Oakland

24 Hr. Oakland Parent Teacher CC #1, 4700 E. 14th St., (510) 532-0574

24 Hr. Oakland Parent Teacher CC #2, 3500 E. 9th St., (510) 261-0162

ACTS Full Gospel Christian Acad., 1127 62nd Ave., (510) 638-1978

ACTS Full Gospel Christian Acad., 1034 66th Ave., (510) 568-3333

Advance DCCtr., 2236 International Blvd., (510) 434-9288

Adventure Time-Chabot, 6686 Chabot Rd., (510) 655-8151

Adventure Time-Glenview Elem. Sch., 4215 Lacresta Ave., (510) 530-6081

Adventure Time-Joaquin Miller, 5525 Ascot Dr., (510) 531-7782

Adventure Time-Kaiser, 25 S. Hill Ct., (510) 845-3371

Agnes Memorial, 2372 E. 14th St., (510) 533-1101

Ala Costa Ctr., 3400 Malcolm St., (510) 383-3200

Apple Garden Montessori, 5667 Thornhill Dr., (510) 339-9666

AOCS-Ellen Sherwood, 3021 Brookdale Ave., (510) 261-1077

Arroyo Viejo-Oakland Pub. Sch., 1895 78th Ave., (510) 879-0802

Auntie Carla's CC and Presch., 2421 Kingsland Ave., (510) 534-4545

Beacon Day Sch., 2101 Livingston St., (510) 436-4466

Bernice & Joe Playschool, 7001 Sunkist Dr., (510) 638-3529

Blossom Day Sch., 4701 Market St., (510) 658-5892

Booth Memorial DC, 2794 Garden St., (510) 535-5088

Broadway Children's Sch., 394 Adams St., (510) 763-9337

Building Blocks, 2370 Grande Vista Pl., (510) 434-7990

CCUMC Nursery Sch., 321 8th St., (510) 268-8210

Chatham Sch., 4359 39th Ave., (510) 531-1534

Chinese Comm. Nursery, 321 8th St., (510) 268-8210

Claremont Day Nurseries, 5830 College Ave., (510) 658-5208

Color Me Children, 8115 Fontaine St., (510) 430-1322

Color Me Children Presch., 3625 MacArthur Blvd., (510) 482-7507

Cornerstone Lrng. Ctr., 3731 MacArthur Blvd., (510) 530-3546

Daisy CDCtr., 5016 Daisy St., (510) 531-6426

Duck Pond, 4426 Park Blvd., (510) 530-0851

Duck's Nest Piedmont, 4498 Piedmont Ave., (510) 428-0901

East Hills Ext. DCCtr., 12000 Campus Dr., (510) 531-6908

Felicia's Giant Step Presch., 3261 Martin Luther King Jr. Way, (510) 652-8110

First Covenant-Treehouse Presch., 4000 Redwood Rd., (510) 531-0320

First Step Children's Ctr., 111 Fairmount Ave., (510) 239-0880

Four C's CDCtr., 756 21st St., (510) 272-0669

Gan Avraham Nursery Sch., 330 Euclid, (510) 763-7528

Gan Mah Tov Presch., 3778 Park Blvd., (510) 530-2146

Giggles, 6009 Colby St., (510) 601-6526

Grace Children's Acad., 993 53rd St., (510) 653-1115

Grand Lake Montessori, 466 & 472 Chetwood St., (510) 836-4313

Grand Lake Montessori, 281 Santa Clara Ave., (510) 836-4313

Growing Light Montessori Sch., 4700 Lincoln Ave., (510) 336-9897

Halimah's Presch., 1150 63rd St., (510) 654-7381

Head Start-55th Ave., 1800 55th Ave., (510) 273-3164

Head Start-85th Ave., 8501 International Blvd., (510) 544-3821

Head Start-92nd Ave., 9202 E. 14th St., (510) 568-1406

Head Start-Arroyo Viejo Park, 7701 Krause Ave., (510) 635-4035

Head Start-Brookfield, 9600 Edes Ave., (510) 615-5737

Head Start-De Colores, 155 35th Ave., (510) 535-6112

Head Start-Eastmont Mall, 7200 Bancroft Ave., (510) 636-1153

Head Start-Fannie Wall, 647 55th St., (510) 658-0960

Head Start-Franklin Ctr., 1010 E. 15th St., (510) 238-1306

Head Start-Frank Mar, 274 12th St., (510) 238-3165

Head Start-Lockhaven, 1327 65th Ave., (510) 615-5798

Head Start-Manzanita, 2701 22nd Ave., (510) 535-5627

Head Start-Maritime Ctr., Oakland Army Base, Bldg. #655, (510) 238-3165

Head Start-San Antonio, 2228 E. 15th St., (510) 535-5639

Head Start-San Antonio Park, 1701 E. 19th St., (510) 535-5737

Head Start-Seminary, 5818 International Blvd., (510) 615-5585

Head Start-Sungate, 2563 E. 14th St., (510) 535-5649

Head Start-Tassafaronga, 975 85th Ave., (510) 639-0580

Head Start-Virginia, 4335 Virginia Ave., (510) 261-1479

Head Start-Willow, 1682 7th St., (510) 238-2268

Horizon Sch., 9520 Mountain Blvd., (510) 635-7470

Ile Omode Sch., 8924 Holly St., (510) 632-8230

Jewish Comm. Svcs., 412 Monte Vista Ave., (510) 658-9222

Kidango-Chestnut, 1058 W. Grand Ave., (510) 893-0456

Lake Merritt CCCtr., 301-345 12th St., (510) 834-3399

Lake Sch., 304 Lester Ave., (510) 839-4227

Lakeshore Children's Ctr., 3518-3546 Lakeshore Ave., (510) 893-4048

Lakeview - Oakland Pub. Sch., 746 Grand Ave., (510) 879-0857

Lakeview Presch., 515 Glenview Ave., (510) 444-1725

Laney College Children's Ctr., 900 Fallon St., (510) 464-3575

Little Elephant Mont., 5782 Miles Ave., (510) 597-1963

Little Folks Presch., 360 W. MacArthur Blvd., (510) 653-4650

Little Stars Presch., 169 14th St., (510) 839-9600

Lockwood CDCtr.-Oakland Pub. Sch., 1125 69th Ave., (510) 879-0823

Lossieland, 8130 Plymouth St., (510) 569-8150

Manzanita CDCtr.-Oakland Pub. Sch., 2618 Grande Vista Ave., (510) 879-0829

Martin Luther King, Jr. CDCtr.,-Oakland Pub. Sch., 960-A 10th St., (510) 879-0822

Maxwell House, 4618 Allendale Ave., (510) 261-5210

Merritt College Children's Ctr., 12500 Campus Dr., (510) 436-2436

Merritt College Presch. Practicum, 12500 Campus Dr., (510) 436-2588

Mills College Children's Sch., Mills College Campus, (510) 430-2118

Monroe's Lrng. Ctr., 3415 Maple Ave., (510) 531-2781

Montclair Comm. Play Ctr., 5815 Thornhill Dr., (510) 339-7213

Mountain Blvd. Presch. Lrng. Ctr., 4432 Mountain Blvd., (510) 482-2850

My Own Montessori Sch., 5723 Oak Grove Ave., (510) 652-5979

New Day Presch. & Lrng. Ctr., 460 W. Grand Ave., (510) 465-8591

Northern Light Sch., 4500 Redwood Rd., (510) 530-9366

Oakland Montessori Sch., 3636 Dimond St., (510) 482-3111

Oakland Progressive DC, 733 Beatie St., (510) 835-0131

OUSD-Bella Vista, 2410 10th Ave., (510) 879-0805

OUSD-Brookfield CDCtr., 401 Jones Ave., (510) 633-0462

OUSD-Cox, 9860 Sunnyside St., (510) 879-0807

OUSD-Emerson CDCtr., 4801 Lawton Ave., (510) 879-0811

OUSD-Golden Gate, 6232 Herzog St., (510) 879-0814

OUSD-Harriet Tubman, 800 33rd St., (510) 547-1832

OUSD-Hawthorne PreK, 2920 E. 18th. St., (510) 879-1326

OUSD-Highland, 1322 86th Ave., (510) 879-0815

OUSD-Hintil Kuu Ca, 11850 Campus Dr., (510) 879-0840

OUSD-Howard, 8755 Fontaine St., (510) 635-7517

OUSD-International CDCtr., 2825 International Blvd., (510) 879-4236

OUSD-Jefferson, 1975 40th Ave., (510) 436-3700

OUSD-Lafayette, 1700 Market St., (510) 879-1290

OUSD-Piedmont, 86 Echo Ave., (510) 652-5740

OUSD-Prescott, 800 Campbell St., (510) 893-5882

OUSD-Santa Fe, 5380 Adeline St., (510) 879-0837

OUSD-Woodland CDCtr., 1029 81st Ave., (510) 879-0190

OUSD-Yuk Yau, 291 10th St., (510) 893-1659

OUSD-Yuk Yau Annex, 314 E. 10th St., (510) 832-4388

Pacific Coast Montessori Prog., 326 51st St., (510) 653-3129

Parker CDCtr.-Oakland Pub. Sch., 7901 Ney Ave., (510) 879-0828

PCDCI-First Presbyterian, 2619 Broadway, (510) 452-0492

PCDCI-Great Beginnings, 1643 90th Ave., (510) 635-1690

PCDCI-Little Learners, 690 18th St., (510) 451-8459

PCDCI-Sch. Age CDCtr., 1094 56th St., (510) 653-2065

PCDCI-Small Citizens, 6203 Avenal Ave., (510) 562-0777

Peter Pan Coop. Nursery Sch.-Pilgrim's Enrichment & Presch. Prog., 3900 35th Ave., (510) 531-3715

Rainbow Sch., 5918 Taft Ave., (510) 658-2034

Renaissance Sch., 3668 Dimond Ave., (510) 531-8566

Rockridge Montessori, 5610 Broadway, (510) 652-7021

Sequoia Nursery Sch., 2666 Mountain Blvd., (510) 531-8853

Sequoyah Presch., 4292 Keller Ave., (510) 632-3481

Skyline Presch., 12540 Skyline Blvd., (510) 531-8212

Smiles Day Sch., 5621 Thornhill Dr., (510) 339-3830

Smiles Day Sch., 5701 Thornhill Dr., (510) 339-9660

Snow White Presch., 214 W. MacArthur Blvd., (510) 655-8353

Spanish Speaking-De Colores, 1155 35th Ave., (510) 535-6112

Spanish Speaking-Foothill Square Parent Child Ctr., 10700 MacArthur Blvd., (510) 553-9926

Spanish Speaking-Fruitvale Parent Child Ctr., 1266 26th Ave., (510) 535-6112

SSUC-Thurgood Marshall Early Head Start, 1117 10th St., (510) 836-0543

St. Leo's PreK, 4238 Howe St., (510) 654-7828

St. Mary's Ctr. Presch., 635 22nd St., (510) 893-4723

St. Vincent's Day Home, 1086 8th St., (510) 832-8324

Starlite CDCtr., 246 14th St., (510) 238-8809

Stonehurst CDCtr.-Oakland Pub. Sch., 901 105th Ave., (510) 879-0838

Supporting Future Growth #1, 3208 San Pablo Ave., (510) 658-7606

Supporting Future Growth #2, 860 30th St., (510) 834-5267

Supporting Future Growth #3, 1466 Havenscourt Blvd., (510) 635-9268

Supporting Future Growth #4, 8401 Birch St., (510) 633-3031

Supporting Future Growth #5, 5410 Fleming Ave., (510) 534-4808

Supporting Future Growth #6, 5909 Camden St., (510) 567-8362

Supporting Future Growth #8, 936 32nd St., (510) 834-5267

Temple Sinai Presch., 2808 Summit St., (510) 451-2821

Therapeutic Nursery Sch., 6117 Martin Luther King Jr. Way, (510) 428-3406

Tilden CDCtr.-Oakland Pub. Sch., 4655 Steele St., (510) 879-0841

24 Hour Parent/Teacher CCCtr., 3500 E. 9th St., (510) 261-0162

Webster Acad.-Oakland Pub. Sch., 7980 Plymouth St., (510) 879-0842

Wee Li'l People Presch., 650 Alma St., (510) 433-0288

YMCA-Y-Kids, 3265 Market St., (510) 654-9622

YMCA-Y-Kids-Hoover, 890 Brockhurst, (510) 428-0749

YMCA-Y-Kids Presch. & CDCtr., 1106 Madison St., (510) 444-6586

YMCA-Y-Kids Presch., 3265 Market St., (510) 654-9622

Piedmont

Highlands Presch., 400 Highland Ave., (510) 547-4242

Linda Beach Presch., 400 Highland Ave., (510) 547-4432

Piedmont Play Sch., 401 Hampton Ave., (510) 654-4371

Piedmont Schoolmates-Beach Sch. , 100 Lake Ave., (510) 420-3077

Piedmont Schoolmates-Havens Sch., 1800 Oakland Ave., (510) 420-3078

Pleasanton

Adventures In Lrng., 3200 Hopyard Rd., (925) 462-7123

CAPE Head Start- Hill N'Dale Presch., 4150 Dorman Rd., (925) 426-8341

Carden-West Sch., 4466 Black Ave., (925) 484-6060

Child Day Schools, 883 Rose Ave., (925) 462-1866

Children's World Lrng. Ctr., 7110 Koll Center Pkwy., (925) 462-2273

Early Years Children's Ctr., 1251 Hopyard Rd., (925) 462-2202

Extd. Day CC-Walnut Grove, 5199 Black Ave., (925) 484-3312

Hacienda CDCtr., 4671 Chabot Dr., (925) 463-2885

KinderCare, 3760 Brockton Dr., (925) 846-1240

Kinderkirk Christian Presch., 4300 Mirador Dr., (925) 846-2465

La Petite Acad., 5725 Valley Ave., (925) 462-7844

Quarry Lane Sch., 3750 Boulder St., (925) 846-9400

Shining Light Presch., 4455 Del Valle Pkwy., (925) 846-6622

Sonshine Enrichment Ctr. Presch., 1225 Hopyard Rd., (925) 417-8411

St. Clare's Christian Presch., 3350 Hopyard Rd., (925) 462-0938

YMCA-Pleasanton CD Prog., 4775 Bernal Ave., (510) 451-8039

YMCA Y-Kids-Fairlands, 4151 W. Las Positas, (925) 426-1992

YMCA Y-Kids-Lydiksen, 7700 Highland Oaks Dr., (925) 426-9784

YMCA Y-Kids-Mohr, 3300 Dennis Dr., (925) 484-9429

San Leandro

Adventure Time-Corvallis, 14790 Corvallis St., (510) 352-5782

Adventure Time-James Madison, 14751 Juniper St., (510) 658-7412

Adventure Time-Jensen Ranch, 19501 Carson Ln., (510) 728-9933

Avenue Presch., 1521-41 159th Ave., (510) 276-1700

Beth Sholom Presch., 642 Dolores Ave., (510) 357-7920

Davis St. CC at Garfield Sch., 13050 Aurora Dr., (510) 567-0322

Davis Street CCCtr., 1190 Davis St., (510) 635-5437

Davis Street Comm. Ctr., 951 Dowling Blvd., (510) 777-9317

Davis Street-Jefferson, 14311 Lark St., (510) 483-3637

Footprints Presch., 14871 Bancroft Ave., (510) 352-8351

Head Start-Jefferson, 14432 Bancroft Ave., (510) 895-5107

Head Start-Madison, 14811 Juniper St., (510) 483-2924

ICRI- Early Childhood Ctr., 13305 Doolittle Dr., (510) 357-1588

Montessori Sch., 16492 Foothill Blvd., (510) 278-1115

Montessori Sch., 14795 Washington Ave., (510) 278-1115

Noah's Ark Presch., 1699 Orchard Ave., (510) 483-8940

Our Future Tots, 963 Manor Blvd., (510) 352-7400

Principled Acad., 2305 Washington Ave., (510) 351-6400

St. James Christian Presch., 993 Estudillo Ave., (510) 895-9590

St. Leander PreK, 451 Davis St., (510) 351-4144

Stepping Stones Growth Ctr., 311 MacArthur Blvd., (510) 568-3331

San Lorenzo

Adventure Time-Bay Sch., 2001 Bockman Rd., (510) 276-5406

Adventure Time-Del Rey, 1510 Via Sonya, (510) 482-0610

Adventure Time-Grant, 879 Grant Ave., (510) 658-7412

Calvary Lutheran Presch., 17200 Via Magdalena, (510) 278-2598

Challenger Sch., 2005 Via Barrett, (510) 481-8690

Comm. Church Presch., 945 Paseo Grande, (510) 276-4808

Lighthouse Kiddie Kingdom, 16053 Ashland Ave., (510) 276-9114

Lollipop Lane Presch., 341 Paseo Grande, (510) 481-2114

Union City

Adventure Montessori Acad. & Sch., 4101 Pleiades Ct., (510) 489-4191

Free to Be Presch., 188 Appian Way, (510) 471-0731

Head Start-Decoto Plaza, 500 E St., (510) 489-8211

Kidango-Alvarado CDCtr., 31100 Fredi St., (510) 675-9326

Kidango-Cabello Presch. Dev. Ctr., 4500 Cabello St., (510) 489-4141

Kidango-Decoto CDCtr., 600 G St., (510) 489-2185

Kidango-Eastin CDCtr., 34901 Eastin Dr., (510) 475-9630

Kidango-Kitayama CDCtr., 1959 Sunsprite Dr., (510) 675-9350

Kidango-Logan Presch., 33809 Syracuse Ave., (510) 487-1689

Kidango-Pioneer CDCtr., 32737 Bel Aire St., (510) 487-4530

Kidango-Searles CDCtr., 33629 15th St., (510) 471-2772

Little Peoples Presch. & DC, 33700 Alvarado-Niles Rd., (510) 489-8650

Merced County

Atwater

Atwater Head Start, 1791 Grove Ave., (209) 358-0811

Atwater-Bellevue Head Start, 1020 E. Bellevue Rd., (209) 357-5171

Atwater Migrant CDCtr., 9200 W. Westside Blvd., (209) 357-7382

Castle Head Start, 2050 Academy, (209) 388-1785

Fruitland Christian Presch., 2100 Fruitland Ave., (209) 358-7981

St. Anthony Presch., 1801 Winton Way, (209) 358-3341

Delhi

Delhi Head Start & State Presch., 16249 Delhi Ave., (209) 668-6126

Gustine

Gustine Pioneer Head Start, 1500 Meredith Ave., (209) 854-1744

Our Lady of Miracles Presch., 370 Linden Ave., (209) 854-6692

Hilmar

Hilmar Christian Children's Ctr., 20037 W. American Ave., (209) 632-2273

Le Grand

Le Grand Head Start, 13071 E. LeGrand Rd., (209) 389-4182

Planada Migrant CDC & Inf. Ctr., 8880 E. Gerard Ave., (209) 382-1036

Livingston

Livingston CDCtr., 848 Prusso St., (209) 394-3115

Livingston Head Start, 847 Prusso Ave., (209) 394-4280

Livingston Head Start, 1001 B St., (209) 723-4771

Walnut CDCtr., 2600 Walnut Ave., (209) 394-5485

Los Baños

Learning Ctr., 975 E. B St., (209) 826-0154

Los Banos Campus Head Start, 16570 S. Mercy Springs Rd., (209) 826-7226

Los Banos CDCtr., 945 I St., (209) 826-2934

Los Banos Head Start, 805 Texas, (209) 826-3483

Los Banos CDCtr., 16570 S. Mercy Springs Rd., (209) 826-7521

Los Banos San Luis Head Start, 129 7th St., (209) 826-7559

Pennington's Little Friends, 805 Texas, (209) 826-2818

Playdaze Presch., 162 F St., (209) 826-9535

Yellow Brick Road Presch. & DCCtr., 725 I St., (209) 827-0679

Merced

Ada Givens Presch., 2900 Green St., (209) 385-6378

Alexander Street Montessori Sch., 201 E. Alexander, (209) 383-1232

Alicia Reyes Presch., 123 S. N St., (209) 385-6761

Bear Country Presch. & DC, 2115 Wardrobe Ave., (209) 722-2327

Buhach Discovery Ctr., 2606 N. Buhach St., (209) 358-0177

Castle Land Acad., 220 S. Canal St., (209) 726-1409

Charles Wright Sch., 900 E. 20th St., (209) 385-6615

Franklin Presch., 2736 N. Franklin Rd., (209) 385-6623

Galen Clark Presch., 211 E. 11th St., (209) 385-6619

John C. Fremont Sch., 1120 W. 22nd St., (209) 385-6000

John Muir Presch., 300 W. 26th St., (209) 385-6667

John O'Bannion CDCtr., 401 Lecher Dr., (209) 726-3154

La Petite Acad., 3190 Collins Dr., (209) 384-1157

Leontine Gracey Presch., 945 West Ave., (209) 385-6710

Luther Burbank Presch., 609 E. Alexander Ave., (209) 385-6674

Margaret Sheehy Presch., 1240 W. 6th St., (209) 385-6676

Merced CDCtr., 720 & 724 S. Hwy. 59, (209) 723-1046

Merced CDCtr., 2759 N Santa Fe, (209) 724-0335

Merced College CDCtr., 3600 M St., (209) 384-6245

Merced Head Start, 213 E. 11th St., (209) 383-6428

Merced Head Start, 541 R St., (209) 722-8547

Merced Head Start, 900 Martin Luther King Jr. Way, (209) 722-4785

Merced Montessori Sch., 424 & 436 W. 21st St., (209) 722-9823

Our Lady of Mercy Presch., 1400 E. 27th St., (209) 722-7496

Sch. Dist. CDCtr., 1900 G St., (209) 385-6440

Sierra Ctr. Presch., 1730 E. Brookdale Ave., (209) 385-6772

St. Luke's Episcopal Sch., 350 W. Yosemite Ave., (209) 723-3907

St. Paul's Evangelical Lutheran, 2916 N. McKee Rd., (209) 383-3301

Weaver Presch. & DCCtr., 3076 E. Childs Ave., (209) 725-7122

Planada

Granada Migrant CDCtr., 9732 E. Haskell Ave., (209) 382-1042

Planada Head Start, 26 N. Fremont, (209) 723-4771

Planada Head Start, 1541 N. Plainsburg Rd., (209) 382-0851

Planada Village CDCtr., 551 N. Plainsburg Rd., (209) 382-2245

Santa Nella

Santa Nella Head Start, 13233 W. Comet, (209) 826-8902

Snelling

Snelling Head Start, 2241 W. Turlock Rd., (209) 563-6501

South Dos Palos

South Dos Palos Head Start, 8540 Christian, (209) 392-3103

South Dos Palos Migrant CD & Presch., 22380 S. 7th St., (209) 392-2722

South Dos Palos State Presch. & CDCtr., 22380 S. 7th St., (209) 392-1129

Stevinson

Stevinson Head Start, 19977 W. 3rd Ave., (209) 634-1356

Winton

Frank Sparkes Presch., 7265 W. Almond Ave., (209) 357-6180

Winton Head Start, 7160 W. Walnut Ave., (209) 357-8744

San Joaquin County

Acampo

Acampo CD Migrant Ctr., 20942 N. Oak St., (209) 368-9351

Banta

Bird's Nest CDCtr., 22345 El Rancho Rd., (209) 832-5772

Escalon

Children's Christian Presch., 1830 Jackson Ave., (209) 838-7185

Country Kids CDCtr., 1301 Miller Ave., (209) 838-1600

Escalon CDCtr., 18950 S. Van Allen Rd., (209) 838-6141

Escalon Head Start, 1998 E. Yosemite Ave., (209) 838-6515

Learning Tree Presch., 2216 Edmart, (209) 838-3955

French Camp

Artesi II Migrant CCCtr., 777 W. Mathews Rd., (209) 983-0655

Artesi III CDCtr., 333 W. Mathews Rd., (209) 982-0520

Lathrop

Lathrop Head Start, 850 J St., (209) 858-4615

Learning Tree Presch., 15551 7th St., (209) 858-5965

Linden

Linden Community Presch., 19147 E. Main St., (209) 887-3253

Linden Head Start, 18100 W. Front St., (209) 887-2589

Lockeford

Kids Carousel Presch. & DC, 19600 Jack Tone Rd., (209) 727-5791

Lodi

Adelita Migrant CDCtr., 14320 E. Harney Ln., (209) 368-2087

Camp Hutchins-Lodi Memorial Hospital, 125 S. Hutchins St., (209) 334-2267

Century Presch., 550 W. Century Blvd., (209) 334-3230

Dorothy Mahin Early Head Start, 5080 Armstrong Rd., (209) 331-7812

Grace Presby. Presch., 10 N. Mills Ave., (209) 333-1811

Happy Hours Nursery, 444 N. Turner Rd., (209) 369-8462

Heritage Head Start & State Presch., 509 E. Eden, (209) 466-5541

James O. Linn Children's Ctr., 701 N. Calaveras St., (209) 331-7252

Joe Serna Elem., 19 S. Central, (209) 430-9543

La Petite Acad., 1910 W. Kettlemen Ln., (209) 368-0303

Lawrence Sch. Head Start, 721 Calaveras St., (209) 466-5541

Lawrence State Presch., 701 Calaveras St., (209) 331-7252

Little Methodist Presch., 200 W. Oak St., (209) 368-5111

Live Oak Sch. Head Start, 5099 Bear Creek Rd., (209) 331-7943

Lodi Boys & Girls Club Head Start, 1050 S. Stockton St., (209) 466-5541

Lodi Day Nursery Sch., 760 S. Ham Ln., (209) 334-6884

Lodi Head Start, 701 S. Hutchins, (209) 369-5072

Lodi Lutheran Presch., 701 S. Pleasant Ave., (209) 368-8488

Montessori Villa, 2525 S. Stockton St., (209) 366-1012

St. Peter Presch., 2400 Oxford Way, (209) 333-2225

Vinewood Comm. Presch., 1900 W. Vine St., (209) 334-4302

Washington Sch. Head Start, 831 W. Lockeford, (209) 331-7292

Manteca

Always Friends Presch. & CC, 907 Davis St., (209) 239-9330

Creative Kids, 115 S. Powers Ave., (209) 825-5437

Hansel & Gretel DCCtr., 1014 W. Center St., (209) 823-6525

Kids Acad., 680 Industrial Park Dr., (209) 823-9944

Kinder Camp Acad., 340 Mission Ridge Dr., (209) 239-5237

Lion N' Lambs Presch., 815 W. Lathrop Rd., (209) 239-1345

Manteca Head Start Ctr., 115 Walnut, (209) 239-6676

McFall Sch. Head Start, 1810 Hoyt Ln., (209) 825-4783

Noah's Landing, 786 Button Ave., (209) 239-4512

Pine St. Head Start, 1130 E. Pine St., (209) 239-5461

St. Anthony's Presch., 323 N. Fremont Ave., (209) 823-3959

St. Paul's United Meth. Presch., 910 E. North St., (209) 239-5848

United Lutheran Presch., 649 Northgate Dr., (209) 823-1971

Ripon

Almost Home, 733 W. 2nd St., (209) 599-7034

Bird's Nest CDCtr., 20700 River Rd., (209) 599-5714

Cornerstone Country Presch., 25067 S. Mohler Rd., (209) 599-9969

Ripon Grace Christian CCtr., 734 W. Main, (209) 599-2345

Ripon Head Start, 415 Oregon St., (209) 466-5541

Stockton

A Child's Smile Acad., 6 W. Main St., (209) 463-6220

Adams Elem. Head Start, 6402 Inglewood Ave., (209) 955-0429

Annunciation Presch., 1110 N. Lincoln St., (209) 465-2961

Barbara J. Brown Head Start, 24 E. Euclid, (209) 463-6676

Barnett House Head Start, 347 E. Poplar St., (209) 467-1359

Blessed Beginnings Presch., 3535 N. El Dorado, (209) 466-1577

Brookside State Presch., 2962 Brookside Rd., (209) 953-8642

Busy Days Nursery Sch., 2629 N. Pershing Ave., (209) 462-3093

Central Meth. Ch. Day Nursery Sch., 3700 Pacific Ave., (209) 462-5127

Child Abuse Prevention Council, 31 E. Vine St., (209) 644-8322

Children's Discovery Ctr., 1234 William Moss Blvd., (209) 982-1212

Children's World Lrng. Ctr., 8121 Don Ave., (209) 951-2273

Clairmont State Prsch., 8282 Lemans Ave., (209) 953-8284

Colonial Heights State Presch., 8135 Balboa Ave., (209) 953-8734

Connie Romena Head Start Ctr., 2295 E. Fremont St., (209) 462-7153

Council for the Spanish Spkng., 1606 Hammertown Dr., (209) 957-9435

Creative CC, 981 Cherokee Rd., (209) 478-2087

Creative CC, 742 Dallas Ave., (209) 465-3851

Creative CC, 1700 E. 11th St., (209) 465-4557

Creative CC, 3293 E. Morada Ln., (209) 478-2087

Creative CC, 10038 N. Hwy 99, (209) 478-2087

Creative CC, 6650 Inglewood, (209) 478-2087

Creative CC, 1700 Porter Way, (209) 478-2087

Creative CC, 17 E. Poplar Way, (209) 462-2282

Creative CC-University Park, 1105 N. Sacramento St., (209) 478-2364

Creative Head Start, 7505 Tam O'Shanter, (209) 956-2686

Creative Pastime Nursery Sch., 1039 Porter Ave., (209) 951-4558

Creekside Head Start & State Presch., 2515 Estate Dr., (209) 957-1732

Delta Head Start, 5151 Pacific Ave., (209) 954-5700

Delta Island Sch. Head Start, 11022 W. Howard Rd., (209) 463-4361

Edison HS Head Start & Presch., 1425 S. Center St., (209) 464-9542

Even Start Ctr., 4401 Manchester, (209) 477-3296

First Step, 31 E. Vine St., (209) 644-5323

Franklin Head Start, 300 N. Gertrude Ave., (209) 953-4197

Garden Acres Head Start, 607 Bird Ave., (209) 466-5686

Garden of Eden DCCtr., 405 Pine St., (209) 474-6648

Gemini Head Start, 1807 E. 10th St., (209) 466-7907

Gianone Park Head Start, 1509 N. Golden Gate, (209) 467-4936

Grace United Meth. Head Start, 1625 N. Lincoln St., (209) 465-6671

Grant Village Head Start, 2040 S. Grant St., (209) 463-5727

Growing Tree Presch., 1904 Quail Lakes Dr., (209) 478-2220

Immanuel Luth. Head Start, 2343 Country Club Blvd., (209) 481-9599

Kennedy Park Head Start, 2800 S. D St., (209) 948-1394

Kiddie Kingdom Presch., 1121 S. Oro Ave., (209) 462-2477

Kids Junction, 6311 Pacific Ave., (209) 951-5437

KinderCare, 7801 Mariners Dr., (209) 477-3723

Kohl Sch. Head Start, 6324 N. Alturas Ave., (209) 951-6725

Latin American Club Head Start, 548 S. Wilson Way, (209) 463-5616

Learning Experience CCCtr., 9389 Davis Rd., (209) 475-1715

Leo Gloria Head Start, 215 W. 5th St., (209) 948-6981

Lincoln Head Start, 1700 Porter Way, (209) 951-7664

Lincoln State Presch., 6844 Alexandria Pl., (209) 476-9046

Lincoln Village Acad., 6608 Grigsby Pl., (209) 957-1021

Little Learners Presch., 3588 Brookside Rd., (209) 954-7656

Madison Elem. State Presch., 2939 Mission Rd., (209) 953-4268

Marjorie Rosera Head Start, 4140 E. Hammer Ln., (209) 476-0715

Martin Luther King CDCtr., 2850 E. Lafayette, (209) 943-2403

McKinley Elem., 30 W. 9th St., (209) 953-4235

Merryhill Sch., 7204 Shoreline Dr., (209) 474-0518

Miz B's Presch. & DC, 2220 W. Alpine, (209) 942-3514

Monroe Sch., 2236 E. 11th St., (209) 944-4120

Montessori Children's House, 2448 Country Club Blvd., (209) 477-1980

Montezuma Sch. & Head Start, 2843 Farmington, (209) 464-9526

Morada Oaks Sch., 5035 Hickory Ln., (209) 931-3117

New World Montessori Sch., 2367 Waudman Ave., (209) 952-8854

Newday Nursery Sch., 4910 Claremont Ave., (209) 957-4089

Nightingale Presch. & Head Start, 1721 Carpenter Rd., (209) 983-9182

Oakwood Head Start, 1315 Woodcreek Way, (209) 953-8399

One Nation Head Start, 1610 N. Sierra Nevada, (209) 463-3406

Park Village Head Start, 3820 N. Alvarado, (209) 464-1162

Parklane State Presch. & Head Start, 8405 Tam O'Shanter, (209) 953-8415

Parvin's Hopeland Presch., 5965 N. Pershing Ave., (209) 474-9144

Quail Lakes Baptist Ch., 1904 Quail Lakes Dr., (209) 952-2267

Rainbow Sch., 1801 W. Bristol Ave., (209) 464-7301

San Joaquin Delta College CDCtr., 5151 Pacific Ave., (209) 954-5700

Sandra Anselmo Head Start, 1091 W. Mendocino, (209) 946-2025

Santa Fe Head Start, 634 Worth St., (209) 943-7268

Sister Diane's DC, 1636 E. Main St., (209) 943-0353

Small World Nursery Sch., 6600 Grigsby Pl., (209) 477-8970

Snell's PreK, 9371 N. Lower Sacramento, (209) 478-6161

St. Basil Presch., 920 W. March Ln., (209) 478-5252

St. Benedict's Head Start, 348 S. Los Angeles, (209) 944-5920

St. Bernadette's Head Start, 2455 Country Club Blvd., (209) 466-1145

St. Luke's Catholic Presch., 4005 N. Sutter St., (209) 465-5368

St. Mathew's Head Start, 305 S. F St., (209) 943-5750

St. Michael's Presch., 5882 N. Ashley Ln., (209) 931-0639

Taft Sch. Head Start, 419 Downing, (209) 953-2011

Taylor Sch. & Head Start, 1101 Lever Blvd., (209) 466-6195

Temple Israel Presch., 5105 N. El Dorado, (209) 474-8662

Tiny Tot DC, 703 E. Swain Rd., (209) 477-4442

Trinity Lutheran Presch., 444 N. American St., (209) 463-9113

Tully C. Knoles Presch., 6511 Clarksburg Pl., (209) 953-8776

Tyler Sch., 3830 Webster, (209) 953-4581

Van Buren Elem. DC & Head Start , 1628 E. 10th St., (209) 953-4804

Wagner Holt Sch. & Head Start, 8778 Brattle Pl., (209) 742-9943

Webber Tech. Presch. & Head Start, 302 W. Webber St., (209) 467-7054

Wee Care Presch., 5211 Barbados Circle, (209) 954-7657

Wee Tech Care, 6221 Harrisburg Pl., (209) 474-0748

Westgate Townhomes Head Start, 6119 Danny Dr., (209) 956-1992

Westwood DC & Head Start, 9444 Caywood, (209) 953-8001

White Rose Head Start, 2340 S. Pilgrim, (209) 464-9227

Write-Start Lrng. Center, 4453 Precissi Lane, (209) 956-5437

YMCA of San Joaquin Co.-Glenwood, 2005 N. Alpine Rd., (209) 467-2444

YMCA of San Joaquin Co.-Julia Morgan, 3777 A.G. Spanos Blvd., (209) 467-2444

Thornton
Thornton Head Start, 8633 Mokelumne Ave., (209) 794-2809

Tracy
Bella Vista Christian Acad., 1635 Chester Dr., (209) 835-8803

Children's Ctr., 125 Berverdor, (209) 832-5437

Great Beginnings Presch., 330 E. Acacia St., (209) 835-1321

Hawkins-Thompson CDCtr., 18 E. 1st, (209) 835-7877

KinderCare, 265 W. Grantline Rd., (209) 835-9247

Little Country CC, 1820 W. Grantline Rd., (209) 833-7882

McKinley Village CDCtr., 2105-2123 Tracy Blvd., (209) 832-7844

Melville S. Jacobson CDCtr., 1750 Kavanagh St., (209) 832-8799

Montessori Sch. of Tracy, 100 S. Tracy Blvd., (209) 833-3458

Mt.View Townhomes Head Start, 377 W. Mt Diablo St., (209) 833-1136

Sunshine Ctr., 340 W. 4th St., (209) 834-8990

Tender Loving Care, 475 Darlene Ln., (209) 839-1313

Tender Loving Care, 2324 Parker Ave., (209) 835-9088

Tender Loving Care, Defense Depot, S. Chrisman Rd., (209) 832-8686

Tender Loving Care, 1001 Cambridge Pl., (209) 836-8948

Tracy Head Start, 11157 W. Larch Rd., (209) 835-6773

TUSDS-West Park Elem., 501 W. Mount Oso, (209) 831-5320

Villalovoz Sch. Age CDCtr., 1550 Cypress Dr., (209) 834-1850

Wanda Hirsch State Presch. & CDCtr., 1280 Dove St., (209) 836-0977

Wee Care DC, 1790 Sequoia Blvd., (209) 835-2783

West Hills CDCtr., 500 N. Corral Hollow Rd., (209) 835-4386

Stanislaus County
Ceres
Carroll Fowler Head Start, 2611 Garrison Ave., (209) 537-4505

Don Pedro State Presch., 2300 Don Pedro Rd., (209) 541-0205

Grandview CDCtr. Head Start, 1317 Grandview Ave., (209) 537-3615

Kiddie Kingdom, 3900 Morgan Rd., (209) 537-8944

Lil Pals Learning Ctr., 2531 W. Whitmore Ave., (209) 531-0892

MAA Helping Hands, 2020 Academy Pl., (209) 538-6443

Walter Thompson CDCtr., 2003 Glenda Way, (209) 537-9032

Denair
Denair Elem. State Presch., 3460 Lester Rd., (209) 632-8887

Empire
Empire Head Start, 5201 1st St., (209) 579-1681

Pearlene Reese CDCtr., 5124 South Ave., (209) 529-2322

Hughson
Hughson Elem., 7201 E. Whitmore Ave., (209) 883-4412

Keyes

Keyes State Presch., 5680 7th St., (209) 537-1504

Modesto

Alberta Martone Ctr., 1413 Poust Rd., (209) 576-4077

Bethel DCCtr., 2361 Scenic Dr., (209) 521-5454

Big Valley Christian Sch., 4040 D Tully, (209) 527-3481

Burbank Family Lrng. Ctr., 1135 Paradise Rd., (209) 576-4709

Calvary Temple Presch. & DC, 1601 Coffee Rd., (209) 529-2531

Capistrano Head Start, 400 Capistrano Dr., (209) 521-2800

Centenary Christian Presch., 1911 Toyon Ave., (209) 527-5441

C.F. Brown Head Start, 1401 Celeste Ave., (209) 525-4937

Children's Crisis Ctr., 133 Downey Ave., (209) 577-0138

Children's Crisis Ctr., 1244 Fiori Ave., (209) 577-0138

Childtime, 2320 Floyd Ave., (209) 551-0255

Childtime, 3912 Honey Creek, (209) 545-1664

Chrysler Head Start, 2818 Conant Ave., (209) 525-4937

Community Christian Presch., 1442 Tully Rd., (209) 522-5601

Early Intervention & State Presch., 1336 Stonum Ave., (209) 531-0604

El Vista Elem. & Head Start, 450 El Vista Ave., (209) 576-4665

Emanuel Lutheran DC, 324 College Ave., (209) 549-0672

Empire Head Start, 400 Capistrano Dr., (209) 527-9865

Empire Head Start-Hughes, 512 N. McClure Rd., (209) 571-2486

Fairview Elem. Head Start, 1937 W. Whitmore Ave., (209) 576-4893

Foundations Acad. Prsch., 820 H St., (209) 579-0338

Franklin Head Start, 150 S. Emerald Ave., (209) 575-7362

Franklin Family Lrng. Ctr., 905 Byron Ln., (209) 576-4688

Garrison Presch., 1811 Teresa St., (209) 576-4182

Geneva Presby. Small Fry Nursery, 1229 E. Fairmont Ave., (209) 524-5630

Grace Lutheran Sch., 617 W. Orangeburg Ave., (209) 522-6393

Green Oak Christian Presch., 1308 Coffee Rd., (209) 529-3000

John Muir Preformal Ctr., 1215 Lucerne Ave., (209) 575-7370

Kairos CDCtr., 304 E. Coolidge Ave., (209) 578-5778

Kindercare, 2825 W. Rumble Rd., (209) 529-1995

Kindercare, 1237 Oakdale Rd., (209) 521-5351

Lighthouse Presch., 913 Floyd Ave., (209) 557-0458

Maryis Baddell CDCtr., 641 Norseman Dr., (209) 576-4600

Merryhill Country Sch., 3301 Coffee Rd., (209) 544-3155

Merryhill Country Sch., 133 E. Roseburg Ave., (209) 527-2310

Methodist Tiny Tots, 850 16th St., (209) 525-8687

Modesto Christian Presch., 921 Woodrow Ave., (209) 527-2250

Modesto Jr. College Children's Ctr., 2201 Blue Gum Ave., (209) 575-6952

Modesto Jr. College Lab. Presch., 2208 Blue Gum Ave., (209) 575-6343

Modesto Parent Coop. Presch., 1341 College Ave., (209) 571-2161

Montessori Sch. of Modesto, 3501 San Clemente Ave., (209) 567-1115

Muncy Head Start, 2410 Silviare Ave., (209) 525-4937

My Pride and Joy, 4825 Stratos Way, (209) 548-9111

Orangeburg Christian Sch., 313 E. Orangeburg Ave., (209) 577-2575

Orville Wright Head Start, 1602 Monterey St., (209) 576-4821

Parkwood Christian Presch., 301 Claratina Ave., (209) 557-9510

Perkins Head Start & Sch. Age CDCtr., 3900 Bluebird Dr., (209) 545-0339

Robertson Rd. Childrns Ctr., 1111 Hammond Ave., (209) 524-1447

Salvation Army CDCtr., 601 I St., (209) 522-3209

Stonum CDCtr., 1336 Stonum Rd., (209) 581-9181

Shackelford Elem. Head Start, 100 School St., (209) 576-2824

MUSD Child Development, 1017 Reno, (209) 576-4688

Small World Presch., 1024 6th St., (209) 523-4388

Sonshine Children's Ctr., 3936 Dale Rd., (209) 545-1992

St. Dunstan's Christian CCCtr., 3242 Carver Rd., (209) 529-8243

St. Paul's Sch., 1528 Oakdale Rd., (209) 527-3382

St. Peter Luth. Ch. & Sch., 3461 Merle Ave., (209) 551-4963

St. Stanislaus Presch., 1416 Maze Blvd., (209) 524-9036

Sylvan Head Start, 2908 Coffee Rd., (209) 525-4937

Tender Hearts CCCtr., 2118 Woodland Ave., (209) 527-7995

Trinity Presby. Nursery Sch., 1600 Carver Rd., (209) 578-5625

Tuolomne Christian DC, 133 Tuolomne Blvd., (209) 522-7019

University/Maris Ext. Care, 3313 Coffee Rd., (209) 480-3177

Westport State Presch., 5218 S. Carpenter Rd., (209) 538-0148

Wright Start Preformal Ctr., 801 Empire Ave., (209) 576-4077

Newman

Newman Coop Nursery Sch., 1147 R St., (209) 862-2744

Newman CDCtr., 655 Hardin Rd., (209) 526-5255

Starkids, 151 S. Hwy 33, (209) 862-4227

Von Renner CDCtr., 1388 Patchett Dr., (209) 581-9000

Oakdale

Children's Crisis Ctr., 246 W. F St., (209) 577-0138

House of Tykes, 217 N. 3rd St., (209) 848-0257

Learning Tree, 1480 Poplar Ave., (209) 838-3955

Little Star Presch., 140 Johnson Ave., (209) 847-4628

Oakdale Head Start, 1235 E. D St., (209) 847-5889

Rockey's Rainbow Rompers, 345 N. 6th Ave., (209) 848-4769

Patterson

Del Puerto CDCtr. & State Presch., 640 M St., (209) 892-1610

Kids Haven, 625 L St., (209) 892-7200

Northmead State Presch., 640 M St., (209) 892-4550

Patterson House of Children, 650 N. 2nd St., (209) 892-2759

Patterson CDC, 456 Eureka St., (209) 892-8130

Sacred Heart Presch., 505 M St., (209) 892-5525

Walnut Acres Presch., 456 Eureka St., (209) 892-3700

Riverbank

Judy's Presch. & DC, 3419 Atchison, (209) 863-1824

Riverbank Head Start, 6200 Claus Rd., (209) 558-8580

Riverbank CDC, 6200 Claus Rd., (209) 869-0973

Salida

Boer Sch. Head Start & State Presch., 4801 Gold Valley Rd., (209) 545-8592

Salida CDC, 4519 Finney Rd., (209) 545-3728

Tender Years, 4718 Broadway Ave., (209) 545-6500

Turlock

A Special Place, 2490 N. Walnut, (209) 667-0322

CSU Stanislaus CDCtr., 801 W. Monte Vista Ave., (209) 667-3036

Chatom Elem. Presch., 7221 Clayton Ave., (209) 664-8003

Covenant Park Children's Campus, Laurel and High St., (209) 667-7622

Crane Sch. Head Start, 1100 Cahill Ave., (209) 632-1043

Crowell State Presch., 118 North Ave., (209) 667-0885

Cunningham Elem. Head Start, 324 W. Linwood, (209) 668-7594

Turlock Lrng. Ctr., 1620 Colorado Ave., (209) 667-0668

Monte Vista Children's Ctr., 1619 E. Monte Vista Ave., (209) 632-8477

Northview Christian Presch., 200 North Ave., (209) 634-8083

Osborne Head Start, 201 N. Soderquist Rd., (209) 667-2938

Sacred Heart Presch., 1250 Cooper Ave., (209) 634-8578

Turlock CDCtr., 400 N. Kilroy Rd., (209) 669-6374

Turlock Christian Presch., 700 E. Monte Vista Ave., (209) 632-2391

Turlock Christian Sch., 2006 E. Tuolumne Rd., (209) 669-2192

Turlock Parent Part. Nursery Sch., 415 Grant Ave., (209) 667-7501

Wakefield Head Start, 400 South Ave., (209) 667-0895

Waterford

Byron F. Todd Christian Sch., 116 E St., (209) 874-2145

Waterford CDC, 319 N. Reinway, (209) 874-3301

Westley

Grayson State Presch., 301 Howard Rd., (209) 894-3470

Westley CDC, 601 Livingston Cir., (209) 894-5191

Chapter 11

Hospitals & Health Care

GOOD HEALTH CARE. You want it. Where, how, do you get it? The question is particularly puzzling these days because so many changes are taking place in medicine and medical insurance.

The "operations" of a few years ago are the "procedures" of today, done in the office, not the surgery, completed in minutes, not hours, requiring home care, not hospitalization.

Large insurance companies, through their health maintenance plans, are setting limits on what doctors and hospitals can charge, and — critics contend — interfering with the ability of doctors to prescribe what they see fit. The companies strongly deny this, arguing they are bringing reforms to a profession long in need of reforming. In 2001, money arguments between insurance firms and hospitals and medical groups forced many people to change HMO plans.

Many hospitals are merging, the better to avoid unnecessary duplication and to save money by purchasing supplies and medicine in larger amounts.

Universal health insurance having failed to clear congress, about 44 million Americans are not covered by any medical plan. Unable to afford medical bills, many ignore ailments and illnesses. Another big issue, the cost of prescriptions, especially for the elderly. In 2004, Congress is supposed to pass some relief. We'll see.

This chapter will give you an overview of Northern California health care and although it won't answer all your questions — too complex a business for that — we hope that it will point you in the right directions.

For most people, health care is twinned with insurance, in systems that are called "managed care." But many individuals, for a variety of reasons, do not have insurance. This is a good place to start: with nothing, all options open. Let's use as our seeker for the best of all health-care worlds — on a tight budget — a young woman, married, one child. Her choices:

No Insurance — Cash Care

The woman is self-employed or works at a small business that does not offer health benefits.

Because | *There are castles to build.*

That's why it's important to choose a doctor affiliated with Eden Medical Center.

At Eden Medical Center, we know there's a lot more to your life than health care. That's why we're constantly working to provide our communities with access to quality medical and surgical care. By combining advanced technology and clinical expertise with personal care and compassion, we have become a leader in emergency and trauma care, neurosurgery, vascular surgery, cancer care, maternity and women's health, psychiatry and rehabilitation. And as a part of the Sutter Health family, we're able to share ideas, resources and expertise with other doctors and hospitals throughout Northern California. So you can relax and get on with life.

Castro Valley Campus	San Leandro Campus
20103 Lake Chabot Road	13855 East 14th Street
Castro Valley, CA 94546	San Leandro CA 94578
(510) 537-1234	(510) 357-6500

To find a physician near you, visit www.edenmedcenter.org

She comes down with the flu. When she goes into the doctor's office, she will be asked by the receptionist, how do you intend to pay? With no insurance, she pays cash (or credit card), usually right there. She takes her prescription, goes to the pharmacy and pays full cost.

If her child or husband gets sick and needs to see a doctor, the same procedure holds. Also the same for treatment of a serious illness, to secure X-rays or hospitalization. It's a cash system.

Medi-Cal

If an illness strikes that impoverishes the family or if the woman, through job loss or simply low wages, cannot afford cash care, the county-state health system will step in.

The woman fills out papers to qualify for Medi-Cal, the name of the system (it's known elsewhere as Medicaid), and tries to find a doctor who will treat Medi-Cal patients.

If unable to find an acceptable doctor, the woman could turn to a county hospital or clinic. There she will be treated free or at very low cost.

Drawbacks-Pluses of Medi-Cal

County hospitals and clinics, in the personal experience of one of the editors — who has relatives who work at or use county facilities — have competent doctors and medical personnel. If you keep appointments promptly, often you will be seen with little wait. If you want immediate treatment for, say, a cold, you register and you wait until an urgent-care doctor is free.

If you need a specialist, often the county facility will have one on staff, or will be able to find one at a teaching hospital or other facility. You don't choose the specialist; the county physician does.

County facilities are underfunded and, often, inconveniently located — a major drawback. Some counties, lacking clinics and hospitals, contract with adjoining counties that are equipped. You have to drive some distance for treatment.

County hospitals and clinics are not 100-percent free. If you have money or an adequate income, you will be billed for service. Some county hospitals run medical plans designed for people who can pay. These people can ask for a "family" doctor and receive a higher (usually more convenient) level of care.

Let's say the woman lacks money but doesn't want to hassle with a long drive and, possibly, a long wait for treatment of a minor ailment. She can sign up for Medi-Cal to cover treatment of serious illnesses, and for the colds, etc., go to a private doctor for treatment and pay in cash, ignoring Medi-Cal.

There are many ways to skin the cat, and much depends on circumstances. For the poor and low-income, Medi-Cal is meant to be a system of last resort.

Medicare — Veterans Hospital

If our woman were elderly, she would be eligible for Medicare, the federal insurance system, which covers 80 percent, with limitations, of medical costs or allowable charges.

Many people purchase supplemental insurance to bring coverage up to 100 percent (long-term illnesses requiring hospitalization may exhaust some benefits.)

If the woman were a military veteran with a service-related illness, she could seek care at a Veteran's Administration clinic or hospital.

Indemnity Care

Usually the most expensive kind of insurance, this approach allows complete freedom of choice. The woman picks the doctor she wants. If her regular doctor recommends a specialist, she can decide which one, and if she needs hospital treatment, she can pick the institution. In reality, the choice of hospital and specialist often will be strongly influenced by her regular doctor but the patient retains control. Many indemnity plans have deductibles and some may limit how much they pay out in a year or lifetime. Paperwork may be annoying.

Managed Care

This divides basically into two systems, Preferred Provider Organizations (PPO) and Health Maintenance Organizations (HMO). Both are popular in California and if your employer provides health insurance, chances are almost 100 percent you will be pointed toward, or given a choice of one or the other.

PPOs and HMOs differ among themselves. It is beyond the scope of this book to detail the differences but you should ask if coverage can be revoked or rates increased in the event of serious illness. Also, what is covered, what is not. Cosmetic surgery might not be covered. Psychiatric visits or care might be limited. Ask how emergency or immediate care is provided. Ask about drug costs.

Preferred Provider

The insurance company approaches certain doctors, clinics, medical facilities and hospitals and tells them: we will send patients to you but you must agree to our prices — a method of controlling costs — and our rules. The young woman chooses her doctor from the list, often extensive, provided by the PPO. The physician will have practicing privileges at certain local hospitals. The young woman's child contracts pneumonia and must be hospitalized. Dr. X is affiliated with XYZ hospital, which is also signed up with the PPO plan. The child is treated at XYZ hospital.

If the woman used an "outside" doctor or hospital, she would pay extra — the amount depending on the nature of the plan. It is important to know the doctor's affiliations because you may want your hospital care at a certain institution.

Hospitals differ. A children's hospital, for instance, will specialize in children's illnesses and load up on children's medical equipment. A general hospital will have a more rounded program. For convenience, you may want the hospital closest to your home.

If you need specialized treatment, you must, to avoid extra costs, use the PPO affiliated specialists. The doctor will often guide your choice.

Besides the basic cost for the policy, PPO insurance might charge fees, co-payments or deductibles. A fee might be $5 or $10 a visit. With co-payments, the bill, say, comes to $100. Insurance pays $80, the woman pays $20.

Deductible example: the woman pays the first $250 or the first $2,000 of any medical costs within a year, and the insurer pays bills above $250 or $2,000. With deductibles, the higher the deductible the lower the cost of the policy. The $2,000 deductible is really a form of catastrophic insurance.

Conversely, the higher the premium the more the policy covers. Some policies cover everything. (Dental care is usually provided through a separate insurer.) The same for prescription medicines. You may pay for all, part, or nothing, depending on the type plan.

The PPO doctor functions as your personal physician. Often the doctor will have his or her own practice and office, conveniently located. Drawback: PPOs restrict choice.

Health Maintenance Organization (HMO)

Very big in California because Kaiser Permanente, one of the most popular medical-hospital groups, is run as an HMO. The insurance company and medical provider are one and the same. All or almost all medical care is given by the HMO. The woman catches the flu. She sees the HMO doctor at the HMO clinic or hospital. If she becomes pregnant, she sees an HMO obstetrician at the HMO hospital or clinic and delivers her baby there.

With HMOs you pay the complete bill if you go outside the system (with obvious exceptions; e.g., emergency care). HMOs encourage you to pick a personal physician. The young woman wants a woman doctor; she picks one from the staff. She wants a pediatrician as her child's personal doctor; the HMO, usually, can provide one.

HMO clinics and hospitals bring many specialists and services together under one roof. You can get your eyes examined, your hearing tested, your prescriptions filled, your X-rays taken within a HMO facility (this varies), and much more.

If you need an operation or treatment beyond the capability of your immediate HMO hospital, the surgery will be done at another HMO hospital within the system or at a hospital under contract with the HMO. Kaiser recently started contracting with other facilities to provide some of the services that it used to do in its own hospitals or clinics. One example: Kaiser contracts with

Children's Hospital in Oakland for treatment of some illnesses afflicting children. HMO payment plans vary but many HMO clients pay a monthly fee and a small per visit fee. Often the plan includes low-cost or reduced-cost or free prescriptions.

Drawback: Freedom of choice limited. If HMO facility is not close, the woman will have to drive to another town.

Point of Service (POS)

Essentially, an HMO with the flexibility to use outside doctors and facilities for an extra fee or a higher deductible. POS systems seem to be popular with people who don't feel comfortable limiting themselves to an HMO. They pay extra but possibly not as much as other alternatives.

Tiered Plans

One of the latest wrinkles. Because hospital stays make up a large part of insurance bills, insurers are shifting some of these costs onto employers and consumers. This approach divides hospitals, based on their costs, into three tiers or price levels. When a patient is admitted to a hospital, he or his plan pays extra, the amount depending on the tier rating.

Choices, more information

If you are receiving medical insurance through your employer, you will be limited to the choices offered. In large groups, unions often have a say in what providers are chosen.

Some individuals will base their choice on price, some on convenience of facilities, others on what's covered, and so on.

Many private hospitals offer Physician Referral Services. You call the hospital, ask for the service and get a list of doctors to choose from. The doctors will be affiliated with the hospital providing the referral. Hospitals and doctors will also tell you what insurance plans they accept for payment and will send you brochures describing the services the hospital offers.

For Kaiser and other HMOs, call the local hospital or clinic.

A PPO will give you a list of its member doctors and facilities.

Ask plenty of questions. Shop carefully.

Here's some advice from a pro on picking a health plan: Make a chart with a list of prospective health plans in columns across the top.

Down the left side of the chart, list the services or attributes that you think are important. Review the health plans and check off the "important" services in each plan. Choose or investigate further those plans that have the most check marks.

Common Questions

The young woman is injured in a car accident and is unconscious. Where will she be taken?

Generally, she will be taken to the closest emergency room or trauma center, where her condition will be stabilized. Her doctor will then have her admitted into a hospital. Or she will be transferred to her HMO hospital or, if indigent, to a county facility.

If her injuries are severe, she most likely will be rushed to a regional trauma center. Trauma centers have specialists and special equipment to treat serious injuries. Both PPOs and HMOs offer urgent care and emergency care.

The young woman breaks her leg. Her personal doctor is an internist and does not set fractures. What happens?

The personal doctor refers the case to a specialist. Insurance pays the specialist's fee. In PPO, the woman would generally see a specialist affiliated with the PPO. In an HMO, the specialist would be employed by the HMO.

The young woman signs up for an HMO then contracts a rare disease or suffers an injury that requires treatment beyond the capability of the HMO. Will she be treated?

Often yes, but it pays to read the fine print. The HMO will contract treatment out to a facility that specializes in the needed treatment.

The young woman becomes despondent and takes to drink. Will insurance pay for her rehabilitation?

Depends on her insurance. And often her employer. Some may have drug and alcohol rehab plans. Some plans cover psychiatry.

The woman becomes pregnant. Her doctor, who has delivered many babies, wants her to deliver at X hospital. All the woman's friends say, Y Hospital is much better, nicer, etc. The doctor is not cleared to practice at Y Hospital. Is the woman out of luck?

With a PPO, the woman must deliver at a hospital affiliated with the PPO — or pay the extra cost. If her doctor is not affiliated with that hospital, sometimes a doctor may be given courtesy practicing privileges at a hospital where he or she does not have staff membership. Check with the doctor.

With HMOs, the woman must deliver within the HMO system.

Incidentally, with PPOs and HMOs you should check that the doctors and specialists listed in the organization's booklets can treat you. Some plans may restrict access to certain doctors. Some booklets may be out-of-date and not have an accurate list of doctors.

The young woman goes in for minor surgery, which turns into major surgery when the doctor forgets to remove a sponge before sewing up. Upon reviving, she does what?

Some medical plans require clients to submit complaints to a panel of arbitrators, which decides damages, if any. The courts are starting to take a skeptical look at this requirement. Read the policy.

The woman's child reaches age 18. Is she covered by the family insurance?

All depends on the insurance. Some policies will cover the children while they attend college. (But attendance may be defined in a certain way, full-time as opposed to part-time.) To protect your coverage, you should read the plan thoroughly.

At work, the woman gets her hand caught in a revolving door and is told she will need six months of therapy during which she can't work. Who pays?

Insurance will usually pay for the medical costs. Workers Compensation, a state plan that includes many but not all people, may compensate the woman for time lost off the job and may pay for medical costs. If you injure yourself on the job, your employer must file a report with Workers Comp.

You wake up at 3 a.m. with a sore throat and headache. You feel bad but not bad enough to drive to a hospital or emergency room. You should:

Call the 24-hour advice line of your health plan. This is something you should check on when you sign up for a plan.

While working in her kitchen, the woman slips, bangs her head against the stove, gets a nasty cut and becomes woozy. She should:

Call 9-1-1, which will send an ambulance. 9-1-1 is managed by police dispatch. It's the fastest way to get an ambulance — with one possible exception. Lately in the Bay Area, 9-1-1 calls placed on cellular phones have been running into delays. If you are on the road and in need of emergency help and your cellular phone keeps getting busy signals, try one of the emergency call boxes.

What's the difference between a hospital, a clinic, an urgent-care center and a doctor's office?

The hospital has the most services and equipment. The center or clinic has several services and a fair amount of equipment. The office, usually, has the fewest services and the smallest amount of equipment but in some places "clinic-office" means about the same.

Hospitals have beds. If a person must have a serious operation, she goes to a hospital. Hospitals have coronary-care and intensive-care units, emergency care and other specialized, costly treatment units.

When hospitals are purchased by the same group, usually each hospital is kept open but instead of, say, two hospitals in the same region offering obstetrics, the service might be consolidated in one hospital.

Some hospitals are contracting out certain treatments — for example, neonatal care — to other hospitals that specialize in this type care. In recent years, hammered by rising costs, hospitals have been looking for ways to avoid duplications and cut expenses. Some of their reductions have drawn criticism. Opponents contend they erode the quality of care.

Many hospitals also run clinics for minor ailments and provide the same services as medical centers.

Urgent care or medical centers are sometimes located in neighborhoods, which makes them more convenient for some people. The doctors treat the minor, and often not-so-minor, ailments of patients and send them to hospitals for major surgery and serious sicknesses. Some doctors form themselves into groups to offer the public a variety of services.

Some hospitals have opened neighborhood clinics or centers to attract patients. Kaiser has hospitals in some towns and clinic-offices in other towns.

The doctor in his or her office treats patients for minor ailments and uses the hospital for surgeries, major illnesses. Many illnesses that required hospitalization years ago are now treated in the office or clinic.

Some hospitals offer programs outside the typical doctor-patient relationships. For example, wellness plans — advice on how to stay healthy or control stress or quit smoking.

Major Hospitals in & near Alameda County

Alameda County Medical Center, 1411 E. 31st. St., Oakland, 94602. Ph. (510) 437-4800. Also includes a facility at1¡```5400 Foothill Blvd., San Leandro, 94578. Ph. (510) 667-7800. Drop-in clinic, internal medicine, primary care, AIDS, pediatric clinic, specialty clinics, Alzheimer day care services, outpatient rehabilitation services, physical therapy, occupational therapy, speech pathology and audiology, inpatient acute rehabilitation services, skilled nursing facility, 229 beds.

Alameda Hospital, 2070 Clinton Ave., Alameda, 94501. Ph. (510) 522-3700. ICU, CCU, OB-GYN, emergency services, acute care, surgical services, outpatient surgery, physical referral, physical therapy, radiology, sub-acute care, cardial rehabilitation. General acute care hospital.135 beds.

Alta Bates Medical Center, Ashby Campus, 2450 Ashby Ave., Berkeley, 94705. Herrick Campus, 2001 Dwight Way, Berkeley, 94704. Ph. (510) 204-4444. ICU, CCU, OB/GYN, birth center, NICU, women's center, mental health center, heart & vascular center, comprehensive cancer center, burn center, skilled nursing, home health care, orthopedics, neurosciences, emergency services, chest pain emergency center, respiratory services, surgery & surgical subspecialties, health education & support groups. Physician referral and 24-hour audio health library with over 400 recorded health topics: (800) 606-2582. 548 beds.

Alta Bates, Summit Campus, (formerly Merritt Peralta Medical Center and Providence Hospital), 350 Hawthorne Ave., Oakland, 94609. Ph. (510) 655-4000. CCU, ICU, cardiac care, work hardening and cardiac rehabilitation, OB, GYN, perinatology, 24-hour emergency services, alcohol and chemical dependency, orthopedics, physical therapy, physician referral, diagnostic imaging, diabetes treatment center, health access/health screening and wellness program, health resource library, oncology, ophthalmology, outpatient surgery/subacute, sports medicine, surgery, geriatrics, radiology, ambulatory treatment center, skilled nursing facility, adult day health care, lifeline emergency response program, respiratory care. 534 beds.

Children's Hospital Oakland, 747 52nd St., Oakland, 94609. Ph. (510) 428-3000. Only pediatric hospital in Alameda County. Regional pediatric trauma center, pediatric ICU and level 3 intensive care nursery. 30 subspecialties, including pediatric cardiology, sickle-cell center, burn center, pulmonology, neurology, hematology/oncology, gastroenterology and infectious disease, rehabilitation, child development center, prenatal diagnosis and craniofacial. Inpatient/outpatient care. Children's health advice line. 171 beds. Subspecialty services in Fremont, Pleasanton, Brentwood and Walnut Creek.

Eden Medical Center, 20103 Lake Chabot Rd., Castro Valley, 94546. Ph. (510) 537-1234. ICU, CCU, OB, GYN, level II intensive care nursery, trauma center, emergency services, chest pain emergency unit, physical/occupational/speech therapy, hand therapy clinic, acute rehabilitation, skilled nursing facility, women's health services, maternity education, home care, geriatric services, senior housing and transportation, cancer treatment, inpatient and outpatient surgery, laser optics, adult psychiatric services, cardiac catheterization, cardiopulmonary services and rehabilitation, nuclear medicine, radiology, wellness programs, support groups. 275 beds. **See ad page 113**.

Highland General Hospital, 1411 E. 31st St., Oakland, 94602. Ph. (510) 437-4800. ICU, CCU, OB-GYN, trauma center, emergency care, pediatric services, radiology, geriatric services, cancer treatment. Clinics include services for AIDS, allergy, arthritis/rheumatology, cardiac, dermatology, gastroenterology, geriatrics, hematology/oncology, internal medicine/general medicine, endocrinology, neurology, renal. Special services: Rape crisis center, START prenatal care, healthy infant program, community adult day health care, death and dying project, chaplaincy project, triage project, pediatric van services. Acute care hospital. County facility. Division of Alameda County Medical Center. 316 beds.

John Muir Medical Center, 1601 Ygnacio Valley Rd., Walnut Creek, 94598. Ph. (925) 939-3000. Regional Trauma Center, 24-hour emergency services, physician referral, neuroscience ICU, medical/surgical ICU, CCU, Birth Center, OB-GYN, Level III neonatal intensive care nursery, pediatrics, physical medicine and rehabilitation, neurosciences, orthopedics, cardiac services, cancer services, Breast Center and Cancer Resource Library, Diabetes Center, senior services (information and referral), full range of outpatient services. Private, not-for-profit, 321 beds. Part of John Muir/Mt. Diablo Health System.

Kaiser Permanente Medical Center, 27400 Hesperian Blvd., Hayward, 94545. Ph. (510) 784-4000. Typical hospital services, medical social work, pharmacy, optical sales, eye care, OB/GYN, internal medicine, health education. Also emergency care, hospice, chronic pain, postgraduate training program in orthopedic physical therapy. 210 beds.

Kaiser Permanente Medical Center, 280 W. MacArthur Blvd., Oakland, 94611. Ph. (510) 752-1000. Typical hospital services. Also emergency care, HIV services, MRI nuclear medicine, occupational medicine, pediatric intensive care, Sports Injury Clinic, health education services, NICU, home care, hospice, genetic & prenatal counseling, lithotripsy. 235 beds.

Kaiser Permanente Medical Offices-Fremont, 39400 Paseo Padre Pkwy., Fremont, 94538. Ph. (510) 795-3000. Allergy, ambulatory surgery, dermatology, dietary, optometry, ophthalmology, health education, optical sales, general medicine, internal medicine, lab, neurology, OB/GYN, orthopedics, pediatrics, pharmacy, physical therapy, podiatry, psychiatry, radiology, otolaryngology.

Kaiser Permanente Medical Offices-Pleasanton, 7601 Stoneridge Dr., Pleasanton, 94588. Ph. (925) 847-5000. Allergy, ambulatory surgery, dermatology, dietary, optometry, ophthalmology, optical sales, general medicine, internal medicine, laboratory, neurology, OB, GYN, orthopedics, pediatrics, pharmacy, physical therapy, podiatry, psychiatry, radiology, surgery, otolaryngology.

Kaiser Permanente Medical Offices-Union City, 3555 Whipple Rd., Union City. Ph. (510) 784-4000. Sports medicine, psychiatry, pharmacy, radiology, alcohol and drug abuse programs.

Kindred Hospital, 2800 Benedict Dr., San Leandro, 94577. Ph. (510) 357-8300. ICU, physical therapy, radiology, extended acute care focused on high acuity ventilator-dependent patients. An intensive care hospital. 100 beds.

Mt. Diablo Medical Center, 2540 East St., Concord, 94520. Ph. (925) 682-8200. 24-hour emergency services, ICU, CCU, Chest Pain Center, The Heart Institute, cardiac catheterization laboratory, Cardiac Emergency Network, cardiac rehabilitation, Regional Cancer Center, respiratory services, pulmonary rehabilitation, Breast Health Center, senior services (information and referral), HIV/AIDS Services, Lymphedema Center, Grief Services, Health and Fitness Institute, wellness programs, Center for Diabetes, in/outpatient physical, occupational and speech therapy; industrial medicine, Diablo Valley Outpatient Surgery Center, physician referral, Laser Technology Center, pharmacy. 254 beds. Part of John Muir/Mt. Diablo Health System.

St. Rose Hospital, 27200 Calaroga Ave., Hayward, 94545. Ph. (510) 264-4000. OB-GYN, family birthing center, ICU, CCU, emergency care, radiology services, occupational health services, physical therapy, hand therapy, cardiopulmonary rehabilitation programs, transitional care, skilled nursing, home health care, cancer treatment, breast-care center. Community Mobile Clinic, Silva Pediatric Clinic. 175 beds.

San Leandro Hospital, 13855 E. 14th St., San Leandro, 94578. Ph. (510) 357-6500. 24-hr. emergency care, in/out patient rehabilitation services, general acute care for inpatients, transitional care unit, ICU, CT, MRI, CCU, in/out patient surgical services, endoscopy/special procedures. 122 beds.

ValleyCare Medical Center, 5555 West Las Positas Blvd., Pleasanton, 94588. Ph. (925) 847-3000. Acute care hospital, a ValleyCare Health System facility. ICU/CCU, surgery, OB, GYN, birth center, level 2 NICU, pediatrics, outpatient surgery, inpatient & outpatient physical therapy, diagnostic imaging, MRI, radiation therapy, home health agency, outpatient drug & alcohol treatment, sports medicine, occupational health services, wellness programs, community health education programs, health resource library, physicians referral, 24-hr. emergency room, cardiac catheterization lab, cancer care, digestive care services, CAT, nuclear medicine, 141 beds.

Valley Memorial Hospital, 1111 E. Stanley Blvd., Livermore, 94550. Ph. (925) 447-7000. A ValleyCare Health System Facility. Physical therapy, skilled nursing, diagnostic imaging, digestive disorders, geriatric psychiatric services, pulmonary rehabilitation, cardiac rehabilitation, cancer care, physicians referral, home health agency, outpatient drug & alcohol treatment, wellness programs, urgent care center, occupational health services, digestive care services, MRI, CAT, nuclear medicine, acute care hospital. 95 beds.

Veterans Affairs Medical Center, 4951 Arroyo Rd., Livermore, 94550. Ph. (925) 373-4700. 120-bed nursing home care unit for qualified veterans, long-term care, geriatric care, physical rehabilitation, skilled nursing care, home care, outpatient psychiatry, outpatient surgery. 45 beds.

Washington Hospital Healthcare System, 2000 Mowry Ave., Fremont, 94538-1716. Ph. (510) 797-1111. ICU, CCU, OB, GYN, birthing center, emergency services, psychiatric care, physician referral, pediatric services, alcohol & chemical dependency, walk-in clinics, outpatient surgery, radiology, radiation-oncology, physical therapy, heart institute, free-standing heart outpatient catheterization lab, cardiac surgery, cardiac rehabilitation, mental health, outpatient rehabilitation center, geriatric services, diagnostic labs, health & prenatal education. 337 beds.

Key: ICU, intensive care unit; CCU, coronary care unit; OB, obstetrics; GYN, gynecology; MRI, magnetic resonance imaging; NICU, neonatal intensive care unit; CAT, computerized axial tomography.

Directory of Hospitals Central Valley

Bloss Memorial Hospital–Castle Clinic, 3605 Hospital Rd., Atwater. (209) 381-2000.

Kindred Modesto Hospital, 730 17th St., Modesto. (209) 593-9006.

Dameron Hospital, 525 West Acacia, Stockton. (209) 944-5550.

Del Puerto Hospital, 821 E. St., Patterson. (209) 892-8781.

Doctor's Hospital of Manteca, 1205 E. North St., Manteca. (209) 823-3111.

Emanuel Medical Center, 825 Delbon Ave., Turlock. (209) 667-4200.

Kaiser Permanente Hospital, 7373 N. West Ln., Stockton. (209) 476-2000.

Kaiser Permanente Hospital, 1777 W. Yosemite Ave., Manteca. (209) 825-3700.

Kaiser Foundation Clinic, 1625 I St., Modesto. (209) 557-1004.

Kaiser Foundation Clinic, 1721 W. Yosemite Ave., Manteca. (209) 824-5051.

Lodi Memorial Hospital, 975 S. Fairmont Ave., Lodi. (209) 334-3411.

Lodi Memorial West, 880 S. Lower Sacramento Rd., Lodi. (209) 334-3411.

Los Banos Memorial Hospital, 520 West I St., Los Banos. (209) 826-0591.

Memorial Medical Center, 1700 Coffee Rd., Modesto. (209) 526-4500.

Mercy Hospital, 2740 M St., Merced. (209) 384-6444

Mercy Medical Center, Merced Campus, 301 East 13th St., Merced. (209) 385-7000.

Northern California Women's Facility Hospital, 7150 E. Arch Rd., Stockton. (209) 943-1600.

Oak Valley Hospital, 350 S. Oak St., Oakdale. (209) 847-3011.

St. Joseph's Behavior Health Center, 2510 N. California St., Stockton. (209) 461-2000.

St. Joseph's Medical Center, 1800 N. California St., Stockton. (209) 943-2000.

San Joaquin General Hospital, 500 W. Hospital Rd., French Camp. (209) 468-6000.

Stanislaus Surgical Hospital, 1421 Oakdale Rd., Modesto. (209) 572-2700.

Sutter Tracy Community Hospital, 1420 N. Tracy Blvd., Tracy. (209) 835-1500.

BUY 10 OR MORE & SAVE!

If you order 10 or more books of any mix, price drops by about 50 percent.
1-800-222-3602. Or fill out form and send with check to:
McCormack's Guides, P.O. Box 190, Martinez, CA 94553. Or fax
order to (925) 228-7223. To order online go to www.mccormacks.com

1-800-222-3602

Next to title, write in number of copies ordered:

No.	McCormack's Guide	Single	Bulk
___	Alameda & Central Valley 2006	$13.95	$6.25
___	Contra Costa & Solano 2006	$13.95	$6.25
___	Orange County 2006	$13.95	$6.25
___	Greater Sacramento 2006	$13.95	$6.25
___	San Diego County 2006.	$13.95	$6.25
___	San Francisco, San Mateo, Marin, Sonoma 2006	$13.95	$6.25
___	Santa Clara & Santa Cruz 2006	$13.95	$6.25
___	How California Schools Work	$15.95	$6.25

Subtotal $ _____

CA sales tax (8.25%) _____

Shipping* _____

Total Amount of Order $ _____

*For orders of 10 or more, shipping is 60 cents per book. For orders of
fewer than 10, shipping is $4.50 for first book, $1.50 per book thereafter.

Circle one: Check/Visa/MC/Am.Exp. or Bill Us

Card No. _____ Exp. Date _____

Name _____

Company _____

Address _____

City _____ State _____ Zip _____

Phone: (_____) _____ Fax (_____) _____

The following guides are available online at www.mccormacks.com:
Los Angeles County 2006, Riverside County 2006, Ventura County 2006,
San Bernardino County 2006 and Santa Barbara County 2006.

☐ **Check here to receive advertising information**

Chapter 12

Newcomer's Guide

FOR NEWCOMERS to Alameda County here are tips on getting started in your new town and answers to frequently asked questions.

Voter Registration

You must be 18 years and a citizen. Go to the nearest post office and pick up a voter registration postcard. Fill it out and pop it into the mail box. Or pick up the form when you register your vehicle or secure a driver's license.

For more information on voting, call the elections office at (510) 272-6993.

Before every election, the county will mail you a sample ballot with the address of your polling place.

Change of Address — Mail

The change-of-address form can also be picked up at the post office but to assure continuity of service, fill out this form 30 days before you move.

Dog Licensing — Missing Pets

License fees vary by jurisdiction. Animal services often provide low-cost spaying or neutering, disposal of dead animals, and pet adoptions. Dog bites should be reported to animal services.

Typical fees run $10 to $25 a year. The price is reduced if the dog is fixed or the owner is elderly. Bring proof of rabies vaccination. For information on where to register, call your city hall. Phone numbers can be found at the beginning of the white pages in phone directories.

Vehicle Registration

California has the most stringent smog requirements in the country. If your car is a few years old, you may have to spend a couple of hundred dollars to bring it up to code.

You have 20 days from the time you enter the state to register your vehicles. After that you pay a penalty, and face getting a ticket-fine.

For registration, go to any office of the Department of Motor Vehicles. Bring your smog certificate, your registration card and your license plates.

If you are a California resident, all you need to do is complete a change of address form, which can be obtained by calling the Department of Motor Vehicles at: (800) 777-0133

If going for a driver's license, ask to have the booklet mailed to you or pick it up. Study it. Almost all the questions will be taken from the booklet.

Driver's License

To obtain a driver's license, you must be 16 years old, pass a state-certified Driver's Education (classroom) and Driver's Training (behind-the-wheel) course, and at Department of Motor Vehicles a vision test and written and driving tests.

Once you pass the test, your license is usually renewed by mail. Retesting is rare, unless your driving record is poor. High schools used to offer free driving courses but these have all but disappeared due to state budget cuts. Private driving schools have moved in to fill the gap, at a cost of about $100.

Teenagers older than 15 1/2 years who have completed driver's training can be issued a permit. New law restricts driving hours for young teens to daylight hours and, unless supervised, forbids them for six months to drive other teens. Law also requires more parental training and extends time of provisional license. Purpose is to reduce accidents.

If no driver's education program has been completed, you must be at least 18 years old to apply for a driver's license. Out-of-state applicants must supply proof of "legal presence," which could be a certified copy of a birth certificate. New law allows illegal immigrants to secure driver's licenses and register vehicles.

Turning Rules and Insurance

If signs don't say no, you can turn right on a red light (after making a full stop) and make a U-turn at an intersection.

Stop for pedestrians. Insurance? Must have it to drive and to secure a license.

Earthquakes

They're fun and great topics of conversation, until you get caught in a big one. Then they are not so funny. At the beginning of your phone book is some advice about what to do before, during and after a temblor. It's worth reading.

Garbage Service

The garbage fellows come once a week. Rates vary by city but figure $12 to $20 a month for one can.

Grocery Prices

Item	Store one	Store two	Average
Apple Juice, 1 gal. store brand	4.79	3.96	4.38
Almonds, whole, 2.25 oz.	2.49	2.17	2.33
American Cheese, Kraft, 1 lb.	5.19	5.19	5.19
Apple Pie, Sara Lee	6.49	5.99	6.24
Apples, Red Delicious, 1 lb.	1.99	1.00	1.50
Aspirin, cheapest, 250 count	4.49	4.99	4.74
Baby Shampoo, Johnson's, 15 fluid oz.	4.39	4.19	4.29
Bacon, Farmer John Sliced, 1 lb.	4.99	5.79	5.39
Bagels, store brand, half doz.	2.99	3.08	3.04
Bananas, 1 lb.	.79	.79	.79
Beef, round tip boneless roast, 1 lb.	4.59	4.49	4.54
Beef, ground round, 1 lb.	4.49	2.49	3.49
Beer, O'Douls 6-pack bottles	5.99	5.99	5.99
Beer, Coors, 12-pack, cans	10.99	10.69	10.84
Bisquick batter, 2 lbs. 8 oz.	2.99	2.99	2.99
Bleach, Clorox, 96 oz.	2.69	2.59	2.64
Bok Choy, 1lb.	.99	.99	.99
Bread, sourdough, Colombo, 1.5 lb.	3.89	3.87	3.88
Bread, wheat, cheapest 1.5 lb.	.99	.99	.99
Broccoli, 1 lb.	1.99	1.00	1.50
Butter, Challenge, 1 lb.	5.49	5.49	5.49
Cabbage, 1 lb.	.99	.69	.84
Cantaloupe, 1 lb.	.99	1.29	1.14
Carrots, fresh, 1 lb.	.59	.69	.64
Cat Food, store brand, small can	.49	.55	.52
Cereal, Grapenuts, 18 oz.	4.89	4.99	4.94
Cereal, Wheaties, 18 oz.	4.99	4.89	4.94
Charcoal, Kingsford, 10 lbs.	4.99	4.99	4.99
Cheese, Cream, Philadelphia, 8 oz.	2.89	2.59	2.74
Cheese, Mild Cheddar, 1 lb.	4.99	3.69	4.34
Chicken breasts, Foster Farms bone/skinless, 1 lb.	5.99	5.99	5.99
Chicken, Foster Farms, whole, 1 lb.	1.59	1.29	1.44
Chili, Stagg, with beans, 15 oz. box	2.29	2.29	2.29
Cigarettes, Marlboro Lights, carton	48.99	48.99	48.99
Coca Cola, 12-pack, 12 oz. cans	4.99	5.29	5.14
Coffee, Folgers Instant Coffee, 6 oz.	5.99	5.99	5.99
Cafe latte, Starbucks, 1 cup	2.30	2.30	2.30
Coffee, Starbucks, 1 cup	1.35	1.35	1.35
Cookies, Oreo, 18 oz. pkg.	3.99	3.99	3.99
Diapers, Huggies, size 2, (42-pack)	16.99	9.99	13.49
Dishwashing Liquid, Dawn, 25 oz.	3.99	3.69	3.84
Dog Food, Pedigree, 22-oz. can	1.39	1.54	1.47
Eggs, large, Grade AA, 1 doz.	3.19	2.69	2.64
Flour, Gold Medal, 5 lbs.	2.39	2.39	2.39
Flowers, mixed	4.99	4.99	4.99
Frozen Dinners, Marie Callendar's	4.59	4.59	4.59
Frozen Yogurt, Dreyer's, half gallon	5.99	5.99	5.99
Gatorade, 64 oz.	3.29	2.99	3.14
Gerber's baby food, fruit or veg., 4 oz.	.57	.50	.54
Gerber's baby food, meat, 2.5 oz.	.79	.79	.79
Gerber's baby food, cereal, 8 oz.	1.69	2.08	1.89
Gin, Gilbeys, 1.75 Ltrs.	18.99	18.99	18.99
Ginger Root, 1 lb.	2.99	1.99	2.49
Granola Bars, 10-bar box	3.99	3.79	3.89
Grapes, Red Seedless, 1 lb.	2.99	2.99	2.99

Grocery Prices

Item	Store one	Store two	Average
Ham, Dubuque, 5 lb., canned	14.39	13.99	14.19
Ice Cream, Dreyers, half gal.	$5.99	$5.99	$5.99
Ice Cream, Haagen Daaz, 1 pint	3.99	3.99	3.99
Jam, Mary Ellen, strawberry, 18 oz.	4.99	3.86	4.43
Ketchup, Del Monte, 36 oz.	2.99	3.11	3.05
Kleenex, 144-count box	2.59	2.53	2.56
Laundry Detergent, Tide, 87 oz.	9.29	8.99	9.14
Lettuce, Romaine, head	1.29	1.49	1.39
Macaroni & Cheese, Kraft, 14.5 oz	2.25	2.29	2.27
Margarine, tub, Brummel & Brown	2.39	2.39	2.39
Mayonnaise, Best Foods, 1 qt.	3.99	3.49	3.74
Milk, 1% fat, half gal.	1.29	1.29	1.29
Milk, soy, half gal.	2.99	2.39	2.69
M&M Candies, plain, 2 oz.	.65	.65	.65
Mushrooms, 8 oz. package	2.29	2.29	2.29
Olive Oil, cheapest, 17 oz.	6.39	5.99	6.19
Onions, yellow, 1 lb.	.99	1.69	1.34
Oranges, Navel, 1 lb.	.69	.99	.84
Orange Juice, Tropicana, 64-oz., Original Style	4.59	4.79	4.69
Paper Towels, single pack	.99	1.18	1.09
Peanuts, cocktail, Planter's, 12 oz.	4.19	4.19	4.19
Peas, frozen, 16 oz.	2.39	3.00	2.70
Peanut Butter, Jiff, 18 oz.	3.19	3.29	3.24
Pizza, Frozen, Di Giorno, 1 lb. 13 oz.	7.59	6.29	6.94
Popcorn, Orville Reddenbacher, 3-pack	3.49	3.55	3.52
Pork chops, center cut, 1 lb.	4.99	3.99	4.49
Potato Chips, Lays, 12 oz.	2.99	2.99	2.99
Potatoes, Russet, 10 lbs.	2.99	2.99	2.99
Raisins, 2 lbs.	4.99	3.99	3.49
Reese's Mini-Peanut Butter Cups, 13 oz.	3.99	3.29	3.39
Rice, cheapest, 5 lbs.	3.69	3.39	3.54
Salmon, fresh, 1 lb.	4.49	5.99	5.24
Seven-Up, 6-pack, cans	2.99	2.99	2.99
Soap, bar, Zest, 3-pack	2.89	2.89	2.89
Soup, Campbell, chicken noodle, 10-oz. can	.99	1.85	1.42
Soup, Top Ramen	.25	.37	.31
Soy Sauce, Kikkoman, 10 oz.	2.29	2.19	2.24
Spaghetti, Golden Grain, 2 lbs.	2.79	2.79	2.79
Spaghetti Sauce, Prego, 12 oz.	1.99	1.99	1.99
Sugar, cheapest, 5 lbs.	1.99	1.99	1.99
Tea, Lipton's, 48-bag box	2.99	4.21	4.10
Toilet Tissue, 4-roll pack, cheapest	1.79	3.29	2.54
Tomatoes, on the vine, 1 lb.	3.69	3.49	3.59
Toothpaste, Colgate 6.4 oz	2.99	2.99	2.99
Tortillas, flour, cheapest, 10-count pack	2.59	1.99	2.29
Tuna, Starkist, Chunk Light, 6 oz.	1.99	.99	1.49
Vegetable Oil, store brand, 64 oz.	3.79	4.41	4.10
Vegetables, mixed, frozen, 1 lb.	2.39	2.50	2.45
Vinegar, 1 gallon	3.39	3.83	3.61
Water, 1 gallon	1.49	1.29	1.39
Whiskey, Seagrams 7 Crown, 750ml.	13.49	13.49	13.49
Wine, Cabernet, Glen Ellen	9.99	9.99	9.99
Yogurt, Frozen, Dreyers, half gal.	5.99	5.99	5.99
Yogurt, Yoplait Original, single	.99	.85	.92o

Garbage companies, for suburban neighborhoods, use wheeled plastic containers designed to be picked up and emptied by mechanical arms attached to the truck. These carts come in several sizes, the most popular 32 and 64 gallons. Almost every home will receive recycling bins or carts for plastics, glass and cans and garden trimmings. Pickup weekly, usually the same day as garbage.

To get rid of car batteries and motor oils and water-soluble paints, call your garbage firm and ask about disposal sites. Or call city hall. Don't burn garbage in the fireplace or outside. Don't burn leaves. Against law.

Property Taxes

Property taxes are paid in two installments — due by April 10 and December 10. They generally are collected automatically through impound accounts set up when you purchase a home, but check your sale documents carefully. Sometimes homeowners are billed directly.

Property taxes for new buyers vary by taxing jurisdiction but most come in under 1.5 percent of market value at time of purchase. This means generally that the buyer of a $200,000 house will pay property taxes of about $3,000 a year, and the buyer of a $300,000 house will pay $4,500 a year.

After the base rate is established, property tax increases, no matter how high property values soar, are limited to no more than 2 percent a year — unless local voters approve an increase.

Some cities, to fund parks and lights and other amenities in new subdivisions, have installed what is called the Mello-Roos tax. Realtors are required to give you complete information on all taxes. If you buy a resale home in an established neighborhood, Mello-Roos almost never enters the picture.

Sales Tax

In Alameda County, it is 8.75 percent. If you buy something for $1 you will pay $1.09 (8% rounded up) and if the item costs $100, you will pay $108.75. Food is not taxed, except in restaurants. The sales tax in Merced is 7.25 percent, San Joaquin, 7.75, Stanislaus, 7.375,

State Income Taxes

See chart on page 283.

Disclosure Laws

California requires homes sellers to give detailed reports on their offerings, including information on flood, fire and earthquake zones.

Cigarette — Tobacco Tax

Sin tax, passed a few years ago, 50 cents on a pack of cigarettes, plus usual taxes. Many Californians load up on cigarettes in Nevada or Mexico or order over Internet.

Gas and Electricity

Most homes are heated with natural gas. No one, or almost no one, uses heating oil. Up until recently, Pacific Gas and Electric (PG&E) reported that gas bills, year round, averaged about $30 a month, and electric bills $60 a month. The bill for an average three-bedroom home ran $130 to $140 a month.

Rates have been increased but structured to reward conservation. Low consumption will see zero increases, medium 7 percent, medium plus 18 percent, heavy 37 percent. Read your utility bill to see how the system works. The energy crisis is not over; more rate changes may be coming.

Almost never between May and September, and rarely between April and October, will you need to heat your home. Air conditioners are used in the summer but on many days they are not needed.

Cable TV Service — Internet Service

Almost all East Bay homes are served by cable. Rates vary according to channels accessed. Installation is extra. For clear FM radio reception, often a cable connection is required. Many changes in this field; price competition.

High-speed internet service is generally available.

Phone Service

SBC charges $33.01 to run a line to your house. It charges $120 for the first jack and $40 per additional jack. If you're handy, you can do the jack wiring and installation yourself. Many homes will have the jacks in place. The basic monthly charge is $10.69 but with taxes, access to interstate calling, and other miscellaneous items the true cost jumps way up.

Bottled Water

If the direct source for your town's water is the Sierra, then you may not need bottled water. If the source is the Delta or ground water, many people take the bottled.

Love and Society

San Francisco often flaunts its sexuality, hetero, homo and trans. Except in rare instances, the suburbs don't but the cosmopolitan virtues apply. In the Bay Area, consenting adults, in sexual matters, are generally free to do what they want as long as it doesn't harm others.

In Alameda County, same-sex couples attend office parties and social events, and usually no subterfuge is put up to disguise the relationship.

If you act out in the suburbs, if you slobber over your loved one, no matter what the sexual orientation, you won't be stoned but you might be shunned.

If you want the society of men or the society of women or both, numerous groups exist to help to make connections.

Smoking

In public places, increasingly frowned upon and in the workplace forbidden. In 1998 a state law took effect forbidding smoking in saloons, one of the last bastions of smoking. Bars in restaurants comply. Saloons enforce sporadically but many people refrain from smoking and those that do, often hide the cigarette under the table. In San Francisco, people smoke in neighborhood bars but social pressures are curbing the practice. In some towns, notably Berkeley, no smoking rules are enforced.

If visiting socially, you are expected to light up outside.

Dress

For almost all social occasions, even in some circles weddings and funerals, the dress is casual. The person who wears a tie to a restaurant on Friday or Saturday often stands out (depends a little on the town).

Dress formal for dinner in San Francisco and the theater and opera (but even here, many men go in sports coats, no tie; women in slacks).

Age a factor: Older men and women often dress up more than younger. And if your business situation calls for suits, then suits it is. Supposedly, we are entering a more conservative, more serious era where suits might make a comeback. Remains to be seen.

For the coast bring a jacket or sweater. It's often chilly, even during the day.

CALIFORNIA TAX RATES 2005
Single Married Filing Separate Returns

Taxable Income		Basic Tax	Plus
Over	But Not Over		
$0	$6,147	$0.00 +	1% over $0.00
$6,147	$14,571	$61 +	2% over $6,147
$14,571	$22,997	$230 +	4% over $14,571
$22,997	$31,925	$567 +	6% over $22,997
$31,925	$40,346	$1,103 +	8% over $31,925
$40,346	And Over	$1,776 +	9.3% over $40,346

Married Filing Jointly & Qualified Widow(er)s

Taxable Income		Basic Tax	Plus
Over	But Not Over		
$0	$12,294	$0.00 +	1% over $0.00
$12,294	$29,142	$123 +	2% over $12,294
$29,142	$45,994	$460 +	4% over $29,142
$45,994	$63,850	$1,134 +	6% over $45,994
$63,850	$80,692	$2,205 +	8% over $63,850
$80,692	And Over	$3,553 +	9.3% over $80,692

Heads of Households

Taxable Income		Basic Tax	Plus
Over	But Not Over		
$0	$12,300	$0.00 +	1% over $0.00
$12,300	$29,143	$123 +	2% over $12,300
$29,143	$37,567	$460 +	4% over $29,143
$37,567	$46,494	$797+	6% over $37,567
$46,494	$54,918	$1,332 +	8% over $46,494
$54,918	And Over	$2,006 +	9.3% over $54,918

Example

John and Jackie Anderson have a taxable income of $125,000.

Taxable Income	Basic Tax	Plus
$125,000	$3,553 +	9.3% over $80,692

They subtract the amount at the beginning of their range from their taxable income.

```
$125,000
 -80,692
 $44,308
```

They multiply the result by the percentage for their range.

```
$ 44,308
 x .093
 $ 4,121
```

Total Tax

Basic	$3,553
% +	+4,121
Total	$7,674

Note: Amounts rounded off. This chart is not a substitute for government forms. If you have questions, consult tax authorities or your tax advisor.   '06

How **much** is your **house worth?**

Go to www.dataquick.com to find the latest sale prices in your neighborhood. DataQuick products provide sale price and trend information, comparable sales and local crime reports in minutes from your computer.

Instant Access to **Property Information**

Complete property ownership information on every parcel in California and most properties across the U.S.

Perfect for lenders, appraisers, insurance providers, Realtors®, investors and investigators.

Available via the Internet, CD-ROM, list and dial-up network.

DataQuick is the nation's leading provider of real estate information products combining timely, in-depth real estate, consumer and business information with over 20 years of experience in product and technological innovation.

Call us today at 888.604.DATA
3 2 8 2

or visit www.dataquick.com

Chapter 13

Rental Housing

AFTER SEVERAL YEARS of double-digit increases, rents are stabilizing and in some Bay Area counties decreasing.

Local rents are greatly influenced by what happens in Santa Clara County (Silicon Valley) and San Francisco-San Mateo. Between about 1996 and 2001, these counties boomed and added thousands of jobs. But lacking buildable land, they failed to provide housing, both homes and apartments, for the newcomers.

Southern Alameda County, particularly Fremont, Union City and Newark, border or are within a short drive of Santa Clara County. Hayward and San Leandro are just a bridge away from central San Mateo and San Francisco International Airport. Oakland, Emeryville and Berkeley are separated from downtown San Francisco by another bridge, a drive for many of just 10 to 15 miles.

Very quickly people flocked to Alameda County, particularly the mentioned cities, and drove up the rents. Some cities, notably Oakland, rushed into apartment construction to meet demand.

When the dot-coms tanked and the high-tech firms foundered, many jobs disappeared and the apartment shortage evaporated. The Sept. 11 terrorist attack discouraged many from flying and cost jobs at the airport and the hotel-service industry in the City and in San Mateo — further weakening demand and lowering rents.

For a long time, Berkeley was painfully short of available apartments and its rents were very high. For decades Berkeley had wrapped itself in rent control and this discouraged apartment construction.

The courts forced Berkeley to change its laws to allow market increases when apartments change hands. People who have held apartments for a long time are paying comparatively low rents; people who recently rented or will rent apartments are paying or will pay much higher rents. services or web and newspaper classified ads to find apartments.

With the law changed, developers built more apartments in Berkeley and the university added more dorms. The result: students have many choices.

For information about dorms and family housing for students, check with the university, which has family housing in Albany.

Many students and adults in Berkeley-Oakland put up in shared rentals. For $500 to $600 a month, you can find something about two miles from the campus.

Older cities with older complexes will offer studios and single apartments for $600 or $700 a month. No pool, no spa, no extras.

If you want the modern apartment with pool and security gates, then you're looking at $1,200 plus. If the apartment complex is located near a BART (commute rail) station, if it's in a safe and nice neighborhood, if it offers extra amenities, the rents will often start over $1,200. Dublin is building many new apartments.

When thinking about rental or temporary housing, apartments come quickly to mind but there are other choices.

For those new to the region and shopping for homes, a hotel might do the trick. Over the last 20 years or so, the major chains have built large and small

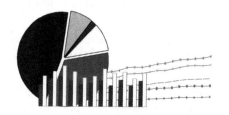

Average Rents

Alameda County

City	Average Rents
Alameda	$1,219
Castro Valley	1,058
Dublin	1,433
Fremont	1,211
Hayward	1,091
Livermore	1,107
Newark	1,269
Oakland	1,281
Pleasanton	1,333
San Leandro	1,022
Union City	1,140

San Joaquin County

Manteca	$845
Stockton	807

Stanislaus County

Modesto	$779
Turlock	748

Source: REALFACTS, Novato, CA. Average rents as of December 2004.

hotels in the suburbs, many of them near freeway exits and a few smack in the middle of residential neighborhoods. Prices range from $80 to well over $100 a night, the higher amount buying more of the extras: pools, game rooms, etc.

Residency hotels offer a slightly different experience. They combine the conveniences of a hotel — maid service, continental breakfast, airport shuttle — with the pleasures of home: a fully-equipped kitchen and a laundry room (coin-operated). They may also have a pool, a spa, a sportscourt, a workout room. Some offer free grocery shopping and in evenings a social hour.

Residency hotels welcome families. Typically, guests remain at least five days and often much longer. At a certain stage, a discount will kick in.

Renting an apartment in California is probably little different from any other place in the country.

You will be asked for a security deposit and for the first month's rent up front. State law limits deposits to a maximum two months rent for an unfur-

Rental Sampler from Classified Ads

Alameda
- Apt., 2BR/1BA, small office, $1,200
- Apt., 1BR/1BA, remod., $900

Berkeley
- Apt.,2BR/1BA, near shops, $1,090
- Apt.,2BR/1BA, craftsman, $1,595
- Home, 4BR/2BA, nr. frwy., $2,300
- Home, 3BR/2BA, form. DR, $3,200

Castro Valley
- Apt., 2BR/1BA, upstrs., $1,040
- Home, 3BR/1BA, porch, $1,450

Dublin
- Apt., 1BR/1BA, loft, $1,400
- Home, 3BR/2BA, brand new, $2,100

Emeryville
- Apt., 1BR/1BA, open flr. plan, $895
- Apt., 2BR/1BA, live/work loft, $2,250
- Home, 2BR/1BA, quiet, $1,200

Fremont
- Apt., 1BR/1BA, upgrds., $899
- Apt., 2BR/1.5BA, townhome, $1,495
- Home, 3BR/2BA, near trans., $1,695

Hayward
- Apt., 2BR/1BA, nr. dwntwn., $995
- Home, 3BR/2BA, hrdwd. flrs., $1,800

Livermore
- Apt., 2BR/1BA, A/C, $1,100
- Home, 4BR/3BA, brand new, $1,395

Newark
- Apt., 2BR/1BA, carport, $1,000
- Home, 3BR/2BA, frplc., $1,750

Oakland
- Apt., 1BR/1BA, priv. deck, $1,145
- Home, 4BR/3BA, yard, $2,000
- Apt., 2BR/1BA, storage, $1,350

Pleasanton
- Apt., 1BR/1BA, condo, $1,025
- Home, 4BR/2BA, nr. schs., $2,195
- Apt., 2BR/1BA, pool, $1,450

San Leandro
- Apt., 2BR/1.5BA, remod., $1,100
- Home, 3BR/1BA, garage, $1,600

San Lorenzo
- Home, 3BR/2BA, corner lot, $1,875
- Home, 3BR/1BA, frplc., $1,650

Union City
- Apt., 2BR/1BA, pool, $1,300
- Home, 4BR/3BA, lrg. yrd., $2,200

nished apartment and three months for a furnished (This includes the last month's rent.)

If you agree to a year's lease, some places will add an extra month free. If you move out before the lease is up, you pay a penalty.

Some apartments forbid pets, some will accept only cats, some cats and small dogs. Many will ask for a pet deposit (to cover possible damage). Some complexes set aside certain units for people with pets.

To protect themselves, many landlords will ask you to fill out a credit report and to list references.

The Fair Housing laws will apply: no discrimination based on race, sex, family status and so on. But some complexes will be designed to welcome one or several kinds of renters. A complex that wants families, for example, might include a tot lot. One that prefers singles or childless couples might throw Friday night parties or feature a large pool and a workout room but no kiddie facilities.

Renters pay for cable service, electricity or gas and phone (in some instances, deposits may be required to start service.)

Some large complexes will offer furnished and unfurnished apartments or corporate setups, a variation of the residency hotel.

If hotels or apartments are not your cup of tea, you might take a look at renting a home. Some homeowners handle the details themselves, others use a professional property manager. In older towns, many of the cottages and smaller homes in the older sections will often be rentals. If you see a "For Sale" sign in front of a home that interests you, inquire whether the place is for rent. You might be pleasantly surprised. Some realty firms double as rental agencies.

What about rates? They vary by town but in a middle-class town you often can rent a three-bedroom home for $2,000 to $2,500 a month. Older, smaller homes in some neighborhoods will go from $1,200 to $1,500.

When you're out scouting for a rental, check out the neighborhood, do a little research, and think about what you really value and enjoy. If you want the convenient commute without the hassle of a car, pick a place near a BART line or bus stop. If it's the active life, scout out the parks, trails and such things as bars and restaurants and community colleges. Say the first thing you want to do when you arrive home is take a long run. Before you rent, get a map of local trails from the city recreation department.

Rental Sampler from Classified Ads

Merced County

Merced
•Apt., 2BR/1BA, $675
•Home, 4BR/2BA, near UC, $1,200

San Joaquin County

Escalon
•Home, 2BR/1BA, almond trees, $875

Lathrop
•Home, 4BR/2BA, nr. sch., $1,800

Manteca
•Apt, 2BR/1BA, quiet, $650
•Home, 3BR/2BA, pool, $1,300

Mountain House
•Home, 3BR/2BA, loft, $1,800

Stockton
•Townhouse, 3BR/1.5BA, $895
•Home, 4BR/2BA, 2 story, $1,800

Tracy
•Apt., 2BR/1.5BA, new crpt., $1,050
•Home, 3BR/2.5BA, form. DR, $1,950

Stanislaus County

Ceres
•Apt., 2BR/1BA, $749
•Home, 4BR/2.5BA, brand new, $1,500

Modesto
•Apt., 2BR/2BA, luxury, $850
•Home, 3BR/2.5BA, cul-de-sac, $1,295

Patterson
•Home, 4BR/3BA, $1,200

Turlock
•Apt., 2BR/1.5BA, patio, $850
•Home, 3BR/2.5BA, hrdwd., $1,350

For parents, your address will usually determine what public school your child will attend. If you want a high-scoring school, see the in this book before making a decision. Always call the school before making a renting decision. Because of crowding, some schools are changing attendance zones. You may not be able to get your child into the "neighborhood" school. See chapter on How Public Schools Work.

The same advice applies to day care. Make sure that it is available nearby before signing a lease. Happy hunting!

Chapter **11**

New Housing

SHOPPING FOR A NEW home? This chapter gives an overview of new housing underway in Alameda and nearby counties.

If you know where you want to live, drive that town or ask the local planning department, what's new in housing. Or go to www.newhomesmag.com.

Prices change. Incidentals such as landscaping fees may not be included. In the 1980s, to pay for services, cities increased fees on home construction. Usually, these fees are included in the home prices but in what is known as Mello-Roos districts, the fees are often assessed like tax payments (in addition to house payments).

Nothing secret. By law, developers are required to disclose all fees and, in fact, California has some of the toughest disclosure laws in the country. But the prices listed below may not include some fees..

This information covers what's available at time of publication. For latest information, call the developers for brochures.

If you have never shopped for a new home, you probably will enjoy the experience. In the larger developments, the builders will decorate models showing the housing styles and sizes offered.

You enter through one home, pick up the sales literature, then move to the other homes or condos. Every room is usually tastefully and imaginatively decorated — and enticing.

An agent or agents will be on hand to answer questions or discuss financing or any other aspect you're interested in. Generally, all this is done low-key. On Saturdays and Sundays, thousands of people can be found visiting developments around the Bay Area and Northern California.

Developers call attention to their models by flags. When you pass what appears to be a new development and flags are flying, it generally means that units are available for sale.

ALAMEDA COUNTY

Livermore

Cresta Blanca, Signature Properties, 2394 Peregrine St., (925) 960-9220, single family homes, 3-6 bedrooms, from high $800,000.

Station Square, Signature Properties, 1832 Railroad Ave., (925) 245-0760, townhomes, 2-3 bedrooms, from low $500,000.

Private Reserve, Signature Properties, 5436 Stockton Loop, (925) 373-3440, single family homes, 4-5 bedrooms, from low $1 million.

Oakland

Harborwalk, Signature Properties, 3090 Glascock St., (510) 532-8843, townhomes, 1-3 bedrooms, from high $400,000.

The Estuary, Signature Properties, 2909 Glascock St., (510) 535-0120, townhomes, 2-3 bedrooms, from low $600,000.

MERCED COUNTY

Merced

University Park, Morrison Homes, 1339 Irvine Ct., (209) 388-0611, single family homes, 3-4 bedrooms, from mid $300,000.

SAN JOAQUIN COUNTY

Stockton

Fox Hollow, Morrison Homes, 2352 Etcheverry Dr., (209) 954-1305, single family homes, 3-4 bedrooms, from high $300,000.

Tracy

Redbridge, Standard Pacific, 2624 Redbridge Rd., (209) 833-7000, single family homes, 3-4 bedrooms, from mid $500,000.

STANISLAUS COUNTY

Patterson

Bella Flora at Patterson Gardens, Morrison Homes, 1256 Fawn Lily Dr., (209) 895-4034, single family homes, 4-5 bedrooms, from mid $400,000.

Turlock

Ventana, Morrison Homes, 4077 Enclave Dr., (209) 632-0025, single family homes, 3-4 bedrooms, from high $300,000.

SHE'S NOT JUST COMING FOR A LITTLE STAY

Life is really full of surprises. But we don't think home buying should be. So we do all we can to ease you through every step of buying your new home. From selecting your floor plan through closing escrow. Even after move in. Which shouldn't be surprising, considering we've spent over 39 years doing our best to make home buying as easy as possible.

STANDARD PACIFIC HOMES
Making You Right At Home™

1-877-STNDPAC (786-3722)
www.standardpacifichomes.com

 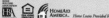

CONTRA COSTA COUNTY
Brentwood

Cedarwood, Signature Properties, 502 Richdale Ct., (925) 513-1057, single family homes, 3-5 bedrooms, from low $600,000.

Garin Landing, Signature Properties, 570 Almanor St., (925) 240-1585, single family homes, 3-4 bedrooms, from mid $500,000.

San Pablo

Abella Villas, Signature Properties, 102 Carmel St., (510) 236-8215, condominiums, 2-3 bedrooms, from mid $400,000.

SOLANO COUNTY
Fairfield

Andalucia, Standard Pacific, 3001 Pebble Beach Cir., (707) 422-3199, single family homes, 2-4.5 bedrooms, from $700,000.

Vacaville

Lantana at Alamo Place, Standard Pacific, call for address, (707) 450-0178, single family homes, 4-6 bedrooms, from lower $600,000.

MARIN COUNTY
San Rafael

The Forest at Redwood Village, Signature Properties, 36 Apricot Ct., (415) 479-8808, townhomes, 2-3 bedrooms, from high $500,000.

NAPA COUNTY
American Canyon

Vintage Ranch, Standard Pacific, 59 Toscana Dr., (707) 552-5034, single family homes, 3-7 bedrooms, from mid $500,000.

SACRAMENTO COUNTY
Rancho Cordova

Anatolia, Morrison Homes, 4008 Kalamata Way, (916) 869-5779, single family homes, 3-4 bedrooms, from high $300,000.

Sacramento

Silver Hollow, Morrison Homes, 8151 Stallion Way, (916) 525-3945, single family homes, 4-5 bedrooms, from high $800,000.

Chapter 15

Fun & Games for Kids

ALTHOUGH REGIONAL amusements are popular with children, the great majority find most of their fun in their backyard or local activities.

When children are very young, parents and day-care centers or preschools will do most of the entertaining. Oh, there are other activities but generally they are of the type that demands the presence of a parent; e.g., tot swimming.

Many cities have built tot lots or installed jungle gym-type equipment in their parks. These are popular with the kids. On weekends, the petting zoo at the Oakland Zoo and the merry-go-round at Tilden Park will be clogged with children.

The Bay Area has zoos, museums, great parks, merry-go-rounds, theme parks (Six Flags Marine World, Great America), musical events (the Nutcracker is a favorite annual). All welcome children.

Activities for Youths

As the children grow older, more activities and sports come into play for the simple reason that the kids are strong enough to handle the running and kicking and throwing, etc., and mature enough to follow directions.

Alameda County and its cities and various organizations offer a great variety of sports and activities but the most popular probably are soccer, Little League baseball, basketball, Pop Warner football, softball, and swimming.

How they are played and who plays them varies by sex and age and happenstance. Sometimes, a local tradition or the presence of a facility will influence what the kids choose.

Dublin, Berkeley, Oakland and Fremont have ice-skating rinks. Ice-skating is more popular in these towns than elsewhere and when Kristi Yamaguchi of Fremont won an Olympic gold for skating, the sport got a boost.

Changes in the law have all but absolved cities for injuries incurred at public skate parks. In recent years, many cities have opened skate parks.

How Local Sports Are Organized

It's a mixed bag but once you ferret out a few networks, the rest will fall into place.

Sports are generally organized through parent groups, through traditional national groups, such as Little League, through schools and churches, through city recreation departments, through special agencies that in effect function as city recreation departments and through private groups. Some examples:

- Soccer. This sport has become very strong in the last 30 years. In many towns, the leagues are formed through parent groups but often they enlist city rec. departments and schools for help, especially in securing fields.

- Baseball. Again, parent groups, organized through Little League, which provides instructional material on how to manage, raise funds, etc.

- Basketball. For younger children, often informal leagues are organized through churches and middle schools.

- Pop Warner football. Like Little League. Very popular in California among boys. Girls often acquire cheerleading skills in Pop Warner football.

- Swimming. When the kids are young, generally through parent groups who set up and manage swim clubs. Often the clubs are built around a city or a neighborhood association pool or a school pool, leased from a school district.

  When the kids hit the teen years, generally they move into high school programs.

- Wrestling. Generally through the middle schools and high schools.

- Volleyball. The schools.

- Gymnastics. Sometimes through the schools but frequently through city programs and private businesses that open schools in converted stores.

- Skating. Through the local rinks, roller and ice.

- Dance. Through the city programs and private businesses.

- Track. Through the schools, generally beginning in junior high.

- Tennis. Schools and rec. departments. Some private.

Some Rules of the Games

- When the children are young, they all play. Soccer, baseball and football are set up to train the boys and girls in the sport. What if the kid has two left thumbs and can't kick straight? He or she will play at least two innings, at least two quarters, etc.

The more skillful kids will play more but no one is shut out. But ask about the rules, and if you don't think your kid will get a fair shake, shop for another team or league.

When the kids hit the teen years, skill and talent get rewarded more. At high school, many kids sit on the bench.

- Girls and boys play soccer and baseball together. The swim teams are mixed. Football is generally a boys' game. Many girls favor gymnastics and cheerleading.

As the kids get older, they are broken out more by sex. At high school, after school, the girls generally play softball, the boys baseball. The girls will field their own soccer, basketball and volleyball teams. Swimming teams will still be mixed but boys race boys, and girls race girls.

Theoretically and legally, the girls may try out for football and wrestling. In the real world, few do.

During regular school hours, in physical education, the sexes are often mixed in a variety of sports: baseball, track, etc. But these activities are not organized for intense competition.

- Many of the teams and leagues are grouped according to age. As the children grow older, they move up into different leagues.

- Yes, you have to shell out — for uniforms and equipment. And yes, you have to volunteer for the snack shack, and the annual dance and buy tickets for this or that raffle. And eat pizza until it's coming out of your ears (because your league, for a few benefit bucks, has cut a deal with the local pizzeria). It's part — burp! — of the game.

What if you don't have the money? Get one of the team officials aside and ask about a reduced fee. Maybe you can spend a few extra hours in snack shack. These people are not out to exclude kids.

Where to Get Information

- Start with your local recreation department, which works out of city hall. Almost all will publish a schedule of activities and sports. Here's where you get a lot of information about activities for the toddlers. Many cities offer parenting classes.

- Hayward, Castro Valley and San Lorenzo formed the Hayward Area Recreation District to provide fun and games. For information, phone (510) 881-6700.

- Check with the schools about the activities they offer.

- Some church schools, notably the Catholics and the Mormons, run their own basketball leagues and organize other activities for the kids.

- Just stop and ask. You're driving down the road and you see a soccer team playing. You want your kids to play soccer. Ask the coach for a contact phone number for signing up.

Miscellaneous

- Scouting is often run as a private activity or an activity affiliated with a church. You don't have to join the church to get your kid into the Scouts. For scouting information, call (510) 522-2772.

- Your city or town doesn't offer the sport your kid wants. The next town does. Sign him or her up in the next town; generally, no problem, except you'll have to drive farther.

- Schools still offer music instruction but many programs have been cut back. For lessons, often you have to go to private sources. Many are listed in the phone book.

- For some activities, ballet and advanced gymnastics, you have to look to the private schools that specialize in these activities — phone books.

- Fishing. Kids under age 16 fish free. Plenty of water around here.

- Skiing. The Sierra is 4-5 hours from the Bay Area. When the winters are wet, the skiing is very good. Many resorts offer training for kids.

- Ocean swimming. You can try but even in summer the water is quite cold, the result of an arctic current that bubbles up along the Northern California shore. Watch the waves! Dangerous, especially off San Francisco. City of Alameda has a public beach.

- Boys and Girls Clubs, YMCA's. Some towns have them. Good sources for activities for kids.

- Miniature golf, water slides, video game emporiums, comic book stores, book stores — they're all out there. Check the Yellow Pages.

- Community colleges. Almost all run child development programs and offer summer academic enrichment programs for kids. See list of colleges in job chapter.

- Often some activities lead to other activities. The Lawrence Hall of Science and the Chabot Space and Science Center offer activity and enrichment classes for kids. You take your kid to one of these classes, meet other parents, they tell you about other activities, and so on.

- Summer camps. Many city recreation departments put together day camps. The kids play under the supervision of an adult (often an older teen) and you pick them up in late afternoon.

  Many parents send their kids away to camps for a week or two. Prices vary widely; this may be an experience you can afford. Check with YMCA or pick up a Parents Press or Valley Parent. Often they carry camp advertise-ments.

Fun-Educational Places to Visit

This is a partial list of attractions-amusements in or close to Alameda County. For more on parks, see Adult Fun, the following chapter.

- **Chabot Space and Science Center.** Planetarium, telescope, biology garden, classes, activities. Rebuilt and opened in 1999. If you're interested in science and want to get kids interested, good place to visit. Located at 4917 Mountain Blvd. near the MacArthur and Warren freeways. Call for schedule. (510) 336-7300

- **Children's Fairyland.** Nestled within Lakeside Park, located off Grand Avenue at the north end of Lake Merritt in downtown Oakland. Favorite kid spot for decades.

  Featuring children's favorites — Mother Goose, Alice in Wonderland, the Cheshire Cat, the Cowardly Lion, the Owl and the Pussycat, Pinocchio, Willie the Whale, Humpty Dumpty, and Mary's Little Lamb — Fairyland is best suited to younger children. Rides include the Jolly Trolly, Lakeside Park Toy Train, the Wonder-Go-Round and Magic Web Ferris Wheel. In addition to puppet and clown shows, youngsters have myriad slides and mazes to entertain their wanderings. (510) 238-6876.

- **Magnes Museum Berkeley,** 2911 Russell St., Berkeley. Shows. Art and artifacts of Jewish culture. Library, history. (510) 549-6950.

- **Lakeside Park.** Located off Grand Avenue at the north end of Lake Merritt in downtown Oakland. Kiwanis Kiddie Korner of the park features children's attractions such as a sea horse swing or an octopus slide. The outdoor aviary and zoo holds turkey vultures, barn owls, great horned owls, hawks, sand-hill cranes, opossums, porcupines, skunks and other small animals. In addition, Lake Merritt is a wild duck refuge. Pelicans frequently entertain by diving into the lake for food.

  The Rotary Nature Center shows free nature films on occasion, in addition to its regular fare of science exhibits. An outdoor bandstand is the site of old-fashioned Sunday summer concerts, and smooth green courts provide hours of entertainment for lawn bowlers. Open year round. Details are available by calling (510) 238-3739.

- **Lawrence Hall of Science.** Great science museum for adults and children. Hands-on fun, computers, rabbits, snakes, brain games, astronomy, Nobel medals, classes, all fortified by strong connection to UC-Berkeley. Store has science toys.

  Located in the Berkeley hills. Take Highway 24 to Fish Ranch Road, right at top of hill onto Grizzly Peak Road, follow for about three miles, left on Centennial Drive. Also can be reached from Canyon Road in back of UC Berkeley, to Centennial Drive. Phone (510) 642-5132 for hours of operation.

- **Lawrence Livermore National Laboratory.** Located two miles south of Interstate 580 on Greenville Road in Livermore, is an advanced research and development complex operated by the University of California for the U.S. Department of Energy. The newly refurbished Visitors Center offers updates on scientific programs, featuring hands-on displays as well as printed materials, films, videotapes and large color photos. Call (925) 423-3272 for hours.

- **Meek Estate.** This renovated and furnished five-story 1869 national historic monument can be found at Hampton and Boston roads in Hayward. You can relive the Victorian era in the nostalgic ballroom, library, solarium, bedrooms, nursery and servants' quarters. The grounds feature acres of park and playground equipment and a barbecue in the picnic area.

- **Mission San Jose.** Located at 43300 Mission Blvd. in Fremont, Mission San Jose was founded June 11, 1797, and destroyed in the earthquake of 1868. Recently restored, this is one of the most picturesque buildings in Alameda County and possesses genuine historic value.

  Starkly simple outside, ornate within, the mission superbly captures the spirit of the Franciscans and Indians. Chandeliers, altars, statues, bells, tile floors — what was not salvaged from the old mission or from the era was accurately duplicated.

  Slide show, artifacts, some history of the Ohlone Indian, a small gift shop. For hours of operation, call (510) 657-1797.

- **Mormon Temple,** 4770 Lincoln Ave., in Oakland hills. Striking edifice, beautiful grounds. Visitor center, daily tours. Non-Mormons welcome. Phone (510) 531-3200.

- **Oakland Museum.** Located at 1000 Oak St. in downtown Oakland, the Oakland Museum focuses on California art, California history and California natural history. The excellence of its collection has given it the reputation as "California's Smithsonian."

  Art from the days of the Spanish explorers to the present is included, featuring panoramic views of San Francisco, cowboys and Indians, Oriental art and modern canvases.

  Natural sciences include exhibits on botany, birds, ecology, paleontology and geology, in addition to an aquarium and dioramas of animals in their natural settings.

  California's history begins with the Indians and walks through the rooms of history from the Spanish explorers, the Californios, the gold miners and cowboys, the pioneers and turn-of-the-century Californians. Phone (510) 238-2200.

- **Oakland Zoo.** Located at Knowland State Park at the MacArthur Freeway connection with Golf Links Road and 98th Avenue.

Underfunded for years, the zoo won state financial support and made a great comeback. The Jungle Lift takes you over the African veldt, past the high ground where elk, deer, lions, flamingo, elephants and buffalo graze in a natural setting. Fascinating acrobatics by the gibbons.

Easy viewing. One of the major features is the Baby Zoo, where children can wander and feed or pet llamas, goats, rabbits, geese, ponies and calves. Phone (510) 632-9525.

- **Sulphur Creek Nature Center.** Located at 1801 D St. in Hayward, this little-known nature center is a great place to introduce children to the wonders of nature. Hawks, foxes, coyotes and opossums are on display in outdoor cages. Plants, trees and fungus-bearing logs are neatly labelled along a nature trail.

Museum is small but informative. Focus is native wildlife. Animal-lending library. Phone (510) 881-6747.

- **Hornet.** The carrier "Hornet" was commissioned in 1943 and saw service in World War II and other conflicts. Decommissioned, the carrier is now a museum. Located at naval station in Alameda. Open daily 10 a.m. to 5 p.m. Closed Tuesdays. Phone (510) 521-8448.

- **East Bay Regional Park District.** Runs most of the major parks in the East Bay and many nature or historic attractions. Phone (510) 562-PARK.

Chapter 16

Fun & Games for Adults

ALAMEDA COUNTY boasts professional baseball (the Athletics), basketball (the Warriors) and football (the Raiders) and college sports. It has a first-class museum and a renovated zoo.

When famous classical musicians or dance troupes tour, they often play UC Berkeley. Thanks to the foresight of its early residents, the county set up one of the first park districts in the state with the happy result that thousands of acres have been set aside in regional parks.

Within a drive of 15-20 minutes for many residents, San Francisco yields most of its cultural and artistic treasures. For Fremont, Newark and Union City residents, the San Jose Arena and professional hockey (the Sharks) are within a half-hour drive. California Cuisine was invented in Berkeley by Alice Waters of Chez Panisse. Excellent restaurants abound. Livermore and Pleasanton are part of the wine country.

As impressive as all this sounds, it needs some perspective. The average resident, looking for fun, dabbles in the above: a concert here, a Warrior game there, a night out in San Francisco once or twice a year. For the most part, people take their recreation in their back yards: in games, exercise, classes, local activities. A typical summer Saturday might include a short jog and a stop at the farmer's market. Some suggestions:

- Local recreation. Get on the mailing list of the local city or special-district recreation department. This will keep you up on the activities offered in or near your neighborhood.

- If your school district offers adult education, get on that mailing list. Adult schools, for a very reasonable fee, mix the practical (typing, bookkeeping) with the entertaining (how to dance).

- Subscribe to a local newspaper. It will carry, usually on Friday, a calendar of events, both local and regional. When you attend an event, say a local theater production, you often wind up on a mailing list and will be notified of future events.

- For regional parks, call the East Bay Regional Park District (510) 562-PARK and ask for brochures on parks, activities and trails. The district includes Alameda and Contra Costa County and owns about 53 parks covering about 69,000 acres. Golf courses, nature areas, about 800 miles of trails, lakes — a lot.

- For local parks, see city hall or the recreation district.

- For local organizations — flower societies, social and hobby clubs — chambers of commerce often will publish a directory of local groups. See also the yellow pages under Associations.

- Golf. Very popular in the Bay Area. Many courses. Yellow pages. Bookstores carry books with descriptions of courses.

Colleges and Universities

Community colleges offer a variety of courses — academic, vocational, and recreational or personal enrichment: music, art, etc.

Both California State University, Hayward, and the University of California offer many classes through their extension programs. Many of the classes are oriented toward business: how to set up a small business, bookkeeping, computer systems, etc. But many fall in the category of personal enrichment, the arts, literature.

See Chapter 14 for a list of colleges and phone numbers.

Private Groups

These include YMCA's, Nautilus exercise clubs, racquetball clubs, and so on. They fill a need; otherwise they would not be in business. Some run 24 hours daily and at 3 a.m. you'll find a few people pumping iron. Check the yellow pages.

How Things Work

Take softball, very popular in the suburbs. The city or special district provides the organizing framework (umpires, fields) but usually does not recruit the teams.

At the job or in the neighborhoods, someone will say, "Let's get a team together." A roster is submitted, practice held (according to the ambitions of the players) and they're off. Sounds simple, but someone must do the organizing.

If you're not affiliated with a team, check with the recreation department to see if some spots are open. City recreation sponsors volleyball. You show up and find in the gym that the nets have been set up and the balls provided. You do the rest: choose sides, keep score, etc.

You join the Sierra Club, get a monthly magazine, and a list of Sierra Club hikes in the Bay Area. You choose your hike.

The trick is to get a toehold in the group or activity you like, tap deeper into the information on activities and pick what you like.

Singles Clubs

Many are organized through churches and religious groups but if this is not your cup of tea there are dozens of groups in the Bay Area. The groups sponsor parties, dances and excursions. Often for a fee, some clubs are heavily into matchmaking and, in fact, if you go into almost any major job setting in the Bay Area you'll find people who have met their spouses through matchmaking services.

The clubs are too many and too diverse to list but you might start with the singles magazine, Possibilities. Phone (415) 507-9962. This is all strictly buyer-beware. McCormack's Guides does not investigate or study these clubs.

Gambling

California has lottery games and allows limited gambling at race tracks and at card parlors but the "legal" card games are few in number, usually a variation of draw poker. No Blackjack. No slots. Nonetheless, the parlors are increasing in number, quality (food, decor) and popularity. Look in the Yellow Pages under Card-Playing Rooms.

For the high-powered stuff, people head usually for Reno or the Nevada side of Lake Tahoe. There you will find the big casinos and the top entertainers. The casinos often advertise their shows in the more popular newspapers. Indian casinos with Las Vegas games and slots have opened in Sonoma County and in Placer County. The City of San Pablo, north of Berkeley, has a casino that is affiliated with a tribe and may soon offer slots and the Nevada games — a first for the Bay Area.

If you want to sample the Nevada palaces without getting behind the wheel, Amtrak and local bus companies offer gambler specials. The bus companies will usually throw in some freebie coupons to sweeten the deal. See Yellow Pages under Tours.

Skiing

On Fridays during the winter, Interstates 680 and 580 out of the Bay Area are filled with people heading for the Sierra and first-class skiing.

For tickets, information, coupons, visit local ski shops and read the Friday entertainment sections of the newspapers. Even if you don't ski, a winter trip to the Sierra is often a great frolic.

Restaurants and Dining Out

In the suburban cities, the chains are popular — Sizzler, Chevy's, etc. — but you'll have no trouble finding tablecloth restaurants and fine dining.

Berkeley is in a class itself, many excellent restaurants, and Oakland and Albany are not far behind. San Francisco, of course, has many fine restaurants. The Livermore-Pleasanton wine country is winning a reputation for fine dining.

Regional Recreation

There's a lot out there: the Napa wine country, the coast, fishing, sailing, the arts. For information in depth on what Northern California has to offer, see the guides listed in the back of this book.

Here are some of the major local attractions. Please note that almost all the large parks and many of the trails and nature attractions are in the East Bay Regional Park District. To receive a brochure about the district and its offerings, call (510) 562-PARK.

- **Chabot Regional Park.** 4,684 acres east of Oakland-San Leandro. Off Skyline Boulevard, south of Redwood Road, you reach an Equestrian Center with horses for rent and access to equestrian, hiking, jogging trails.

  Off Redwood Road between Oakland and Castro Valley, you'll find group camping areas available by reservation, a 67-acre motorcycle hill area, a marksmanship range and backpacking access to East Bay Skyline National Trail. Here you also have access to Chabot Family Camp, with 73 trailer, tent, and hike-in sites overlooking Lake Chabot with showers, self-guiding nature trails and hiking-fishing access to Lake Chabot. For more conventional activity, there is also the 18-hole Willow Park Public Golf Course and driving range.

  Off Lake Chabot Road east of Fairmont Avenue, you'll discover Lake Chabot Marina (315-acre stocked lake with rental boats), fishing, coffee shop, boat tours, picnicking, large turfed play areas, horseshoe pits, hiking, bicycling, jogging and running trails.

- **Coyote Hills Regional Park.** 1,039 acres in Fremont near the eastern approach to the Dumbarton Bridge. Take Patterson Ranch Road. Bicycling, hiking, jogging and running trails, birdwatching, picnicking, kite and radio-controlled model glider flying (requires club membership), visitor center, boardwalk view areas of freshwater marsh, self-guided nature trail and reservable group camping.

  Special features include interpretive programs and guided tours of 2,300-year-old protected Indian shell mounds and reconstructed Indian village. There's also access to Alameda Creek Regional Trail and San Francisco Bay.

- **Del Valle Regional Park.** 3,868 acres, 10 miles south of Livermore. Take South Livermore Road and Mines Road out of Livermore. Del Valle includes a 750-acre lake planted with fish on a regular basis. In season, swimming from two sandy beaches when lifeguards are on duty, visitor center, self-guided nature trail and interpretive programs.

  Year-round group picnicking and camping by reservation, four-lane boat ramp, sailboating, motor boats and rental boats. Also available are tour boat, fishing, hiking, equestrian, jogging and running trails.

Del Valle Campground offers complete family camping service year-round and connects with the Ohlone Wilderness Trail. Reservations required.

- **Redwood Regional Park.** 1,829 acres in Oakland and Contra Costa County. Take Skyline Boulevard or Redwood Road out of Oakland. Picnicking, equestrian field and trails, hiking, jogging and running trails, playfields, volleyball court, children's play area, exercise course, amphitheater fire circle, reservable group picnicking and youth group camping areas. Accessible to backpackers and horseback riders via East Bay Skyline National Trail.

- **Tilden Regional Park.** 2,078 acres in Berkeley hills, an excellent park. At Lake Anza in season, swimming, sandy beach, bathhouse complex, large turfed area, food concession. Year-round fishing.

  Environmental Education Center and Nature Area, interpretive programs, exhibits, puppet shows, Little Farm, Jewel Lake and all-weather nature trails.

  At Tilden Public Golf Course, an 18-hole course and driving range, pro shop and Tee Clubhouse restaurant.

  In other park areas, a merry-go-round, food concession and children's playhouse, Redwood Valley Railroad and Golden Gate Steamers (scale model steam locomotives), playfields, horseshoe pits, picnicking, Regional Park Native Plant Botanic Garden and Visitor Center, Inspiration Point, hilltop vistas and reservable areas for group picnicking and youth group camping.

  Hiking, jogging, bicycling and equestrian trails throughout. Backpacking access via East Bay Skyline Trail.

- **Ardenwood Regional Preserve.** 203 acres in Fremont including the former Patterson Mansion. Take Newark Boulevard north of Highway 84. A glimpse of ranch life at the turn of the century. Horse-drawn railroad and hay wagons. Picnicking.

- **Mission Peak Regional Preserve.** 2,596 acres atop Mission Peak and Monument Peak east of Ohlone College in Fremont. Climbing to the top on a clear day yields views of the entire region. Birdwatching, hiking, equestrian, jogging and running trails, kite flying, interpretive programs. Staging areas are at the end of Stanford Avenue, with space to park horse trailers. Connects with Ohlone Regional Wilderness Trail.

- **Ohlone Regional Wilderness.** 6,758 acres in southeastern Alameda County between Sunol Regional Wilderness and Del Valle Regional Park. Enter via trail from Sunol and Del Valle. Ponds, waterfalls, nature trails. Connects with Ohlone Wilderness Trail.

- **Cull Canyon Regional Recreation Area.** 360 acres in Castro Valley. Take Cull Canyon Road. In season, swimming lagoon, sandy beach, turfed play area, bathhouse and food concession open Wednesday through Sunday. In other park areas year-round fishing, hiking and equestrian trails, picnicking.

- **Don Castro Regional Recreation Area.** 100 acres between Castro Valley and Hayward. North end of Woodroe Avenue. In season, swimming in lagoon, sandy beach, bathhouse and food concession open daily. Year-round lake fishing, hiking trails, limited horseback riding, picnicking, turfed areas, group picnic areas available by reservation.

- **Roberts Regional Recreation Area** and Redwood Bowl. 100 acres in Oakland at the western boundary of Redwood Regional Park. Take Skyline Boulevard. In season, swimming (Tuesday through Sunday) at heated outdoor swimming pool with bathhouse and food concession.

  Year-round group picnicking by reservation, family picnic areas, playfields, volleyball court, hiking, bicycling, jogging and running trails. Children's play area and wading pool.

- **Shadow Cliffs Regional Recreation Area.** 249 acres in Pleasanton. In season, swimming off a sandy beach with bathhouse, food concession and paved ramp to the lake for disabled. The Giant Rapids Waterslide operates April through Labor Day.

  Year-round fishing in the lake, picnicking, volleyball courts, horseshoe pits, hiking, equestrian, jogging and running trails. Group picnicking by reservation. Rental boats available. Connects with Alameda County bicycle trail along Stanley Boulevard between Pleasanton and Livermore.

- **Sunol Regional Wilderness.** 6,758 acres south of Pleasanton and Livermore. Take Calaveras Road to Geary Road. Picnicking, birdwatching, interpretive programs, group overnight camping by reservation, family camping, backpack loop available by reservation, hiking, equestrian, running and jogging trails.

- **Temescal Regional Recreation Area.** 48 acres in Oakland. In season, swimming off sandy beach. Crowded on hot days. Bathhouse, food concession. Year-round fishing, picnicking, turfed play areas, children's play areas, bicycling, hiking, jogging, group picnicking by reservation.

Shorelines

- **Crown Memorial State Beach.** 383 acres in city of Alameda. Bathhouse and food concession, reservable youth-group day camps, turfed play areas, beach. Estuary and reserve, wading, swimming, windsurfing, fishing.

- **Hayward Regional Shoreline.** 816 acres in Hayward at end of West Winton Avenue. Birdwatching, hiking and interpretative programs. Visitor center off Highway 92.

Trails

Lineal parkland for walking, jogging, bicycling and horseback riding. Five hundred miles of trails are within parks, plus the following 106 miles which connect the parks:

- **Alameda Creek Regional Trail.** 458 acres form parallel trails along Alameda Creek Flood Control Channel from the mouth of Niles Canyon through Union City, Newark and Fremont with several staging areas.

- **Cull Canyon Regional Trail.** This is the first portion of the Chabot to Garin Trail. Combined length of trail is 4.5 miles.

- **East Bay Skyline National Trail.** This 31-mile regional trail, suitable for hiking, backpacking and horseback riding full length and for bicycling in part, connects six regional parks. Beginning at Wildcat Canyon in Richmond, it progresses through Tilden, Sibley Volcanic, Huckleberry Botanic, Redwood and Chabot regional parks.

- **San Lorenzo Shoreline Regional Trail.** A five-mile trail connecting Hayward Regional Shoreline with San Lorenzo and San Leandro Park and Marina. Staging areas for the trail at the west ends of West Winton Avenue, Hayward, and Grant Avenue, San Lorenzo.

Around the Cities

- **Berkeley**. Theater district, Berkeley Rep, plays, foreign movies, shopping, bookstores, cafes, restaurants. Good town for strolling. For shopping, Shattuck Avenue, Telegraph Avenue, Fourth Street. Berkeley Rep, (510) 204-8901. Visitors bureau, (510) 549-7040.

- **Dunsmuir House & Garden.** A beautiful colonial revival mansion, with 37 rooms, 40 acres with garden in Oakland, available for touring for $3. Located at 2960 Peralta Oaks Ct., you can find it by taking the 106th Avenue exit from Highway 580. Phone (510) 615-5555.

- **Golden Gate Fields Racetrack.** They're off and running — from late January to June. Thoroughbred racing. Golden Gate is located in Albany — take the Gilman Street exit off Interstate 80. Phone (510) 559-7300.

- **Jack London Square.** Located at the foot of Broadway in Oakland, you'll find waterfront stores, movies, Barnes and Noble bookstore, restaurants and night clubs, and an ever-changing view of ships in the Oakland Estuary. For information about what's happening in Oakland, look at cityofoakland.com and check activities.

- **Judah L. Magnes Memorial Museum,** 2911 Russell St., Berkeley. Shows. Art and artifacts of Jewish culture. Library, history. (510) 549-6950.

- **McConaghy House,** 18701 Hesperian Blvd., Hayward, next to Kennedy Park. Furnished Victorian farmhouse. (510) 276-3010.

- **Meek Estate.** Renovated and furnished five-story 1869 mansion at Hampton and Boston roads in Hayward. Relive the Victorian era in the ballroom, library, solarium, bedrooms, nursery and servants' quarters. Park with playground equipment and a barbecue in the picnic area.

- **Mission San Jose.** Located at 43300 Mission Blvd. in Fremont, Mission San Jose was founded June 11, 1797, and destroyed in the earthquake of 1868. One of the most picturesque buildings in Alameda County. (510) 657-1797.

- **Oakland-Alameda Coliseum.** One of the premiere sports-exhibition complexes in the country, the Coliseum is located off the Nimitz Freeway at Hegenberger Road. Home of the Oakland A's, Golden State Warriors, Oakland Raiders. Site of many rock concerts and major exhibitions. (510) 569-2121

- **Oakland Museum.** 1000 Oak St. This museum focuses on California art, history and natural history. The excellence of its collection has given it the reputation as "California's Smithsonian." Art from the days of the Spanish explorers to the present is included, featuring panoramic views of San Francisco, cowboys and Indians, Oriental and modern art.

  Natural sciences include exhibits on botany, birds, ecology, paleontology and geology, and an aquarium and dioramas of animals in natural settings. California's history begins with the Indians and goes through the Spanish explorers, the Californios, the gold miners and cowboys, the pioneers and turn-of-the-century Californians. (510) 238-2200.

- **Paramount Theater.** One of best examples of "Art Deco" architecture on West Coast. Parquet floors, gold ceiling teeming with sculptured life and elegant 1930s embellishments. Used for concerts, plays. (510) 465-6400.

- **Toot-Toot.** The Pacific Locomotive Association, a group of train buffs, has rebuilt an abandoned line near Sunol and twice a month offers rides to the public on its old trains. Phone to confirm trains are running (925) 862-9063. Sunol is located off I-680, just south of Pleasanton.

- **University of California, Berkeley.** Bookstores, magnificent libraries, museums, lectures, concerts — it's one of the intellectual capitals of the world. Phone (510) 642-6000. The Campanile and Sather Gate are famous landmarks. Top dance and musical events. The Greek Amphitheater is spectacular. Great spectator sports, including football, basketball, track. Go Bears! To get on the Cal Performances mailing list, call (510) 642-6000.

Art guilds and galleries, dance schools, bands, symphonies, choral groups, little theater — Alameda County has them all. Every town is hooked to cable television. Local theaters offer a good variety of movies. IMAX (big screen) movie theater in Dublin.

Chapter 17

Commuting

DESPITE NUMEROUS COMPLAINTS, many Alameda residents have a short commute, thanks to the presence of so many local jobs. If you take BART or buses to work and travel a long distance, you will often find the ride tiring but endurable.

In some ways, the commute is getting better. In 2002, a new San Mateo Bridge opened and in 2003, BART completed its extension to San Francisco International Airport.

Oakland International Airport is spending $1.5 billion to improve its roads and terminals. The job is far from finished but already it is much easier, from the freeway, to get to and from the airport.

Diamond (car pool) lanes are turning up more and more in Bay Area freeways. If you car pool, these lanes will speed you to your destination. Not every time. They have their choke points.

The lose-your-cool, insane commutes boil down to only two: solo drives to San Francisco or to the old Silicon Valley (San Jose, Sunnyvale, Santa Clara, etc.).

To get to San Francisco, you have to grind your way through the approaches to the Bay Bridge toll plaza, then through the metering lights, then over the bridge and into downtown San Francisco.

Damaged in the 1989 earthquake, the east span of the bridge is to be replaced over the next five or so years — construction delays. Many improvements have been made to freeways leading up to the Bay Bridge. Many more will be made. But no matter how many or how great the changes, this bridge will always snarl. Just too many vehicles trying to fit into too narrow a space.

San Francisco has never been friendly to freeways. Following the 1989 earthquake, the City decided not to rebuild the Embarcadero freeway and tore down several heavily used ramps in the downtown.

Further, to push people into public transit, San Francisco is not building parking anywhere close to what it needs.

Nonetheless, many East Bay residents still drive solo to the City. If you are one or thinking about becoming one, at least give BART and the other alternatives a try. The mind you save may be your own.

Riding the Rails, ala BART

In 2004, BART completed a $1.2 billion renovation to its system, including upgrading car interiors and overhauling fare gates, ticket machines, escalators and elevators.

Coupled with opening of the SFO Airport BART station, and expansion in Contra Costa, Alameda and San Mateo counties, the improvements have upped both system efficiency and customer satisfaction. Ridership on BART now averages close to three million passenger trips every month.

In the 1990s and in 2000, Silicon Valley generated jobs by tens of thousands and homes by the dozens and the hundreds. Prices soared and even with the recession are still quite high.

Many people moved to places like Livermore and Pleasanton in Alameda County and Tracy and Manteca and Merced out in the Central Valley, about 75-plus miles from San Jose. Three freeways lead from these places to San Jose:

• Interstate 580. It collects traffic from the Tracy and Central Valley and from east Alameda and Contra Costa counties and feeds it into the Bay Area and Interstates 680 and 580.

• Interstate 680. This freeway intersects I-580 at Pleasanton-Dublin and travels down the east side of Fremont to San Jose and Silicon Valley. In 2002, car-pool lanes were added between, roughly, Pleasanton and Fremont. This has helped moved things along. Another plus, if you want to call it that, fewer jobs in Silicon Valley, less traffic on the roads.

• Interstate 880, Bayshore freeway. It travels along the shore — Oakland, San Leandro, Hayward, Union City, Fremont — to San Jose and connecting freeways. Always being improved but frequently jamming. Serves Oakland Airport and Coliseum complex and, over the Hayward-San Mateo Bridge, San Francisco International Airport and its job centers.

San Joaquin, Stanislaus, Merced Counties

The problem is not the local freeways. Highway 99 and Interstates 580 and 5 don't roar along at peak hours but they keep moving. Some of the smaller roads — Highway 132 out of Modesto and Highway 152 out of Los Banos — will creep along at peak hours because they are two lane and overloaded with traffic. Highway 152 is being improved but slowly.

The real problems concern distance and Bay Area congestion. Many people in the Central Valley are driving over 90 and 100 miles, one way, to their jobs. Even if no delays were encountered, these are long drives.

Traffic in the Bay Area is often congested. From the Central Valley, it's not bad to places like San Ramon, Dublin, Livermore or Pleasanton. These towns, which have many jobs, are located on the periphery of the Bay Region.But to San Francisco and Silicon Valley, often it's stop and go. Or just stop. The Bay Bridge and its approaches, despite many improvements, bring traffic to a halt. Interstate 680 between Pleasanton and San Jose often hangs up.

The Good News—Central Valley

Key improvements have been made or soon will be made. Interstate 680 added another lane. Some bottlenecks are being widened along Interstate 880. Work on the interchange at Pleasanton, another mess, was finished in 2002. The Bay Area has been adding diamond (car pool/bus) lanes for years and it finally has enough of them to run buses in a speedy way. More buses are being purchased.

Caltrain runs commute trains from Gilroy to San Jose and other Silicon Valley cities. If you're coming from Los Baños and Merced, it might be worth while to park at Gilroy and take the train to work.

The Altamont Commuter Express (ACE) runs commute trains from Stockton to San Jose with stops in Manteca, Tracy, Livermore, Pleasanton, Fremont and Santa Clara.

Central Valley Buses

Bus service throughout Stanislaus, Merced and San Joaquin counties is limited to internal destinations. For more information:

- Stanislaus Regional Transit (800) 262-1516.

- San Joaquin Regional Transit (209) 943-1111

- Merced County, The Bus, (800) 345-3111

- Buses and school kids. Many California school districts do not provide busing. The few that do often charge. Check with school district. Some bus companies offer discounted fares for students. Varies by town.

- Altamont Commuter Express, commute trains from Stockton to Silicon Valley with stops along the way. (800) 411-7245

- Be wary of winter fog on freeways. Central California gets some horrible smashups when tule fog sets in.

Other Improvements

- After years of work, the rebuilding of the freeway interchange at Dublin-Pleasanton was completed in 2002. Big difference.

- FasTrak, automated tolls. Now installed at all bridges in the Bay Area. Proving popular and a time saver.

- BART to SFO. As popular as Oakland Airport is, many East Bay residents depend on SFO or work at the airport or in the vicinity.

Driving Miles to Bay Bridge

City/Location	On I-580	On I-880
Alameda	NA	9
Albany	NA	5
Berkeley*	5	4
Castro Valley	20	NA
Coliseum	NA	9
Dublin	29	NA
Emeryville	NA	2
Fremont	NA	23
Hayward	20	17
Livermore	37	NA
Newark	NA	22
Oakland Airport	NA	10
Pleasanton	29	NA
San Leandro	17	11
San Lorenzo	NA	15
Union City	NA	21

Note: These are approximations. A traveler from Fremont, a large city, could easily add another five miles depending upon his starting point within the city. Of bridges, the Bay Bridge is a little over 8 miles long, the San Mateo about 7, the Dumbarton about 3. **Key:** NA, not applicable. Either exits were not available or the freeway was judged to be too distant for a reasonable measurement. *I-580 route applicable mostly to residents in south and southeast Berkeley who use Highway 24.

• More money. In 2000, Alameda County renewed a half-cent sales tax to pay for transit projects and Santa Clara County passed a half-cent sales tax for transit. Much of the Santa Clara tax will go to extending BART from Fremont to San Jose and the remainder for local jobs.

As for the Alameda tax, it's going to fund a variety of jobs around the county, some long-term, some immediate. Another shot of cash: tolls were raised by a $1.

Shortcuts and Commuting Strategies

Nothing ventured, nothing gained. Do some experimenting.

• Change routes. If the Bay Bridge is driving you batty, take BART or drive the Hayward-San Mateo Bridge.

Switch freeways. Instead of I-880, try I-680. Or Highway 13 in the Oakland hills.

• Buy a good map book and keep it in the car. The editor favors Thomas Guides. Sooner than later you will find yourself jammed on a freeway or about to be jammed and in dire need of an alternate route. They're out there.

San Pablo Avenue will get you through Berkeley, Emeryville and Oakland; Hesperian Boulevard parallels I-880 through the south county;

Mission Boulevard in Fremont will take you off I-880 and place you on the usually faster I-680.

For people shopping for new homes, Thomas is indispensable. Many foldout maps sold locally are several years old. Often they don't show the new tracts.

- Listen to traffic reports on radio. The info is timely and will give you a chance to take alternate routes.

- Buy your BART tickets at Safeway or Albertsons. This will speed you through the gate. BART is studying new ways to ticket riders.

- Call 5-1-1, the universal number for travel information. Almost all the services we list here can be accessed by calling 5-1-1. Also helpful: the web sites, www.BART.gov and www.ACtransit.org

- Join a car pool. The Bay Bridge and local freeways have set aside

BART Discounts

• Blue Ticket. Discounts up to about 6 percent when purchased in amounts over $30. Example, $30 ticket gets $32 in rides, $45 ticket, $48 in rides.

• Red Ticket, 75 percent discount. For disabled and children 5-12. Students on field trips. Requires appropriate identification.

• Green Ticket, 75 percent discount. For people over age 65. Need to show identification.

• Orange Ticket, 75 percent discount. Middle, junior high and high school students, ages 13 to 18. Available only through participating schools. For more information call (510) 464-6406.

• BART Plus. Discounts for riders transferring to other transit systems, including WHEELS, Union City Transit and San Francisco Muni.

• Other discounts are available, including one subsidized by certain employers. Visit BART web site, www.bart.gov.

Chapter 18

Job Training & Colleges

IF YOU ARE looking for a job but need training or additional education, local colleges, public adult schools and private institutions have put together a variety of programs, ranging from word processing to MBA degrees.

Many institutions have devised programs for working adults or parents who must attend the duties of school and child rearing.

In many instances, jobs and careers are mixed in with personal enrichment. At some colleges, you can take word processing, economics and music.

This chapter lists the major local educational and training institutes. All will send you literature, all welcome inquiries.

Adult Schools

Although rarely in the headlines, adult schools serve thousands of local residents. Upholstery, microwave cooking, ballroom dancing, bookkeeping, computers, cardiopulmonary resuscitation, aerobics, investing, art, music, how to raise children — these and more are offered in the adult schools.

These schools and programs are run by school districts and by cities. Many schools also run adult sports programs, basketball, volleyball, tennis. Call your local school or city for a catalog.

Getting the Older Students

As the public's needs have changed, so have the colleges. The traditional college audience — high school seniors — is still thriving but increasingly colleges are attracting older students and working people.

Many colleges now offer evening and weekend programs, especially in business degrees and business-related subjects. Some programs — an MBA — can take years, some classes only a day. Here is a partial list of local colleges and specialty schools.

- University of California, Berkeley. Bachelor's, master's and doctorate degrees. Call (510) 642-6000. Extension program, all sorts of classes for the public. (510) 642-4111. The Extension service has a center in Fremont. Phone (510) 440-9090.

- California State University, East Bay. Popular with adults returning for degree or seeking master's. Day and evening classes. Branch campus in Contra Costa County. Phone (510) 885-3000. Many extension classes. (510) 885-3605.

- Mills College, Oakland. Women's college, coed grad school. (510) 430-2255 or (510) 430-3309 for graduate school information.

- Holy Names University, 3500 Mountain Blvd., Oakland, 94619. Coed. Four-year college.

  Also offers weekend college for working adults. Bachelor's degrees in Humanities, Liberal Studies, Human Services, Business Administration, Nursing (for registered nurses). Master's in Business Admin., English, Education. Teaching credentials and certificates. (510) 436-1000.

- Heald College, Oakland. Business. (510) 444-0201.

- College of Arts and Crafts, Oakland. 1,100 students. Design, arts, architecture, ceramics, graphics, film. (510) 594-3600.

- Northwestern Polytechnic University, 117 Fourier Ave. Fremont. Bachelor and master degrees in computer science, computer systems engineering, electronic engineering, business. (510) 657-5913.

- University of San Francisco-San Ramon Campus. Bachelor's and master's programs in San Ramon. Phone (925) 867-2711.

- Silicon Valley College-Walnut Creek, 41350 Christy St., Fremont. Computer, high-tech, medical programs. 800-750-5627

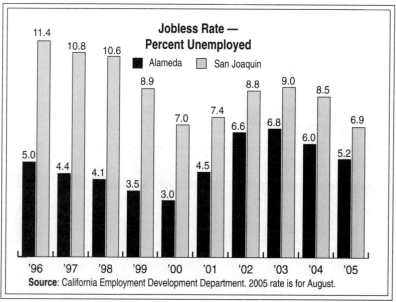

Jobless Rate — Percent Unemployed

■ Alameda ☐ San Joaquin

	'96	'97	'98	'99	'00	'01	'02	'03	'04	'05
Alameda	5.0	4.4	4.1	3.5	3.0	4.5	6.6	6.8	6.0	5.2
San Joaquin	11.4	10.8	10.6	8.9	7.0	7.4	8.8	9.0	8.5	6.9

Source: California Employment Development Department. 2005 rate is for August.

- St. Mary's College. Bachelor's degrees in Liberal Arts, Economics, Business Administration, Education. Also offers special programs, including master's in business, for working adults. Credentials in education and extension programs. Phone (925) 631-4224.

Community Colleges

Many students attend these two-year public colleges then transfer as juniors to state universities or University of California schools. Community colleges also have diverse selections for people interested in occasional classes or in job-related classes. These colleges also offer associate degrees for vocational programs and certificate and license training, e.g., registered nurses.

- College of Alameda, 555 Atlantic Ave., City of Alameda 94501. Ph: (510) 522-7221.

- Laney, 900 Fallon St., Oakland 94607. Ph: (510) 834-5740.

- Merritt, 12500 Campus Dr., Oakland 94619. Ph: (510) 531-4911.

- Vista, 2020 Milvia St., Berkeley 94704. Ph: (510) 981-2800.

- Chabot, 25555 Hesperian Blvd., Hayward 94545. Ph: (510) 723-6600.

- Las Positas, 3033 Collier Canyon Rd., Livermore 94550. Ph: (925) 373-5800.

- Ohlone, 43600 Mission Blvd., Fremont 94539. Ph: (510) 659-6000.

Central Valley

- California State University, Stanislaus. 801 W. Monte Vista Ave., Turlock. 95382 Ph. (209) 667-3811.

- Merced College, 3600 M St., Merced 95348. Ph. (209) 384-6000.

- Modesto College, 435 College Ave., Modesto 95350. Ph. (209) 575-6067.

- San Joaquin Delta Community College, 5151 Pacific St. Stockton 95207. Ph. (209) 954-5151.

- University of California, Merced, 5200 No. Lake Road, Merced, 95343. Ph. (209) 724-4400.

- University of the Pacific, 3601 Pacific Ave. Stockton 95211. Ph. (209) 946-2211.

Chapter 19

Crime

EVERY neighborhood or city in this country suffers from some crime. Even communities surrounded by gates and patrolled by guards will on occasion see domestic violence or pilfering by visitors.

So the question to ask when shopping for a home or apartment is not: Is this neighborhood safe? But rather, how safe is it compared to other places?

In California, crime often follows demographics: High-income neighborhoods generally have low crime, middle-income places middling crime, and low-income towns and neighborhoods high crime.

In many instances, these figures mislead. You can probably take every high-crime city in the country and find within it low-crime neighborhoods.

The demographic connection also can mislead. Many peaceful, law-abiding people live in the "worst" neighborhoods. But these neighborhoods also contain a disproportionate number of the troubled and criminally inclined.

Why does crime correlate with income and demographics? In many countries, it doesn't. Japan, devastated after World War II, did not sink into violence and thievery. Many industrialized nations with lower standards of living than the U.S. have much less crime. In 1990, according to one study, handguns killed 10 people in Australia, 22 in Great Britain and 87 in Japan. The count for the U.S. was 10,567. (But in recent years Europeans have seen more burglaries, robberies, etc. In fact, in some categories, the U.S. is doing better than some European nations. The big exception: handgun deaths.)

Sociologists blame the breakdown of morals and the family in the U.S, the pervasive violence in the media, the easy access to guns, and other forces. Any one of these "causes" could be argued into the next century but if you're shopping for a home or an apartment, just keep in mind that there is a correlation between demographics and crime.

How do you spot a troubled neighborhood?

Crime is a young person's game, particularly boys and men. In one of its annual studies, the FBI determined that 61 percent of all the people arrested were under age 30. For every female arrested four males were arrested, the same study noted.

Crime Statistics by City

City	Population	Violent Crimes	Homicides
Alameda	74,581	342	1
Albany	16,743	42	1
Berkeley	104,543	557	4
Dublin	39,931	83	0
Emeryville*	8,261	118	0
Fremont	210,445	454	5
Hayward	146,027	588	9
Livermore	80,723	140	2
Newark	43,708	142	0
Oakland	412,318	5,151	83
Piedmont	11,055	1	0
Pleasanton	67,650	90	0
San Leandro	81,442	489	4
Union City	70,685	348	1

Crime in Other Northern California Cities

City	Population	Violent Crimes	Homicides
Concord	124,798	393	5
Danville	43,273	49	0
Fairfield	105,026	754	3
Mountain View	72,033	263	1
Palo Alto	61,674	89	2
Richmond	103,012	1,080	35
Sacramento	450,472	4,730	50
San Francisco	772,065	5,757	88
San Jose	944,857	3,379	24
San Ramon	51,027	47	0
Stockton	265,593	3,700	40
Sunnyvale	133,086	161	2
Vacaville	96,735	331	2
Walnut Creek	66,501	115	1

Source: Annual reports from FBI, 2004 data. Homicides include murders and non-negligent manslaughter. The FBI does not break out towns with fewer than 10,000 residents. The state often does but its 2004 figures were not available at time of publication. For this reason, the italicized cities show figures from 2003.

Take a look at the academic rankings of the neighborhood school. Very low rankings indicate that many children are failing or dropping out, that they will have difficulty finding jobs — conditions that often breed crime.

In middle-scoring towns, the failures are fewer. In higher scoring towns, fewer still.

Drive the neighborhood. The signs of trouble are often easily read: bars on many windows, security doors in wide use.

Crime in Other Cities Nationwide

City	Population	Violent Crimes*	Homicides
Anchorage	273,714	2,164	15
Atlanta	430,066	7,922	112
Austin	683,298	3,589	27
Birmingham	238,167	3,261	59
Boise	193,864	745	0
Boston	580,087	6,917	61
Chicago	2,882,746	NA	448
Cleveland	462,260	5,983	78
Dallas	1,228,613	16,165	248
Denver	563,688	4,490	87
Hartford, Conn.	125,109	1,514	16
Detroit, MI	914,353	15,913	385
Honolulu	906,589	2,507	26
Houston	2,043,446	23,427	272
Jacksonville, FLA	790,972	6,533	104
Las Vegas	1,239,805	9,783	131
Little Rock	185,870	3,048	40
Milwaukee	590,874	4,637	87
Miami	385,186	6,461	69
New York City	8,101,321	55,688	570
New Orleans	471,057	4,467	264
Oklahoma City	525,094	4,321	39
Philadelphia	1,484,224	20,902	330
Phoenix	1,428,973	9,465	202
Pittsburgh, PA	334,231	3,739	46
Portland, OR	543,838	4,034	29
Reno	201,981	1,480	9
St. Louis, MO	335,143	6,897	113
Salt Lake City	182,768	1,328	15
Scottsdale, AZ	224,357	468	4
Seattle	575,816	3,798	24
Tucson	522,487	4,873	55

Source: Annual 2004 FBI crime report. *Number of violent crimes.
Key: NA (not available).

Should you avoid unsafe or marginal neighborhoods? The troubled neighborhoods often carry low prices or rents and are located near job centers. Some of the best commute neighborhoods are run down and have crime problems. Some landlords have made their complexes safer and more assuring by hiring guards and installing cameras and security devices.

Many towns and sections are in transition; conditions could improve, the investment might be worthwhile. What's intolerable to a parent might be acceptable to a single person. If you don't have the bucks, often you can still buy safe but you may have to settle for a smaller house or yard.

Whatever your neighborhood, don't make it easy for predators.

Crime in States

States	Population	Homicides	Violent Crimes	Rate*
Alabama	4,530,182	254	19,324	427
Alaska	655,435	37	4,159	635
Arizona	5,743,834	414	28,952	504
Arkansas	2,752,629	176	13,737	499
California	35,893,799	2,392	198,070	552
Colorado	4,601,403	203	17,185	374
Connecticut	3,503,604	91	10,032	286
Delaware	830,364	17	4,720	568
Florida	17,397,161	946	123,754	711
Georgia	8,829,383	613	40,217	456
Hawaii	1,262,840	33	3,213	254
Idaho	1,393,262	30	3,412	245
Illinois	12,713,634	776	69,026	543
Indiana	6,237,569	316	2,294	325
Iowa	2,954,451	46	8,003	271
Kansas	2,735,502	123	10,245	375
Kentucky	4,145,922	236	10,152	245
Louisiana	4,515,770	574	28,844	639
Maine	1,317,253	18	1,364	104
Maryland	5,558,058	521	38,932	701
Massachusetts	6,416,505	169	29,437	459
Michigan	10,112,260	643	49,577	490
Minnesota	5,100,958	113	13,751	270
Mississippi	2,902,966	227	8,568	295
Missouri	5,754,618	354	28,226	491
Montana	926,865	30	2,723	294
Nebraska	1,747,214	40	5,393	309
Nevada	2,334,771	172	14,379	616
New Hampshire	1,299,500	18	2,170	167
New Jersey	8,698,879	392	30,943	356
New Mexico	1,903,289	169	13,081	687
New York	19,227,088	889	84,914	442
North Carolina	8,541,221	532	38,244	448
North Dakota	634,366	9	504	79
Ohio	11,459,011	517	39,163	342
Oklahoma	3,523,553	186	17,635	501
Oregon	3,594,586	90	10,324	298
Pennsylvania	12,406,292	650	50,998	411
Rhode Island	1,080,632	26	2,673	274
South Carolina	4,198,068	288	32,922	784
South Dakota	770,883	18	1,322	172
Tennessee	5,900,962	351	41,024	695
Texas	22,490,022	1,364	121,554	541
Utah	2,389,039	46	5,639	236
Vermont	621,394	16	696	112
Virginia	7,459,827	391	20,559	276
Washington	6,203,788	190	21,330	344
West Virginia	1,815,35	68	4,924	271
Wisconsin	5,509,026	154	11,548	210
Wyoming	506,929	11	1,163	230
Washington D.C.	553,523	198	7,590	1,371

Source: FBI 2004 Figures.

Crime In Other California Cities

City	Population	Violent Crimes*	Homicides
Anaheim	345,317	1,530	10
Bakersfield	274,162	1,948	23
Fresno	456,663	3,496	53
Huntington Beach	200,763	421	6
Riverside	285,537	1,777	17
Los Angeles	3,864,018	42,785	518
San Diego	1,294,032	6,774	62
Santa Ana	351,697	1,858	25
Santa Barbara	89,269	264	0

Source: Annual reports from FBI, 2004 data. Homicides include murders and non-negligent manslaughter.
*Number of violent crimes.

Lock your doors, join the neighborhood watches, school your children in safety, take extra precautions when they are called for.

U.S. Crime

• In 2004, the FBI reports, 16,137 people were murdered in the United States. Of these, the FBI was able to assemble data on 14,121. The following is based on these 14,121 deaths. Of them, 9,326 or 66 percent were shot, 1,866 stabbed, 663 beaten with a blunt instrument, 933 assaulted with feet, hands or fists, 11 poisoned, 15 drowned, 114 killed by fire and 155 strangled. Narcotics killed 76 and asphyxiation 105. In 856 homicides, weapons were not identified.

• Of total murdered, 10,990 were male, 3,099 female and 32 unknown.

• In murders involving guns, handguns accounted for 7,365 deaths, rifles 393, shotguns 507, and other guns or type unknown 1,161.

• Of the 14,121 murdered in 2004, the FBI reported that 3,976 lost their lives in violence stemming from arguments or brawls. The next largest category was robbery victims, 988 homicides. Romantic triangles led to 97 homicides, narcotic drug laws 554, juvenile gang violence 804, gangland violence 95, rape 36, arson 28, baby-sitter-killing-child 17, burglary 77, prostitution 9, gambling 7.

• In 2004, there were 666 justifiable homicides in the U.S. — 437 by police officers, 229 by private citizens.

• In 1993, the U.S. recorded 24,526 homicides. There then began dramatic decreases. By the year 2000, total homicides numbered 15,586. Among possible reasons for decline: better emergency-trauma care, locking up more people, prosperity, more cops and according to the author of the book, "Freaknomics," abortions.

California Crime

Of the 2,394 homicides in 2004, guns, mostly pistols, accounted 73 percent of the total, knives 12 percent, blunt objects such as clubs 4 percent, hands and feet other personal weapons 6 percent, and unidentified weapons 5.

Megan's Law

For a list of registered sex offenders by town or city, go to www.meganslaw.ca.gov.

Crime Statistics by City
Central Valley Counties
San Joaquin County

City	Population	Violent Crimes	Homicides
Escalon*	6,912	26	0
Lathrop	12,565	NA	0
Lodi	62,467	279	1
Manteca	61,927	250	2
Ripon	13,241	28	0
Stockton	279,513	3,700	40
Tracy	78,307	129	2
County Total	653,333	5,431	55

Stanislaus County

Ceres	38,813	171	2
Hughson	5,942	3	0
Modesto	207,634	1,291	19
Newman	9,134	21	0
Oakdale	17,439	47	2
Patterson	16,158	21	0
Riverbank	19,988	38	0
Turlock	67,009	372	4
Waterford	7,897	48	0
County Total	504,482	2,875	42

Merced County

Atwater	26,693	166	1
Dos Palos	4,854	43	0
Gustine	5,311	25	0
Livingston	12,344	63	0
Los Banos	32,380	265	0
Merced	73,610	602	12
County Total	240,162	1,612	16

The FBI does not break out towns with fewer than 10,000 residents. The state often does but its 2004 figures were not available at time of publication. For this reason, the italicized cities show figures from 2003.

Chapter 16

Weather

THE WEATHER of Alameda County can be accurately described as almost delightful. The qualifying "almost" is necessary because there will be days when you will curse the heat, bewail the fog and wish the rain would cease. But these days will be few and the days of balm many.

Broad Weather Patterns

Although erratic, Alameda weather does hold to broad patterns. Rain almost never falls in the summer. September and October will usually usher in fall with several spells of heat. Snow every few years will powder the mountain tops.

Livermore in the summer will be warmer than Newark and Newark will be warmer than Berkeley. In the winter, the reverse will show: Berkeley cool, Newark cooler, Livermore coolest.

Understanding how the weather works — an easy task — will make you appreciate it all the more. There is a perverse but charming logic to the play of the elements.

If you are shopping for a home in the Bay Area, knowledge of the weather can save you from buying in a place unsuitable to your temperament.

Five actors star in weather extravaganza: the sun, the Pacific, the Golden Gate, the hills and the Central Valley.

The Sun's Role

In the spring and summer, the sun moves north creating a mass of ocean air called the Pacific High. The Pacific High blocks storms from the California coast and dispatches winds to the coast.

In the fall the sun moves south, taking the Pacific High with it. The winds slough off for a few months, then in bluster the storms. Toward spring, the storms will abate as the Pacific High settles into place.

The Fog Machine

Speeding across the Pacific, the spring and summer winds pick up moisture and at the coast, strip the warm water from the surface and bring up the frigid. Cold water exposed to warm wet air makes a wonderfully thick fog.

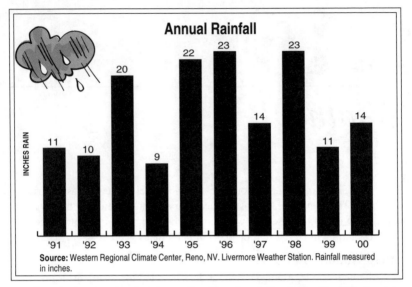

Annual Rainfall

Source: Western Regional Climate Center, Reno, NV. Livermore Weather Station. Rainfall measured in inches.

In summer months, downtown San Francisco often looks like it is about to be buried by mountains of cotton candy. This candy entrances many and depresses not a few coastal residents. Week after week of chilly fog, which happens occasionally, wears on some nerves.

The Golden Gate

This fog would love to scoot over to the East Bay but Mount Tamalpais and the hills running up the San Francisco peninsula stop or greatly impede its progress — except where there are openings. Of the half dozen or so major gaps, the biggest is that marvelous work of nature, the Golden Gate.

The fog shoots through the Golden Gate in the spring and summer, visually delighting motorists on the Bay Bridge, and bangs into the Berkeley-Albany hills. Some of the cooler air will drift toward Oakland, and the other gaps will admit the cool air to the lower Bay. But Berkeley gets the most, which is why Berkeley and Oakland in the summer are cooler than Newark.

A Mountain Barrier

A mile or so inland, the east shore ascends to a mountain range, which traverses Alameda County. These mountains perform the same function as the coastal mountains: they impede the cool air and fog from traveling on to Pleasanton and Livermore.

The next summer day you drive Interstate 580 from Hayward to Pleasanton, let your hand hang out the window. As you crest the ridge and descend, the air will become noticeably warmer. You have left the coastal pattern and entered the continental, warmer and dryer — which is why, in summer, Livermore is warmer than Newark or Berkeley (see chart).

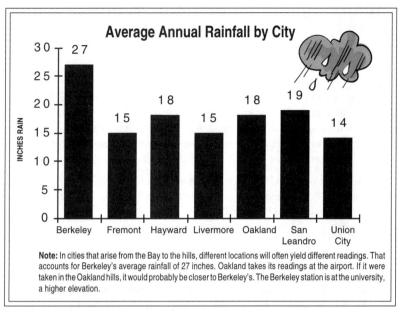

Average Annual Rainfall by City

Note: In cities that arise from the Bay to the hills, different locations will often yield different readings. That accounts for Berkeley's average rainfall of 27 inches. Oakland takes its readings at the airport. If it were taken in the Oakland hills, it would probably be closer to Berkeley's. The Berkeley station is at the university, a higher elevation.

But although weakened, the coastal pattern retains enough strength to take the edge off the Livermore-Pleasanton-Dublin summer. As with the coastal range, the East Bay range has its gaps, foremost the Carquinez Strait near Martinez, and the Hayward gap, which opens to Pleasanton-Livermore. Into these gaps runs the cooler air, hurried along by the last actor, the San Joaquin Valley.

Valley Air Pump

The San Joaquin Valley is also known as the Central Valley. Located about 75 miles inland, the vast Central Valley lies within the continental pattern. In the summer, this means heat. Hot air pulls in cold air like a vacuum. The Central Valley sucks in the coastal air through openings in the East Bay hills, and even over the hills.

You are driving down Interstate 680 south approaching Dublin. The sky is blue, the temperature high. To your left, the horizon is clear. To your right, a great surprise: snow white fog billowing over the hills and through the gaps, cooling the air while you gawk in wonder.

When the cool coastal air neutralizes the Central Valley heat, the Valley says to the coast: no more cool air, thank you. The suction disappears and the winds taper off.

With the winds down, the ocean fog stays offshore, and San Francisco, Berkeley and the East Bay shore towns enjoy some sunny days. Livermore and Pleasanton, in the grasp of the continental pattern, endure considerably more heat.

Meanwhile, lacking the cooling fog, the Valley heats up again, creating the vacuum that pulls in the cool air and renews the cycle. This cycle has its daily counterpart. As the sun's rays weaken in the late afternoon, the fog will often steal across and down the Bay to be burned off the following morning by the robust sunlight.

In the fall and winter, the temperatures are reversed. The Central Valley grows colder and the Pacific Ocean, which is warmer than the land in winter, sends its balmy breezes over the coast. Again the hills impede the coastal flow. San Francisco, in the winter, is warmer than Berkeley, which is warmer than Newark, which is warmer than Livermore (see temperature chart).

Also in the winter, Central Valley fog, attracted to warm air, moves toward the shore cities but, except at openings like the Hayward gap and the Carquinez Strait, is usually blocked by the hills.

Rain Patterns

Besides blocking the fog, the hills greatly influence the rain pattern.

When storm clouds rise to pass over a mountain, they cool and drop much of their rain. Mt. Diablo, a landmark of the region, gets an average of 25 inches annually at its summit, 3,849 feet. But at the ranger station about a 1,000 feet lower, the average drops to 22 inches.

For the most part, the average rainfall ranges between 14 and 19 inches for most Alameda County cities. But in cities that rise from the Bay to the mountains, different locations will often yield different readings. That accounts for Berkeley's average rainfall of 27 inches.

Oakland, which averages 18 inches, takes its reading at the airport. If it were taken in the Oakland hills, it would probably be closer to Berkeley's. (The Berkeley station is at the University, a higher elevation.) Berkeley, opposite the Golden Gate, also gets visited by more rain-bearing clouds than Oakland, which is sheltered by San Francisco.

Drenched by Fog

Fog drip can sometimes be as heavy as rain. One of the editors recalls attending a summer picnic in a redwood grove in the Oakland hills. He and his family arrived about 11 a.m. to find the air cold and the drip heavy enough to soak their clothes. Parents bundled up children, plastic tablecloths were used as rain jackets. Two hours later the fog had burned away and they were playing softball in a hot sun.

In this instance, the trees were squeezing the fog, forcing it to give up its moisture, another example of the neighborhood diversity of Bay Area weather. Fog drip in the Berkeley hills has been measured over 10 inches in a summer.

That, basically, is how the weather works in the Bay Area (see, that wasn't hard). But unfortunately for regularity's sake, the actors often forget their lines

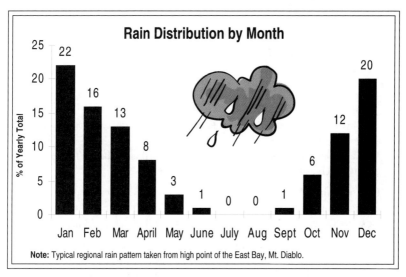

Rain Distribution by Month

Note: Typical regional rain pattern taken from high point of the East Bay, Mt. Diablo.

or fail to show up. Rainfall over the 10 recent seasons shows how undependable nature can be (see chart).

Up and Down Years

During the drought years of 1975 through 1977, rainfall averaged 14 inches or less and dropped as low as 8 inches in 1976.

Between 1981 and 1983, El Niño tricked the Pacific into forgetting the summer fogs. The Bay Area enjoyed unusually warm summer weather. Rainfall also zoomed to 35 inches in 1983, causing widespread flooding and damage. Then years of droughts followed. Then two years ago the rains came back.

Even when erratic, however, the weather is almost always mild. Rainy winters cause slides and road washouts but Bay Area residents count their blessings when they sit in front of the television and see what havoc Nature raises in the rest of the nation.

Weather Tidbits

*   When San Francisco built Candlestick Park, it chose the junction of several wind funnels coming through a gap in the Pacific hills. Pop flies, when they could be seen, flitted around like demented bugs. The new baseball stadium, located near the downtown, is sheltered by coastal hills. It catches some fog but is not as wild and windy as Candlestick.

    Conversely, Candlestick is a great football stadium. Winter breaks down the fog, abates the winds.

*   September and October are the best months to go swimming in the ocean. The upwelling of the cold water has stopped. Often the fog has gone. Sunshine kisses the water and the coast.

Average Daily Temperatures

City	Ja	Fb	Mr	Ap	My	Ju	Jy	Au	Sp	Oc	No	De
Berkeley	50	53	54	56	59	62	63	63	64	62	55	51
Livermore	47	51	54	58	63	68	72	72	70	63	54	47
Newark	50	54	56	60	63	66	68	69	67	64	56	49
Oakland	51	55	56	59	61	63	65	66	66	64	57	51

Note: Figures derived from 1971-2000 records, National Climatic Center, Asheville, North Carolina.

While cooler, the coast is also delightful in April and May. Winter has departed. The summer fogs have yet to arrive.

- Like sunshine? You are in the right place. Records show that during daylight hours the sun shines in New York City 60 percent of the time; in Boston, 57 percent; in Detroit, 53 percent; and in Seattle, 43 percent.

In San Francisco, the sun shines during 66 percent of daylight hours. Atop Mt. Tamalpais in Marin County, where conditions are comparable to Alameda County, the sun shines 73 percent of daylight hours.

- Of Alameda County's two types of fog, one is much more dangerous than the other.

The coastal fog often forms well above the Pacific and, pushed by the wind, generally moves at a good clip. In thick coastal fog, you will have to slow down but you can see the tail lights of a car 50 to 75 yards ahead.

In winter, valley or tule fog blossoms at shoe level when moist air rests atop the cold ground. Tule fog rarely penetrates west of the Berkeley-Oakland-Fremont mountain ranges. But it is a problem east of these hills.

When you read of chain accidents in the Altamont area (east Alameda County) or in the Central Valley, tule fog is almost always to blame.

- During the summer and fall, the Pacific High will occasionally loop a strong wind down from Washington through the Sierra and the hot valleys, where it loses its moisture, and into the Bay Area.

Extremely dry, these northeasters, which are now called "Diablos," will tighten the skin on your face, cause wood shingle roofs to crackle and turn the countryside into tinder.

The October 1991 fire that destroyed 2,500 homes and apartments in the Berkeley-Oakland hills and killed 25 was caused by a Diablo.

On Sept. 27, 1923, a northeaster fire roared down upon North Berkeley, destroying homes, libraries, students' clubs, hotels and boarding homes — 584 buildings in all.

If you buy in the hills, take a look at fire prevention tactics.

Temperatures for Selected Cities
Number of Days Greater than 90 Degrees in Typical Year

City	Ja	Fb	Mr	Ap	My	Ju	Jy	Au	Sp	Oc	No	Dc
Berkeley	0	0	0	0	0	0	0	1	0	0	0	0
Fremont	0	0	0	0	0	3	4	10	5	0	0	0
Livermore	0	0	0	0	1	6	14	21	11	0	0	0
Oakland	0	0	0	0	0	0	1	0	0	0	0	0

Temperatures for Selected Cities
Number of Days 32 Degrees or Less in Typical Year

City	Ja	Fb	Mr	Ap	My	Ju	Jy	Au	Sp	Oc	No	Dc
Berkeley	2	0	0	0	0	0	0	0	0	0	0	4
Fremont	1	0	0	0	0	0	0	0	0	0	0	6
Livermore	11	2	0	0	0	0	0	0	0	0	0	12
Oakland	0	0	0	0	0	0	0	0	0	0	0	1

Source: National Weather Service

Central Valley Weather

• Rain rare between May and September. January usually is the wettest month. But by wet, we're talking 2 to 3 inches in that month. In some years, the annual rainfall can be as low as 4 inches or as high as 24.

• Temperatures. Here are some average lows and highs for the Manteca area which is typical of the Valley: January-March, 46 low, 61 high; April-June, 53 low, 78 high; July-September, 62 low, 92 high; October-December, 48 low, 75 high.

• Pollution. A problem in many parts of Central and Sacramento Valley. The region sits in a bowl. After much argument, air quality rules were tightened for farm machinery and agricultural burnings. Because air pollution is a major problem in so many parts of the state, especially Los Angeles, California is forcing major changes in vehicle emissions. Many arguments.

• Modesto. Annual average rain over 30 years, 1950-1980, is 12 inches. The same or close to for Merced and Stanislaus.

• Allergies. They often kick in during the spring and in October. During the spring, the grasses pop their buds and many trees release pollen. In the fall, the Diablos dry out the trees and cones and pollen fills the air. Hanky time.

• Rain is rain, generally welcome all the time in dry California. But some rains are more welcome than others. Storms from the vicinity of Hawaii turn Sierra slopes to slush and, in the upper elevations, deposit soft snow that sinks under the weight of skis. Alaskan storms bring snow to the lower mountains and deposit a fine powder, ideal for skiing. When snow caps Mt. Diablo and the mountains above Fremont, thank Alaska.

Subject Index

BUY 10 OR MORE & SAVE!

*If you order 10 or more books of any mix, price drops by about 50 percent.
1-800-222-3602. Or fill out form and send with check to:
McCormack's Guides, P.O. Box 190, Martinez, CA 94553. Or fax
order to (925) 228-7223. To order online go to www.mccormacks.com*

1-800-222-3602

Next to title, write in number of copies ordered:

No.	McCormack's Guide	Single	Bulk
___	Alameda & Central Valley 2006	$13.95	$6.25
___	Contra Costa & Solano 2006	$13.95	$6.25
___	Orange County 2006	$13.95	$6.25
___	Greater Sacramento 2006	$13.95	$6.25
___	San Diego County 2006	$13.95	$6.25
___	San Francisco, San Mateo, Marin, Sonoma 2006	$13.95	$6.25
___	Santa Clara & Santa Cruz 2006	$13.95	$6.25
___	How California Schools Work	$15.95	$6.25

Subtotal $ _____

CA sales tax (8.25%) _____

Shipping* _____

Total Amount of Order $ _____

**For orders of 10 or more, shipping is 60 cents per book. For orders of
fewer than 10, shipping is $4.50 for first book, $1.50 per book thereafter.*

Circle one: Check/Visa/MC/Am.Exp. or Bill Us

Card No. _____ Exp. Date _____

Name _____

Company _____

Address _____

City _____ State _____ Zip _____

Phone: (_____) _____ Fax (_____) _____

*The following guides are available online at www.mccormacks.com:
Los Angeles County 2006, Riverside County 2006, Ventura County 2006,
San Bernardino County 2006 and Santa Barbara County 2006.*

☐ **Check here to receive advertising information**

Advertisers' Index

To advertise in McCormack's Guides, call 1-800-222-3602

BUY 10 OR MORE & SAVE!

*If you order 10 or more books of any mix, price drops by about 50 percent.
1-800-222-3602. Or fill out form and send with check to:
McCormack's Guides, P.O. Box 190, Martinez, CA 94553. Or fax
order to (925) 228-7223. To order online go to www.mccormacks.com*

1-800-222-3602

Next to title, write in number of copies ordered:

No.	McCormack's Guide	Single	Bulk
____	Alameda & Central Valley 2006	$13.95	$6.25
____	Contra Costa & Solano 2006	$13.95	$6.25
____	Orange County 2006	$13.95	$6.25
____	Greater Sacramento 2006	$13.95	$6.25
____	San Diego County 2006	$13.95	$6.25
____	San Francisco, San Mateo, Marin, Sonoma 2006	$13.95	$6.25
____	Santa Clara & Santa Cruz 2006	$13.95	$6.25
____	How California Schools Work	$15.95	$6.25

Subtotal $ _____

CA sales tax (8.25%) _____

Shipping* _____

Total Amount of Order $ _____

**For orders of 10 or more, shipping is 60 cents per book. For orders of
fewer than 10, shipping is $4.50 for first book, $1.50 per book thereafter.*

VISA MasterCard *Circle one: Check/Visa/MC/Am.Exp. or Bill Us*

Card No. _____ *Exp. Date* _____

Name _____

Company _____

Address _____

City _____ *State* _____ *Zip* _____

Phone: (____) _____ *Fax (____)* _____

*The following guides are available online at www.mccormacks.com:
Los Angeles County 2006, Riverside County 2006, Ventura County 2006,
San Bernardino County 2006 and Santa Barbara County 2006.*

☐ **Check here to receive advertising information**